The Spectral Arctic

The Spectral Arctic

A History of Dreams and Ghosts in Polar Exploration

Shane McCorristine

UCL PRESS

First published in 2018 by
UCL Press
University College London
Gower Street
London WC1E 6BT

Available to download free: www.ucl.ac.uk/ucl-press

A CIP catalogue record for this book is available from The British Library.

ISBN: 978–1–78735–247–6 (Hbk.)
ISBN: 978–1–78735–246–9 (Pbk.)
ISBN: 978–1–78735–245–2 (PDF)
ISBN: 978–1–78735–248–3 (epub)
ISBN: 978–1–78735–249–0 (mobi)
ISBN: 978–1–78735–250–6 (html)
DOI: https://doi.org/10.14324/111.9781787352452

Epigraphs

There can be no question that in the frozen wastes and snowy wildernesses lurks a powerful fascination, which proves almost irresistible to the adventurous spirit. He who has once entered the Arctic World, however great his sufferings, is restless until he returns to it. Whether the spell lies in the weird magnificence of the scenery, in the splendours of the heavens, in the mystery which still hovers over those far-off seas of ice and remote bays, or in the excitement of a continual struggle with the forces of Nature, or whether all these influences are at work, we cannot stop to inquire. But it seems to us certain that the Arctic World has a romance and an attraction about it, which are far more powerful over the minds of men than the rich glowing lands of the Tropics (Adams, 1876, iii).

NOT HERE! THE WHITE NORTH HAS THY BONES; AND THOU
HEROIC SAILOR-SOUL
ART PASSING ON THINE HAPPIER VOYAGE NOW
TOWARD NO EARTHLY POLE
(Tennyson's epitaph to Franklin, Westminster Abbey)

They were walking inland, walking the mainland – the nunamariq – 'the real land'. They were a raggedy bunch and their clothing was not well made. Their skins were black and the meat above their teeth was gone; their eyes were gaunt. Were they tuurngait – spirits – or what? (Towtongie qtd. in Eber 2008, xi).

Acknowledgements

Thanks to Michael Bravo for his guidance, input and friendship throughout this project; to Chris Morash for his support in Ireland; to Heather Lane, Naomi Boneham, Lucy Martin, Naomi Chapman, Kate Gilbert, Rosie Amos, Julian Dowdeswell, Bryan Lintott and the entire staff of the Scott Polar Research Institute for providing a supportive and scholarly home in Cambridge for many years; to Claire Warrior at the National Maritime Museum for her kind assistance; to Janice Cavell, Russell Potter and my anonymous reviewers for sharing their knowledge and expertise with me; to Chris Penfold at UCL Press, who was a pleasure to work with; and to my wife and family.

This research was undertaken while I was a scholar at the Rachel Carson Center for Environment and Society (LMU Munich), Maynooth University and the Scott Polar Research Institute. This book was made possible by an Irish Research Council CARA Marie Curie Fellowship, for which I am immensely grateful.

Sections of chapter 6 appeared previously as: 'The Spectral Presence of the Franklin Expedition in Contemporary Fiction', in *Critique: Studies in Contemporary Fiction*, 55:4 (2014) (reprinted with the permission of Taylor & Francis Ltd, http://www.tandfonline.com); and 'Searching for Franklin: A Contemporary Canadian Ghost Story', in *British Journal of Canadian Studies*, 26:1 (2013) (reprinted with the permission of the Licensor through PLSclear).

Contents

List of illustrations

Introduction
Arctic dreams

In 1893, while frozen in the Arctic ice aboard his expedition ship the *Fram*, the Norwegian explorer Fridtjof Nansen reflected on the environment around him:

> Nothing more wonderfully beautiful can exist than the Arctic night. It is dreamland painted in the imagination's most delicate tints; it is colour etherealised. One shade melts into the other, so that you cannot tell where one shade ends and the other begins, and yet they are all there. No forms – it is all faint, dreamy colour music, a far-away, long-drawn-out melody on muted strings (Nansen, 1897).

In popular myth Nansen is the archetypal Scandinavian polar explorer – a manly, no-nonsense hero with little time for the sentimentality or plodding amateurism of his British contemporaries.[1] However, Nansen's account of this expedition, *Farthest North* (1897), reveals someone with a deeply romantic outlook whose musings on the Arctic 'dreamland' have much in common with the thoughts and ruminations of other nineteenth-century polar explorers. Nansen's was a book, moreover, that did not just appeal to other explorers, for it was massively popular too, selling some 40,000 copies shortly after its publication in English (Huntford, 1997, 442).

Some years later in a busy household in Vienna, the psychiatrist Sigmund Freud read the German translation of *Farthest North* after noting that his family were 'hero-worshipping' Nansen: 'Martha [Freud's wife] because the Scandinavians obviously fulfil a youthful ideal of hers, which she has not realized in life, and Mathilde [Freud's daughter] because she is transferring her allegiance from the Greek heroes she has hitherto been so full of to the Vikings'. Freud was in the midst of writing *The Interpretation of Dreams* when he read Nansen, and had recently begun an intense period of self-analysis. It was in this context that he thought he could make use of the 'practically transparent' polar dreams that Nansen wrote down (qtd. in Lehmann, 1966, 388).

Although they never met, Freud and Nansen shared more than an appreciation for dreams. Like Freud, Nansen was an early investigator in neuroanatomy and in his doctoral dissertation on the central nervous system – defended in 1888 – Nansen cited and challenged some of Freud's ideas. While Nansen soon after launched a successful expedition to cross Greenland on skis, Freud was forced to shelve his neuroscientific research and earn a living as a specialist in private practice. As a psychologist he was fascinated by the motivations of polar explorers and was impressed by their heroic feats; but in the case of Nansen – a rival neuroanatomist who became internationally famous only a few months after graduating – his feelings were notably ambivalent (Anthi, 2016).

After reading *Farthest North* Freud described Nansen's mental state as 'typical of someone who is trying to do something new which makes calls on his confidence and probably discovers something new by a false route and finds that it is not so big as he expected' (qtd. in Lehmann, 1966, 388). On a conscious level Freud identified with the polar explorer as a fellow pioneer and intellectual adventurer – someone whose theories about reaching the North Pole by drifting with the Arctic ice had been originally dismissed by incredulous scientific authorities in Britain. On an unconscious level, however, Freud conflated his own doubts about discovering something new with Nansen's daring voyage into the unknown. In a materialisation of these feelings, Freud himself dreamt of being in a 'field of ice' with Nansen and giving 'the gallant explorer galvanic treatment for an attack of sciatica from which he was suffering'. During this self-analysis Freud realised he had recovered a childhood memory of confusing *Reisen* [travels] with *Reissen* [gripes] and this awareness disclosed repressed anxieties he had about travelling (Lehmann, 1966, 389).

This is one example of the way that dreams travelled from the Arctic through narratives and were picked up by dreamers who then travelled back to the Arctic with them – a magical loop that mixed together cultural productions of the polar regions with actual experiences. In this book I argue that, just like the proverbial iceberg of psychoanalysis, the narratives of modern Arctic exploration we are all familiar with today are just the tip of the iceberg: they actually disguise the great mass of mysterious and dimly-lit stories that lie beneath the surface of the water. Nansen's 'dreamland' musings and Freud's fascination with polar dreams were not isolated behaviours: rather, they indicate a core set of perspectives on the Arctic that drew upon actual experiences and cultural imaginings of dreams and other supernatural phenomena in the far North.

Nineteenth-century explorers and their audiences, of course, spent hours dreaming each and every night (see Figure 0.1). When awake, they lived in the everyday spiritual worlds that included religious reflection, creative imagination and supernatural belief. People's presence in the Arctic – whether real or imagined – inspired an outpouring of texts, images and performances that attempted to express the strangeness and magic of polar experience. Maddeningly, commentators were unable to pin down exactly how this experience might be described (in the first epigraph to this book several words were used: 'fascination'; 'spell'; 'mystery'; 'romance'; 'attraction'). This book focuses on one pervasive mode of expressing the relationship between people and place in the Arctic – the spectral.

Throughout the nineteenth century, ghosts and shadowy interlocutors featured in the narratives of British explorers in the Arctic and their audiences back home. Taking the history of Sir John Franklin's last Arctic expedition from the 1840s as my central focus, in this book I examine how spectral experiences such as dreaming, clairvoyante travel, reverie, spiritualism and ghost-seeing informed ideas of the Arctic

Figure 0.1 'A Vision of Home'. Source: Richard W. Bliss. *Our Lost Explorers: The Narrative of the Jeannette Expedition as Related by the Survivors, etc.* Hartford, Connecticut: American Publishing Co., 1883.

and the searches for a Northwest Passage through the Arctic. The role of spectral experiences in this geographical quest has not been adequately addressed before and I argue that integrating them into the cultural history of exploration revises traditional accounts of polar discovery that focus mainly on 'men and maps'. This book, then, is about the cultural production of the spectral in Arctic narratives and what this can tell us about Victorian exploration and its legacies.

* * *

Today people from western cultures who visit the Arctic enter places that have long been imagined as somehow dreamlike or magical. 'Ice', 'wilderness' and 'sublime' register as keywords in a Eurocentric vocabulary that continues to inform the way that we think about what is Arctic and what is not Arctic. Much of this can be traced back to the particular colonial and capitalist development of a few northern European states that looked north for riches in the early modern period. Despite the fact that our engagement with the Arctic has always been contingent – depending on how we see, move and reflect on the environment in a given historical context – long-held associations mean that its landscape is consistently imagined as enchanting and magical.[2]

So far this will not be news to most readers, but there is a large gap between recognising this as simply a descriptive vocabulary and putting forward arguments for its core importance in the cultural history of Arctic exploration. As humans we dream as we live, with our eyes and ears open to the world and there are social and material histories of the apparently immaterial – dreams and reveries of air, earth, water and the ghosts that haunt the Arctic. I came to this subject after realising that no one took seriously the fantastic icebergs that lurk under the surface of Arctic narratives – the ways in which Arctic explorations were historically represented by people in Britain as dreamlike or ghostly enterprises, whether in canonical sources (like the published journals of explorers) or peripheral sources (like poetry in periodicals or pulp fiction).[3]

Robinson notes that 'stories, more than specimens or scientific observations, constituted the real currency of Arctic exploration' (2006, 6). In contrast to oft-told tales of derring-do and disaster, this book aims to do something new for the cultural history of the Arctic. It looks at stories of dreaming and haunted explorers, of reveries and visits to Inuit shamans and of the entranced female clairvoyants who travelled to the Arctic in search of the lost expedition led by Franklin, which departed Britain in 1845 in search of a Northwest Passage. By highlighting the oscillating movements between absence and presence, these 'hidden histories' of exploration (Driver, 2013) reflect the complex ways that men and women actually thought about the far North in the past. The Arctic is imagined here as a zone of loss, disappearance and fragility, but also of haunting, uncanny returns and frozen permanence (see Figure 0.2). Stories of Arctic dreams, ghosts and haunting are not just literary decorations: they force us to question who had cultural authority over the Arctic during the nineteenth century. They also help us to make sense of current cultural and political concerns in the Canadian Arctic about the disappearance and reappearance of the Franklin expedition.

Therefore, my first key argument is that British Arctic explorers – such as those on the Franklin expedition – recognised and reflected on the spectral aspects of being in the Arctic. This included having strange dreams, reveries, hallucinations and other supernatural experiences. Highlighting their spectral stories complicates the pervasive idea that explorers were always, or always thought of themselves as, rational actors in a wild region. In doing so we are forced to think about Arctic exploration historically as a practice that involved supernatural experiences: this is an important revision given the power of Victorian exploration in current conceptions of the Arctic (in politics, geography and tourism for example).

My second key argument is that, for many people, the Arctic became so much more than an unknown, empty space waiting to be discovered and mapped by elite men. Rather, nineteenth-century audiences saw the Arctic as a dreamlike zone that overflowed the cartographic and literary space in which it was traditionally bounded by that tiny group of men who promoted and handled polar exploration. Because of the spectral power of the Arctic as an idea, it could be sensed remotely, dreamed about, imagined and consumed by people who were at a great distance from the Arctic geographically and politically (see Figure 0.3). This was especially so for British women: although they had no formal access to the exclusively male expeditions, from the 1840s women began to feature as ghostly presences in Arctic fiction and poetry, haunting the journeys of men and adding emotional dimensions to cultures of exploration. Alongside this literary development, young women were able to psychically travel to the Arctic in search of lost explorers through the popular techniques of clairvoyance, mesmerism and spiritualism. So where did ideas about a spectral Arctic come from?

British and Canadian travellers, writers, scientific collectors and policy-makers have long used a predetermined set of stereotypes, dreams and political strategies when discussing the Arctic – frequently termed

From a painting by Albert Operti

LOST ON THE ICE-CAP

Figure 0.2 'Lost on the Ice-Cap', from a painting by Albert Operti. Source: Rudolf Kersting. *The White World: Life and Adventures Within the Arctic Circle Portrayed by Famous Living Explorers*. New York: Lewis, Scribner & Co., 1902.

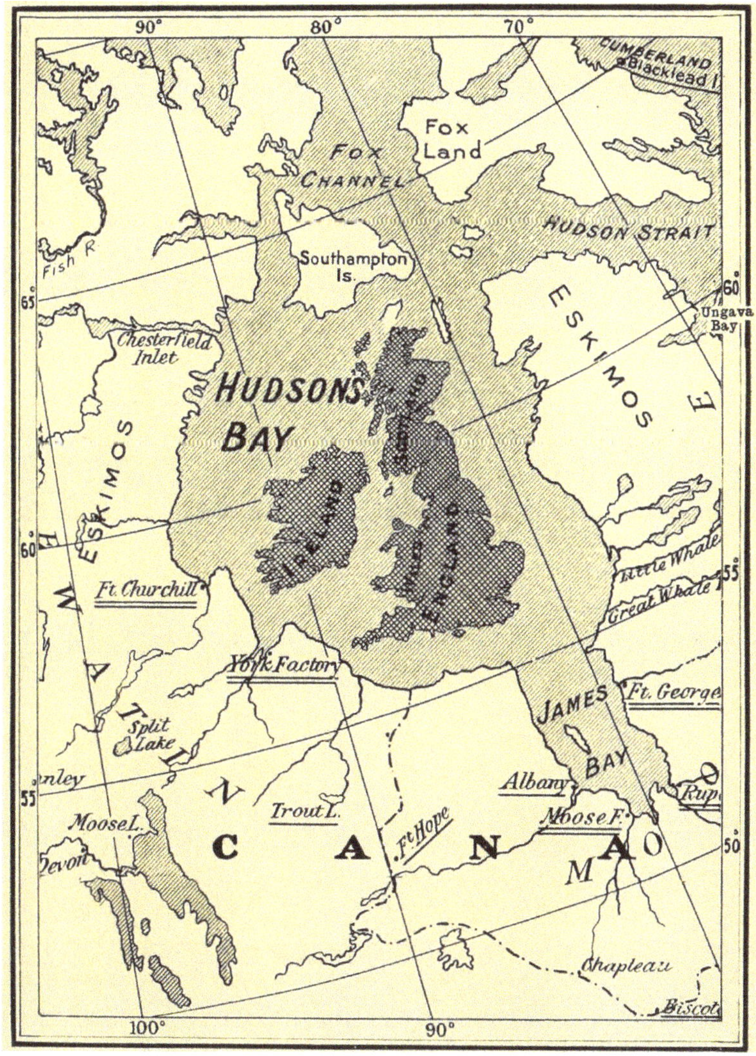

Figure 0.3 'Map of the Diocese of Moosonee'. Source: Arthur Lewis. *The Life and Work of the Rev. E.J. Peck Among the Eskimos*. New York: A.C. Armstrong & Son, 1904.

'ideas of the north'. To take a poetic example, the Arctic was a place where, as Robert Service suggested,

> There are strange things done in the midnight sun
> By the men who moil for gold;
> The Arctic trails have their secret tales
> That would make your blood run cold (1907a, 35).

Such ideas of Arctic strangeness, however, should be traced to their sources in culture – they are not simply given. In fact, there are many cultural-historical reasons for why people thought of the Arctic as an exceptional place, not least the sense of a geographic and aesthetic distance between Britain and the Arctic. The spatial and perceptual differences between the Arctic and other British imperial possessions meant that explorers could imply that voyages to the frozen north were 'pure' in a way that voyages to India, for example, were not. After all, on the face of it, Arctic exploration did not involve the warfare, women, or 'weakening' climate associated with Britain's tropical colonies.[4] Furthermore, unlike the southern regions of Canada, the Arctic was not a scene of settler colonialism or political integration during the period. As a space of radical difference in the British imperial imagination, the Arctic was therefore easily exoticised by explorers.

This exoticism was reinforced by the way that people wrote about the Arctic. The American explorer Elisha Kent Kane criticised others for speaking of the Arctic environment in 'language as exact and mathematical as their own correction tables. It almost seems as if their minute observations of dip-sectors and repeating-circles had left them no scope for picturesque sublimity' (1854, 67). However, accounts by Arctic explorers actually suggest that there was a lot of scope for this 'picturesque sublimity'. Take the artist and photographer William Bradford, who travelled to Greenland in the 1860s and believed he had experienced 'the revelation of a new world, a new phase of life and nature, which is accompanied by the feeling of being in the presence of the Eternal God' (1885, 123). Kane would also have had no complaint with the narrative style of a fellow American, Frederick Cook, who described the ice fields he encountered on his North Pole expedition:

> Through vapor-charged air of crystal, my eyes ran over plains moving in brilliant waves of running colors toward dancing horizons. Mirages turned things topsy-turvy. Invented lands and queer objects ever rose and fell, shrouded in mystery. All of this was due to the atmospheric magic of the continued glory of midnight suns in throwing piercing beams of light through superimposed strata of air of varying temperature and density (1911, 277).

Other explorers, writers and their audiences equally sought out examples of polar 'glamour', as Arthur Conan Doyle put it (2012, 319), but does this mean that they were anything more than literary devices? Explorers may have described some of the weird things that lay beneath the surface of the ice, but how might this lay the groundwork for a revisionist historical account?

To start to take people's accounts of the spectral Arctic seriously we must realise that, in any society, things like hallucinations, visions and dreams are more than just symptoms of mental disorder or irrational experiences. Rather, when they are used by people in describing feelings, beliefs, or experiences, they perform significant cultural work, just like the 'psychic realities' that Freud saw as the keys to the unconscious.

Polar explorers frequently used dreams and dreaminess to explain what motivated them to travel to the poles. Isaac Israel Hayes, an officer under Kane and then an Arctic commander in his own right, described an 'intuitive feeling that my destiny would lead me to the North and under the influence of this feeling I set to work the harder and graduated a year earlier than I otherwise would have done' (qtd. in Wamsley, 2009, 73). The Norwegian explorer Roald Amundsen wrote of how finding the Northwest Passage was a 'dream' of his boyhood (1908, I 5; II 125) and how reading stories of Arctic endeavour created a 'strange ambition' within him to endure the same sufferings as the lost explorer John Franklin (1927, 2) (see Figure 0.4). As a child, the Antarctic explorer Ernest Shackleton was also well-read in the mysterious disappearance of the Franklin expedition, and he later claimed that a specific dream inspired him to think of polar exploration:

> [S]trangely enough, the circumstance which actually determined me to become an explorer was a dream I had when I was twenty-two. We were beating out to New York from Gibraltar, and I dreamt I was standing on the bridge in mid-Atlantic and looking northward. It was a simple dream. I seemed to vow to myself I would go to the region of ice and snow and go on and on till I came to one of the poles of the earth, the end of the axis upon which this great round ball turns (qtd. in Huntford, 1986, 24).[5]

Strange coincidences like this pop up now and again, shimmering in the accounts of polar explorers, but it is important to note that whalers and ordinary seamen also dreamt of the Arctic and these accounts were occasionally also disseminated to wider audiences (see 'Dream Fortunes', *Western Times*, 1903; 'Long Arctic Experiences', *Daily Mail,* 1902). The widespread circulation of dreams and dream language in exploration narratives fed into constructions of the Arctic as a strange and spectral place.

Figure 0.4 'The Late Sir John Franklin'. Source: Wellcome Library, London.

These dreams could be thought of in a theatrical way, as simple enactments of desire or compulsion, but they could also be more place-specific and attuned to ideas of the north.[6] In his unpublished memoirs the Scottish naval commander John Ross recorded some of the 'amusing' applications for positions he received while planning his *Victory* expedition in search of a Northwest Passage (1829–33). In one instance a man wrote to Ross telling him that:

> a person appeared to me in a Dream and said 'go with Captain Ross he will be crowned with Success' and not having the smallest thought of such things before, and reading of Dreams have led to great Discoverys [sic], I put some confidence in this and make [haste] to offer my services (SPRI, MS 655/3; BJ).

Ross wrote in his journal how he might normally have taken such a letter as a joke, but he actually needed a cook and, as the man provided a good reference, he arranged an interview. However, before this could take place Ross received another letter, this time from the man's irate wife:

> I have just found out that my husband have made an engagement with you to join your Expedition through a dream without consulting me, I must beg to tell you Sir that he shall not go, I will not let him have his Cloaths, he must be mad ever to think of leaving a comfortable home, to be frozen in with ice, or to be torn to pieces with Bears [sic throughout] (SPRI, MS 655/3; BJ).

Dreams and coincidences, as well as the ideas of polar glamour or of the 'magnetic' North, were not just used by people as incidental justifications for voyages. Rather, they revealed important assumptions held about Arctic space that have been missed or downplayed by most scholars.

Dreams have many geographical characteristics but, as Freud argued, the particular maps dreamers use can be 'worked at' to improve waking lives. This thought echoes the way that some geographers now think about space, as something that is not solid and tied to a location, but is in motion, unbounded and worked into being by humans through a range of emotional practices (see Thrift, 2006, 143). The notion of relationality is important here – the idea that space is actually an assemblage, 'a subtle folding together of the distant and the proximate, the virtual and the material, presence and absence' (Amin, 2007, 103). Dreams of space, therefore, involve a dream-work that draws bodies together into relation with one another.

Although Ross's tone was comic, the use of his dream narrative relates to my second key argument, that many people saw the Arctic as overflowing the maps and textual space in which it was traditionally bounded. Certainly, those who could afford to could share in the magic felt by Arctic explorers by reading their expensive quarto narratives, but most people's knowledge of the Arctic was mediated through newspapers, periodicals, poetry or ballads. This extended discursive field encouraged the idea that British people were, or should be, intimately linked with what happened in the Arctic. Even if they were not told about the strange things explorers sensed beneath the surface, they had more than enough raw materials to imagine it for themselves. For example, in February 1850 Jane Franklin received a letter from Southsea detailing a 'remarkable dream' which the correspondent believed could aid in the rescue of her husband:

> I saw in my dream two Air Bloon's a great distance off rising just like the moon. I said in my dream to myself [this is] Sir J. Frankland. I looket the second time as the Bloon's [rises?] on their journey looking beautiful an as I looket all in a moment one Banishet like a Pillar of Smoke. The second Bloon still going on its journey it gets to a place where I saw the inhabitants living People I saw in the my dream a Lady beautiful Dressed looking at them I said in my dream their is Lady Frankland but with this dream I saw nothing but snow as it fell amongst the inhabitants of these two Bloon's [sic throughout].

The correspondent, who signed off 'a Humble and true dreamer', explained that the balloons represented the ships and that the first one was destroyed. The second one 'stands well' and 'Providence will bring them back again' (SPRI, MS 248/335; D). Although the letter is a rare surviving example of the type of correspondence that Jane Franklin and her companion Sophia Cracroft were receiving at the time, this allegorical vision sent by a semi-literate dreamer shows how for many ordinary men and women, especially after 1849, the Arctic became more than a space of geographical exploration and imperial imaginings. It became a space where intense bundles of dreams, bodies and spirits gathered, were sensed and were then expressed emotionally and artistically in high and popular cultures.

Far from being disconnected or distant from reality, this sense of the dreamlike was actually bound up with the weird things that happened to the bodies of explorers at the poles. The idea of 'sensed presences' has received some attention from environmental psychologists looking at human experience in Antarctica (Suedfeld and Mocellin, 1987; Geiger, 2010), but there has been little attention given to the rich qualitative data on strange Arctic experiences. For British explorers weird, supernatural or uncanny feelings were part of what it was like to be there, as it also was for other non-native inhabitants, such as whalers, missionaries and fur traders. Indeed, almost every nineteenth-century polar narrator touched on the subjects of mirages and illusions, whether referring to the shifting shapes of the ice or the strange way that sound travelled, or how small things in the distance seemed enormous (see Figure 0.5). It is clear from the sources available that the fantastic atmospheric phenomena in the Arctic put into question the reliability of human perception, especially that of commanders (see Belcher, 1855, I, 266; Huish ed., 1835, 2; Godfrey, 1857, 134; Rees, 1988; McCorristine, 2013; Simpson-Housley, 1996). As I will discuss in chapter 1, these doubts challenge the idea that explorers were somehow separate from, and sovereign over, the environments they passed through.

Figure 0.5 'A strange animal was bounding along within a cable's length from the ship'. Source: Jules Verne. *At the North Pole; or, The Adventures of Captain Hatteras*. Philadelphia: Porter & Coates, 1874.

What kind of strange things happened on polar expeditions? A classic case of Arctic phantasmagoria occurred on 6 April 1853 during Robert McClure's *Investigator* expedition in search of the Franklin expedition in the region of the Arctic that is now part of Canada (and mostly comprising the federal territory of Nunavut, created in 1999). The expedition had been frozen-in for three winters at a place McClure named Mercy Bay and was in a woeful state. Having just dug a grave for their first fatality, the crew suddenly caught sight of a faint figure in the distance:

> The stranger came quietly on, and we saw that his face was as black as ebony, and really at the moment we might be pardoned for wondering whether he was a denizen of this or the other world, and had he but given us a glimpse of a tail or a cloven hoof, we should have assuredly have taken to our legs: as it was, we gallantly stood our ground, and, had the skies fallen upon us, we could hardly have been more astonished than when the dark-faced stranger called out, – 'I'm Lieutenant Pim, late of the "Herald", and now in the "Resolute". Captain Kellett is in her at Dealy Island!' (McClure, 1857, 290).

Bedford Pim's transformation from otherworldly demon to human and fellow explorer eventually led to the rescue of McClure's expedition. After abandoning the *Investigator* in June, the crew made their way east to the *Resolute* and most survived to return home to Britain in 1854. For entering the Arctic from the west, and leaving it through the east (though not in the same ship), McClure and his expedition were, controversially, given the £10,000 parliamentary award for achieving a Northwest Passage.

But one did not even need to be outdoors for the ghostliness of the Arctic to be sensed and made manifest. An account by the French Oblate missionary Émile Petitot speaks of visual and auditory hallucinations in the Arctic and also of a persistent haunting throughout the 1860s at Fort Yukon, then a Hudson's Bay Company (HBC) trading post in Russian America (2005, 22, 36–9). Many years earlier the fur trader David Thompson memorably described playing draughts with the Devil while overwintering by himself at York Factory (1962, 43–4).

The logging of strange dreams and unaccountable events was something that Arctic travellers and explorers shared with those overwintering in Antarctica. Tryggve Gran, a Norwegian member of Robert Falcon Scott's 1910–13 Antarctic expedition – known amongst his colleagues as a believer in white magic – recorded a dream he experienced on 15 December 1911:

> I dreamed I had a telegram reading: 'Amundsen reached Pole, 15-20 December'. [I lay in the tent dozing in a kind of half sleep. Suddenly it appeared as though a picture materialized on the tent canvas of four men, at day-break, in front of a tent with two flags fluttering ... I jumped up and Taylor awoke ... 'The Norwegians have got to the Pole this minute' ...] (1984, 153).

Struck by this, Gran's colleague Thomas Griffith Taylor let him write it in his copy of Robert Browning's poems (Taylor, 1916, 434–5). Amundsen and his men had actually reached the South Pole on 14 December, making Gran's dream-telegram an amazing (if not entirely accurate) coincidence. As for Amundsen himself, in 1898, during the ill-fated *Belgica* expedition off Antarctica, he recorded hearing 'three or four terrible, long screams'. Of the ship's crew, two other colleagues said they also heard the noises, which remained a mystery. 'I do not know what it was', wrote Amundsen, 'but I have recorded this incident as accurately as possible for a number of reasons' (2009, 90–1). Amundsen kept these reasons to himself, but these kinds of experiences were meaningful in that they constituted a form of dream-work for explorers.

However, the Arctic differed from Antarctica in being an historically inhabited region that formed part of the economies and cultural imaginations of northern Atlantic states. Although it was a region well-visited by explorers, whalers and missionaries, a good part of being in the Arctic meant experiencing spectral moments, of seeing the familiar become the strange and of having to work out how absent people seemed to have presence. Remembering an 1880 whaling trip in *The Strand*, Arthur Conan Doyle tried to put some bones on this spectrality, writing of the 'peculiar other-world feeling of the Arctic regions – a feeling so singular, that if you have once been there the thought of it haunts you all your life' (2012, 333). Linear narratives of geographic achievement or failure, then, were only the beginnings of the cultural appreciation for Arctic exploration. Ghostly experiences meant a lot to explorers and their audiences. These stories, and the dream-work they represent, enrich our understanding of exploration as a complex set of practices that did not simply involve the activities of explorers in the field.

Today the Arctic is no longer merely thought of as a space of geographical distance and difference; rather issues of climate change, oil and gas resources and cultural loss dominate the way the region appears in the international media. Yet the language of the magical Arctic, so prominent among narrators in the nineteenth century, has retained its allure among contemporary scholars, newspaper editors and writers. So it behoves us to look at what fertilised this language. Where does it come from and what does it mean for our historical understandings of Arctic exploration? What happens when we move beyond describing the consumption of Arctic enchantments and start to delve deeper into the actual dreams of explorers, archiving their ghost stories and mapping their reveries?

The overall aim of this book is to re-think some of the stories that explorers, readers and consumers told themselves about Arctic exploration. In researching the topic, I have visited relevant archives and libraries but I have also accessed newspaper and periodical materials that have only recently been digitised. This has uncovered a fresh range of sources that have allowed me to take quite a different approach to what has become relatively well-trodden ground. In what follows I move from well-known accounts of Arctic expeditions to lesser known stories, from events that took place in the Arctic to the imaginative forces travelling from different parts of the British Empire. Taken together, my explorations of the spectral Arctic present new ways of reading traditional accounts of exploration and resuscitate reports, stories and other neglected narratives about ghostly or dreamlike travel in the Arctic.

One inherent value in this approach is that it fundamentally questions the standard narrative of polar exploration, which recounts how a rational male hero either conquers or is conquered by an inanimate and alien nature. While this challenge might sound like old news, every week articles and books continue to be published that rehearse the familiar 'heroic man versus harsh environment' myth. Although this myth still influences commentary on Antarctica, such 'whitewashing' is more disturbing when it appears in work on Arctic exploration, where it is still common for indigenous people to be written-out of expeditions, or appear only as background actors in a Eurocentric drama. Such a pervasive dichotomy not only ignores the everyday dreaming and religious or 'superstitious' behaviour which explorers carried with them, but it also obscures the messy spiritual values that were sensed by people in polar landscapes, whether through atmospheric phenomena such as the Aurora Borealis or the embodied spiritual journeys of Inuit shamans and British clairvoyants across vast distances. Both Inuit oral testimonies and the published journals of explorers tell us that shamanism and spiritual forces played a key role in the encounters between strangers in the Arctic, as did Inuit guides, interpreters and map-makers.

It is high time that we start to 'provincialise' the types of behaviours, thoughts and emotions that British people had with regard to the Arctic. This might mean thinking of expeditioners as if they were tribesmen on wooden boats – people with extremely local habits, outlooks and assumptions who (by a kind of sleight of hand linked to colonial power) routinely managed to think of themselves as normal and civilised and to think of indigenous inhabitants as odd and uncivilised. Over the centuries expedition narratives told stories of ships and crews moving about the Arctic like chess pieces on a blank board, but readers of these accounts should never forget that there were plenty of witnesses to the arrival of these flagships, plenty of interlocutors with the men in woollen clothes who ate strange food and sought a sea route west.

Oral history records the inhabitants of Baffin Island thinking that the British strangers they encountered in 1576 were 'dressed in rags': 'How come they dress like this?' It's very cold; their clothes are not fit for this kind of weather. They used to wonder … They were ghostly' (qtd. in Eber, 2008, 4).[7] Where were their women and children? Why were these pale men journeying to an unknown location? How could a commander explain his quest to an Inuk and not be thought of as strange? For too long we have looked at the encounter scene through the eyes of *qallunaat* [Inuktitut: white people] alone and this has blinded us to their trickery. For instance, it was common for British explorers to mention the smells and stinks coming from Inuit bodies, and how women spat in a disgusting manner. Yet if we were to depend only on official accounts, we might be forgiven for thinking that British expeditioners were perennially clean and never went to the toilet or suffered bowel disorders.[8]

It is in unpublished diaries and journals that we get some indications of the everyday habits of this particular European tribe. For example, Arthur C. Horner, surgeon and naturalist on the *Pandora* Northwest Passage expedition of 1875, advised his ill commander against taking a warm bath:

> It is a mistake to wash one's body in this climate. It is much better to let the oily secretion + dirt remain for they are its natural protectives … A healthy person should be able when he digs his fingers into the skin of his chest … to feel his skin greasy & almost scrape off the grease. If the skin is dry and harsh you are not in good health (SPRI, MS 713).

Other people's homes always smell different but it takes a certain mindset to believe that your home is the way that all homes should smell. In another long-standing bit of trickery, European explorers had fun showing the Inuit their reflections in mirrors and looking-glasses for the first time (Huish ed., 1835, 201; Fisher, 1821, 56). But what if we could turn those mirrors around so that the explorers saw their own strangeness for the first time? Interestingly, Inuit oral history records how they refused the caribou meat offered to them by an explorer because of the 'white man's smell' (qtd. in Eber, 2008, 47). White men's excrement even looked out of place to locals: in recollections this *anaq* appears as the organic matter of strangeness (Woodman, 1995, 64).

Given these stories, in *The Spectral Arctic* I argue that we might think of Arctic exploration less as a stable, visible and slowly moving ship on the horizon – solid, manly and upright in its appearance. Rather, in the chapters that follow I show that it was more like a mutable, unpredictable and opaque force which shadowed the ship, occasionally revealing its hidden presence through the sound of repressed and ghostly voices. These dark, icy depths tell us how the Arctic haunted minds and bodies, stretching our concept of exploration beyond simply one of 'boots on the ground' and into the more dynamic realm of dreams and ghostly forces.

1
Toward no earthly pole: Otherworldly quests for a Northwest Passage

John Barrow's Arctic explorer

We can trace much of the magical vocabulary attached to polar exploration, at least in Anglophone cultures, back to the modern era of the search for a Northwest Passage in British naval history (1818–59). For centuries before this a diverse set of monarchs, traders, naturalists and explorers yearned for a navigable maritime passage through the Arctic and into the Pacific Ocean, a route imagined as a short-cut to Asian markets that would benefit Britain commercially and politically. This dream of an Arctic passage became interlaced with English imperial visions of naval dominance in the north Atlantic during the heyday of Martin Frobisher and the magus Dr John Dee in the late sixteenth century (see Trattner, 1964) (see Figure 1.1). The disappearance and search for Franklin's expedition of 1845 stands out as the most famous and politically useful story in this long quest for a Northwest Passage, inspiring the detailed mapping of the Arctic in its wake as well as a legacy of sovereignty claims by Canada. Yet this expedition only came about after centuries of intermittent state, commercial and scientific interest in Arctic discovery or, as Craciun puts it, 'an uneven series of exploration booms punctuated by decades of inactivity and the occasional catastrophe' (2016, 15).

In this chapter I examine the way that the quest for a Northwest Passage was originally launched and narrated. I then turn to some of the otherworldly dreams associated with the quest – 'otherworldly' because they came about through embodied practices of transcendence, such as wandering, reverie, dreaming and remote sensing. After this I critique the influential myths associated with the body of the explorer – myths

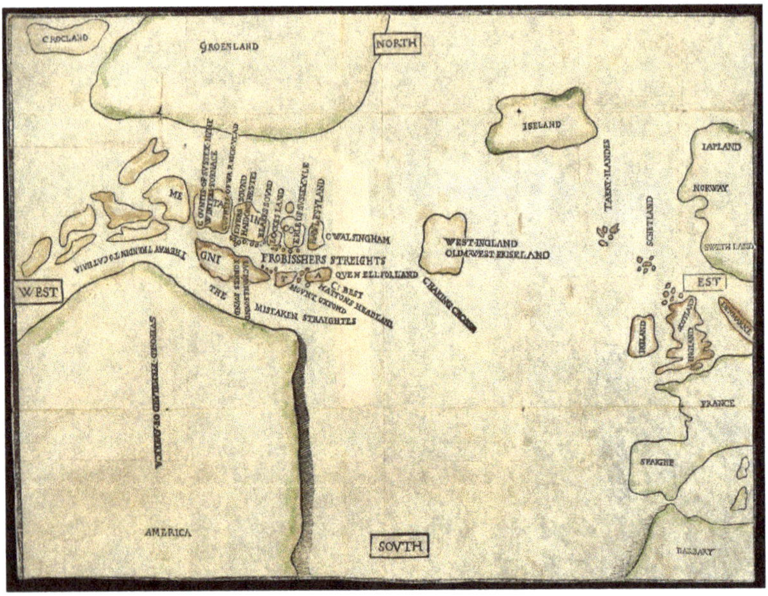

Figure 1.1 Untitled Map of Arctic and Northwest Passage (1578) by George Best and James Beare. Source: Osher Collection, www.oshermaps.org/map/309.

that underwrote the quest in the nineteenth century – before looking at the themes of place, the spectral and mobility in thinking about Arctic exploration.

* * *

For most of the eighteenth century the Hudson's Bay Company, a fur-trading corporation which had been granted the vast and inhabited North American territories known as 'Rupert's Land' by King Charles II in 1670, discouraged voyages in search of a maritime passage to the Pacific as it sought to protect its monopolies and territorial interests. When it did explore northwards and westwards of its trading posts along Hudson Bay, the Company generally sent small groups with limited, mostly commercial, aims. This caused ex-HBC employees, as well as armchair explorers like the Irish politician Arthur Dobbs, to agitate for larger government-funded geographical expeditions farther north (see Williams, 2002).[1] Things began to change later in the century when overland explorers started to map the lands up to the Arctic and Pacific coasts and the region took on a new significance in British strategic and scientific thinking.

The figure of the British Arctic explorer we are familiar with today emerged soon after the Napoleonic Wars ended in 1815. This Arctic explorer was a new figure associated not with the Hudson's Bay Company (HBC), but with the perquisites of naval authority, mostly created out of the imagination of the influential civil servant John Barrow, Second Secretary of the Admiralty (1764–1848) (Craciun, 2011; Cavell, 2008, 53–70). From London, Barrow used his influence on the Admiralty Board to oversee a series of attempts at a Northwest Passage between 1818 and 1845, launching the careers of explorers such as John Franklin, George Back, James Clark Ross and William Edward Parry (see Fleming, 1998).

Aside from appointments and direction, Barrow's authority on Arctic exploration was exerted through his influential writings (see Cameron, 2007). Barrow was a prodigious contributor of global exploration and travel narratives in the *Quarterly Review*, an influential conservative journal, and his privileged political position meant that he literally fashioned an historical account of the quest for *the* Northwest Passage, portraying it as something 'liberal and disinterested' but also as 'an object peculiarly British' (1818, 378, 364). Barrow always had to contend with alternative and critical voices and part of his strategy in creating this quest was to tune out these voices in order to choreograph a consistent and legible history of British enterprise in a new national space. This was a space that was separate from the commercial (and less glorious) spaces of the whalers and fur traders – rather a northern stage that connected the navigators of the sixteenth century – whom Barrow found so courageous – with the new breed of nineteenth-century heroic naval officers.

Barrow's historical survey of previous Arctic voyages, *A Chronological History of Voyages into the Arctic Regions* (1818), began the modern programme to chart a Northwest Passage. This book was published just a few months after two expeditions departed London on voyages of northern discovery: one, under the command of John Ross, went in search of a Northwest Passage via Baffin Bay and the other, under the command of David Buchan, went in search of the North Pole by way of Spitsbergen. The specific context of these expeditions was information received from whalers, especially the Whitby scientist-whaler William Scoresby, which suggested a dramatic decline in seasonal sea ice (Barrow, 1818). The moribund eighteenth-century parliamentary reward scheme for geographical achievements in the Arctic was rebooted and, with the enthusiastic support of scientists like Joseph Banks and the Royal Society, Barrow was able to launch the quest.[2]

In *A Chronological History* Barrow framed these expeditions as the latest efforts in an imagined linear narrative of 'dangers and difficulties and progressive discoveries' ('Preface') from the accounts of English navigators like Martin Frobisher and Henry Hudson. With these antecedents, Barrow's Arctic explorer emerged as a man challenged to continue an adventure while inscribing British power and its ideals of enterprise and knowledge on an ever-unfinished map of the circumpolar region. Where these ideals were not realised, Barrow criticised the explorer as if he were an aberration, someone who had failed to live up to national expectations.

One candidate who retrospectively dropped Barrow's baton was Thomas James, the leader of a Bristol merchant expedition whose account of overwintering in 1631 at the southern end of Hudson Bay was lambasted as 'a book of "Lamentation and weeping and great mourning"' (Barrow, 1818, 250; for revisionist accounts of James's expedition see MacLaren, 2013; James, 2014). Barrow was disturbed by James's dark and melancholic descriptions of the Arctic winter as well as his belief that the Northwest Passage did not in all likelihood exist.

Belief in the Northwest Passage was a prerequisite for Barrow, but scientific observation was another priority and it was to this end that Banks offered influential institutional support for the Northwest Passage campaign (Bravo, 1992). The study of terrestrial magnetism was a particularly important scientific agenda for the Royal Society and this overlapped with geographical expeditions to the Arctic, as can be seen from the experiments of George Fisher, Edward Sabine and John Franklin (see Levere, 1993; Lambert, 2010). In the context of the increased professionalisation of science in Barrow's time, an explorer's connections to scientific networks and his competent use of instruments like the dip circle were paramount. For instance, in *A Chronological History* Barrow criticised the narrative by the HBC trader and explorer Samuel Hearne, *A Journey from Prince of Wales's Fort in Hudson's Bay to the Northern Ocean in the years 1769, 1770, 1771 and 1772* (1795). Hearne travelled with a band of Chipewyan Indians from Fort Prince of Wales (now Churchill) on the western shore of Hudson Bay to the Arctic Ocean between 1769 and 1772, but the narrative of this expedition is generally believed to have been sensationalised by a ghostwriter years after the events took place (MacLaren, 1991; Cameron, 2015). In addition to this, Hearne was criticised for the erroneous scientific observations he took which, for Barrow, disparaged his credibility as an Arctic authority (1818, 301–3). By 1818, aside from the practical duties to extend maritime, magnetic and cartographic knowledge, Barrow's Arctic explorer would also function as a more compliant author than Hearne, having been trained in taking accurate observations using instruments recommended by the Royal Society and publishing his account in a more prescribed way.[3]

This creation of the Arctic explorer implied a repression of emotional and ecstatic states. Stephen Greenblatt has written that wonder is the 'central figure in the initial European response to the New World, the decisive emotional and intellectual experience in the presence of radical difference' (1991, 14). Although he drew on the early modern navigators for a myth of Britain's northern, Arctic destiny, Barrow had no place for the kinds of descriptions of wonder and superstition narrated by figures like James.

Although it was not stressed by Barrow in *A Chronological History*, wonder certainly featured in accounts of Northwest Passage voyages during the sixteenth century where it became a feature of Inuit-British relations. Take Martin Frobisher's expedition to Baffin Island in 1576, which established the first of the Northwest Passage 'contact zones' between the British and different regional groups of Inuit (Pratt, 1992, 4). It is significant that the expedition's first thoughts about local Inuit were that they were 'porposes or seales, or some kinde of strange fish' (Collinson ed., 1867, 73). Another wonder recorded a year later was that of a large dead fish found on a small island which was thought to be a 'sea Unicorne' (Collinson ed., 1867, 134): spiders were placed by the sailors in the horn – a legendary test to see if it was genuine (Settle, 1577, 32).

Strange disappearances were also a feature of Arctic exploration at this time. Memories were still fresh about Hugh Willoughby's Northeast Passage expedition of 1553. This ended in disaster after Willoughby's ships were separated from each other off the coast of Norway. It was not until the summer of 1554 that Russian fishermen came across a horrific cargo of frozen men in a Lapland bay. So when, after visits and exchanges between the English and the Inuit in 1576, five of Frobisher's men ignored orders and ventured on to the land, probably seeking to trade more 'tryfles' for fur, the Arctic once again became a haunted place. These men did not return to their ship 'and were never since hearde of to this daye againe' as a contemporary noted (Collinson ed., 1867, 73). This disturbing incident poisoned relations between the two groups on Frobisher's subsequent voyages to Baffin Island in 1577 and 1578.

In an act of revenge, Frobisher kidnapped three people as hostages in 1577, all of whom died shortly after arriving in Bristol. One of them – 'Calichoughe' as he was known – became a medical wonder and he was the subject of an autopsy in Bristol by Dr Edward Dodding. Where Frobisher's chroniclers wrote of the '*Anthropophagi*' and 'monstrous Islandes of yce' in the Arctic (Settle, 1577, 55, 27), Dodding claimed that Calichoughe's appearance showed evidence of *Anglium diceres metum* ['Anglophobia'], an ailment that, in a psycho-geographical manner, contributed to his death (Collinson ed., 1867, 190). After this the female captive, Arnaq, was forced to attend his burial and watch the body 'completely covered over with earth' in order to demonstrate that the English did not practise cannibalism (Collinson ed., 1867, 191). Arctic and non-Arctic tribal customs were here mutually strange and dangerous.

Other examples of strange and wondrous Arctic experiences include Frobisher's men stripping an old Inuk 'whome divers of oure Saylers supposed to be eyther a Divell, or a Witche' to see if she was cloven-hoofed (Settle, 1577, 35) while, in his account of Humphrey Gilbert's disastrous voyage back from Newfoundland in 1583, Edward Hayes wrote of how he '[omitted] to recite frivolous reports by them in the frigate, of strange voices the same night, which scared some from the helm' (1910, 298). Later, on his voyage in search of a Northeast Passage in 1608, Henry Hudson soberly reported that two of his men had seen a mermaid while east of Greenland (see Figure 1.2):

> From the navill upward her backe and breasts were like a womans, as they say they saw her, but her body as big as one of us. Her skin very white, and long haire hanging downe behind of colour blacke. In her going downe they saw her tayle, which was like the tayle of a porposse, and speckled like a macrell. Their names that saw her were Thomas Hilles and Robert Rayner (qtd. in Janvier, 1909, 21–2).

Later in the seventeenth century Thomas James particularly played up the ancient idea of the far north as the realm of Satan (see Franklin, 2008; MacLaren, 1984a), while a German whaler named Christian Bulle reported seeing the Devil's fleet several times, ready to collect the souls of northern voyagers. Also, while overwintering on Spitsbergen with six men, Bulle and his company set the table for eight, instead of seven, so that the Devil could dine with them (Hacquebord, 1991, 152).

These characterisations of the Arctic as a place of wonder and supernatural beings became more subtle as later narrators took on more scientific and objective ways of writing about exploration, but we do know that a base level of religious beliefs, superstitions and taboos continued to inform the everyday thought of whalers and seamen on discovery service, a profession that came with the risks of death, shipwreck or severe accident.[4] John Ross may be considered unusual for mentioning his sailors' 'harmless fondness for omens' (1819, 30) because, from at least the eighteenth century on, clergymen

Figure 1.2 Mermaid sighted by Hudson's crew at 75° 7'N.
Source: Thomas A. Janvier. *Henry Hudson: A Brief Statement of his Aims and Achievements*. New York: Harper, 1909.

desperately sought to combat superstitious beliefs among seamen by promoting 'Christian Spirit and Behaviour' and respect for the workings of Providence (Woodward, 1806, 36).

Ross, however, was not adverse to writing about Arctic omens and even recorded a strange solar phenomenon which made the sun appear like a medal of the Order of the Bath: 'If there was any one on board who imagined that this appearance was ominous of that, or any other knighthood, to any of us, the secret was kept ... though, by a very singular coincidence, it has been accomplished on the very day that the correction of this sheet, in passing through the press, enables me to add its fulfilment [December 24, 1834]' (1835, 222). Although we might smile at Ross's very personal vision, there was sometimes a very thin line between a personal faith in Providence and the transformation of the Arctic seas into regions of divine manifestation. Take William Scoresby, an evangelical Christian and committed Sabbatarian who saw signs of God's approval and disapproval in things like the number of whales captured, ice movements, near-escapes and storms avoided or endured (see Scoresby, 1850a). Shipwrecks also lent themselves to providential and supernatural interpretations, and popular accounts of disasters at sea disclosed national, class, gender and racial identities (Lincoln, 1997).

By the nineteenth century, the records of expedition commanders were supposed to be sober narrations of events, rarely interrupted by references to the author's body, emotions or passions (see Parry, 1826, 41). Partly, this was due to the fact that officers' journals and diaries were no longer purely their own, as they were collected by the naval commander on returning home and given to the Admiralty Board and Colonial Office for a period of time.[5] Scientific styles of discourse, including hydrographical, geographical and magnetical data, were privileged and if an officer wanted a promotion or subsequent employment it would be unwise, for instance, to include one's true feelings about the commander or details of the men's violence or sexual involvement with local women. Barrow therefore praised Parry's *Journal of a Voyage for the Discovery of a North-West Passage* (1821) for not including any 'marvellous stories' and for sticking to 'a plain statement of facts and occurrences, and a detail of scientific observations, made with unimpeachable accuracy and recorded in the clearest and most simple and unaffected language' (Barrow 1821, 177). Private correspondence – for example, John Ross's extended letter on his *Victory* expedition to the Hydrographer of the Navy, Francis Beaufort – gives better insight into the personal feelings of explorers (see Holland and Savelle, 1987). For literate crew and officers, shipboard publications and satires also served to express the poetic and dreamlike details of life in the Arctic, details that could not necessarily make it into a published narrative after it had been edited back home (see Figure 1.3).[6]

In the rare cases when accounts containing sensational or dissenting details were published, they tended to be by junior expeditioners seeking to make commercial gains in the literary market.[7] Commanders or expedition journalists with the responsibility for writing the official narrative often looked to James Cook's dispassionate and influential second narrative as a model (see Cavell, 2008, 18; Percy, 1996; O'Sullivan, 2008, 27–35).[8] Where conventions of travel writing were utilised, the contemporary artistic categories of the sublime and the picturesque offered explorers ways of depicting the Arctic and marketing it to readers (see Glickman, 1998). Overall, the important thing for establishing narrative authority for Barrow was to maintain a separation between the subject and the world: even if the explorer became immersed in foreign spaces or societies, his body must always be shown to be under the control of his mind.

Figure 1.3 'The Dream – Midnight – Middle Watch', by George F. MacDougall. Source: Sherard Osborn and George F. MacDougall eds. *Facsimile of the Illustrated Arctic News, etc*. London: Ackermann, 1852.

Otherworldly voices

The log-books and official accounts of naval expeditions were only two types of texts that came out of the searches for a Northwest Passage. We therefore need to look elsewhere to get a more rounded view of the way that the Arctic was imagined and experienced by people. Scholars in recent decades have argued that relying on the writings of explorers and their immediate readerships to understand Arctic exploration is unsound, both historically and methodologically. Challenging the dominance of a particularly constrictive type of historical narration of polar exploration – pioneered by Barrow – scholars have shown that people of all classes in nineteenth-century Britain and North America gained knowledge about the Arctic through visual culture (Potter, 2007), the newspaper and periodical presses (Cavell, 2008; David, 2000; Riffenburgh, 1994) and fiction (Wilson, 2003; Spufford, 1996; Hill, 2008; David, 2000). Things like panoramas, articles in local and national newspapers and assorted works of fiction were more likely to inform the average consumer about the Arctic than the expensive account of an explorer.

A more neglected part of this extended narrative field includes the diverse voyages (poetic, magical and spiritual) taken across the Atlantic Ocean to 'otherworldly' polar environments. In the nineteenth century, there was a lively scientific interest in 'Hollow Earth' hypotheses (see Standish, 2006; Spufford, 1996, 64–74) as well as popular interest in mystical theories of an 'Open Polar Sea' or a polar paradise (see Warren, 1898; Potter, 2004; Wilson, 2003). Frederick Cook's *My Attainment of the Pole* (1911) is particularly noteworthy for its ecstatic descriptions of the polar otherworld. Cook was a self-consciously haunted explorer, enchanted by the 'spectral denizens of the North' and the ghosts of dead explorers that he believed accompanied him on his journey (212–3). In many other cases, otherworldly voyages were more personal and intimate, involving family members back home sensing the presence of loved ones in the Arctic.

For example, in his autobiography, the infamous Victorian medium Daniel Dunglas Home remembered seeing a vision of his brother die during a polar expedition in the 1850s, 'at the very time of its occurrence' (1864, 30). In a similar case, the wife of T.C. Pullen, who served as second-in-command of the Franklin searching vessel the *North Star*, dreamt the following:

> she was standing on the deck of her husband's vessel, which was deserted. The ship was lit up by a thousand pieces of paper, which the lady, impelled by some impulse, picked up. On each she read these words: 'From the log of H.M.S. North Star, September 30, 1852'. Mrs. Pullen kept this date in her memory, and on the next occasion a letter arrived from her husband she read that on that very date he had been saved from death ('A Treasure House of Romance', *The Western Morning News and Mercury*, 1925).

There was a particular cluster of Arctic dreams associated with two disastrous American North Pole expeditions of the 1880s. In December 1881, just after the first news reached St. Petersburg of the tragic end of the American *Jeannette* North Pole expedition, the father of Lieutenant Charles W. Chipp, second-in-command of the ship, told the *New York Times* of a strange dream he had in June of that year. Chipp dreamt that the ship 'was being crushed in the ice': 'He says the whole affair seemed perfectly vivid before his eyes at the time and he thought much about it since' ('Lieut. Chipp's Father's Dream'). The *Jeannette* was indeed crushed by the ice floes on 12 June 1881, hundreds of miles north of the Siberian mainland and Chipp died in the subsequent desperate boat journey towards the Lena delta.

In 1882 the wife of the *Jeannette*'s engineer George W. Melville, who safely reached the Lena delta and then began a search for his lost comrades, told a reporter from the *New York Times* her own strange experience:

> 'On the 10th of last June … I retired to my room late at night. Days of anxious waiting for some news of the Jeannette without bringing a ray of hope had almost caused me to despair of ever again seeing my husband. I had fallen into an uneasy sleep, from which one of the children aroused me. It was, perhaps, more than an hour after this, and while I was wide awake, that I became conscious of a strange presence in the room, and you may well imagine with what mingled feelings of joy and fear I heard George's voice and looking up, saw him standing by the bedside – saw him as plainly as I now see you. He was saying: 'Count the bells! Count the bells!' and as he spoke I distinctly heard the bell of a ship striking … 'Eight bells; the Jeannette is lost!' and vanished from the room. At that moment the sitting-room clock struck the hour of 4 and it was the morning of the 11th of June. At that very hour on that very morning the Jeannette went down into the fathomless depths of the Arctic Ocean and the ice floe closed over her grave. I am no Spiritualist', continued Mrs. Melville, 'nor do I believe in spirits … A few weeks after the occurrence which I have narrated, and at the same hour in the morning, I had arisen for the day, and was in the hall which you see there. Again I saw my husband – nay, I even felt his breath in my face. I was dreadfully startled, but had sufficient courage to call out: 'George, is that you?' when the figure disappeared as if swallowed up in the air' ('Melville's Wife's Story').

Just a few years later another American polar expedition – the Lady Franklin Bay Expedition, led by Adolphus Greely – also ended in death and disaster. This time the mother of an expedition member, Sergeant David Linn, had her son's body examined 'as to the manner of his death, she having dreamed that he was shot in the back' ('The Greely Expedition').

These visions and dreams show how non-explorers could appropriate their own senses and ideas about the Arctic in the nineteenth century. This happened because of a gradual breakdown in cultural authority over the Arctic when diverse audiences, who initially bought into quest narratives like Barrow's, started to interpret exploration differently, 'in accordance with their own needs and preoccupations' (Cavell, 2008, 10). Once these Arctic channels had been opened up for popular cultures, stories of ghosts, dreams and strange coincidences started to appear in letters, texts and images.

It is a given that the narratives of naval explorers spread through popular culture and became central to the way that the Arctic was imagined in the nineteenth century. But alternative voices, sometimes dissenting, gothic or ghostly, were enmeshed in this geographical imagination. These include, for instance, the testimony of 50 psychics who supported Frederick Cook's contested claim that he reached the North Pole region in 1908 ('Spirits for Cook'). I follow previous scholars in looking at the way the Arctic was constructed by different audiences but I look at the dream-work that went into these imaginaries as well. This involves questioning the ontological separation between practice and representation, between the Arctic experiences of explorers and the images, panoramas and literature produced by audiences in Britain. This dream-work of Arctic exploration involved many experiences including reverie, mesmeric travelling and the projection of ghostly desires. Such spectral experiences and practices wove together the spaces of the Arctic and Britain. They could be fragmentary or substantive but, taken together, they challenge the idea of an objective and distant explorer. This has consequences for the way we think about the forms and legacies of Arctic exploration today.

The heterogeneous journals, stories, art and fiction that emerged from this period in the history of the Arctic are still relevant. They inform the way that people engage with the issue of the Northwest Passage today, whether through academic scholarship, popular culture, or the exercise of sovereignty at a state level. Yet taking account of the diversity of voices involved in Arctic exploration requires that we move beyond an exclusive focus on representations to an engagement with the 'non-representational' also. Scholars of global exploration have highlighted the varieties of actors involved in the cultures of exploration but, when it comes to the ways western navigators and travellers thought about exotic and unmapped regions of land and sea, there has been a tendency to focus on the visual or representational – what they 'saw' over what they 'experienced' (see for example Smith, 1985; Stafford, 1999). This focus has undoubtedly brought out cogent themes in histories of imperial discovery (see Rose, 1993) but it has also resulted in a tendency to take bodies for granted.

Members of Arctic expeditions were, after all, living, dreaming, breathing and embodied actors in the midst of strange environments inhabited by strangers who also lived and breathed the same air. Postcolonial analysis in particular has relied on the idea of the person as a spectator at the expense of the idea of a person who, despite forming representations of the environment 'out there', is part of a complex world that impacts on subjectivities (Dubow, 2000). This objectification of colonial space means there is a lack of interest in the emotions or altered states of consciousness among explorers, particularly Arctic explorers.[9]

Analysing representations of the Arctic as dreamlike or ghostly demands an attentiveness to the non-representational, to both everyday practices and to the moments when the body seems to melt away or senses the otherworldly.[10] This double movement, towards and beyond representation, leads me to point out two overarching myths that have underwritten traditional accounts of polar exploration by our British tribe: the integrity of the explorer's body and its edification despite great physical pain. Both reflect the ur-myth that polar space *tests* the explorer on a moral plane.

The explorer's body

A report from 1877, released after the return of yet another failed Admiralty expedition in search of the North Pole, gave Arctic exploration the appearance of a perfect 'bloodless contest' between Britain and other nations which elevated the mind in its 'true and honest ambition' (Johnston, 1877, 7). This understanding of Arctic experience as nationalist, but also enlightened, created a particular set of associations around the body of the male explorer – a coherent, rational actor constituted as heroic by virtue of his clean and selfless activity in a dangerous and unknown region.

At the outset of Barrow's quest, William Scoresby had been clear that if a Northwest Passage was found at all it would be of no practical use due to the prevailing sea-ice conditions that rarely allowed for more than two months of navigation. Yet Scoresby supported Northwest Passage expeditions for their advancement of scientific and geographic knowledge and for their development of the 'adventurous spirit' of British navigators (1820, I, 21–2). Decades later, even after the enormous expense and tragedies associated with the lost Franklin expedition, the President of the Royal Geographical Society, Roderick Murchison, similarly praised the quest as 'the best school for testing, by the severest trials, the skill and endurance of many a brave seaman. In her hour of need – should need arise – England knows that such men will nobly do their duty' (qtd. in McClintock, 1859, xxii). Barrow's construction of the Northwest Passage quest implied that, despite the tragedies and limitations of exploration, failure was something that could be reconfigured by explorers and the media into a kind of national capital – a repository of noble action. This framework meant that many nineteenth-century narratives were, consciously and unconsciously, cast in a military rhetoric that appealed to national masculine values.[11]

While it is dangerous to assume that all journalists and naval authorities were enamoured of Arctic exploration (see Cavell, 2008), where commentators were positive about the benefits of northern expeditions a rather disembodied mythology of heroism predominated. Less well publicised were the bodily and ignoble incidents that lurked beneath the epic stories: these included Martin Frobisher receiving an Inuk arrow in his buttocks (Collinson ed., 1867, 131); bitter rows about smoking in a tent (Ross and Savelle, 1992, 181); the suggestion that John Ross should mend a state-of-the-art steam-boiler with 'dung and potatoes' (Braithwaite, 1849, 13); an expeditioner dying in the snow with his trousers down (Bray, 1992, 120); and a survivor of the Franklin expedition who was nicknamed *Qoitoyok* by his Inuit hosts [Inuktitut: 'he who pisses a lot'] (Eber, 2008, 86).

While on this note, it is important to remember that Arctic explorers were not at all immune to satire and derision (Spufford, 1996, 55–7): John Ross's 1818 expedition was particularly pilloried by sections of the press and he became the subject of the ribald book *Munchausen at the Pole* (1819) (see Potter, 2007, 48–51). Even the great Arctic commander William Edward Parry – lionised by Barrow at every opportunity – was at the receiving end of criticism and satirical verse from the pens of Thomas Hood and Samuel Taylor Coleridge (see Cavell, 2013a, 60–1, 64–5). Panorama shows also offered audiences myth-busting moments of Arctic humour, especially if compèred by a talented showman capable of making fun of the audience's assumptions of heroism (see 'Moving (Dioramic) Experiences', 305).

The poetry of Alfred Tennyson is a touchstone in the more familiar mythology of polar heroism: indeed, Tennyson was John Franklin's nephew and composed the epitaph for the Franklin monument at Westminster Abbey, unveiled in 1875:

> NOT HERE! THE WHITE NORTH HAS THY BONES; AND THOU
> HEROIC SAILOR-SOUL
> ART PASSING ON THINE HAPPIER VOYAGE NOW
> TOWARD NO EARTHLY POLE.

In this piece, Tennyson looked back to the loss of Franklin's last Arctic expedition with a sentimental vision of an environment transcended through heroic death. It is no coincidence, therefore, that a line from another Tennyson poem, 'Ulysses' (1842), was later used to commemorate another polar disaster – the tragic end to Robert Falcon Scott's *Terra Nova* Antarctic expedition.[12] Before they left Antarctica, the surviving members of Scott's expedition erected a memorial cross inscribed with Tennyson's line 'To strive, to seek, to find, and not to yield', a citation deeply redolent of the British mythology of polar heroism. In this imagination, the struggles and will-power of the explorer are emphasised, sometimes at the expense of environmental knowledge or adaptation. Jen Hill (2008) shows how the myth of a blank, empty Arctic made sense as a figurative and literal testing ground for British masculinity and patriotism, one where the body and its characteristics were placed at risk.

In his 'Message to the Public', Scott famously declined to write of the 'hardihood, endurance and courage of my companions which would have stirred the heart of every Englishman. These rough notes and our dead bodies must tell the tale' (1913, I, 417). In the discourses of polar heroism, the British body overcame the environment through a denial of, or victory over, pain and suffering. In defeat, death remained as an emblem of victory, a form of national possession or inscription and remembering the final moments of explorers was part of this resistance. Take, for instance, the following passage, which imagines the afterlife of Franklin:

> No green turf covers the grave of Franklin. The drifting snow and benumbing ice shroud his remains, and the howling Arctic blast for ever and ever represents his requiem, and spreads its wailing dirge over the desolation where the gallant seaman is laid to rest. His enterprise is over. Those elements against which he persevered with such daring constancy vanquished him at last; and he has only given an immortal name and interest to a spot which human foot can rarely tread, and human sympathies but faintly penetrate (Jerdan, 1866, 220).

Such representations, and the myths they mask, continue to influence the way Arctic exploration is thought of to the present day.

Franklin's first Arctic land expedition along the Coppermine River (1819–22) is important here as a disaster that was transformed through narrative into an heroic journey. In his account of the expedition in *Narrative of a Journey to the Shores of the Polar Sea* (1823), Franklin created a narrative distance from the everyday bodily pain he and his men experienced by constructing an 'ideological, mythic, national' body

(Hill, 2008, 45). Franklin deployed this over-determined symbol in his discussion of the killing of Michel Terohaute, an Iroquois voyageur member of the expedition who was suspected of murdering the Englishman Robert Hood and cannibalising his colleagues. Readers of these sensational events could frame the British naval explorer as rational, civilised and reasonable, in contrast to the wild, irrational and unstable landscape and its indigenous inhabitants. As a later biographer of Franklin put it, this story was an 'Iliad in prose' and the incidents of chivalry, devotion and struggle that it related 'are all tales which should be household words by every English fire-side' (Osborn, 1860, 23–4). In the emergent myth of British polar exploration it was not just the conquering of space that was at stake, therefore, but the unfolding and testing of patriotic duty and spirituality in the face of disaster.

At the time of Hood's death, the expeditioners had eaten their moccasins and scraps of leather and were surviving on *tripe de roche*, a kind of edible moss scattered throughout the barren grounds of northern Canada. This suffering brought the British explorers and their Canadian voyageurs a shared sense of their fragility. The expedition's naturalist, Dr John Richardson, almost drowned when crossing a river and had to be stripped and rolled in blankets. 'I cannot describe', Franklin wrote of this incident, 'what every one felt at beholding the skeleton which the Doctor's debilitated frame exhibited. When he stripped, the Canadians simultaneously exclaimed, "Ah que nous sommes maigres"' ['ah how very thin we are'] (1823, 424).

However, in comparison to the voyageurs, the bodies of the British were failing even more alarmingly: they were unable even to gather *tripe de roche*. The ultimate difference between the two groups, according to Franklin, was a moral one, for the British refused to give in to despair and instead relied on God. As an example of this, Franklin praised his subordinate seaman, John Hepburn, who, 'animated by a firm reliance on the beneficence of the Supreme Being, tempered with resignation to his will, was indefatigable in his exertions to serve us' (Franklin, 1823, 427). Richardson's narrative of how he realised that Terohaute had killed, and probably cannibalised, three of the other voyageurs also contrasted British spiritual solace with the spiritual poverty of the native. Richardson described how he and Hood gained 'incalculable benefit' from reading to each other from religious books (Franklin, 1823, 449). To make the differences even plainer, when Hood was shot by Terohaute he had been reading *Bickersteth's Scripture Help*, while Terohaute's principles, 'unsupported by a belief in the divine truths of Christianity, were unable to withstand the pressure of severe distress' (Franklin, 1823, 458–9). For Barrow, this episode was useful in defining the noble characteristics of the British explorer *in extremis*:

> [O]ut of fifteen individuals enured from their birth to cold, fatigue, and hunger, no less than ten (native landsmen) [voyageurs] were so subdued by the aggravation of those evils to which they had been habituated, as to give themselves up to indifference, insubordination, and despair, and finally, to sink down and die; whilst of five British seamen, unaccustomed to the severity of the climate, and the hardships attending to it, *one* only fell, and that one by the murderous hand of an assassin. A light buoyant heart, a confidence in their own powers, supported by a firm reliance on a merciful Providence, never once forsook them, nor suffered the approach of despondency, but brought them safely through such misery and distress as rarely, if ever, have been surmounted (1846, 332).

Perseverance despite bodily pain is a theme that runs through Barrow's summary of this classic age of British Arctic exploration, *Voyages of Discovery and Research within the Arctic Regions, from the Year 1818 to the Present Time* (1846). Here Barrow argued that what made men like Parry, Franklin, Back and James Clark Ross legitimate representatives of British endeavour was the moral energy to keep going without complaining, confident in the guidance of Providence. Ignoring the physical and psychological torment suffered by voyageurs and other indigenous guides, Barrow celebrated the commanders'

> patient endurance of extreme suffering, borne without murmuring, and with an equanimity and fortitude of mind under the most appalling distress, rarely if ever equalled, and such as could only be supported by a superior degree of moral courage and resignation to the Divine will – of displaying virtues like these of no ordinary cast, and such as will not fail to excite the sympathy and challenge the admiration of every right-feeling reader (Barrow, 1846, vii).

Polar exploration was an opportunity for British men to prove themselves, to display the virtues that legitimated their global position. The definition of success and failure in the Arctic was therefore dependent on who was narrating stories of exploration, and what use they had among different popular or elite audiences. For some, John Ross's expedition of

1818 was a notorious failure for having returned back to Britain after sighting the illusory 'Croker Mountains' that blocked Lancaster Sound, causing Ross to cast doubt on the existence of a Northwest Passage. The following year Parry, Barrow's favourite, breezily sailed through this blockage, thereby making Ross appear a foolishly pessimistic navigator and a symbol of retreat in the Northwest Passage quest. Although Buchan's expedition of 1818 also failed in its objectives, 'unlike the other,' Barrow wrote, 'it was not owing to any want of exertion, zeal, or intelligence' (1846, 62–3). George Lyon's expedition of 1824 also failed in its objectives, but it similarly displayed 'a fine example of manly resolution under the most distressing difficulties, and of pious resignation to the Divine will' (Barrow, 1846, 230). For Barrow, Ross was unfit for discovery service because of his lack of perseverance, for 'running away home' after a journey that any yachtsman could have accomplished (Barrow, 1846, 49). By contrast, Parry possessed 'the true character and spirit of a British sailor – open, straightforward, and upright' (Barrow, 1846, 119): needless to say, Parry shared Barrow's optimism about the Northwest Passage quest.[13]

Aside from disputes about mapping and discovery, then, there were different 'cultural cartographies' (Gieryn, 1999) of Arctic exploration at work. This meant that boundaries were policed and discipline was enforced precisely because definitions were so important. During his overwintering expedition of 1819–20, Parry was able to keep the bodies and minds of his men active through exercise and education, thereby displaying the kind of persevering and enterprising spirit that Barrow thought central to British maritime power. James Clark Ross, John Ross's nephew, was another favourite of Barrow's, who said he had 'bodily powers of no ordinary kind' and united 'an ardent love of enterprise, a determined perseverance in the attainment of his object, and a mind undaunted by difficulty or danger' (Barrow, 1846, 329–30). Crucially, in Barrow's system, scientific progress and perseverance were joined by the idea of Divine Providence: Parry described it as 'the only rational source of true fortitude in man' (1826, 183). For Barrow, religious faith performed the work of distancing (if not separating) the body from the painful realities of exploration and guided the mind toward the edifying powers of hope and spiritual assurance (see Elce, 2002a).

What Barrow did not go into was the way that religious belief was not just something that Arctic explorers took with them, but was something that emerged through practices in the field. There was a routine religiosity to exploration comprised of daily prayers, grace before meals and Sunday services. On Parry's 1819–20 expedition, divine service was a systematic part of the daily regime of activities and Sunday service was a time for discipline and surveillance. '[R]esignation to the Divine will' was thus the result of practices in which bodies came together and it was more contingent than Barrow would have realised. It was not a case of bodies becoming inured to the challenges of an Arctic winter through faith and discipline, but a case of living, breathing men *becoming* explorers every day, again and again, through the very processes that seemed habitual and orderly.

Several expeditioners mentioned the importance of adapting prayers and sermons to Arctic situations, so that the men could use religious discourse in their everyday lives (see Parry, 1821, 126; Osborn, 1852, 121). This was the result of the evangelical Anglicanism that spread through the Royal Navy during the Napoleonic Wars, mostly through the efforts of officers known as 'Blue Lights'. These pious officers worked for moral renewal on warships by organising prayer meetings, literacy classes and religious discussions with men on the lower decks (see Blake, 2008). Although many officers in the Royal Navy distrusted the evangelicals by the end of the Wars, several low church and evangelical Christian officers quickly attained leadership roles in the Northwest Passage quest. Parry, Franklin and Richardson were 'Blue Lights' and for them the quest became an opportunity to integrate faith with exploration. Christianity, it was thought, could play a key role in managing the health and well-being of their men during the long and stressful Arctic winters (see Blake, 2014, 187–211). Furthermore, in the absence of chaplains, it was usual for commanders to conduct prayer services on expedition and whaling ships in the Arctic. While explorers like Parry and Franklin were therefore responsible for the spiritual health of their men – maintained through public observance – they were also concerned with a deepening of their private faith while in the Arctic.

Parry turned from conventional Anglicanism to evangelical Anglicanism while overwintering at Port Bowen in 1824–5. During this period, he immersed himself in the New Testament and formed a close religious bond with his purser, William Harvey Hooper. He even managed to convert two seamen to his faith (Parry, 1858, 201). Also, as Cavell shows (2010), Franklin's experience in the Arctic between 1819 and 1822, and his representation of it later, were influenced by his evangelical faith. In the aftermath of this expedition, Franklin wrote, 'I have never experienced Such ... happiness from the comforts of religion as in the moments of greatest distress, when there scarcely appeared any reason to hope that my existence could be prolonged beyond a few days' (qtd. in Cavell, 2008, 96). Bodies in the Arctic were also religious bodies and although Christian rhetoric was used to buffer the body from harsh realities, in practice, faith was expressed and acquired in the body's everyday performance and rhythms. Indeed, Parry was certain that the men 'who were always called upon in a time of especial difficulty and danger, – were, without exception, those who had thought the most seriously on religious subjects' [sic] (qtd. in Parry, 1858, 208).[14] Faith was therefore very important to how suffering was both experienced privately and represented to wider audiences. As Cavell notes:

> Without the image of the stoical Christian explorer-hero who would, if necessary, die with a prayer on his lips and a religious book in his hand, it is unlikely that the long, frustrating search for the Northwest Passage could have caught the public's attention and held it for so many decades (2010, 139).

It is also important to note the connections between evangelicalism and colonialism in the Arctic: Franklin and other officers were supportive of early missionary attempts to convert the Inuit to Christianity (see Craciun, 2016, 104).

The Arctic as a testing ground for 'national bodies' (Hill, 2008, 29–52) was a myth that was transferable to other geographical quests, but it also had currency among non-British explorers. Underwriting it were ways of thinking about polar environments that ranged from the idea of space as blank and awaiting discovery, to the idea of space as a treacherous agent that could resist discovery and swallowed up explorers. This latter sense of a struggle between the enlightened but fragile male and an alien, nonhuman nature, came up again during the race for the North Pole with Frederick Cook writing of:

> the terrible oppression of that raging, life-sucking vampire force sweeping over the desolate world. Disembodied things – the souls of those, perhaps, who had perished here – seemed frenziedly calling me in the wind. I felt under me the surge of the sweeping, awful sea. I felt the desolation of this stormy world within my shuddering soul; but, withal, I throbbed with a determination to assert the supremacy of living man over these blind, insensate forces; to prove that the living brain and palpitating muscle of a finite though conscious creature could vanquish a hostile Nature which creates to kill. I burned to justify those who had died here; to fulfill by proxy their hopes; to set their calling souls at rest. The storm waked in me an angry, challenging determination (1911, 229).

Innumerable examples from other polar narratives could be cited which reiterate this basic, and extremely problematic, separation between body and nature.

It is on the basis of such understandings of polar exploration that the concept of discovery was internalised as a kind of self-discovery with little to do with the actualities of the worlds travelled through. Rather, exploration was imagined by many as something more than the sum of its parts – even as ecstatic experience. This partly came out of the Romantic interest in armchair travelling (see Stiegler, 2013) – the practice of exploring by wandering around a room, going through material collections, or ruminating over memories. This is what Henry David Thoreau wrote about the loss of the Franklin expedition:

> Is not our own interior white on the chart? Is it ... a North-West Passage around this continent, that we would find? ... Is Franklin the only man who is lost, that his wife should be so earnest to find him? ... Be rather the Mungo Park, the Lewis and Clarke and Frobisher, of your own streams and oceans; explore your own higher latitudes, – with shiploads of preserved meats to support you, if they be necessary; and pile the empty cans sky-high for a sign (1895, 343).

One of the most striking invocations of the transcendental type of polar journey is the Latin inscription over the bust of Scott at the entrance to the Scott Polar Research Institute in Cambridge, England, which reads *Quaesivit arcana poli, videt dei* ['he sought the secret of the pole, but saw God']. Given the rhetoric of suffering and edification in polar narratives, references to ghosts and dreams could easily be taken to be mere poetic devices, appeals to divine-human relations that stood for a torturous worldly relationship with the body-in-pain. But to do so would be to ignore the actual role of space.

In the traditional account of polar exploration as narrated by Barrow and others, the Arctic was merely a sublime backdrop, a stage upon which humans left their mark or were put to the test. Barrow, like, most popular commentary on polar exploration, continues to place an emphasis on mythic change through linear time, on heroic adventures in a depthless, unchanging and depoliticised space. Here, time conquers space, a fact shown in the progressive mapping of 'empty' space.[15] The Arctic in these narratives is discussed in terms of discovering and naming. Thinking about Arctic space and place in a more dynamic and relational manner, by contrast, shows us the ways that explorers actually moved through an environment that was haunted: by inhabitants, spirits and sensed presences.

Making Arctic place

British explorers in the Arctic, particularly those who produced and circulated knowledge, were bound by fundamental somatic and environmental conditions. These conditions influenced the way they behaved, they way they moved and they way they thought. A question frequently asked of someone researching polar history is 'Have you been there?' The implication is that physical presence in the Arctic or Antarctic – however these locations are defined – provides access to knowledge and feelings that libraries and archives do not offer, but must form part of any analysis. But how is place really being made here and by whom?

The explorer's body, located at the centre of knowledge production, something that so impresses people who imagine the polar regions to be inaccessible, is also a dreaming body: 'I work, read, think, and dream' wrote Nansen of his Arctic routine onboard the *Fram* (1897, I, 260); elsewhere he quoted Edvard Grieg in describing the environment: '[T]hat is where the reality became a dream, and the dream became reality!' (Nansen, 1897, 202). Nansen put his finger on precisely the kind of perception I am interested in – a dreamlike perception that was tied up with people's Arctic encounters. Comments such as this suggest that in experiences like polar dreaming or armchair travelling to the Arctic from Britain, people's travel involved bodily movements and the sensing of otherworlds beyond the body.

In western imaginations the Arctic was something constructed over time, an assembly of myths and testimonies that marked out the region as exotic. For Europeans, biblical ideas of the North as the domain of Satan were succeeded by the medieval ideas of Ultima Thule and early modern visions of gold or quick access to the Indies (Franklin, 2008). By the era of the Northwest Passage quest, the attribution of a type of non-human agency to the Arctic regions was common in British culture. The strangeness of the light, the flashes of the Aurora Borealis and, above all, the phantasmagoric ice contributed to the idea of the north as a realm of fantastic spectacles. Just as there came to be a way that Africa or the African 'should look' (Neumann, 1998, 1), popular representations of the Arctic tended to cluster around the idea of a sublime wilderness.[16]

Although describing a voyage to the Antarctic regions, Samuel Taylor Coleridge's *The Rime of the Ancient Mariner* (1798) was in part inspired by Arctic sources and therefore reproduces many of the stereotypical and aesthetic features of the icescape:

> Listen, Stranger! Storm and Wind,
>   A Wind and Tempest strong!
> For days and weeks it play'd us freaks –
>   Like Chaff we drove along.
>
> Listen, Stranger! Mist and Snow,
>   And it grew wond'rous cauld:
> And Ice mast-high came floating by
>   As green as Emerauld.
>
> And thro' the drifts the snowy clifts
>   Did send a dismal sheen;
> Ne shapes of men ne beasts we ken –
>   The Ice was all between.
>
> The Ice was here, the Ice was there,
>   The Ice was all around:
> It crack'd and growl'd, and roar'd and howl'd –
>   Like noises of a swound. (2011, 63–4)

The 'otherness' in such representations of ice suggests the currency of colonial readings of the Arctic as a place of desire and dread. Like other colonial locations, the Arctic was already cognitively mapped before it was explored, painted with a palette of British preconceptions and visions. At the beginning of Mary Shelley's *Frankenstein; or, The Modern Prometheus* (1831 (original 1818)) Captain Walton writes to his sister that he tried in vain 'to be persuaded that the pole is the seat of frost and desolation; it ever presents itself to my imagination as the region of beauty and delight' (Shelley, 1831, 3). Walton's fantasies of geographic and scientific discovery were incubated by the narratives of Arctic exploration he found in his uncle's library, but it is significant that he was directly inspired to voyage north by *The Rime of the Ancient Mariner*:

> I have often attributed my attachment to, my passionate enthusiasm for, the dangerous mysteries of ocean, to that production of the most imaginative of modern poets. There is something at work in my soul, which I do not understand. I am practically industrious – pains-taking; – a workman to execute with perseverance and

> labour:– but besides this, there is a love for the marvellous, intertwined in all my projects, which hurries me out of the common pathways of men, even to the wild sea and unvisited regions I am about to explore (Shelley, 1831, 9).

Walton's reading reminds us of the predetermined nature of Arctic dreams. These textual representations were extremely influential in framing the way future British explorers and audiences described the North. Ships were also floating libraries and, as Urban Wråkberg (2007) points out, the work of the explorer also entailed sitting in an armchair and sifting through the accounts of previous navigators (explorers were also voracious readers of polar fiction and poetry; see Karamanski, 1984). When an explorer returned to Britain, his narrative would undergo further processes of mediation and translation, through what Bill Bell terms 'filters of technology and taste' (2013). The search for sublime Arctic experiences – Walton's 'love for the marvellous' – must therefore be thought of as something that involved intertextual dream-work. Explorers travelled through ice-fields of narrative, past bergs hiding masses of latent myths beneath their surface, all of which formed a 'constellation of ideas' that determined how the region was imagined (Said, 1995, 5; see also Driver, 2001).

The spectral Arctic

This notion of the spectral in this book is drawn from a research theme in the humanities and social sciences that reflects on the power of haunting as a figurative and non-figurative force. As explored variously by scholars in literary studies (Wolfreys, 2002), sociology (Gordon, 1997), philosophy (Derrida, 2006) and geography (Holloway and Kneale, 2008; Lipman, 2014), haunting is linked to questions of justice and exclusion. We all enjoy a good ghost story but how can we believe that the dead or disappeared have social agency in the cold light of day? The ghost is a sign that the past has returned to the present, revealing, in Jacques Derrida's formulation, the 'non-contemporaneity of the present time with itself' (2006, 29). The spectral locates the traces and effects that are left when something that was present becomes absent. This theme looks at how power (or lack of power) in the past becomes manifest in the present and it is seen as particularly relevant to modernity.

But why should ghosts be around in the present, supposedly a secular and disenchanted time? In recent years scholars have tackled the 'disenchantment of the world' thesis famously propounded by the sociologist Max Weber, who understood it to be a process that emerged with the scientific revolution and Protestant Reformation (Landy and Saler eds., 2009). For Weber, modernity is characterised by a process in which the natural world becomes less mysterious and more knowable, impersonal and predictable. On this account, secularisation and the decline of magic followed the increased power of the formal rationalities of science and bureaucracy. By contrast, revisionist scholars in the historical disciplines highlight the significance and continuity of uncertainty in scientific systems of knowledge and look at themes like the urban 'magical imagination' (Bell, 2012) or 'occult' Enlightenment science (Harvey, 2005).

These revisionist accounts show that audiences do not simply have one attitude (believing) or another (disbelieving) when they attended séances, magic shows or lectures on animal magnetism. Rather, consumers of spectacles, just like Arctic explorers in the field, displayed a range of responses, many incommensurable and self-consciously enchanting. Oppositional scholarly notions like the spectral, the uncanny, or 'cycles of re-enchantment' (Walsham, 2008), suggest that modernity can be seen as 'haunted': they challenge the idea of the rational western savant as somehow above the spectrum of spiritual, spectral and anomalous beliefs we encounter in everyday life.

My own interest in spectralities has previously centred on the sense of a haunted self (McCorristine, 2010). In this book I turn to the cultural production of the spectral. An obvious advantage of such an approach is that it creates a ground for dialogue between the inhabitants of the present and the past. In the case of Canada, this ground lies between European settlers and native inhabitants. The ghostliness of the Arctic has a long history, originating in the ways that British settlers made indigenous people part of a 'gothic' wilderness, on the borders of civilisation. As I will mention in chapter 6, critics using the notion of the spectral argue that Canada as a settler nation is indisputably haunted by the legacies of its colonial past (which it inherited from Britain) – a theme that figures heavily in contemporary Canadian literature, art and film. Despite this and even if we recognise the obvious differences between Britain's possessions in the Arctic and its possessions in southern Canada, ghosts and ghostliness are strangely absent from historical scholarship on the Northwest Passage.

The Franklin expedition is a presence that looms large in this book, a feature that it shares with some other recent studies (Potter, 2007; Davis-Fisch, 2012; Cavell, 2008). Franklin left London in 1845 in command of an expedition in search of a Northwest Passage made up of 128 men onboard HMS *Erebus* and *Terror*. After stopping at Disko Bay in Greenland, the ships entered Baffin Bay where they were last seen by Europeans in July. Searchers later discovered that the expedition wintered on Beechey Island that year (where it buried three crew members who died – John Torrington, William Braine and John Hartnell), before sailing in a south-westerly direction into an unmapped region. By September 1846, the ships were frozen in the ice off the coast of King William Island (see Figure 1.4). According to a note discovered in a cairn on this island in 1859 by Francis Leopold McClintock's expedition, Franklin died on 11 June 1847 and the icebound *Erebus* and *Terror* were abandoned in April 1848. Led by the second-in-command Francis Crozier, the note stated that the surviving 105 men were about to commence a march south towards the Great Fish River – although whether this was intended as a final march by a single group of men is currently a hot topic of debate.

It is likely that this was the first of several breakouts as the *Erebus* was probably re-manned in late 1849 and piloted south by a small company before it sunk in shallow waters in Queen Maud Gulf. In any case, this torturous southern escape route proved fatal for ill-equipped men who, by this stage, had split into different groups and were probably debilitated by scurvy (Cyriax, 1939). Evidence from Inuit testimony recorded the sightings of bands of starving white men ('all black, no fur'; Eber, 2008, xx) who 'fell down and died as they walked along' (McClintock, 1859, 275). The Inuit reported that these *qallunaat* carried iron, acted strangely and ate human flesh (Eber, 2008, 80).

McClintock's discovery of skeletons and relics years later failed to dampen interest in the mysteries of the expedition. Almost immediately Arctic veterans like Richard King and William Parker Snow campaigned for further expeditions, although it was several years before another explorer returned to the King William Island region in search of survivors, tombs, testimony or any paper records. In the late twentieth century, scientists and archaeologists confirmed Inuit accounts of cannibalism (see Beattie and Savelle, 1983; Keenleyside, Bertulli and Fricke, 1997; Potter, 2016), while in the last few years, teams sponsored by the Canadian government launched annual searches for the wrecks of the *Erebus* and *Terror*. These proved successful in 2014 and 2016.

Whilst retaining it as a central story, I will say some new things about the Franklin expedition in an effort to make sense of its complex and spectral legacies in history and literature. In chapters 3 and 4 this involves taking seriously the stories of 'clairvoyants, visions, dreams, and revelations' that McClintock dismissed in the search for Franklin ('A Strange Tale of Handwriting on the Wall', *Pall Mall Gazette*, 16 May,

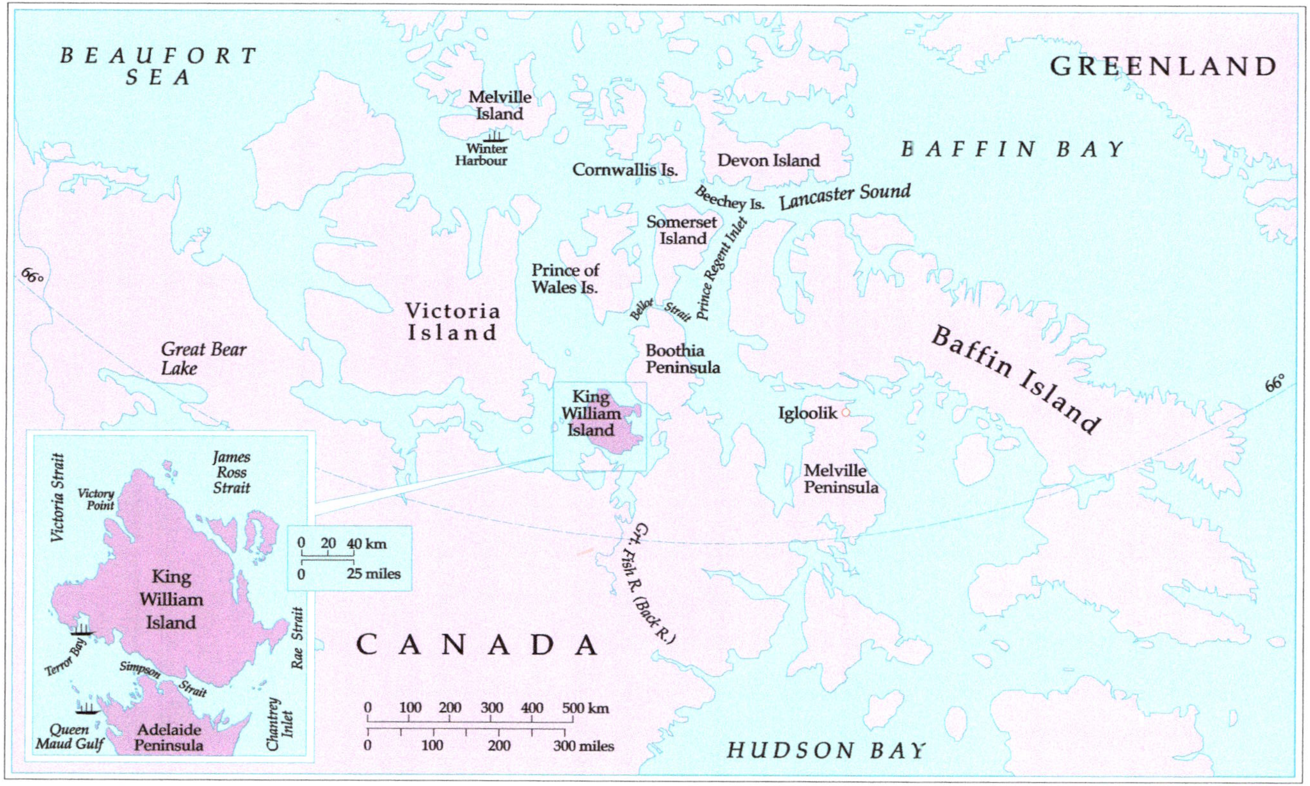

Figure 1.4 Map of the Canadian Arctic with inset.

1889). Looking at stories of dreams and ghosts promotes a shift in the scale of exploration, from the grand histories of naval commanders to the fractured and intimate voyages of writers, mummies, dreamers and clairvoyants. These dreams and visions did not come out of nowhere; they formed part of the social reality of Arctic exploration as a diverse set of practices that did not simply consist of narratives of manly endeavour meant for respectable readers.

My approach also implies a shift in our notion of sequentiality: to quote Hamlet, time is 'out of joint' in the Arctic. History does not stop at one point and begin at another, nor do injustices or memories rot in the ground. What we think of as securely consigned to the past reappears and there is a 'return of the repressed' in both dreams and bodily movements – the repetitive disruption of what Freud termed the 'uncanny'. In this book I show how non-explorers – those whom Barrow would have denigrated – created or gained access to the otherworldly Arctic. One advantage of a refusal to separate the spheres of men and women in this context is to further draw out the relations between home and Arctic, the ways that distance and loss came to be expressed and managed through the emotions. Through the materiality of the séance, the ghost story or the politics of haunting, people shared in the imaginaries and legacies of Arctic exploration.

Whether through déjà-vu, the idea of home, or the practice of visiting old 'haunts', most of us occasionally feel that a place means more than what can be seen and consciously felt. The accounts of Arctic explorers show that they also sometimes recognised that ghosts and dreams were part of how place was felt.

During a search for the Franklin expedition, the Arctic commander Edward Belcher mentioned seeing a wolf hanging around his ship that the men considered 'charmed'. Some even thought the wolf was one of the officers of the *Erebus*: 'It is a ridiculous feeling; yet who is free from it?' Belcher wrote: 'Indeed, I have been so far, at times, a victim to some such feeling, as even to attach the name of one of my friends to this cunning visitor!' (1855, II, 128). Some years later the HBC trader Roderick MacFarlane removed the body of a colleague, Augustus Richard Peers, from Fort Good Hope for burial at Fort Simpson, as was his wish. MacFarlane reported hearing a voice directing the dog team on this journey and felt a 'spiritual or supernatural presence of the late Mr. Peers' at Fort Simpson: 'The feeling, however, came on so very suddenly and scaringly that I instantly covered my face with the blanket and remained speechless' (qtd. in Colombo ed., 2008, 162–3).

Although polar explorers dreamed every night, the transcription of remembered dreams in their narratives was rare.[17] When they were recorded, dreams tended to involve food, warmth and home – the 'manifest content', we might say (see Hall, 1879, 211; Kane, 1856, I, 265; II, 42; Osborn, 1852, 219; 'Arctic Dreams of Food'). Kane went into a bit more detail on this subject, mentioning how the men of the first Grinnell expedition (1850–1) talked of their dreams during the dark days around winter solstice time:

> Some had visited the naked shores of Cape Warrender, and returned laden with water-melons. Others had found Sir John Franklin in a beautiful cove, lined by quintas and orange-trees. Even Brooks, our hard-fisted, unimaginative boatswain, told me, in confidence, of having heard three strange groans out upon the ice. He 'thought it was a bear, but could see nothing!' (1854, 267)

The period of winter was particularly dangerous for most expeditions as it was the time when access to fresh meat from hunting was restricted by the weather. December was therefore usually marked by the onset of scurvy, while the reopening of old scars, frostbite and the threat of fire on the ship were recurring matters of concern. These anxious times were reflected in the psychological disturbances reported by commanders. As men began to spend more time cooped up indoors they could become increasingly irritable and tetchy, while changes in sleep-patterns caused bouts of sleep-talking (Kane, 1856, I, 431; Young, 1875, 14). So when an explorer goes to the trouble of writing down a winter dream, it is not surprising to find that it contains themes of anxiety and conflict.

A good example of this comes from Isaac Israel Hayes, who during an Arctic expedition dreamed about his fellow expeditioner, August Sonntag:

> I had a strange dream last night, which I cannot help mentioning; and, were I disposed to superstition, it might incline me to read in it an omen of evil. I stood with Sonntag far out on the frozen sea, when suddenly a crash was heard through the darkness, and in an instant a crack opened in the ice between us. It came so suddenly and widened so rapidly that he could not spring over it to where I stood, and he sailed away upon the dark waters of a troubled sea. I last saw him standing firmly upon the crystal raft, his erect form cutting sharply against a streak of light which lay upon the distant horizon (1867, 182).

Hayes's dream occurred on 22 December 1860, during a period of prolonged darkness and gloominess at his expedition's encampment at Port Foulke, west Greenland. This was a time Hayes described as 'awe-inspiring and unreal' (172). In November an Inuk member of the expedition, Peter, mysteriously ran away from the camp, an incident which Hayes attributed to the rivalry between him and another Inuk, the veteran hunter Hans Hendrik. Hayes worried about the fate of Peter for weeks after his disappearance and drew analogies between the worsening weather and the fate of his former servant:

> The stiffened ropes which pound against the masts, the wind shrieking through the shrouds, the crashing of the snows against the schooner's sides, are sounds of terror echoing through the night; and when I think that this unhappy boy is a prey to the piercing gale, I find myself inquiring continually, What could possibly have been the motive which led him thus to expose himself to its fury? (170)

One answer came later from Hendrik, who recorded in his memoir the belief that Peter had turned into a 'Kivigtok' [*Qivittoq*] – a person who abandons the community and wanders the wilderness, perhaps as a ghost and possibly because of paranoia or feelings of alienation among his colleagues (1878, 37).

Following the disastrous deaths of most of the expedition's dogs it was arranged that Sonntag, who had served with Hayes previously, along with Hendrik, would sledge to the Inuit of the Northumberland Island region to purchase replacement dogs. Setting out on 21 December 1860, Sonntag and Hendrik encountered dreadful weather and the next day they resolved to return to camp. However, Sonntag fell through a sheet of ice and, although pulled out, was left, according to Hendrik, barely breathing in a blocked-up snow-house while Hendrik unsuccessfully sought help. News reached Hayes of Sonntag's death in late January and Hayes's mistrust of Hendrik again resurfaced. Although he never discussed the coincidence, the prescience of the dream of 22 December foreseeing Sonntag's death must have forcibly struck him and exposes for us a material imagination which attributes magical status to the ice – the 'crystal raft' of the dream. It also hints at an ingrained culture of anxiety among explorers who overwintered. Although the recording of dreams of death was quite common among Euro-Americans back home in the nineteenth century (McCorristine, 2010, 162), the particular image of an expeditioner floating away on ice actually reflects a realistic risk factor that Arctic explorers shared with indigenous inhabitants. Sonntag's body was eventually recovered and buried in March 1861: although Hayes recounted the dream in his narrative of the expedition, the burial site shows that he resisted naming 22 December as the exact date of his friend's death.

Strange experiences like these clearly affected explorers, but Arctic narratives also contain less dramatic moments where the narrator drifts into a reverie, at times inspired by wandering through a landscape. During this activity, place is suddenly recognised as being populated by absent forces and it is at this moment that the notion of the Arctic as somehow spectral is drawn out. This involves the recognition that reveries and dreaming are not simply abstract and disembodied experiences for people, but forms of practice, like religious worship, inextricably linked to the various rhythms and tempos of space and time. The spectral Arctic, in other words, emerged through the interactions between people and places that felt strange to them.

Arctic mobilities

Another research trend of recent years looks at mobilities, a set of approaches that conceives of the human world on the move, physically and imaginatively (Sheller and Urry, 2006). Taking a mobilities perspective on Arctic exploration offers obvious insights into the way we think of naval bodies onboard a ship. It also shows how traditionally neglected 'unbounded' spaces such as the air and the ocean can be brought into debates about human-environmental interaction and shown to have their own landmarks and histories (Adey, 2010). For instance, Percy Bysshe Shelley's valorisation of balloon travel across 'unknown countries' was informed by the way that Enlightenment ideology and technology had informed the imagination of the geographies of 'unhappy' lands (qtd. in Fulford, Lee and Kitson, 2004, 1). Similarly, after the return of Parry's first expedition in search of a Northwest Passage in 1820, the poet John Keats spoke of how the sailors' eyes:

> ... were so fatigued with the eternal dazzle and whiteness that they lay down on their backs upon deck to relieve their sight on the blue sky. [They described] the dreadful weariness at the continual day – the sun ever moving in a circle round their heads – so pressing upon him that he could not rid himself of the sensation even in the dark Hold of the ship (1899, 339).

On departing the Arctic for more southerly latitudes, Keats also mentioned that the sailors rushed upon deck to gaze at the stars which they had yearned to see all summer. So, while lunar bearings, stargazing and other meteorological observations were obviously part of a wider geographical concern to the officers, incidents such as this serve to remind us that the cosmic worlds above the horizon were neither peripheral nor superfluous in the everyday lives of sailors on Arctic discovery service.

The field of exploration need not be taken as purely earthbound – it can extend to our atmosphere. During the searches for the Franklin expedition, there were many desperate and imaginative attempts to communicate with the lost men. One scheme was the release of messenger balloons filled with hydrogen and attached to a slow-match. The idea was that the match burned off and caused colourful slips of paper to drop off the balloon at regular intervals. Other attempts included one, initiated by some 'English ladies', where dolls containing information about the location of rescue ships were distributed to Inuit women with the hope that they would one day make their way into the hands of the missing expeditioners (Bray, 1992, 21–2). Still another scheme was to release captured Arctic foxes that wore copper collars with rescue details attached (Osborn, 1852, 138). All of these mobilities reflect an understanding of the existence of different layers of place within a space to which British bodies had no access. Signs, rumours and visions of the Franklin expedition cropped up again and again, but their actual location in the Arctic was discussed in spectral terms as a result of their prolonged and haunting absence. The idea of maintaining links with absent explorers carried on into the twentieth century in the form of telepathic and spiritualistic experiments.

In 1921, Danish explorer and anthropologist Knud Rasmussen, about to commence his epic Fifth Thule Expedition across the Arctic, 'promised to place either himself or a sensitive Greenlander at the disposal of those engaged in psychical research, for an experiment in the receipt and despatch of telepathic reports' ('Telepathic Experiment', *Lancashire Evening Post*, 1921). In 1937–8 the Australian polar explorer Hubert Wilkins participated in an extended long-distance telepathic experiment during his search for the Soviet aviator Sigizmund Levanevsky, who went missing during a flight over the North Pole (Wilkins and Sherman, 1942). Finally, in the 1950s the Norwegian polar aviator Hjalmar Riiser-Larsen attempted to contact the spirit of Roald Amundsen, a close friend and colleague who disappeared in the Arctic during an air expedition in search of Umberto Nobile's airship the *Italia* in 1928. Riiser-Larsen was prevented from taking this course by the Amundsen family, not because of their aversion to spiritualism, but because Riiser-Larsen had been excommunicated from Amundsen's circle for posing for a photograph with his rival Nobile before Amundsen left on his last voyage (Berg, 2006, 132). Indeed, Amundsen himself professed to have telepathic powers around the time of this expedition (Anthi, 1999, 1002).

Telepathic communications across great polar distances were one thing, but mobility matters in other ways too. The naval expeditions and whaling voyages moving through Arctic seas were 'ship-shaped'. The ship has long been recognised in nautical traditions as an extension of the sailor's body and far from being background noise, the songs and sea-shanties sung aboard critically informed the movement and tempo of sailors' bodies (see Mack, 2011, 136–64; Podruchny, 2006; *Arctic Miscellanies*, 1852, 9–10). Like sailors, Admiralty ships in search of a Northwest Passage had to adapt to northern service. This called for technical and scientific (especially magnetic) instruments; air, filtration and cooking systems featured alongside preserved food (artificially extending potential subsistence durations); and a cultural stowage made up of libraries and theatrical equipment to combat boredom and restlessness. In all of these ways ships emerge not just as vehicles but as key material spaces in Arctic exploration, transporting, housing, healing and entertaining their inhabitants. These complex spaces were points of departure for 'spectral geographies' of the Arctic during the early phase of Barrow's quest for a Northwest Passage.

2
Spectral geographies of the Arctic: Shamanism, reveries, wandering

Introduction

In what ways did explorers encounter the Arctic world in all its strangeness and complexity?

In this chapter, firstly I challenge the traditional assumption in histories of the Arctic that only indigenous people engaged with supernatural experiences. Among the Inuit, shamans were traditionally consulted when a *qallunaat* ship was sighted and it was they who dictated the terms of the encounter following a séance (see Eber, 1989, 3–4). Although it is not surprising to learn that Inuit occasionally thought that British commanders were shamans, given their power and leading spiritual role as religious celebrants onboard the ship, it might surprise some to discover that explorers were active participants in shamanic séances. On these occasions, British explorers adopted nuanced positions on the supernatural, indicative of both scepticism and a degree of enchantment regarding indigenous claims for spirit-travelling. Far from being flim-flam, I show that shamanism and dreaming played a key role in the relations between the British and the Inuit during Northwest Passage expeditions.

Secondly, I thread together some connections between embodied practices and senses of the spectral in the Arctic. I do this by focusing on the ways that movement through the Arctic was thought of as something that was dreamlike and ghostly, which involved spectral senses of co-presence. Reflecting on the reveries of some British explorers can deepen our understandings of Arctic exploration. Reveries were a part of how the world was encountered and a means by which explorers made sense of their environments – the way that they 'flirted with space' (Crouch, 2001, 62). I focus on William Edward Parry's account of his 1819–20 Northwest Passage expedition because this set the model for overwintering that subsequent expeditions followed.

* * *

During voyages of imperial discovery, British explorers frequently adopted a panoramic 'monarch-of-all-I-survey' perspective on the world, encompassing the environment in a sweeping and possessive manner. In the Arctic, part of this strategy of incorporation involved naming places after family, friends, patrons or home locations – indeed, in one case, John Ross felt the need to invent some small islands to name after several members of the royal family (Ross, 1994, 185). This possessive strategy also relied on the importation of British aesthetic categories for its power in Arctic narratives.

The idea of Arctic exploration as something disinterested, in which British explorers – like astronauts – inscribed their visions and achievements on empty space, was a performance that denied the incoherence of everyday life in the Arctic and the historically inhabited landscapes people moved through. Using the language of the sublime or picturesque assumed a disentangled relationship between the British and the Inuit, and between the human and the non-human, both of which promoted the pervasive concept of the Arctic as an untamed wilderness beyond society. This was in contrast to Inuit perspectives, which did not take the environment as something to be contemplated or fought against but rather as something interrelated with social and emotional life.

Landscapes are more than just inert substances, capable of being inscribed upon by a powerful, gazing, and contemplative explorer. They are cumulative processes rather than simply projections, made in and through practices. In this chapter my arguments about exploration are not drawn solely from the thoughts emanating from the minds of explorers – I am interested in different and more complex forms of disembodiment. Hunter-gatherers and animists like to think of the world in terms of relationships, whereby animals, spirits, humans, rocks and water all have agency through their connections to each other (see Nuttall, 1992): this animist perspective can help us to understand historical episodes of British-Inuit interaction during which spiritual relationships played a role.

For instance, in response to the arrival of white men in 1821, the Inuit of the Igloolik region [Iglulingmiut] told them a story of how *qallunaat* once came to visit them, a story that integrated these aliens with the Inuit and the Indians in a shared creation myth. As the story goes, a girl named Uinigumasuittuq was married to a dog with whom she had six children – two Inuit, two half-dog half-Indian babies, and two half-dog half-white babies. Her father brought the half-Indians – who were feared by the Inuit – to the mainland while the half-whites were put into a boot sole with a stem of grass and let go in the ocean:

> Then all of a sudden there was a fog; there were bells ringing in the air, and the father could see a mast from the grasses, and sails of a boat like the sails of the boat in which Paarri came. You could see this boot sole, with the two babies in it, leaving the shore. There were only the two babies in the boot sole – a girl and a boy – but that's how the white people multiplied; they had children from one another. Uinigumasuittuq created the white people (qtd. in Eber, 2008, 21).

For the Iglulingmiut this explained why the man they called 'Paarri' [Parry] and other expeditioners looked for skulls in old graves and camps – they were seeking the skull of their mother.

A later story told by the Neitchille people relates to the Franklin expedition. In the 1860s the Franklin searcher, Charles Francis Hall, heard the story of how two *qallunaat* ships brought bad luck to the Boothian region and so two shamans performed so much magic that the fish and game stayed away from the area. Hall's informants told him that these shamans were very bad because they wanted the 'Koblunas' (white men) that were in the ice to starve to death. Some time later Inuit found a big tent ashore 'and there saw starved and frozen Koblunas all dead – many with the flesh all cut off the bones' (qtd. in Loomis, 1991, 191). This story echoes others about the Inuit fear of meeting vengeful *qallunaat* spirits on King William Island (Watson, 2017, 227). Supernatural power was a way of making sense of unusual events, and shamans provided a sense of narrative control over such incidents. In any case, examples like these are striking because they push against the grain of traditional accounts of how British explorers came to be in the Arctic and what they did there. They show that, although explorers consciously maintained the modernist dualisms that placed them above other animals and races, they were actually part of a spiritual field of engagement in which their presence was already a co-presence to the local inhabitants and in which their fate was directed by the actions of shamans.

Shamanic otherworlds

In a valuable study, D. Graham Burnett (2000) discusses the way that nineteenth-century explorers of British Guiana engaged with a landscape populated with spirits:

> On the one hand, the explorer was obliged to believe (and demonstrate) that Amerindian claims about geographical spirits were devoid of substance. On the other hand, the explorer's identity as intrepid and courageous, his heroic character, hinged on the imminent potency of the 'hostile forces' he confronted. This ambivalence required subjecting native place-myths and 'superstition' to ridicule while at the same time offering some subtle intimation of their power (185).

Spirits are part of exploration and they certainly played a part in British, French and Spanish cultures of colonialism in the Americas (see Lutz, 2007). The examples I gave in the previous chapter showed that the Arctic could be a spiritual place for explorers. I use the word spiritual here as it can be suggestive of ghosts without necessarily involving judgement or recognition of them, and these were examples that had very little to do with the indigenous cosmologies of the region. Of a different order are the spirits, ghosts and elementals recognised by Inuit in the Arctic, encountered by the shaman and engaged with – albeit ambivalently – by British explorers.

The shaman (the word comes from the Tungus languages of Siberia) or, in the Canadian Arctic, the 'angekok' or *angakkuq* ['moving, or jerking about'], was a communally recognised medium (male or female) who interacted, through trance states and other ceremonies of possession, with the spirit world on behalf of his or her people (DuBois, 2009, 6). These ceremonies, which featured a 'shaking tent' or the harnessing of the shaman with ropes, enacted a soul journey or 'spirit flight', through a multi-levelled cosmos (Crantz, 1767, I, 210–11) (see Figure 2.1). People chanted, sang and danced at the shamanic séance and they recognised the presence of spirits by hearing voices or seeing objects fly around inexplicably.

In European thought, shamanism was particularly associated with Arctic and sub-Arctic peoples and, throughout the eighteenth century, shamanic rituals, while no longer seen as demonological, were derided as obscurantist survivals of superstition among non-Christian and ignorant societies.[1] Furthermore, it was maintained that these rituals could be

Wizard preparing for a "spirit flight." He is bound head to knees and hands behind; the magic drum resting on his foot is beating itself. Bird's wings are fastened to his back.

Figure 2.1 'Wizard preparing for a "spirit flight"'. Source: Knud Rasmussen. *Eskimo Folk-tales*. London: Gyldendal, 1921.

explained or debunked by the attentive observer, wise to the tricks of the shaman. By the time encounters between explorers and shamans took place in the Arctic, the dominant explanation for the strange sounds heard at the séance was ventriloquism, understood as a natural ability or art, not evidence of demonic possession. For instance, writing of the shamans in the 1850s, Elisha Kent Kane could not discover 'any resort to jugglery or natural magic': 'their deceptions are simply vocal, a change of voice, and perhaps a limited profession of ventriloquism, made more imposing by the darkness' (1856, II, 126).

Yet despite this, accounts by explorers demonstrate the way that they adopted a range of ambivalent responses to the shamanic otherworlds in their midst, some of which was related to their own Christian spirituality. For instance, in his 1823 account of Cree and Northern Ojibwa shamanism, the Hudson's Bay Company (HBC) trader George Nelson suggested that true Christian belief required one to take the shamanic séance seriously:

> There are many in the civilized or Christian world who absolutely and positively deny [the shamanic power of conjuring] as being absolutely impossible and at best but absurd and idle stories. Many of the things related of these Conjurings I acknowledge to be so; but at the same time I am as positive and as firmly persuaded of

> the truth of the assertion 'that they have dealings with some supernatural spirit', as I am convinced that I live and breathe in air … To absolutely deny this, we must first deny that there is a Devil, and afterwards deny his pernicious power and if we deny these points, we must descend to a third, more fit for an atheistical wretch and a beast than a Christian, or even rational creature (1988, 82).

Séances were therefore disturbing to those who held to one objective or rational outlook on the matter.

Even if the séance was to their minds debunked, many western observers left with a sense of bafflement, a tense frustration that they were unable to *fully* explain the phenomena that had taken place. Just like the scores of intellectuals and aristocrats astounded by Daniel Dunglas Home's spiritualist performances in the 1850s and 60s, George Francis Lyon, who travelled as Parry's second-in-command on the Northwest Passage expedition of 1821-3, emerged from a shamanic séance at Igloolik with an interested and hesitating attitude.

Lyon's shamanic encounter was with an Iglulingmiut man named Toolemak, a 'cunning and intelligent' (1824, 358) hunter, storyteller and healer who was very friendly with the British. Lyon had heard of Toolemak's 'deceptions' (Lyon, 1824, 289) and 'exhibitions as a conjurer' (Lyon, 1824, 291) and engaged him in a discussion about a vision that Toolemak recently had:

> the sum of which was, that an object had appeared to him, advancing rapidly, and making extraordinary motions; this had first alarmed him, but on a nearer approach he discovered the figure of Lyon, bearing in his hand an axe, which he immediately presented to him. This extraordinary account I answered by the relation of a dream which I had also lately been surprised by; which was, that Toolemak had been turned out of my cabin for begging (Lyon, 1824, 296–7).

Lyon's joke did not affect his friendship with Toolemak and his mannerly concern to share a meal of frozen walrus encouraged the shaman to perform a séance in Lyon's cabin onboard the *Hecla*. On this occasion voices were heard, alternately loud and smothered:

> in about half a minute, a distant blowing was heard very slowly approaching, and a voice which differed from that we at first had heard, was at times mingled with the blowing, until at length both

> sounds became distinct, and the old woman [Toolemak's wife] informed me that Tornga [*tuurngaq*: 'helping spirit'] was come to answer my questions. I accordingly asked several questions of the sagacious spirit, to each of which inquiries I received an answer by two loud slaps on the deck, which I was given to understand were favourable. A very hollow, yet powerful voice, certainly much different from the tones of Toolemak, now chanted for some time, and a strange jumble of hisses, groans, shouts, and gabblings like a turkey, succeeded in rapid order. The old woman sang with increased energy, and, as I took it for granted that this was all intended to astonish the Kabloona [white man], I cried repeatedly that I was very much afraid. This, as I expected, added fuel to the fire, until the poor immortal, exhausted by its own might, asked leave to retire. The voice gradually sank from our hearing as at first, and a very indistinct hissing succeeded: in its advance, it sounded like the tone produced by the wind on the base chord of an Eolian harp; this was soon changed to a rapid hiss like that of a rocket, and Toolemak with a yell announced his return. I had held my breath at the first distant hissing, and twice exhausted myself, yet our conjuror did not once respire, and even his returning and powerful yell was uttered without a previous stop or inspiration of air (Lyon, 1824, 360).

This séance (or meta-séance, given that Lyon and Toolemak shared the awareness that this was a performance) led to a subsequent session at Toolemak's hut in which Lyon could not detect any movement from the shaman, despite the séance lasting an hour and a half:

> for had he done so, I was so close to the skin behind which he sat, that I must have perceived it. Neither did I hear any rustling of his clothes, or even distinguish his breathing, although his outcries were made with great exertion (Lyon, 1824, 367).

By calling the séance an 'exhibition' and the shamans 'professors' who don't disclose each other's secrets, Lyon translated shamanic experience into the language of secular magic. This translation made its way into *Letters on Natural Magic* (1832) by the Scottish scientist David Brewster. This text became something of a guide-book for debunking the supernatural and in it Brewster cited Lyon's first séance with Toolemak as a paradigmatic case of the power of ventriloquism. Yet debunking was not the end of the matter, for both Brewster and Lyon were enchanted by the shaman and found him 'uncannily desirable as well as alien because his voicings declared the limit-point of scientific discourses' explanatory power' (Fulford, 2009, 193). Certainly, ordinary people, as well as influential Victorian intellectuals like Brewster, Charles Dickens and the anthropologist Edward Burnett Tylor, exhibited a whole range of incommensurable responses to spiritualism that went well beyond *either* scepticism *or* belief (see Kaplan, 1975; Lamont, 2006; Stocking, 1971; McCorristine, 2010).

The appearance of *qallunaat* in Toolemak's visions points to further complexity in the relationship between shamans and non-indigenous observers. Both Parry and Lyon became intimate friends of Toolemak, with the shaman greeting Lyon as a 'son' who 'as well as himself was a great Annutko [*angakkuq* or shaman]' (Lyon, 1824, 405). This was not an isolated incident. Some years later, during his *Victory* expedition, John Ross allowed the Neitchille Inuit he encountered to think that he was a shaman. This was apparently in order to:

> impress upon the minds of the poor benighted natives the belief, that the proprietorship of all the seals and walruses was vested in him, and that they were so far under his control that not one should be killed, unless his will ordained it (Huish ed., 1835, 560).

Ross, we are told (by a critical eyewitness, it should be noted), went beyond his 'official capacity, as the commander of the Victory' and went '*Angekoking*' (ie being a shaman) in order to convince the Inuit that he had set the marine animals free (allowing them to hunt) and to prevent thefts on his ship (Huish ed., 1835, 563–4). Taking on shamanic power, then, could be an instrumental act by British explorers, eager for food or knowledge. Lyon and Ross, it seems, were participant-observers in Inuit cosmologies and this entanglement has consequences for the way we think about encounters – traditionally taken as climactic *moments* in Arctic histories.

In a close analysis of the interactions between the British and the Iglulingmiut in the Melville Peninsula region between 1821–3, Michael Bravo has stressed the historic avoidance of *qallunaat* by the Inuit and the consequent reasoning behind *their* discovery of and decision to engage with Parry during these years. In 1821 Parry believed that he was making first contact with an undiscovered tribe of Inuit. This was despite receiving testimony from Toolemak about his communication and trading with 'three kabloona ships' that were whaling around Igloolik a few years previously (Parry, 1824, 436; Bravo, 1992, 196). Parry's belief that he was the first is a fantasy of control that other explorers shared, something that is undercut by indigenous oral histories and non-official textual narratives.[2] These suggest that Parry's expeditioners were actually *too late* in that they encountered peoples who knew they were not alone in the world and who had been entangled with western material cultures and ontologies since, at least, the sixteenth century (see Bird, 2005). Bravo's model of 'premeditated cross-cultural exchanges' (1992, 221), rather than sudden encounters between the Inuit and the British, is drawn from this correction and is also helpful when we turn to the visionary dimension of their interactions.

I have mentioned the 'dream exchange' between Lyon and Toolemak: other sources attest to the fact that Euro-American explorers were already part of shamanic cosmologies. Disrupting the idea of a classic unidirectional encounter with Arctic peoples, Neitchille Inuit oral history recalls how after sighting Ross's expedition at Felix Harbour in 1830, a séance was held at which 'the spirits of the white men themselves arrived behind the curtain and invited all the Eskimos to visit their camp' (Learmonth, 1948, 11).[3] In another account, the first sight of the masts of the *Victory* caused a hunter to worry that 'the white people might think they were spirits – not people' (qtd. in Eber, 2008, 42). These cosmologies featured later the same year when James Clark Ross was nearly killed by an Inuk whose son had suddenly died, apparently due to *qallunaat* witchcraft (Ross, 1994, 145). From the other perspective, British officers sometimes consulted shamans to access their geographical knowledge and it is significant that these consultations could alternately be made in the formal atmosphere of the ship with maps and charts, or during a shamanic séance in a hut.

In his journal of 1822–3 William Harvey Hooper, purser on the *Hecla*, wrote that he wanted Toolemak to perform 'some of the ceremonies of Angetkokism' (ie the work of the shaman). The shaman agreed on condition that Hooper and his colleagues slept in his hut that night. Hooper agreed and during the opening chants of this séance Lyon and Parry were mentioned and a 'general request' was then made for a *qallunaaq* to chant, 'but as we were all diffident of our talents in this way, Mr Hooper proposed to substitute a song' (RGS, SSC/73 4, 877). Hooper held the hand of an Inuk woman throughout who explained what was happening (RGS, SSC/73 4, 895).

Despite Hooper's scepticism regarding Toolemak's 'conjurations', he wanted the shaman to find out if the expedition's ships could achieve a Northwest Passage (RGS, SSC/73 4, 879). Toolemak questioned a *tuurngaq* (calling upon the British officers 'to become his auxiliaries' in this process) who answered that the ships would not be able to reach their destination due to the quantity of ice and would then 'return to

Kabloona-noona' [white man's land] (RGS, SSC/73 4, 881, 885). The expedition was indeed repelled by ice at what Parry called 'Fury and Hecla Strait' and then departed the Arctic for home. Incidents such as this remind us that the point of these séances was not primarily to display supernatural powers for foreign observers but to serve the needs of the community and fulfil requests for information. The *reasons* for going to the shaman in a particular place and time were the key, not the phenomena that he/she could produce.

Despite their own mythologies, and the assumptions underlying traditional approaches to Arctic history, British explorers were actually entangled with indigenous cosmologies. The natural and the supernatural dimensions of life were not easily separated in the Arctic. This was an especially tense terrain for evangelicals like Parry and Hooper who were eager to see signs of God's presence in earthly events but probably encountered accusations that their beliefs tended toward irrational 'enthusiasm' and 'fanaticism' (see Bebbington, 1989, 22; 'Review of New Publications', 609). Inuit testimony tells us that John Ross – a man not particularly known for his piety (see Huish ed., 1835, 487) – visited the Inuit as a spirit before he arrived in physical form. British testimony tells us that he later took on the attributes of a shaman. Ross had disciplinary reasons for *Angekoking*, just as the Inuit controlled events by predicting the arrival of the British. The point here is that otherworldly ideas operate in the context of social practices and it makes no sense to restrict either group to just one epistemological outlook or set of beliefs about what is natural or supernatural.[4]

It was a feint of the explorer to believe that his discovery ship explored the Arctic through inanimate ice-fields, occupying empty space along the way through ceremonies of possession. Whether appearing in dreams, singing during a shamanic séance or collaborating with the Inuit on maps, it is clear that Barrow's idealised Arctic explorers were not above the world. In fact they always inhabited small portions of already-inhabited physical and social worlds, and a large part of growing into these worlds involved something not even necessarily goal-directed or purposive: wandering about in the winter.

Reveries of the solitary explorer

> *The surrounding Scenery began to assume a winter like aspect. The Men in consequence worked with all diligence to prepare the House* (Franklin, 1995, 67).

Arctic explorers tended to be anxious about the environments they passed through. To judge by their diaries and journals, the stillness of the Arctic was something that felt threatening to them and this led to a sense of relief whenever they saw signs of animation. Explorers gave flesh to these moments of strangeness by representing them as reveries or occasions of mental wandering in their narratives. In the western imagination winter was a season particularly conducive to reveries but scholars have not recognised their importance in accounts of Arctic exploration. Reveries are the buoys that mark out how the Arctic became a haunting place for explorers. Parry's narrative of his 1819–20 expedition, in particular, shows how overwintering in the Arctic inspired him to mental wanderings.

In this account, *Journal of a Voyage for the Discovery of a North-West Passage from the Atlantic to the Pacific* (1821), Parry described the technical challenges of finding a place to winter after making significant progress sailing through Lancaster Sound during the summer of 1819. With winter setting in in September, his ships the *Hecla* and *Griper* were towed by the men through ice canals and into a place they called Winter Harbour on Melville Island (diplomatically named after the First Lord of the Admiralty). It is at the point when the ships were anchored that stillness started to become a problem for the expeditioners. In his chapter on this winter, Parry described the way that the social life of the expedition was recalibrated, going through the creative methods by which the crew staved off the creeping boredom (education, theatrical performances and craft work) (1821, 123–7). In a disciplinary sense, Parry had to deal with the consequences of 'the stop' (Appelbaum, 1995), when life turns inward and when hidden tensions come to the fore. This involved combating the abyss of dead time by structuring time into watches, forcing the sailors to perform calisthenics onboard deck and, most noticeably, dancing to the barrel organ.[5] When the weather outside was too harsh for regular exercise to take place, the men were:

> ordered to run round and round the deck, keeping step to a tune on the organ, or, not unfrequently, to a song of their own singing. Among the men were a few who did not at first quite like this systematic mode of taking exercise; but when they found that no plea, except that of illness, was admitted as an excuse, they not only willingly and cheerfully complied, but made it the occasion of much humour and frolic among themselves (Parry, 1821, 124).

This barrel organ, which is held in the Polar Museum at the Scott Polar Research Institute, was taken by Parry on all three of his Northwest Passage expeditions (Holland and Hill, 1972). To modern ears the barrel organ's repertoire of some 40 hymns, reels and fiddle tunes sounds slightly eerie, but the music of this instrument was an important part of how British time was passed during the Arctic winter. It harnessed the bodily rhythms of the men and created activities for the expedition, combating the stillness that explorers found dangerous.

Following the preparations for the winter and the disappearance of the sun, Parry and his men sought to create homeliness in the ships, which were mobile objects that were suddenly transformed into frozen houses. Parry's journal shows that this process was not a given but something that actually involved reveries:

> Perhaps, too, though none of us then ventured to confess it, our thoughts would sometimes involuntarily wander homewards, and institute a comparison between the rugged face of nature in this desolate region, and the livelier aspect of the happy land which we had left behind us (1821, 125).

Affects float between disparate bodies, Parry hints, making proximate what is far and distant. Winter was a poetic device for Parry, a motif that he shared with contemporary Romantic writers who drew on winter melancholy and mystery as part of their sensitivity to locale. The environment around Winter Harbour clearly offered the conditions for mental wandering and dreaming. We are told that wolves approached the ship 'howling most piteously on the beach near us' (Parry, 1821, 116);[6] remarkable varieties of Aurora Borealis appeared, while the stars, moon effects and a meteor drew the eyes skyward; fires were maintained in-between decks and the men largely relaxed and wrote by candlelight. We are dealing with representations here, but also the things that evade representation, what the philosopher Martin Heidegger referred to as 'those attunements which attune us in such a way that we feel as though there is no attunement there at all' (1995, 68).

The phenomenology of this light is a good example of something that exists on the fringes of awareness but is ubiquitous in everyday life nonetheless. Light has been taken for granted in histories of polar exploration, discussed either in a negative sense (lack of light during winter) or a positive sense (return of light in spring). It deserves more attention than this, for people's perceptions and senses of place are transformed when natural light diminishes and we begin to spend more time in enclosed spaces illuminated artificially.[7] George Brown, a petty officer on McClure's *Investigator*, gave some sense of what waking up in the ship during the darkness felt like: 'Rising in the morning to the shrill boason's "lash up hammocks" one gropes about by the light of one dim lamp, then tumbling on deck, finds even less light there from the dull glare of the open candle' (GM, M-141). Of course, darkness was always relative and varied widely from location to location. The Winter Harbour region of the Arctic was never totally dark: moonlight, twilight and light reflected from the snow gave some sense of illumination to expeditioners.

Despite the hardships that expeditioners endured, ideas of snugness and somnolency emerged from this period of darkness, within the intimate spaces of the winter house. The stillness of the air became alternately impressive or oppressive; sound vibrations paradoxically drew close to the ear but kept their distance; loud noises in the twilight startled listeners. Winter affected explorers' moods also, pushing them inward where the self comes to the fore (see Bessels, 2016, 107). Parry's account of the expedition now became a winter journal – a therapeutic record of thoughts and signs of animation. His thoughts, now 'housed' for the winter, began to wander and reverberate according to the rhythms of memory and emotion (see Bachelard, 1994). It is clear that Parry, who frequently felt the lure of melancholy ('the most delightful sensation I experience', qtd. in Parry, 1858, 30), made efforts to keep the dangerously hypnotising powers of winter solitude at bay, including prematurely opening the stern windows of the *Hecla* during the period of the most intense cold in February 1820 'not less from the impatience which I felt to enjoy the cheering rays of the sun for eight hours of the day, than on account of the saving of candles, the expenditure of which had hitherto been much greater than we could well afford' (1821, 146–7). The issue of light therefore exposes just one of the phenomenological threads which created winter-time.

With the phenomenology of reveries comes a geography of reveries. Not only did Parry fail to achieve a Northwest Passage in 1819 but the expedition had to overwinter in a single location. This was the point at which the overwintering explorers were forced to attune themselves to a new rhythm of waiting, something that was extremely difficult for an expedition that prioritised speed and momentum (Parry, 1821, 54). As mobility was restricted by seasonal conditions, navigation by sea was out of the question, while the explorers could not launch their sledging journeys across land and sea ice until the spring. So creating winter homeliness called for a different form of movement that enacted exploration by mapping out what was not home.

Parry mentioned that he and his officers were in the habit of 'rambling on shore' near the ships to combat the tedious monotony they experienced (Parry, 1821, 124). I take this practice to be central in the place-making imperatives of the expedition, for reconnaissance and other forms of boundary exploration served to set limits to what was canny and where British authority was unchallenged. Underlying this, however, are the flickers and intimations of other uncanny voices in the landscape: Inuit did not pass by Winter Harbour during the period of waiting, so it is on the perimeter where one rambles in search of novel encounters, and it is here, within hearing or seeing distance of the ships, where the reverie can unfold itself.

Not that this part of Melville Island was always strange: the summer landscape was considered picturesque, something that was conducive to reassuring reminders of home. Parry highlighted a place called Bushnan Cove as 'one of the pleasantest and most habitable spots we had yet seen in the Arctic Regions' (Parry, 1821, 199), a place that was sheltered, open to game and had abundant vegetation. A drawing by Lieutenant Frederick William Beechey illustrating this scene, entitled 'Green Ravine. Winter Harbour', portrays the casual rambling postures of two figures walking towards a third in a pastoral-style scene. But a reverie is something more than the pleasant contemplation associated with picturesque aesthetics. The previous winter, Parry's distant view of the ships had inspired dread at the image of home, a position that drew out a reverie in which senses of place and placelessness come to the fore. Crucially, it is the perimeter that creates the settlement, not the other way around:

> When viewed from the summit of the neighbouring hills, on one of those calm and clear days, which not unfrequently occurred during the winter, the scene was such as to induce contemplations which had, perhaps, more of melancholy than of any other feeling. Not an object was to be seen on which the eye could long rest with pleasure, unless when directed to the spot where the ships lay, and where our little colony was planted. The smoke which there issued from the several fires, affording a certain indication of the presence of man, gave a partial cheerfulness to this part of the prospect; and the sound of voices, which, during the cold weather, could be heard at a much greater distance than usual, served now and then to break the silence that reigned round us, a silence far different from that peaceable composure which characterizes the landscape of a

> cultivated country; it was the deathlike stillness of the most dreary desolation, and the total absence of animated existence. Such, indeed, was the want of objects to relief to the eye or amusement to the mind, that a stone of more than usual size appearing above the snow, in the direction in which we were going, immediately became a mark, on which our eyes were unconsciously fixed, and towards which we mechanically advanced (Parry, 1821, 124–5).

This representation has been taken as an example of Parry's '[u]nromantic', 'calm', and 'subdued' take on the 'Arctic sublime' (Loomis, 1977, 101). But at the same time one can sense a panic in this passage that punctures the image of the disinterested observer and acts to entangle the explorer in the landscape.

Parry's motif of smoke rising from a fire in the distance has deep symbolic meaning in nineteenth-century exploration narratives ('a hieroglyphic of man's life' in Thoreau's words (1895, 41)), offering, on the face of it, that primeval reassurance of a place of warmth for the explorer in an empty and strange land.[8] But the motif has the double effect of suggesting vulnerability and exposure to the surrounding darkness and cold. Like a microcosm, the home-fire can represent the power and limits of activity in expedition narratives of this period. For instance, an illustration in Franklin's *Journey to the Shores of the Polar Sea*, 'Manner of Making a Resting Place on a Winter's Night' (1820) (see Figure 2.2), suggests that the border between fire and darkness is less redolent of the picturesque than reflective of an anxiety about the divide between the bustling signs of encampment and the ominous, snow-dappled trees surrounding and enclosing the expedition (Belyea, 1990). Some years later, also in the woods of the sub-Arctic, George Back described a similar tense moment between solitude, stillness and homeliness:

> There is something appalling in the vastness of a solitude like this. I had parted from my companions, and was apparently the only living being in the wilderness around me. Almost unconsciously I reloaded my gun; and then, stepping cautiously along the narrow ridge of the descent, glided silently into the valley, as if afraid to disturb the genius of the place. It was a positive comfort to hear, now and then, the hollow tread of the men as they passed rapidly through the thicket which screened them from sight; and when the white tent was pitched, and the curling smoke rose through the dense green of the forest, it seemed as if the spell of the desert was broken, and the whole landscape was suddenly animated into life and cheerfulness (1836, 72).

Figure 2.2 'Manner of Making a Resting Place on a Winter's Night', engraved by Edward Finden after George Back. Source: John Franklin. *Narrative of a Journey to the Shores of the Polar Sea, in the Years 1819, 20, 21 and 22*. London: John Murray, 1823.

The point here is that British explorers looked at the environment around them in an ambivalent way. The representations of stillness and quietude were sometimes not signs of peace and tranquillity but rather of the uncanny, the unknowable and a reminder of the judgement of God. To go back to Franklin's first land expedition, another officer, John Richardson, wrote to his wife about the sense of place that had overcome him. 'If we pass the threshold of our hut', Richardson wrote:

> and enter the forest, a stillness so profound prevails that we are ready to start at the noise created by the pressure of our feet on the snow. The screams of a famished raven, or the crash of a lofty pine, rending through the intenseness of the frost, are the only sounds that invade the solemn silence. When in my walks I have accidentally met one of my companions in this dreary solitude, his figure, emerging from the shade, has conveyed, with irresistible force, to my mind, the idea of a being rising from the grave. I have often admired the pictures our great poets have drawn of absolute solitude, but never felt their full force till now. What must be the situation of a human being, 'alone on the wide, wide sea!' How

dreadful if without faith in God! An atheist could not dwell alone in the forest of America (qtd. in McIllraith, 1868, 74).

Jumping at one's own shadow; encountering traces of one's own footsteps; meeting companions by chance, now figured as ghosts – this is the language of spectrality in which an inanimate place suddenly becomes alive with forces that might isolate and threaten the individual. Richardson's response to the uncanny stillness is to demonstrate how this threat could be managed by the certainty of religious belief. Parry, desperately seeking visual relief, similarly suggests a sense of panic – despite the sign of fire and hint of warmth – but in contrast to Richardson's resolution, Parry allows it to hover over the scene. There is a realisation of the precariousness of a winter home surrounded by a 'silence that reigned' (Parry, 1821, 125), and a recognition of the 'claustrophobic immensity' that undercuts any harmonious view (Belyea, 1990, 14). The discourse of the picturesque – the importation of local English ways of seeing – therefore unravels 'as though it were a fabric torn and repaired with foreign patches – indications of other knowledge, other values, other discourses' (Belyea, 1990, 22).

The scene of the ships is also a poetic image that echoes Coleridge's descriptions of ice and fearful sounds in *The Rime of the Ancient Mariner* and William Cowper's musings on winter from his blank verse poem *The Task* (1784). Moreover Parry's text was accompanied by an engraving – originally sketched by Beechey – that does express a romantic sensibility, in this case a melancholy reverie. Beechey's sketch was set during an overcast winter's day but the illustration included in Parry's *Journal of a Voyage for the Discovery of a North-West Passage* was an engraving of the sketch by the landscape artist William Westall – well-known for his representations of Australia – who gave the scene a twilight mood (see Figure 2.3). This nocturnal representation of Parry's daytime view of the 'colony' adds strangeness to the scene. Parry's description of 'the deathlike stillness of the most dreary desolation' becomes interrelated with the engraving, emphasising the soul-disturbing darkness of winter. This engraving was widely disseminated through cheaper reprints after the publication of Parry's account (see Snelling, 1831, n.p.; *Northern Regions,* 1826, facing 24) and it became iconic of the British Arctic winter. Lord Byron was particularly taken by Parry's descriptions of these winter experiences, using the explorer's account in his poetry and lightheartedly referring to the cold of 'Parry's polarities' (qtd. in Lloyd-Jones, 1996, 60). Furthermore, if we compare Parry's reverie with Percy Bysshe Shelley's contemporary visionary poem 'Mont Blanc' (1817), we find the

Figure 2.3 'H.M. Ships Hecla & Griper in Winter Harbour', William Westall, after William Frederick Beechey. Source: William Edward Parry. *Journal of a Voyage for the Discovery of a North-West Passage from the Atlantic to the Pacific, etc*. London: John Murray, 1821.

same idea of the interpenetration between nature and mind which is anything but 'subdued':

> Thou art the path of that unresting sound –
> Dizzy Ravine! and when I gaze on thee
> I seem as in a trance sublime and strange
> To muse on my own separate phantasy,
> My own, my human mind, which passively
> Now renders and receives fast influencings,
> Holding an unremitting interchange
> With the clear universe of things around (Shelley, 1901, 348).

In taking Parry's view of the ships as a destabilising reverie it is worth explaining what is meant by reverie a little more. In early nineteenth-century psychiatry, reverie was considered analogous to dreaming in its imagery, but also different in that the person having a reverie exercised some amount of control over their imagination. The Glasgow physician Robert Macnish wrote extensively on reverie during this period, considering it something proceeding from 'an unusual quiescence of the brain' causing the mind to wander, as when one gazes intently at a river (1834, 244):

> The thoughts seem to glide away, one by one, upon the surface of the stream, till the mind is emptied of them altogether. In this state we see the glassy volume of the water moving past us, and hear its murmur, but lose all power of fixing our attention definitively upon any subject: and either fall asleep, or are aroused by some spontaneous reaction of the mind, or by some appeal to the senses sufficiently strong to startle us from our reverie (Macnish, 1834, 245).

Macnish also highlighted walking alone in the country, ennui and the fading candle light on a winter's evening as 'most favourable' for reveries (Macnish, 1834, 245–6). It is no surprise, therefore, that these 'waking dreams', as they were frequently called, were experienced by Arctic explorers who constantly complained of stillness and solitude.

Today, the twentieth-century French philosopher, Gaston Bachelard, is perhaps most associated with the idea of reverie. Bachelard took the reverie to be a creative daydream that, in contrast to the nocturnal dream, occurred during a period of 'relaxed time' (1971, 5). In sympathy with the phenomenological perspective, Bachelard thought of the moment of reverie as a time when subject and object folded into each other, thereby transforming Descartes' famous *cogito* formulation: 'I dream the world, therefore, the world exists as I dream it' (Bachelard, 1971, 158). The reverie, in this understanding, has ontological consequences, for the 'dreamer's being invades what it touches, diffuses into the world … The world no longer poses any opposition to him. In reverie there is no more non-I' (Bachelard, 1971, 167). Reveries, in other words, draw people into a world that entangles but this is not something that occurs in a disembodied manner, for remember that Parry's reverie began as a 'ramble on shore'.

Spectral geographies of walking

Looking closely at the embodied practice of walking allows us to historicise and place Arctic reveries. The Romantics revitalised walking in British culture by celebrating wandering and strolling through the landscape on foot in contrast to the emerging public transport technologies of the nineteenth century (see Solnit, 2002; Wallace, 1993). While pedestrian travel ironically depended on new transport links to picturesque locations, such as the Lake District in England and Connemara in Ireland, walking was re-imagined as an extraordinary rather than mundane activity, which was treasured and celebrated by people in all its sensory richness. Crucially, however, wandering was seen as something that was not necessarily goal-oriented, but was linked to self-discovery. This practice of wandering on foot was symbolised by the solitary male *Rückenfigur* [person seen from behind] in Romantic art and letters, who engaged in contemplation and reverie while on the move: as Jean-Jacques Rousseau put it, 'my mind only works with my legs' (qtd. in Solnit, 2002, 14). The characters in some of Caspar David Friedrich's paintings memorably illustrate this practice.

Reacting against the dominant 'head over heels' position in western culture, Tim Ingold argues that '[l]ocomotion, not cognition, must be the starting point for the study of perceptual activity' (2011, 46). We perceive, in this understanding, not as static beings but rather in our movement along a 'path of observation': the methods, styles, technologies and effectiveness of moving on one's feet through the environment are linked to knowledge and experience of that environment (Gibson, 1979, 195–7). It is no coincidence that the Arctic explorers generally seen as being among the most successful in terms of their communication with indigenous inhabitants – Samuel Hearne, George Back and John Rae – were also celebrated as long-distance walkers. Indeed, a history of cross-cultural communication in the Arctic could be written just on the theme of feet.[9]

Therefore, walking, like the winter landscape, is not ontologically given. It was constructed and performed by people moving through the Arctic. Inuit could absolutely distinguish British tracks from their own due to different footwear and gaits (Woodman, 1991, 258). In contrast to heavy British boots, with their deep heel imprint and long narrow footprint, Inuit footfalls were soft and their gait was pigeon-toed (Woodman, 1995, 15). An Inuk woman told a Franklin searcher that white men could also be spotted by the way they swung their hands while walking (Woodman, 1995, 13). Several explorers, typically taller than Inuit, were named Aglooka by them [*aglukaq*: 'he who takes long strides'] and one *Victory* expeditioner was named Niugitsoq ['the good walker'] (Rasmussen, 1931, 28). One of the exceptional things the Iglulingmiut noticed about Parry was that he 'took very long strides in walking' (RGS, SSC 73/3 367) and, indeed, in a portrait of 'Paarri', probably drawn by the teenager Toolooak sometime between 1821–3, the commander appeared to the boy as tall and thin, with noticeably

Figure 2.4: 'Portrait of Parry, probably drawn by Toolooak'.
Source: Scott Polar Research Institute, University of Cambridge, with permission: SPRI 76/6/2+a (reverse).

elongated limbs (see Figure 2.4). Furthermore, when the Inuit of Cape Bathurst were trying to convince McClure that they had seen Rae they mimicked the walk and manner of Rae so exactly that one expeditioner said immediately 'That's the Doctor – Sir J.R. [sic]' (SPRI, MS 1503/47/1). Despite its universality, different tribes have different ways of walking. Walking changes according to social, environmental and historical contexts and focusing on the 'heels' over the 'head' can help us to think of exploring as akin to dreamy wandering, as much as it involved purposeful travelling.

Not that wandering was something everyone could do. On Arctic expeditions commanders differentiated between the mechanical movements of the men and the more refined, contemplative 'rambles' and 'wanderings' of the officer class. For instance, on John Ross's 1818 expedition, William Harvey Hooper described how he 'rambled, or rather scrambled' up the hills of Disco Bay, Greenland, in search of 'natural productions' (RGS, SSC/73 1 53). In August 1858 Francis Leopold

McClintock recorded a 'delightfully refreshing ramble' which he took by himself on the shore near Bellot Strait in order to make immediate plans for the sailing of the *Fox*: McClintock described this as cogitating 'undisturbed in a leisurely and philosophic manner' (1859, 185). On a darker note, the Moravian missionary Johann Miertsching reported that during the long winter of 1851 Robert McClure was 'oppressed with anxieties' and sought comfort 'by wandering alone on the hill' (1967, 170). McClure was regarded as a particularly irascible man but, while officers were allowed to have moods, they did not separate the explorer from the world around him. The mood is something that the solitary wanderer shares with the world for, as Heidegger points out, the landscape perceived as melancholy or desolate is not in-itself so: it 'merely attunes us in such a way, causes this attunement in us' (1995, 85). With their authority and authoritative voice, explorer-authors had the opportunity to express this radical interlacing of the self and the world.

* * *

I turn now to the walking practices of George Lyon, who interestingly used three different terms to describe this distinctive mobility of the officers: 'ramble', 'stroll' and 'American walk' (1824, 52–3). However, like Hooper, when Lyon described a walk it was usually in connection with an antiquarian adventure, rather than anything cartographic or utilitarian. Moreover, this was a practice that was not exclusive to Arctic exploration for Lyon. Before setting out in command of the *Griper* on his own expedition in 1824, Lyon made the standard stopover for water and supplies at Stromness on Orkney, where he 'walked into the country' in the company of his officers to investigate the 'Druidical remains' of the island.

> The first of these remarkable monuments consisted of three flat slabs of sandstone, standing upright, and from ten to fifteen feet in height. One entire slab lay flat on the ground, and I afterwards heard that it had been intentionally thrown down by some ardently inquisitive antiquary, to ascertain how deeply it had been embedded in the earth; but he was afterwards unable to place it as it was before, to the great chagrin of some of the old Orkney women, who hold these ruins in great reverence (1825, 7).

The disenchanting antiquarianism of this passage reads like the prelude to an M.R. James ghost story, but it is an incident that expresses the very

Figure 2.5 'An Eskimaux Grave', engraved by Edward Finden after George Lyon. Source: George Lyon. *A Brief Narrative of an Unsuccessful Attempt to reach Repulse Bay: Through Sir Thomas Rowe's 'Welcome' in His Majesty's Ship Griper, in the Year 1824*. London: John Murray, 1825.

real sense of connection between walking and the sense of place. In his account of Parry's second Northwest Passage expedition (1821–3), Lyon wrote that readers might feel it strange that he regretted leaving his Arctic winter camp for, though dreary and flat, he had occupied his eight months with walking around and naming landmarks accordingly, such as the 'Promenade' or the 'Causeway' (1824, 208).[10] Lyon's walking was not just a reflection of his position as an officer with spare time, but was something that revealed him to be entangled in an inhabited landscape, for again and again he described rambles when he happened across traces of Inuit encampments, landmarks and sacred sites, uncovering a sense of co-presence in this foreign environment, ideologically figured as uninhabited.

So what did Lyon do with this intimation of other voices? In his 1824 expedition, Lyon described finding an Inuit encampment full of relics and signs of historical inhabitation. After disinterring the corpse of an adult, Lyon excavated the grave of a child (see Figure 2.5):

> Near the large grave was a third pile of stones, covering the body of a child, which was coiled up in the same manner. A snow buntin[11]

> had found its way through the loose stones which composed this little tomb, and its now forsaken, neatly built nest, was found placed on the neck of the child. As the snow buntin has all the domestic virtues of our English red-breast, it has always been considered by us as the robin of these dreary wilds, and its lively chirp and fearless confidence have rendered it respected by the most hungry sportsmen. I could not on this occasion view its little nest, placed on the breast of infancy, without wishing that I possessed the power of poetically expressing the feelings it excited. Both graves lay north-east and south-west. Before going on board I placed boarding-pikes, men's and women's knives, and other articles, which might be useful to the poor Esquimaux, on the huts and various piles of stones (1825, 68–9).

Lyon here dwelt in a place that was crowded with the memories and possessions of the dead and the living. Finding Inuit settlement and grave sites offered explorers more than something colourful and interesting to note and remember; these artefacts were signs of an inhabited landscape intersecting with the places they created through discovery service: this could be deeply affecting for explorers. Coming across these signs during a walk, when chance encounters and discoveries are welcomed, means they become symbols of haunting absences for the walker, traces that are barely there. The walker here becomes spectral, curiously poised between 'one step and the next' (Wylie, 2005, 237).

Lyon's concept of place here seems to be spectral in that it recognises the voices of absent others. Unlike the cartographic vision in which a 'particular kind of boundary between subject and space' is created (Kirby, 1996, 47), Lyon's encounter creates the space for multiple voices to emerge. Lyon connects the present Arctic scene with absent English 'domestic virtues' but beyond this his voice fails, he tells us, to express poetic feeling. Not that this closes off the power of the moment for, years later, John Barrow recalled that he read this passage to 'an accomplished lady' who 'felt a desire to try what *she* could do with so interesting a subject'. 'Georgiana' went on to write a short poem entitled 'To the Snow-bunting' that cited Lyon's analogy with the English robin and suggested that the snow bunting 'cheer'st the wandering seaman's thoughts / With home, his aim and end' (Barrow, 1846, ff 220–1).[12] This moment of grave-digging, therefore, contains so much more than the scientific curiosity of the explorer. Rather, we are dealing with an Arctic made up of multiple voices, an interweaving of presences that jostle among each other. At this scene Lyon leaves some tools for the 'poor Esquimaux' to use, imagining, perhaps, that they might someday wander, like him, by this cache by chance: this is a new horizon that places exotic British materials into circulation with the Inuit, further entangling the work of foreign exploration with the lives, feelings, and voices of indigenous inhabitants. 'To haunt a landscape', John Wylie writes, 'is to supplement and disturb it' (2005, 246).[13]

Happening upon signs of Inuit inhabitation in the Arctic was one thing but the British could also be haunted by their own absence and walking played a significant role in this context. The kind of rambles I have been discussing are what Wallace identifies as 'excursive walks', associated most prominently with the poetry of William Wordsworth, which counter 'the threat of wandering with the promise of return' (1993, 120). For the indigenous inhabitants of the Arctic, the world is so full of spatial references and landmarks that getting lost is something of a temporary disorientation: once a mark on the land, ice or horizon is located the locale becomes familiar again (see Aporta, 2003). What for British explorers might seem like a monotonous and empty landscape outside history was filled with memories, contexts, stories, information and trails for Inuit travellers. By contrast, the British were unfamiliar with the environment and this meant that getting lost was something to be feared.

On Parry's first expedition, in September 1819, a party of seven men from the *Griper* disappeared after following the tracks of some reindeer and musk-oxen. Search parties were sent out but it began to snow:

> which rendered the atmosphere so extremely thick ... that this party also lost their way in spite of every precaution, but fortunately got sight of our rockets after dark, by which they were directed to the ships, and returned at ten o'clock, almost exhausted with cold and fatigue, without any intelligence of the absentees (Parry, 1821, 82).

Parry's apprehensions grew to a 'painful degree' and he had search parties plant pikes with flags and messages in bottles attached in the surrounding area that had the double purpose of guiding themselves *and* the absent party back to the ships (1821, 82). It was three long nights before the men found their way back to the ships and the tale of disorientation and confusion they told impacted on the expedition's sense of place. Living out in the open had nearly killed them and in 'humble gratitude to God for this signal act of mercy', Parry named the place 'Cape Providence' (Parry, 1821, 84). Some weeks later, after anchoring in Winter Harbour, Parry had finger-posts erected 'on all the hills within two or three miles of the harbour' to direct his men to the ships and prevent them becoming lost amid the 'dreary sameness' of the locale (Parry, 1821, 109).

Further rambles drove home just how strange and dangerous Arctic place was for the British. Wandering around was not something that performed possession in a disembodied manner – rather it was something that signalled their vulnerability. After 'a longer walk than usual' in April 1820, Parry's group of ramblers passed a stone three miles north of the ships 'on which was plainly engraved the letter P' (Parry, 1821, 160). This puzzled them as the weather had been so cold that winter as to discount any one man sitting down and taking the time to carve this, 'however desirous he might be of immortalizing himself in this way' (RGS, SSC 73/2 83). This was quite an uncanny moment for the group, akin to when one of the officers reported seeing fresh footprints at a place called Possession Bay the previous July (on examination it became apparent that they were actually made by the shoes of the same men one year previously, when John Ross's expedition had passed by (Parry, 1821, 26)). The mysterious 'P' stone, however, suggested that they 'were not the first visitors of the country' (*Letters Written*, 1821, 84). Bringing the stone back to the ships, they found out that a seaman named Peter Fisher had scratched the initial on it with his bayonet when he was lost the preceding September, some 25 miles from where the ships were now located. 'This circumstance', Hooper noted in his journal, 'throws a good deal of light on the direction which these wanderers took, and shows how little idea they themselves had of their true situation' (RGS, SSC 73/2 83).

The party of seven seamen lost for up to 91 hours was a microcosm for the larger expedition, a pioneer group of men who vanished just at the precincts of homely space. Despite the best efforts of Parry to gather some geographical information from the leader of the lost party it was clear that 'little dependence' was placed on men in those circumstances as they were in 'utter ignorance' about where they were (Parry, 1821, 162). The 'P' stone, much like the 'found objects' celebrated by the surrealists in the 1920s, gained meaning by being something mundane that was made extraordinary. Peter Fisher engaged in serious physical activity in order to mark his presence in a place marked by the 'total absence of animated existence' (Parry, 1821, 125). After carving his first initial he gave up this struggle and wandered off again. The stone he left behind was 'out of place' and was later encountered by chance by passing ramblers who felt that this thing represented a rupture of the unknown in a place that had been extensively walked and mapped during the winter. Like the stone from Parry's reverie that stood out of the blankness, this was a mark towards which they 'unconsciously' and 'mechanically advanced' (Parry, 1821, 125).

For an expedition that particularly sought to guard against any moments of 'uneasiness' among its members (Sabine ed., 1821, vii), such moments were rendered mysterious and, along with occasions of winter dreaminess and reverie, drew out the spectral forces that were present in everyday life. This puts into question assumptions that British explorers somehow disconnected from the world during the winter, bedding-in in homely ships, and continuing the battling work of exploration once the opportunity presented itself again. Actually, explorers who felt a reigning solitude and stillness during winter were already entangled in the world and could not be sealed off from the voices and presences that haunted outside, whether Inuit or people back home. Exploration was always taking place *in* the Arctic, not *on* the Arctic.

3
Mesmerism, clairvoyance and the search for the lost Franklin expedition

> *CLAIRVOYANCE – Any lady or gentleman wishing to try the power of Clairvoyance may receive answers to any five questions relating to the past, the present, or the future, on receipt of a letter enclosing a lock of hair, with the real initials, and a post-office order for 2s. 6d., addressed to Ambrose Delaine, King William-street, City, London. For the satisfaction of all persons, the Clairvoyante assures them that the strictest secrecy may be relied on* ('Clairvoyance', *The Morning Post*, 1850).

Introduction

During the late 1840s the Admiralty faced serious communication problems when sending out successive expeditions to search for the lost Franklin expedition. This was because traversing the long distances to the Arctic through the Atlantic or Pacific oceans meant that Admiralty authorities experienced extended periods of 'dead time', with little or no reliable knowledge of what was occurring in the field. Contemporary newspaper reports reveal the existence of at least a dozen 'clairvoyants' (mostly young women) who spoke out about what they saw currently happening in the Arctic. These clairvoyants, mostly from Britain, but also from Ireland, India and Australia, were put into a mesmeric trance and then described visiting Franklin and his men in the Arctic. Beginning at the time of greatest anxiety regarding the fate of the expedition, these clairvoyant visionaries, and their operators, formed part of a field of speculation and experimentation centred on the haunting disappearance of Franklin. That these women, so socially distant from those who had authority on the Arctic, were able to speak in such forums about the location of missing explorers seems remarkable, but is perhaps less so once we dig deeper.

The lack of information about the expedition created a context that allowed different types of people to make claims about the Arctic. As cultural authority regarding the fate of Franklin broke down, dozens of unlikely leads were investigated by the Admiralty, the newspaper press, and the general public alike, from 1847 until the return of McClintock in 1859 (who brought the document that fixed Franklin's date of death as 11 June 1847) (Ross, 2003b). As a contemporary wrote:

> Every circumstance, however trifling, which could be supposed to emanate from the north, became invested with importance, and linked to the all-absorbing subject. This solicitude was felt from the shores of the Scheldt to North Cape, and from North Cape to the Strait of Behring; but joined to this noble feeling was much wildness of thought as to the probable course and position of the unfortunate Franklin and his companions; hence, however well meant, the feeling, *by its very intensity, often contributed to render confusion more confounded* (Brown, 1858, 272, emphasis in original throughout).

Rumours received at port towns, however bizarre, suddenly gained syndication in the national and international press, while travelling objects like messages in bottles raised hopes in morning editions that were dashed by evening editions. Mysterious reports about Franklin circulated uncontrollably, including one sent from Hong Kong that gave a strange account of 'Esquimaux vibrating from the Asiatic to the American continent and back again, carrying their boats, made of skins and whalebone, over the ice' ('Sir John Franklin and the Clairvoyants', 1852).

In 1848, reports from Canada reached the Admiralty claiming that the 'firing of cannon was heard at the last post on Mackenzie's River both last winter and the winter before. They were probably signals of distress' (DRO, D3311/51/2). On the evening of 28 December 1850, a sensational rumour spread around the theatres of London that the Admiralty had announced that Franklin had been located. This news 'passed like electricity' and sent incessant callers to Whitehall and the homes of members of the Board of the Admiralty ('Rumoured Discovery of Sir J. Franklin', *Kentish Gazette,* 1850).[1] In 1851, meanwhile, a garbled or hoax report circulated in Scotland, apparently issued from a returned Hull whaler, describing how the crew found the bodies of four Franklin expeditioners near Lancaster Sound in 'a large natural amphitheatre among the mountains' ('Sir John Franklin', *The Derby Mercury*, 1851).

Because of this multivocal field, Jane Franklin and her niece and amanuensis, Sophia Cracoft, positioned themselves at the centre of an Arctic information network that quashed some rumours and followed up on others. They managed this network through the intervention of experts, friends and well-wishers, and it was supported by formidable letter-writing and monitoring of the press (see 'Sir John Franklin', *The Standard*, 1850). In many cases, though, rumours and hoaxes travelled through the press faster than sceptical and fact-checked responses ever could. Colonial newspapers, much like the 'vibrating Esquimaux', bounced back their own sensational Franklin-related stories to Britain, raising the tricky problems of time-lags and time-zones.

In this uncertain informational context it seemed that the clairvoyant was a highly sensitive person capable, during mesmeric séances, of collapsing the distance between the explorers and those searching for them through imaginative travelling. This chapter uncovers the remarkable history of how mesmerism and clairvoyance played key roles in Victorian cultures of Arctic exploration.

'Mesmeric mania'

Mesmerism originated in the practices of Franz Anton Mesmer's 'animal magnetism' in the 1770s, and it referred to the many different types of therapies, surgical practices, and entertainments that hypothesised a magnetic fluid emanating from bodies. It typically involved a male mesmerist making 'passes' with his hands over a seated patient (usually a young female), or using materials such as magnets or a candle to place the patient in a state of sleep that ranged from highly sensitive to totally comatose (see Figure 3.1). Mesmerists believed that a universal fluid permeated all existence and that this could be activated and directed for the purposes of healing by the force of the mesmeriser – this connection was conceptualised as *rapport*. As the fluid was thought to be universally distributed, its action could be exerted at a distance, 'without the aid of any intermediate body' as Mesmer put it (qtd. in McCorristine, 2012, II, ix).

Mesmer's sensational group performances of magnetic healing flourished in the context of electrical experimentation in France before the Revolution, but his ideas were taken in different directions after his death. Mesmer's most influential follower, the Marquis de Puységur, made the connection between the magnetic trance and the state of mind when the patient entered natural 'somnambulism', when one was neither fully awake nor asleep. Puységur found that in this sleep state, intelligence

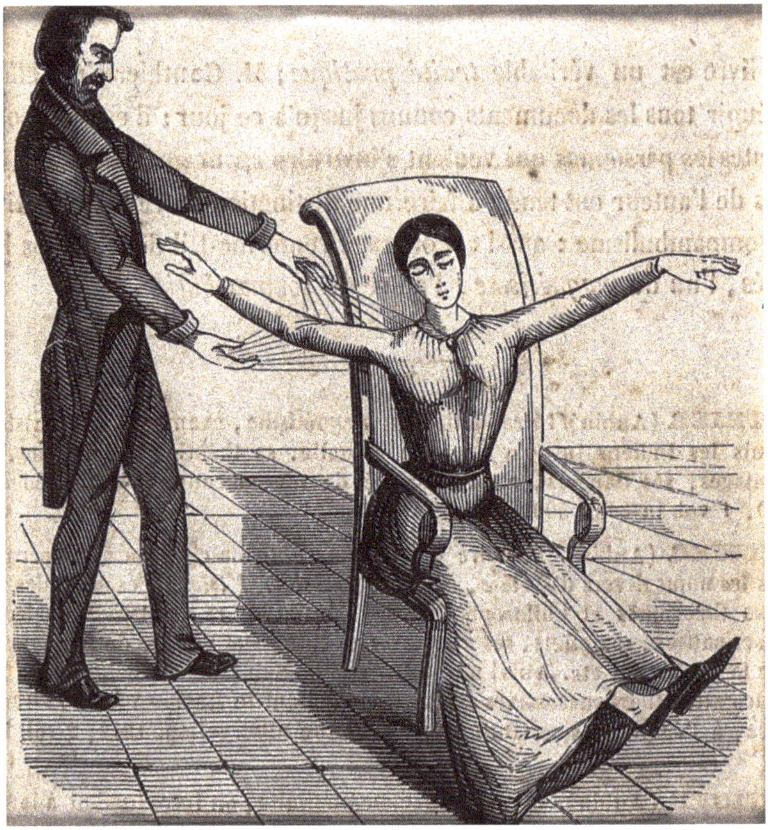

Figure 3.1 'A Mesmerist using Animal Magnetism on a woman who responds with convulsions'. Source: Wellcome Library, London.

and language seemed to be enhanced, but nothing could be remembered upon awakening, suggesting that there were two different forms of consciousness present in the same personality. Crucially, Puységur began to develop a therapeutic approach in which the mood of the patient could be affected and directed by the verbal suggestions of the magnetiser while in a state of apparent trance.

Puységur also had considerable claims to make about the rapport between mesmerist and patient, and the role of transference in their union. Puységur believed in Mesmer's universal fluid and the efficacy of the magnetic passes, but emphasised: 'Our electric organisation is so perfect that with the help of the will alone we can produce phenomena which, while being very physical, have the air of the miraculous':

> The nerves are the conductors of the universal fluid in the human body ... The nerves of the two human beings can, in this instance,

> be compared to chords of two musical instruments placed in the greatest possible harmony and union. When the chord is played on one instrument, a corresponding chord is created by resonance in the other instrument (qtd. in Crabtree, 1993, 50, 59).

For Puységur, a sick person in a state of somnambulism was like a 'magnet needle replaced on its pivot', requiring the mesmerist to 'open a channel' between him and the patient (qtd. in Podmore, 1909, 76).

Puységur was unsettled by the chaotic scenes at Mesmer's communal treatments. He discarded the infamous *chambres des crise* and, instead, recommended subdued and comforting treatment directed through the will of the mesmerist. He found that during these private sessions, his 'somnambule' patient could read *his* thoughts and accurately diagnose an illness he was suffering from. Subsequent somnambules began to diagnose themselves and others, and even direct medical treatments while in a state of magnetic sleep. Although they shared much with Mesmer, Puységur's somnambules expanded magnetic experience by imaginatively travelling across vast distances, and even visiting the moon. This took mesmerism in new, non-materialist, directions.

The sensational travels and diagnoses of somnambules in the mesmeric séance were now mostly termed 'clairvoyant' [French: *clair* (clear), *voyance* (vision)]. As defined by a contemporary, clairvoyance referred to 'the direct and immediate perception of absent or distant objects, without the use of the eyes' (Gregory, 1851, 116). This ability was first noted by mesmerists who recorded that their subjects could 'see' the hand of the mesmerist making the passes, even though their eyes were shut. As their abilities developed, clairvoyants reported being able to see objects held behind them, perceive objects wrapped in boxes, objects held in other rooms and even reported visiting distant places. Clairvoyance, therefore, involved both performing and making geographical claims in front of audiences. Through its relationship with contemporary cultures of what we might call 'remote sensing', clairvoyance was something that resisted being reduced to a single thing. Rather, it was a heterogeneous force in nineteenth-century culture, subversively circulating between public sensation, private medical treatment and magnetic journeys between bodies and across worlds.

During the trance, the identity of the clairvoyant became porous and fragmented, echoing recent notions of subjectivity. Boundaries between power and knowledge were then redrawn as an in-between space emerged: in this, the dynamics of the trance share many features with the processes of transference and counter-transference in psychoanalysis and other forms of psychotherapy. Arctic exploration – the practice of travelling into unknown spaces – was enmeshed in this trance context. This chapter looks at the relationship between the 'geospatial' and the 'geospectral' – between the range of remote sensing techniques present in Victorian Britain and the particular ghostly imaginaries circulating around the lost Franklin expedition.

Most scholarship on the Franklin expedition continues to focus on the history of search and rescue expeditions, or the aftermath of the trauma in Victorian literature and culture. Clairvoyance is perhaps best known in connection with the mystery through its role in the plot of *The Frozen Deep* (1856) – a play written by Wilkie Collins with input from Charles Dickens. The play and its performance have received a significant amount of critical attention in recent years, some of which has focused on the role of second sight (Van Schlun, 2007; Elce, 2002b; Davis-Fisch, 2012, 165–94; Potter, 2007, 137–48; Hill, 2008, 113–50). Scholars have engaged with primary source material dealing with Arctic otherworlds during the Franklin period (Chapin, 2004; Spufford, 1996, 130–7; Ross, 2003a), but this chapter digs deeper into stories of Victorian clairvoyance in order to show how they influenced ideas of a spectral Arctic throughout the nineteenth century and beyond. This chapter brings what was peripheral, disparaged or forgotten in relation to the Franklin era centre stage. This entails thinking about the Arctic in a relational sense.

The argument that follows suggests that mesmerism highlighted notions of 'feeling at a distance' in such a way that it offers substantial insights into the relationship between British people and the Arctic in the nineteenth century. The particular figure of the female clairvoyant (or 'clairvoyante') emerges into view here as a working-class person capable of providing male authorities with information about the Franklin expedition. But, going further, clairvoyance demonstrates the way that Arctic exploration was never just a unidirectional practice involving explorers gathering knowledge abroad and then transmitting it back home. Rather, it involved a series of noisy and contested transferential relationships that, taken together, make attempts to demarcate categories such as home and abroad, mind and body, subject and object, deeply problematic.

* * *

Mesmerism reached Britain in the early nineteenth century through French émigrés, newspaper reports and isolated practitioners but it only developed an indigenous following from the 1830s onwards when medical practitioners began to use mesmeric passes in their therapeutic practices. The most famous case of this was John Elliotson's experiments with Jane and Elizabeth O'Key from 1837.

Elliotson, a respected professor at University College London, conducted the mesmeric treatment of working-class women on the wards, but also demonstrated animal magnetism for his colleagues and the general public (including Dickens). The O'Key sisters were teenage maidservants who suffered from spontaneous fits followed by somnambulism, ecstasy, insensibility and the transposition of the senses. This was a period in European cultural history when female 'hysteric' patients became test cases for a rising class of psychiatric professionals. Elliotson's demonstrations caused a sensation and, as Alison Winter notes, the O'Keys 'stopped being merely patients and became prized experimental subjects, pivotal to medical research. One year later their names would be as well known in fashionable circles as their prestigious doctor's' (1998, 70).

The Lancet soon withdrew its support for Elliotson's experiments, and the ensuing controversies surrounding mesmerism – and the allied practice of phrenology – led to an upsurge in public interest, or 'mesmeric mania', which was seen to reach a climax around 1851 (Bennett, 1851). From hospital wards, to amateur experimentation, to public performances, mesmerism hosted questions about the boundaries of the mind and the permeability of identity. On one occasion Elliotson stood behind the somnambulistic Elizabeth O'Key and waved his arms in a particular manner. O'Key had been instructed to keep her hands clasped but was irresistibly drawn to mimic her mesmerist's motions (Winter, 1998, 74). Such moments performed cultural work by revealing the messiness of the mind/body connection, pointing to shifts in how people understood the way that sensations travelled and how personal autonomy was something contingent and provisional.

Mesmerism soon spread from London to towns and cities throughout the British Isles. One commentator believed the 'mesmeric epidemic' was particularly pronounced in Scotland ('Reviews of *The Mesmeric Mania*', 1851, 161), but port towns and cities with strong maritime infrastructures such as Bristol, Liverpool and Whitby, also featured heavily on the route of travelling lecturers ('Whitby', *Hull Packet and East Riding Times*, 1845). Hospitals, learned societies and apothecary networks were important for local experimentation on mesmeric subjects, but mesmerism was also discussed at more working-class locations such as mechanics' institutes and temperance halls. In the 1840s, travelling mesmerists brought the new techniques and marvels into villages and towns, skirting the boundaries between education and entertainment.

Many were entrepreneurs drawn to the practice by the chance of making money, but others certainly travelled to spread knowledge of magnetic healing and demonstrate what they held to be wonders of the modern age. By the mid-century, these travelling mesmerists had incorporated clairvoyance into their act – a prelude to the 'thought-reading' crazes of the 1870s and 1880s that kick-started international interest in 'telepathy'.

Thus far, this section has surveyed the social history of mesmerism, pointing out its intellectual significance, geographic dispersal and relationship to performance. But what about its relationship to Arctic exploration, another contemporary obsession being discussed and imagined in newspapers, lecture halls and panorama shows?

Clairvoyants were seen as remarkable because they could name locations for audiences, bring back news about the health of the missing explorers and perform Arctic experiences such as cold and hardship. This was thought to be possible through a 'community of sensation', a mesmeric concept that referred to the transference of sensations between mesmerist and subject, and also between material objects and distant bodies. The person in a trance might taste what the mesmerist tasted, smell what he smelled and see what he saw (Gregory, 1851, 102–4). This also extended to community of thought, whereby thoughts, feelings and secrets moved spontaneously between people via a sympathetic connection – something that obviously disturbed power relations.

These clairvoyant reports about Franklin were taken not as factual narratives, but as pieces of information that, like the port town reports, were always *potentially* worthwhile, requiring the passage of time for their confirmation or rebuttal. Clairvoyants described the condition of the men, their emotions and even their location – sometimes in the form of geographic coordinates. At the same time, as they travelled through the international press, these reports were sifted through by experts and Arctic veterans and contested by armchair travellers, mesmerists and sceptics. Clairvoyance therefore drew upon a range of overlapping spaces that moved from the informational to the emotional: the psychic space of the clairvoyant, the Arctic space of the explorers, the medical space of the mesmeriser and the intimate spaces linking clairvoyant, operator and Arctic in a shared field of emotions.

Clairvoyance also reveals the tensions inherent in how geographical knowledge was made credible or incredible during this period. Clairvoyance drew a new map of relations between the Arctic and Britain, providing diverse communities with routes to *terrae incognitae*. Although critics and supporters of clairvoyance used the Franklin episode as a trial or test case to prove or disprove the practice, the voice of the clairvoyant was one element in what was a multivocal culture of Arctic exploration. This was made up of 'legitimate' bodies such as the Admiralty Board and the veterans and experts associated with the unofficial 'Arctic Council' (Ross, 2004a); persons on the peripheries of Admiralty authority, such as John Ross and the surgeon and explorer Richard King (on King see Wallace, 1980); Inuit and local informants in the Arctic; and spectral voices considered by some to be 'illegitimate' by virtue of their social and geographic location and the kinds of presence that they projected onto the Arctic. To be lost in the Arctic was not simply a physical condition – it was also a cultural one that impacted on the mind of every person affected by it (Potter, 2016, xv). Rather than denigrating the reasons why Arctic experts took clairvoyance seriously, it is worth exploring how knowledge about the Arctic came from many sources at this time.

Clairvoyance was a part of the debates that were raging over the validity of trances and their relationship to the mind, technology and the spirit world. Arctic exploration narratives became entangled in clairvoyant practices because of their shared use of remote sensing as a way of locating Franklin. Sensing the Arctic from Britain involved negotiating a great geographical distance, but it also involved remoteness from the established authorities on the Arctic. Paradoxically, for some this remoteness made the voice of the clairvoyant legitimate: how could poor illiterate women who knew nothing about Arctic navigation invent such details about the lost expedition? In an informational context, Jane Franklin, the Admiralty Board and other Arctic authorities could no more dismiss clairvoyance a priori than refuse to investigate other unsolicited sources of information that floated around Britain. In Jane Franklin's own words, the communications were 'too remarkable to be disregarded' (SPRI, MS 248/106). In an emotional sense, the powers of the clairvoyant – to travel, see and reveal what others could not – made her an agent of hope, a powerful thing in cases of disappearance and missing people.

The Bolton clairvoyant

The most celebrated case of Franklin-related mesmerism was that of Emma, the 'Seeress of Bolton' (Hood, 1852, 143), who was the domestic servant of a surgeon-apothecary named Dr Joseph W. Haddock (1800–61). Haddock carried out many mesmeric experiments on his patients and was the author of the pamphlet *Somnolism & Psycheism: Otherwise Vital Magnetism, or Mesmerism: Considered Physiologically and Philosophically*.

Haddock frequently gave lectures on the subject and advertised his services to patients 'desirous that the faculty of Clairvoyance be used as an aid in discovering the cause and nature of their complaints' (1851, xii). He referred to clairvoyance as a kind of 'magnetic vision' or 'internal sight, or sight of the soul' (Haddock, 1851, 63) in which light is projected from within 'as the spark flies from the excited electric machine, so the perception seems, as it were, to *seek* the corresponding sensation' (Haddock, 1851, 66). The role of the mesmeriser was therefore analogous to a machine operator and Haddock referred to the lucid, mesmerised subject as 'a living stethoscope' that assists the judgement of the physician 'just as the astronomer uses his telescope' (Haddock, 1851, 53).

Extending the analogy to the physiology of the brain, Haddock suggested that the wakeful cerebrum of the operator dominates that of the subject 'because they form part, as it were, of the same electric circle' through which thoughts and sympathies may pass unhindered – a community of sensation in which two distinct bodies perform as one. However, unlike the telegraph machine, 'reason or judgement is only at *one end* of the communication' (Haddock, 1851, 60). The clairvoyant, in this understanding, was close to an animal or a child in her ability to express complex thoughts: 'As we have to learn to talk, and even to see, or rather, rightly to interpret what the eye reveals, so, it would appear, do clairvoyants require a continued exercise of their peculiar powers to familiarize them with its use' (Haddock, 1851, 72).

According to Haddock, 'Emma L.' was born around 1826 in Worcestershire and entered his service in Bolton in 1846. She was of a 'nervous-bilious temperament' (Haddock, 1851, 84) and suffered from inflammatory disease as a teenager. On a visit to Bolton to investigate her, Harriet Martineau described Emma as 'a vulgar girl, anything but handsome, and extremely ignorant' (1877, III, 355). In common with other medical physicians, Haddock experimented with ether as an anaesthetic, and hearing that Emma was familiar with it (having been mesmerised with it by a cousin), he decided to test it on her. She soon became insensible to pain, and demonstrated a variety of abnormal states that she did not remember afterwards. Haddock believed she had a remarkable susceptibility to the drug and began reducing the quantity he gave her until he realised that her condition was actually one of mesmeric trance. Haddock's experiments gradually began to cover the traditional spectrum of susceptibility, from the creation of illusions to mesmerism at a distance. As she was illiterate, Haddock decided to test Emma's clairvoyant ability using pictures that, upon being concealed and placed on her head, she was able to faithfully describe. Yet to Emma, they appeared not as pictures 'but *as the things represented*. So that *the picture* of a rose would convey as *vivid* and *real* an idea to her sensorium, as the *rose itself* would do, to an individual in the ordinary state' (Haddock, 1851, 100).

By 1848, Haddock was placing Emma in trances at public lectures where she displayed the ability of 'lucidity' – seeing what had been placed in concealed boxes – and clairvoyance. In July of that year, Haddock brought Emma to Manchester to be examined by the phrenologist William Bally, who said that 'her head was well formed, and that her faculties wanted only cultivation' (Haddock, 1851, 85). Emma's ability to leave her body and travel to exotic places was a practice that Haddock cultivated, but he did note the consequent physical and mental fatigue that followed these 'distant excursions' (Haddock, 1851, 107). The representation of Emma's body as an instrument of wonder continued when Haddock applied a tube to 'the great plexus of organic nerves' near the stomach while she was 'sent away', and discovered that she could hear his voice through her lower body (Haddock, 1851, 108). Apart from these marvels, in July 1848 Emma began to visit and converse with figures in the spirit-world while in mesmeric trance (Haddock, 1851, 185). Although both Emma and Haddock were Presbyterians, doctrinal concerns about spiritualism and clairvoyance were never raised ('Sir J. Franklin and the Clairvoyantes', *Manchester Times*, 1852).

The utility of Emma's ability to collapse distance was put to the test in December 1848 when Haddock used her powers to solve a theft that had taken place at a tea-merchant's in Bolton. Emma was put into rapport with the owner of the shop and she began to describe the thief and the location of the robbed items (Haddock, 1851, 113–7). On confronting the thief, Haddock and the merchant forced him to take Emma's hand: 'She instantly started back convulsively, as if he had been a serpent – evincing great fear, and clinging to me' (Haddock, 1851, 115). In August 1849, Haddock was also consulted in Bolton during an inquiry into missing banknotes to the value of £650. William Lomax, the unfortunate cashier responsible for the loss, believed that clairvoyance could aid in their discovery. Haddock accordingly put Emma into 'a psychic state' and, through the medium of the letter containing the banknotes, she tracked their journey from Lomax's pocketbook to the Bank of Bolton where she insisted they would be found. The following morning, after further searches, 'and among a lot of papers in an inner room at the bank … were found the notes and bill wrapped in paper, just as the clairvoyant had described them' ('A Strange Story', *The Times*, 1849).[2] Haddock was undoubtedly astute at publicity, and press releases of the case were reprinted in specialist journals (*The Journal of*

Health), regional newspapers (*Bolton Chronicle*, *Liverpool Courier*), and the widely-circulated national daily *The Times* (see 'Interesting Case of Clairvoyance', *The Journal of Health*, 1849).

Another aspect of Emma's repertoire was her ability to travel to distant parts of the globe in search of people on request, usually through the medium of connection with some handwriting. As with the pictures, her method was to place a letter over her head and then begin describing the person who wrote it. On one occasion, the writing of a man from Australia was given to her, and 'she was soon mentally there, described the climate and season, and expressed her surprise at finding the *seasons reversed*, when compared with England, having no knowledge of the effect of latitude and longitude in altering season and time' (Haddock, 1851, 180). In November 1849, Haddock reported that Emma was consulted by a merchant who enquired about the business dealings of his partner at the Cape of Good Hope: Emma told the man (correctly as it turned out) that his partner had 'sold one of the guns' (NA, ADM/7/189). Indeed, Emma's travels were not limited to the earth: Haddock sent her on an excursion to the moon where she saw the inhabitants who 'were very small – dwarfs – not larger than children on our earth' (Haddock, 1849, 58). It was in this context of mental travelling to exotic locations that Emma's clairvoyance came to be used as a way to solve the fate of Franklin.

The knowledge Emma provided was given an aura of the marvellous because it came from such an 'uneducated' and naïve source: the key term here is *transference*. Emma was 'sent' on her travels and 'put' into rapport with her mesmerist and distant targets; she was the 'bearer' of information and messages hidden to others, not the source. Her connection with the lost and the missing came about through the transference of their identity through material relics: when Emma wished to leave the trance she asked Haddock, 'will you *have me*?' (Eadon, 1853). Thus, her role as a medium of transmission was something that gave her provisional authority, despite her social exclusion from the centres of Arctic knowledge production.

The clairvoyant might be understood, then, not as a single person but as an assemblage of forces, a community of sensation whose potential power came from the transmission of geographical information. This assemblage confused normative distinctions between legitimate and illegitimate knowledge, as can be seen in the way clairvoyant narratives travelled through the press in the very columns reserved for 'naval intelligence'.

Following the discovery of the Lomax money, Haddock was contacted by 'a naval gentleman' in September 1849 about the possibility of using the clairvoyant to shed light on the Franklin mystery. This gentleman was Captain Alexander Maconochie (1787–1860), who was a penal reformer and had served as a professor of geography at the University of London and secretary of the Royal Geographical Society in the 1830s. Furthermore, Maconochie was a friend of the Franklins, and he served as John Franklin's private secretary during the latter's unhappy time as Lieutenant-Governor of Van Diemen's Land. Despite his falling out with Jane Franklin in Van Diemen's Land, Maconochie was in frequent contact with her throughout 1848, and he made enquiries regarding the lost expedition among clairvoyants in London and Paris 'in concert with different members of Sir John Franklin's family' (NA, ADM/7/189).

About the same time that he read of the Lomax case, Maconochie, by coincidence, dined with Haddock's niece. He soon wrote to Haddock to 'enquire whether he thought that his Clairvoyant cd discover the fate of Sir J. Franklin'. Haddock replied requesting a letter in Franklin's handwriting and a sample of his hair, if possible. Maconochie immediately sent an old letter of Franklin's from 1836, and wrote to 'friends in London' seeking the hair (it appears Maconochie later got this hair sample directly from Eleanor Gell, Franklin's daughter from his first marriage). Although pessimistic about the fortunes of the expedition, Haddock consulted Emma on 21 September and was surprised to hear her state that Franklin was still alive 'with three or four companions'. Emma told him that they were 'clothed in rough skins' and that many of Franklin's men were dead. Emma then:

> looked for the ship, & saw two, one under the water, with very thick timbers, & the other I judge from her language, either abandoned, or a Wreck on a beach. Her manners were highly graphic of the situation, climate etc & could only be appreciated thro' being seen (DRO, D3311/81/1 (iii)).

This tantalising correspondence enticed Maconochie to visit Bolton, and he was present at three séances with Emma. He described her as 'a very plain, ignorant, common looking person' who was unassuming and mannerly. Yet in her 'abnormal state', Maconochie stated that she became 'extremely familiar, almost pert & childish in her whole demeanour' (DRO, D3311/81/1 (iii)). When interrogated, Emma was frequently incoherent and voluble, and her 'ejaculating manner' caused Haddock to hire an assistant to take notes (NA, ADM 7/189). Following a séance in early October, Maconochie sent an account to the *Manchester Guardian*, enclosing his card to 'authenticate' the report, although he did not want his name to be published. This sensational account was circulated in almost every national and local newspaper of note in the British Isles in the following days. In contrast to the earlier séance, at which Emma seemed to suggest there were only four survivors, Maconochie now reported that although she saw 'shells (dead bodies)' [cheap coffins were known as 'shells'] under the snow, Franklin's small party was actually being followed by other parties of men. Franklin, then, was alive and 'comparatively well' although, according to Emma, his cheeks were sunken. She also said that Franklin was in 'good hope of getting to England in nine months and a half', although this was not given as a prophecy, but as 'the impression on his mind, with which she professed to have some mysterious means of communication' ('Sir John Franklin', *Morning Post*, 1849).

Emma's narrative was full of picturesque details regarding Franklin (she correctly stated that he was bald), the ice, marvellous animals and 'many queer looking things'. On one occasion she appeared to imitate Franklin by drinking some fish oil, 'wh produced a great deal of Nausea' (NA, ADM 7/189). For Maconochie, gaining knowledge of the geographical location of Franklin was paramount and he 'very earnestly begged her to ascertain what o'clock it was where Sir J.F. was; & when it was 11.30am with us, she said it wanted 10m to six with him, indicating a difference of long. [longitude] of from 80 to 85 degrees'. In later séances Emma maintained that there was a seven-hour time difference between Bolton and the Arctic, an impression she gained by looking at clocks or timepieces while away. She believed that Franklin's watch kept the 'best time', while Maconochie noted 'Time in Bolton now <u>Greenwich</u> Time, from the Railways' (NA, ADM 7/189). A later observer, William Gregory, thought it 'quite absurd to suppose that this totally uneducated girl has any notion of the longitude to time, or of the difference between an arctic day and one in our latitude' (1851, 305).

Emma was then provided with a map of the Arctic regions, although it was 'very inconveniently bound up in a volume of the *Penny Cyclopaedia*, and required by her to be rested on her head'. The book – a symbol of working-class aspirations to education – was placed on her head, and Emma pointed to a region on the map that corresponded with the north-west side of Hudson Bay. This 'took the bystanders quite by surprise. They had not the least idea of looking for Sir John in this direction'. Maconochie was eager for Emma to locate James Clark Ross's rescue expedition, currently in the Arctic, so he gave her a handwriting sample and asked her to look for him: she 'pointed to Bankes' Land [sic] almost at once, a position full of probability'. Emma claimed that Ross's ships were beset in the ice and that the expedition had not made contact with Franklin ('Sir John Franklin', *The Morning Post*, 1849).

Emma's journey to the Arctic involved her body as she 'arrived' home exhausted (DRO, D3311/81/1 (iii)). As reported by Maconochie, Emma obtained her information from the Arctic through conversations with Franklin, talking 'ideally' as Haddock put it (1851, 146), although there was no suggestion that the actual Franklin was consciously talking with the clairvoyant. At this stage in her seership, Emma was apparently unable to take questions while 'away', although Haddock noted in a letter of December 1849 that 'I can communicate with Emma when away, it saves her strength and enables me to put enquiries' (NA, ADM 7/189). While communicating with Franklin, Emma could also communicate his state of mind to her audience, acting through a kind of emotional transference. For instance, in a séance of 13 January 1850 she reported that Franklin 'Thinks much of Lady F. and some children, not babes … He wonders no one has been to help him – thinks it very strange' (NA, ADM 7/189).[3] Maconochie thought it was premature to rely absolutely on this narrative, 'though in these days, when we make the lightning carry our messages and the sun take our portraits, it is very difficult to draw the precise line betwixt the possible and impossible' ('Sir John Franklin', *Morning Post*, 1849).

Maconochie quickly sent detailed memorandums on Emma's clairvoyance to the Admiralty Board. Far from being ignored, he was contacted by Barrow's successor as Second Secretary of the Admiralty, W.A.B. Hamilton. Hamilton maintained a correspondence with Maconochie on the matter and he procured letters and autographs of some of the officers on the Franklin expedition for Emma's use. In October, Haddock tried Emma with a larger map of the polar regions and she 'two or three times kept feeling with her fingers along Barrow's Straits and Westwards'. On another occasion she decided Franklin's party were at the Parry Islands (now the Queen Elizabeth Islands). Interestingly, at this point in the document sent by Maconochie to the Admiralty, a sceptical reader scribbled 'Gross Humbug' in the margin (NA, ADM 7/189). However, Haddock more tactfully noted that Emma 'appeared to have lost this instinctive sort of power to mark the place, and I found that no reliance could be placed on her in this respect'. In attempting to map out the trajectories of Emma's visions, Haddock believed her confusing references to warmer regions could be explained by Franklin's previous residence in Van Diemen's Land: 'it would seem that she mentally followed him through other climes, and former scenes, to his then situation' (1851, 146).

Why did clairvoyant visions about Franklin suddenly start to emerge in Britain? Late 1849 was a particularly significant period in the search for Franklin. Looking at it closely shows that clairvoyant reports were not anomalous rants, emerging out of nowhere. Rather, they can be thought of as pieces of geographical information that circulated, alongside other reports, rumours and speculations, in private and public where they were harnessed, contested and distributed. By this time it was clear that the authorities nearest the Arctic (HBC, Danish Greenlandic and Russian) had not made contact with the expedition, and that the food supplies taken in 1845 must be almost finished. On 3 October 1849, the *Truelove*, a whaler that sailed the Davis Straits under Captain John Parker, put in at Hull and spread the sensational intelligence that Franklin might be safe and soon rescued. In many newspapers this information appeared above the account of Emma's séance, binding both stories together in a moment of heightened emotion (see, for instance, 'Safety of Sir John Franklin's Expedition', *London Standard*, 1849). As one commentator observed:

> Seizing eagerly on the asserted fulfilment of a long-deferred hope, the press at once announced the actual safety of Sir John Franklin and his party; and as news generally travels with the properties of an avalanche, swelling in importance with every step, many hours had not elapsed before the return of the Erebus and Terror in the course of the present month was spoken of as an almost certain event (qtd. in Ross, 2003b, 142).

As told by Parker, in July of that year a Kircaldy whaling vessel, the *Chieftain*, was visited by Inuit who had been near Prince Regent Inlet. Their account suggested to the whalers that both Franklin's ships and James Clark Ross's ships were beset in the ice (on the west and east sides respectively), and that they had visited both expeditions that March ('Arrival of the "Truelove"', *Hull Packet*, 1849). The Inuit drew a sketch of this scene – the 'Esquimaux chart' – which was sent to Hamilton at the Admiralty and reproduced in the popular *Illustrated London News* on 13 October (see Figure 3.2). Parker's account was, at first, welcomed by the Arctic veterans William Edward Parry, George Back and William Scoresby. Although the report was also 'universally believed among the whaling people' (SPRI, MS 248/247/15), doubts regarding the credibility of the Inuit testimony were soon raised ('Sir John Franklin. Further Revelations by the Bolton Clairvoyante', *Preston Guardian*, 1849; Jacobs, 2015). While instinctively positive, Parry

Figure 3.2 'Esquimaux Chart'. Source: *Illustrated London News*, October 13, 1849.

urged that the Admiralty Board take an extremely cautious response to the report, stating that Inuit informants would 'say almost anything; especially after a little questioning, of which they soon get tired, and would get rid of us by saying 'Yes' to any and every question, thus often contradicting what they had said before'. Maconochie was more dismissive of the report and, in a memorandum, he informed the Admiralty that the information obtained through Emma's clairvoyance was 'the most detailed, coherent, and even probable, that I have received' (NA, ADM/7/189).

The first batch of search and rescue missions had, in fact, achieved little and the expedition led by James Clark Ross, which overwintered at Port Leopold in 1848 (far from Banks Land), was actually making its way out of Baffin's Bay in October, reaching Scarborough on 3 November 1849. Ross's expedition had 'neither heard nor seen anything of Sir J. Franklin' ('Arrival of Sir J. Ross from the Arctic Regions', *Elgin Courier*, 1849), and it did not come into contact with any Inuit, undermining the account of the whalers.[4] For Jane Franklin, this failure, coming at the end of the Arctic season, 'put an almost fatal extinguisher' on the hopes she had placed on this expedition (qtd. in Owen, 1978, 275). Parry summed up the mood in a letter to John Barrow Junior (his father, John Barrow, died in 1848): 'Alas! for poor dear Lady F' (NA, ADM/7/189).

It was not until August 1850 that the first real traces of the Franklin expedition were found on Beechey Island, and October when these discoveries were publicised on the return of that season's ships. The period from the winter of 1849 to the autumn of 1850 was therefore dominated by rampant speculation about the whereabouts of Franklin. At this point, the Admiralty was criticised in the press for its response to the disappearance and Janice Cavell argues that 'broad social and political resentments' now entered public discourse on the back of hard-fought Arctic debates (2008, 183). After the return of James Clark Ross, Jane Franklin commenced her decade-long lobbying campaign for the rescue of her husband or recovery of the ships (see Figure 3.3). The beginning of this quest was also the point when the motif of the hopeful polar wife entered the popular imagination:

> The time for hope was nearly gone by in all hearts save that of the noble wife who *would not* part with hope, – and who, with a sort of heroic confidence which until to-day it was almost as wonderful as it was admirable to witness, is now at the period of the Arctic returns, in the Orkneys, that she may be the first to welcome home her husband! ('Sir John Franklin's Expedition', *The Athenaeum*, 1849).

Emma's clairvoyance was widely reported in the British press in October 1849, reaching the colonies in the early months of 1850. The news reached Orkney where Jane Franklin and Sophia Cracroft were based, awaiting news from the Admiralty expeditions and returning whalers. Cracroft was initially sceptical of Emma's account and suggested that it would be a useful experiment to have several clairvoyants consulted 'on the same day in different parts' (SPRI, MS 248/247/15). Although they first read about Emma's clairvoyance in a newspaper, by 15 October Jane

Figure 3.3 Jane Franklin. Source: James Parton. *Daughters of Genius: A Series of Sketches, etc*. Philadelphia: Hubbard Brothers, 1888.

Franklin and Cracroft had seen a copy of Maconochie's report sent by Eleanor Gell. While Gell thought it 'exceedingly interesting & satisfactory' (SPRI, MS 248/247/17), Cracroft, and apparently Jane Franklin, believed that there was 'a diseased imagination, or over excited nerves, at work' (SPRI, MS 248/247/21). Yet, their opinions changed when they read an account of two séances with Emma (on 16 and 17 October), published on 25 October.

At the first séance, Maconochie requested that Haddock send Emma in search of Franklin, see what time of day it was there, and find out whether the account from the *Chieftain* was correct or not. This time Emma gave a more detailed account of *how* she travelled to the Arctic:

> After a short interval she began to breathe heavily, and said 'Oh! what a wind!' ... 'The first thing I want to know is, whether the snow is higher than when I was here first. But stop, I will go higher up.

> Oh! how cold and slippery it is! ... There, now, I can see the ships, but what a height I shall have to go!'

Emma then began to talk as if Franklin was before her:

> You expect to get out in nine months. Have you seen Sir James Ross? Oh! you have seen his signal, but don't know how to get to him. She then said she would go and visit Sir James Ross, and, after a short interval, during which she complained of the cold, she exclaimed, 'Oh, is it you Sir James? I have been to see Sir John Franklin, and I want to know whether it is your signal, or one from some other party, that Sir John Franklin can see? Oh, I can tell, it is your signal. Have you seen any natives? Then what makes them say you have seen them? Well, I thought so; if they could get over these heaps of ice, you could get over them also'.

During this visit Emma made an effort to get the time from Franklin (he said it was 11.10 p.m.), but Haddock was not satisfied with this, worrying that Emma was unable to read the Roman numerals from a gentleman's watch. For the second séance Haddock gave her an old watch with numerical figures on it 'and told her to set the hands to the time she saw':

> She did so, and placed the hands at five minutes past twelve (noon), the time in Bolton then being thirty minutes past six (evening). She then put the watch at eleven o'clock (morning), for the time with Sir James Ross. Sir John Franklin according to this time, would be in 6h. 30m. west longitude (longitude 97½° west), and Sir James Ross in 7h. 30m. west longitude (longitude 112½° west). A map being shown to her, she put her finger upon Prince Regent's Inlet, saying, 'Sir John Franklin is there'; the longitude being 95° west, which is a near approximation to that indicated by the watch – viz. 97½° ('Sir John Franklin. Further Revelations by the Bolton Clairvoyante', *Preston Guardian*, 1849).

On further discussion with Franklin, Emma named Lowther Island as his location, a claim that greatly impressed Cracroft. In a letter to her mother and sister, Cracroft revealed that she was 'very much inclined to place confidence' in this revelation, and she began the process of cross-comparing Emma's account with the story from the *Chieftain* and some other clairvoyant narratives that she and Jane Franklin had been gathering that year (SPRI, MS 248/247/21).

Hopes, dreams and otherworldly travels

Cracroft was particularly eager to root out some notes she wrote after a visit to a clairvoyant named Ellen Dawson, made with her aunt just a few months previously in May 1849. Like Emma, Dawson was described as a 'young, pale, sickly-looking girl' (qtd. in Esdaile, 1852, 90–1) who looked 'emaciated' (Fawcett, 1860, 282) and apparently suffered from epilepsy. Due to her illnesses, she was referred to Dr Joseph Hands of Grosvenor Square for 'rheumatism and hypertrophy of the left ventricle of the heart' (qtd. in Maitland, 1849, 9). Hands found her to be susceptible to mesmerism, and he soon began testing her clairvoyant abilities, 'travelling' with her to distant locations such as India and New York ('and in crossing the seas she described the waves, the storm, the vessels going up and down' (Hands, 1847–8, 10)).

In 1845, she achieved some publicity among the mesmerist community and the upper classes after she was consulted by Carolina 'Caddy' Boyle, who had been Maid of Honour to Queen Adelaide in the 1830s (Dickens was a close friend of her sister, Mary Boyle, whom he cast in his production of Elizabeth Inchbald's farce *Animal Magnetism* (1788)). Dawson's fame then spread more widely after she performed a diagnosis on one of Hands's patients and located a missing brooch for a wealthy lady ('Extraordinary Case of Clairvoyance', *The New Monthly Belle Assemblée*, 1849). Throughout her career, Dawson was managed by Hands during her mesmeric trances and he charged set fees for consultation: one pound and six shillings for himself and five shillings for Ellen (Fawcett, 1860, 282).[5]

The Franklin family had an extensive interest in clairvoyance during this period. John Franklin's expedition had disappeared in a region that was already exoticised by British commentators. This aesthetic context encouraged a general practice of speculation about what sublime experiences explorers were having in the Arctic. Past experiences and emotional connections were brought to bear on these thoughts, as when Jane Franklin wrote about her husband's second-in-command in 1850: 'My thoughts often dwell on poor Captain Crozier who seemed so ill & dispirited when he left. Some mesmeric clairvoyance, tho' I put no trust in it, clings to my imagination respecting him – and yet all this must be a delusion' (qtd. in Ross, 1994, 313). Francis Crozier's last letters home after departing for the Arctic with Franklin were melancholy and apprehensive, and his lonely mood may have been related to his unrequited love for Cracroft, whom he met in Van Diemen's Land when Franklin was Lieutenant-Governor there (see Smith, 2006; Fluhmann, 1976). Elsewhere, Jane Franklin was also quick to deploy supernatural metaphors, as in her final letter to her husband, picked up by him at Orkney: 'I wish we could see you in a glass as they do in the fairy-tales' (qtd. in Woodward, 1951, 253). In December 1845, she again referred to crystal gazing in a letter to James Clark Ross: 'I sometimes think it is better perhaps that we should thus be in happy ignorance of any disaster that may have happened to them, or of any dreadful difficulty they may have yet to overcome than to be viewing as in a magic mirror in a fairy tale, their daily vicissitudes' (qtd. in Woodward, 1951, 256).

The feeling of hope was something that Jane Franklin and Cracroft kept returning to throughout this decade of searches. Hope and hopefulness punctuated their correspondence, and Jane Franklin was someone who mastered the popular emotions surrounding her husband's loss in order to influence men in positions of power. In a letter to the President of the United States of America, Zachary Taylor, in December 1849 Jane Franklin wrote: 'hope still remained to me that, should the necessity for renewed measures continue to exist, I might look again across the waters for the needed succour' (2009, 80). Earlier in the same year, Jane Franklin probably read the following in *The Athenaeum*: 'The misery is, that if the truth be not *known*, Lady Franklin will nurse for years her frail hope, almost too sickly to live and yet unable to die' ('Our Weekly Gossip', *The Athenaeum*, 1849). Years later, after John Rae had returned with news of the expedition's demise, she was still agitating for British government support for a final search expedition, writing to the Lords of the Admiralty:

> And here I feel compelled to state that, though it is my humble hope and fervent prayer that the Government of my country will themselves complete the work they have begun, and not leave it to a weak and helpless woman to attempt the doing that imperfectly which they themselves can do so easily and well, yet, if need be, such is my painful resolve, God helping me (Franklin, 2009, 131).

Hope became a symbol and a weapon for Jane Franklin once the period of Franklin's expected arrival came and went. On one Sunday in January 1849, some 50,000 worshippers across churches in Britain prayed for the safe return of the expeditioners – a community of sensation that gave Scoresby grounds for 'Christian hope' (1850b, 95). The

Illustrated London News weighed in, praising Jane Franklin's resolve as something which 'touched a strong chord in the national heart':

> the humblest and least-educated reader of the public events of our day, as recorded in the newspapers, indulged in the hope, that, sooner or later, and whether successful or unsuccessful in the great object of his voyage, Sir John Franklin would return to receive the thanks of his countrymen and the renewed affection of his friends and family ('British Adventure', *Illustrated London News*, 241–2).

Hope was something that was also harnessed in the material culture of exploration: in 1852 Jane Franklin embroidered a sledge flag with the motto (drawn from Barrow) 'HOPE ON HOPE EVER', now in the National Maritime Museum in Greenwich. This flag flew from the sledge that was commanded by Bedford Pim when he reached McClure's *Investigator* in April 1853. However, as time passed by, the hopes of the public diminished. By 1854, the Franklin searcher Robert McCormick believed that the time had arrived when he was 'hoping against hope': he even named his boat the *Forlorn Hope* as a representation of this unhappy realisation (*Further Papers Relative*, 1898, 222). Jane Franklin, though, stubbornly remained optimistic and this positive outlook became a core part of her public identity.

People use feelings of hope to maintain connections with the missing. Hope creates a magical space on the horizon that is conjured up by states of anxiety, promises, clues, assumptions, intuition, faith and belief: hope therefore elides the distinctions between positive knowledge and deeply-held feelings. Hope defers disappointment, pushing it into the realm of the 'not-yet' (Bloch, 1998, 341): everything has meaning, and nothing can be ignored. The concept of providence was one way of representing hope, and indeed one of the last letters to reach home from the *Terror* in July 1845 came from the ice-master Thomas Blanky, who wrote to his wife: '*do not allow any person to dishearten* you on the length of our absence, but look forward with hope, that Providence will at length of time restore us safely to you' (qtd. in Coulton, 1853, 388).

It is clear that Jane Franklin and Cracroft were affected by a feeling of 'ambiguous loss', a feeling that is common among people whose loved ones are physically or psychologically missing (as in Alzheimer's disease or comas) (see Boss, 2004). When the boundaries between absence and presence are elided, closure becomes unattainable and this leads to stress and feelings of guilt among loved ones.[6] Listening to clairvoyants was another way of generating hope for those left behind because their words could be used as part of a hopeful narrative, as something that kept those at home and those in the Arctic in the same world. Although the image of Jane Franklin as a devoted wife resonates to this day, recent work suggests she was a self-serving and flawed character who used hope as a political weapon (Jacobs, 2015; McGoogan, 2006; Stone, 1993a; 1993b). With Cracroft, Jane Franklin deployed a network of experts and allies in support of her ideas about the whereabouts of Franklin. They listened to or silenced the voices of whalers and Inuit according to the stories they told, they 'made and discarded alliances as it suited them' (Jacobs, 2015, 4), and as time passed they became the gatekeepers of Franklin's legacy and archive. In 1849 Jane Franklin and Cracroft used hope to bring Franklin closer and they were willing to explore the ability of clairvoyants to embody this potential.

Aside from her metaphorical uses of the spectral, Jane Franklin, like Carolina Boyle, was interested in mesmerism and clairvoyance in the very serious sense of putting this hopeful culture of speculation to use in social situations. Jane Franklin's brother-in-law, Ashurst Majendie (a practising mesmerist and a founding member of the Royal Geographical Society), accompanied her and Cracroft to at least one mesmeric séance in 1849. Jane Franklin also read Haddock's pamphlet on Emma's clairvoyance (SPRI, MS 248/118; BJ), and allowed him to borrow (probably through Maconochie) the last letter sent by Franklin to her to act as a medium for the clairvoyant (Haddock, 1851, 147). Her attitude towards clairvoyance at the time seemed to be sceptical but pragmatic – she kept an open mind and was unwilling to discount any source of information without investigation and consultation with others. For instance, after she was particularly struck by one of Emma's later communications, which described Franklin greeting a grey-haired man in Davis Straits (she guessed this might be the 72-year-old John Ross), she wondered if this was a 'product of the imagination ... a trick of the Mesmeriser, or a foreboding of the truth, or what?' (SPRI, MS 248/184; D). Meanwhile, Franklin's daughter Eleanor Gell – estranged from her stepmother Jane Franklin – was kept informed of Emma's clairvoyance by Haddock and Maconochie. Gell wrote to Parry seeking his advice on the matter. His reply was delayed but to the point:

> With respect to the Clairvoyant, I am sorry that I omitted to answer you, but I was too much occupied with the realities of the case at that time, to allow me to give one thought to what I believe to be mere delusion – for such is the impression, I am free to confess,

> wh. the several Accounts I recd. from Miss Cracroft, have, upon the whole, left upon my mind (DRO, D3311/74/1).

Jane Franklin and Cracroft therefore also discussed Emma's clairvoyance with Parry and both were kept informed about clairvoyants by Maconochie up until at least May 1851 (SPRI, MS 248/107). They also discussed the visions of Ellen Dawson with the hydrographer Francis Beaufort in November 1849, by which time he was also becoming impatient with the lack of action being taken by the Admiralty Board. Beaufort was interested enough in what he heard to arrange to join them at a séance with another 'mesmeric girl', but she failed to show up (Ross, 2004b, 295).

When Cracroft looked over her notes from a visit to Dawson in May 1849 she was trying to make sense of an information network that was distributed, provisional and contested. On this occasion, Hands put Dawson in a trance by 'looking at her steadily for a space of from 6 to 10 seconds, while at a considerable distance from her'. After Dawson had been taken to a different room, and attended to by a mesmeric pupil, Cracroft was invited to sit with her and ask her questions.

> I said 'where have you been this evening?' 'A long way' she replied 'on the sea and into the ice'. I said 'that is where I want to go, and we will travel together – what do you see there?' 'A ship in the ice, – and the sky is deep purple'. 'What do you see in the Ship?' 'Several people – no ladies – only men – several gentlemen, some old, and some young gentlemen'. 'Tell me first about the old gentlemen, what are they like?' 'One of them is rather short, & stout, rather dark, with such a nice face'. 'What hair has he got?' 'It is dark, but he has very little – he is bald'.

Dawson gave details of the situation on one of the ships (the *Erebus* from what Cracroft could gather) and mentioned that there was plenty of salt beef and biscuits, and the men were drinking brandy. Although Cracroft pressed her to tell her what way the ships were going, Dawson said that there was a 'cloud before her'. At the time, Cracroft had been eager to be mesmerised herself, but Dawson told her: 'The reason you are not affected is because you are in trouble, your mind is always working – it is your brain which is nearer still' (SPRI, MS 248/267/1).

After reading of Emma's more detailed travels in October, where she also stated that Franklin was bald, Cracroft decided to return to Hands in November for another séance with Dawson. On this occasion,

Cracroft expressed a desire to 'travel with' Dawson and accordingly she held her hand '& said to her that I felt sure she wd tell me all she knew &, the truth'. With some emotion, Dawson described how one ship was lost and the other was blocked in by the ice and could not get out. Franklin was alive and 'quite well', although he was unhappy he could not send a letter to his wife. At this point, Cracroft sought some detailed geographical information from the clairvoyant:

> 'Now Ellen, think very much before you will tell me what I am going to ask – don't hurry. Look towards the N. Pole – now there is an entrance into that sea where Sir J. Fr. is on the East side, do you see that Entrance?' (she replied that she did) 'is there any other way of getting into that sea?' (After a moment's thought or a searching look) 'Yes, there is one on the west side'. 'Now keep both these passages in your view – that from the E. & that from the W. & tell me wh is Sir J. Fr the nearest to?' 'Nearer to west, but needs help to get out'.

Despite this remote sensing of Franklin's situation, Dawson said that she could not locate the ships on a map as 'nobody has ever been there before – it has no name, it is farther than any body has ever been before' (SPRI, MS 248/267/2).

Although this was clearly an unsatisfactory survey, some further questions elicited responses that were of an intimate nature and caused Cracroft to mark them as 'Confidential' in her notes. Cracroft asked Dawson about the captain of the lost ship – Crozier – who Dawson originally thought was married because he was always thinking about his wife:

> 'but (doubtfully) I do not think he is married – but he loves her more than any person he has ever met with'. 'And how does the lady feel?' (Somewhat carelessly) 'Oh! she loves him too very much'. (Then as if light broke upon her gradually, she continued) 'there is a lady who does not love him, and now I see that is the same person he loves so much. She would not marry him, and that is the reason that he is come away from England, but he intends (or 'intended' I cannot say which) settling when he gets back'. 'Settling what Ellen?' 'Marrying – he will have got more money then'. 'But had money anything to do with it?' 'Oh no, because the lady did not love him, but he will get more money by coming there, and he intends settling'. 'But what will the lady say then?' 'Oh she will say she will marry him, because he has been away'. A pause. 'But are

you sure the ship is lost?' 'Yes, I am sure'. 'And what will the poor lady do?' 'Oh she will be very sorry when she knows it – & she will never marry' (SPRI, MS 248/267/3).

Dawson's prediction here was correct: Cracroft never married.

Consulting dream books, fortune-tellers and clairvoyants for romantic advice was common during this period, but Dawson engaged in some inspired cold-reading when she interwove Crozier's heartbreak with her otherworldly travelling. This shows how emotion featured in the Arctic imagination after the Franklin expedition. The séance, much like the Arctic 'field' that clairvoyants travelled to, was a space where emotional forces circulated and were recognised by people, and we can here gesture towards the dual meaning of 'feeling' as touch and emotion. Cracroft was obviously concerned about her own part in Crozier's motivations and Dawson sensed and expressed these concerns as part of the Franklin narrative. Feelings and emotions were not considered separate from the fate of the expedition. Rather, as Cracroft held Dawson's hand she travelled to the Arctic with her and through her, causing tangible connections to be made between the Arctic and Britain. This conjured up the 'community of sensation' that brought different people and distant locations together in a moment of intimacy. Like the common post-bereavement experience of sensing a loved one's presence, the expedition was no longer lost: it was located, made part of everyday space, and thereby invested with life. Crozier lived on, it seemed, and his mind was still wandering back to Britain and back to Cracroft, his unrequited love.

A time for magic

Underlying people's sceptical reactions to clairvoyant claims were particular concepts of time and anxieties about popular forms of prophecy. Our awareness of time, it is perhaps obvious to point out, is not a given but is something that is socially constructed, expressing the ideological or cosmological concerns of changing political modes. The time-politics associated with the Enlightenment involved a secularised and universalised concept of Judeo-Christian time that created a kind of temporal slope with the future at the top end (modernity, progress, limitless opportunities) and the past at the bottom end (savagery, ignorance, pessimistic reliance on omens, cyclical ills).

Johannes Fabian argues in his influential analysis (1983) that nineteenth-century evolutionary thinkers 'spatialised time', in other words the difference between the modern western and the Other was thought of as something that involved a *distance* in time. This didn't just involve the traditional focus of anthropologists and other scientists on remote and 'uncivilised' societies, but also involved 'time-travelling' in Britain itself. Edward Burnett Tylor, for instance, was one of many evolutionary thinkers to draw equivalences between spiritualism at home and abroad, between the likes of 'the Red Indian medicine-man, the Tartar necromancer, the Highland ghost-seer, and the Boston medium' (1871, I, 141). Even more disturbing for Tylor was the knowledge that he lived within a mile of an astrologer and that the piles of astrological almanacs in bookshops at Christmas 'are a symptom of how much yet remains to be done in popular education' (Tylor, 1871, I, 119).

One of the most consistent tropes in anti-mesmerist and anti-spiritualist writings was the charge that modern 'enlightened' society was being fatally undermined by backward and superstitious people who lacked the will-power or expertise to resist common tricks and ruses. The traditional targets of commentators in this context were those who believed in love magic, astrologers and fortune-tellers. Social reformers particularly identified working-class women as people who paid for predictions about the future or engaged in prophesying about public or private events. Making claims about the future is something that has always been political because it touches on issues of power and authority. For middle-class critics, the search for the secrets of futurity promoted a dangerously fatalistic and heterodox concept of time that placed it at some distance from the dominant rational model of the future as something that is open to progressive change. As Maureen Perkins puts it:

> The blank calendars of the late nineteenth century gave very material form to the idea of progress by replacing the crowded historical chronologies of the traditional almanac with spaces on which to record the precise schedules created by the railroad and steamship companies, as well as the many appointments that a busy, modern life would entail. At the same time, the new calendars also symbolised a *tabula rasa* of opportunity, on which individual members of society could write their futures, increasing the emphasis on individual responsibility (2001, 15).

Yet, contrary to the widely held model, magic (or to use an umbrella term 'magical thinking') did not simply decline with the onset of a modernity characterised by secularism and mass literacy. Recent decades have seen an upsurge of interest in the relationship between nineteenth-century modernity and supernatural beliefs and practices. Keith Thomas's *Religion and the Decline of Magic* (1971) advanced a Weberian account of magic fading away in the face of bureaucratisation and rationalisation but scholars now focus on the cultural, social and intellectual power of things like ghost-seeing, spiritualism, occultism and psychical research in and *with* modernity. Such phenomena are not imagined as 'survivals' within an era of disenchantment but as manifestations of modernist re-enchantment.

For instance, focusing on what he terms the 'plebeian magical imagination', Karl Bell thinks of the supernatural as a tool that channelled dissent, empowered communities, and expressed the tensions of modernisation. Bell draws inspiration from Bronisław Malinowski's functionalist theory of magic and Owen Davies's work on witchcraft (1999), and outlines the pragmatic, even rational, application of fantastical mentalities in an urban environment: 'Unlike elitist efforts … at the popular level the epistemological understanding of ghosts was less important than their communal application, the issue being less about what ghosts were and more about the veracity of the message their stories articulated' (2012, 193). This echoes the point I made about the functions of the shamanic séance in the previous chapter.

In the 1840s and 50s female astrologers and fortune-tellers were easily found in Victorian towns and cities, while a large market in almanacs, astrological guides and cheap dream books offered women advice on things like favourable or unfavourable omens and ways to see a future spouse in a dream (see *Goode's Universal Dream Book*; *The Universal Fortune Teller*). Far from being primitive superstitions, the charms and ceremonies printed in such guides were part of a suite of strategies people used to manage experiences of anxiety, loss or desire. The dividing line between folklore, astrology and weather forecasting was not at all clear during this period. Indeed, Jane Franklin owned almanacs and used moonlore when planning an excursion during her time in Van Diemen's Land (see Perkins, 1996, 200). With their large fees and respectable clientele, private mesmerists (some of whom worked on the prestigious Harley Street in London) offered upper-class investigators like Jane Franklin a less transgressive form of consultation about the future than backstreet fortune-telling. However, clairvoyants and their operators undoubtedly drew on popular associations between 'cunning women' and prognostications. Also, as we have seen, most celebrated clairvoyants attracted national attention because of their apparent ability to locate stolen jewellery and money, something that provided upper-class women especially with a potential strategy for recovery.

Emma and Ellen Dawson provided Jane Franklin and Cracroft with some positive news about the expedition by visiting the Arctic in 'real time'. These messages were attractive because they suggested that though Franklin might be lost in *space*, he was not lost in *time*. Franklin's watch, according to Emma, 'kept the best time' (NA, ADM/7/189) – a potent symbol of regularity and status – and his Arctic time could be calibrated locally, that is, calculated against longitude to locate him in the here and now. This reduced the spatial and temporal distance of the expedition from Britain and gave it a coeval status as an event that loved ones could trace. In an account of her experience with Dawson, Cracroft maintained that the object of clairvoyance was not to look into the future, but 'simply to ascertain that wh. *now is* by means of an extended state of vision' (qtd. in Woodward, 1951, 267). In contrast to the deterministic worldview promoted by astrologers, which social reformers found so disturbing, clairvoyants seemed to keep good time, so to speak, and their predictions about the future tended to be plausible and hopeful (that the Franklin expedition would return next summer after the ships were released from the ice) rather than obscurely prophetic. Indeed, Haddock declared that he would have a watch made for Emma as she would then 'learn the time correctly, and that will be a necessary thing in such enquiries' (NU, WCT 284/83).

Crystal gazers

In 1846, the author of a review of Barrow's *Voyages of Discovery in the Arctic Regions* wrote that he 'dare not indulge in speculation, still less in prophecy, as to the fate and fortunes of those men who have again, under Sir J. Franklin, disappeared through Lancaster Sound' (Egerton, 1846, 47). The author urged his readers to be content to wait for developments and then listed the progressive benefits that Arctic exploration had brought to human knowledge, especially about the 'brute tenants' of the Arctic (Egerton, 1846, 48). Clearly, by 1849, such calls for restraint regarding speculation about the future were ignored by mesmerists who made noisy claims about the mystery. During this period, Cracroft and Jane Franklin continued to receive and monitor information from clairvoyants (see Ross, 2003a), but they also used divination by scrying, or crystal gazing, as a means of making contact with the Franklin expedition from a distance.

In the one instance of which we have evidence, Cracroft and Jane Franklin availed themselves of the services of a 13-year-old boy – the son of Lieutenant Richard Morrison, a retired naval officer and well-known author of bestselling astrological almanacs written under the nom de plume 'Zadkiel'. Morrison caused a sensation in London society during the 1850s through his demonstrations of a crystal ball that once belonged to Marguerite Gardiner, an Irish novelist and socialite better known as Lady Blessington. Blessington was part of a network of writers and intellectuals known as the Gore House Circle. This included Dickens, Edward Bulwer-Lytton and Chauncey Hare Townshend among its members, all of whom were fascinated by mesmerism and the occult. The crystal ball was apparently bought from an Egyptian magician and kept by Lady Blessington as a curiosity. After her death in 1849, Morrison purchased her crystal ball from a dealer in Brompton and began to use this small rock crystal (about four inches in diameter) during séances with his son that attracted aristocrats and became great social occasions. Indeed, during the 1850 season, one commentator wrote that the crystal ball became the 'wonder, the talk, and – with not a few – the belief' of the social elite (Costello, Wills, and Wilson, 1850, 285). Morrison, however, was more than a one-trick pony: he was proud of the fact that he also devised utilitarian proposals to propel ships, add bells to buoys, and bake bread by machine (Cooke, 1863, 8).

In the context of renewed Admiralty plans for rescuing the Franklin expedition in early 1850, Morrison wrote to the highbrow magazine *The Athenaeum* with a challenge. In his letter Morrison described a vision of Franklin obtained from the crystal ball that he wanted to put on the record. He wrote that, after leaving his crystal ball on the mantelpiece on 4 January of that year, his son looked into it and envisioned an Arctic scene:

> 'Mist and snow and rough ice; several parties of sailors on it, all walking in one direction; one party of six, with a tall and slender officer commanding them; a party in the distance with sledges, drawn by dogs, on which was luggage, bags and boxes, and furs, &c.' 'Another party distinct; three sailors waving their hats, as if hurraing. I could see their mouths moving. They seemed thin in the face; *they* were on the *land*'.

According to Morrison, the boy went on to claim that the parties were located at 100° west longitude and 73½° latitude and that 'Sir J. Franklin and his crew are safe, and will be found'. Although the commentator in *The Athenaeum* cynically noted that this was just the type of scene that anyone could imagine ('We ourselves have already seen all these things "as in a glass darkly"' ('Our Weekly Gossip', *The Athenaeum*, 1850a)), it clearly aroused interest elsewhere because, in February 1850, Morrison and his son were visited at least twice by Jane Franklin and Cracroft inquiring about the fate of Franklin.

On one occasion, as transmitted by the boy, the spirit of Orion was called to help and Franklin was located at 'Franklin Island', a place near Melville Island. Franklin was well and making his way home, but one of the inquirers asked: what was his longitude?: 'I do not know – goodbye', the spirit abruptly replied. A second celestial spirit named Gego was then called for and this time questions were asked about James Fitzjames – second-in-command on the *Erebus*:

> 'Where is he'
> 'He is with us'
> 'How long has he been dead?'
> 'This minute'.
> 'What did he die from?'
> 'The Climate' (SPRI, MS 248/267/4).

This type of consultation was a prelude to spiritualist communications with lost explorers in the later 1850s that moved past the framework of mesmerism and began to incorporate the voices of angels and the dead as part of a new cosmological ordering of the otherworldly. Where mesmerists like Haddock imagined themselves as controlling a wonderful new 'natural' machine that could connect with lost bodies at a distance, crystal gazers like Morrison's son began to speak of intercourse with the souls of the dead and spiritual planes of existence beyond this world.

By this stage the Franklin mystery was deeply entangled in a variety of mesmeric, spiritualist and occult networks – circulating as a touchstone of national loss and, for some, a test case of supernatural perception. However, in becoming connected with astrology, the mystery also entered a cultural battlefield regarding the perceived influence prophecies had on society at large. From the 1820s, there had been a push against astrological almanacs in Britain led by the Society for the Diffusion of Useful Knowledge (SDUK), a campaign intended to rationalise this form of knowledge for its popular readership (Perkins, 1996, 55). This gathered support from the professional and political classes and indeed one of the most successful of the SDUK's reforming alamancs – the *British Almanac* of 1828 – was published with the assistance of Francis Beaufort. Beaufort even managed to get the Admiralty to prepare the astronomical tables for the *British Almanac* and had it proof-read by some 'senior wranglers' from the University of Cambridge (Knight, 1864, II, 63). Morrison's connection with the Franklin expedition, and the continuing relationship between high society, naval personnel and the occult therefore became extremely embarrassing when it was brought up some years later during a scandalous court case that received widespread attention.

In 1861, Morrison made a prediction in his *Zadkiel's Almanac* that '[t]he stationary position of Saturn will be very evil for all persons born on or near the 26th August; among the sufferers I regret to see the worthy Prince Consort of these realms' (Woodcock, 1865, 58). Prince Albert, born on 26 August, died the same year and this remarkable story was publicised by the *Daily Telegraph* in January 1862, when it asked 'who is this Zadkiel?' The newspaper received a swift reply from Knight Commander Edward Belcher, a naval officer who had commanded a massive Arctic expedition in search of Franklin ten years previously.

Widely regarded as the 'most unpopular officer in the fleet', Belcher had controversially abandoned four vessels under his command in the summer of 1854, rather than spend a third winter searching in the Arctic. For this, Belcher was court-martialled (as naval policy dictated) and although he was cleared of dishonourable behaviour he never commanded a ship again (Pierce, 1982, 552). In semi-retirement, Belcher published his account of the Arctic expedition and a novel about naval life, but it was his story about Zadkiel's prediction that brought him into the limelight once more. Belcher wrote to the *Daily Telegraph*:

> Sir, – in your impression of this day you ask who is this Zadkiel, and are there no means of ferreting him out and handing him up to Bow-street under the statute as a rogue and vagabond. I will aid you in the scent by first informing you he stands as a lieutenant in the navy list, seniority 1815. Next that he has his admirers about Greenwich Hospital, who fancy him a prophet A1, and that his mischievous propensity is not solely involved in that foolish publication 'Zadkiel's Almanack'. More, I think he gave his name not long since as president of some peculiar society connected with astrology, R.J. Morrison. A friend reminds me that the author of 'Zadkiel' is the celebrated crystal globe seer, who gulled many of our nobility about 1852. Making use of a boy under fourteen years of age or a girl under twelve, he pretended, by their looking into the crystal globe, to hold converse with the spirits of the apostles, and even our Saviour, with all the angels of light, as well as of darkness, and

> tell us what was going on in any part of the world, and drawings were made of the objects seen in those visions. One noble lady gave one of these boys £5 to give her intelligence of her boy, who was in the Mediterranean. The boy peached and let the cat out of the bag. Of course the information was false. He took money, if he really be the same, for these profane acts, and made a good thing of it. If it was deemed sufficiently important, there can be no doubt that he can be satisfactorily trolled out. As to his position as a naval officer, excepting the coast-guard, he has not served afloat since 1815. ANTI-HUMBUG

Morrison discovered that Belcher was the author of this letter and promptly took a case for libel against him, leading to one of the 'most singular trials' of the era. Although Belcher did not appear at the Court of Queen's Bench, Morrison's counsel called upon an array of aristocrats who had attended some of the crystal gazing sessions in the 1850s. To great laughter in the courtroom, Morrison said he had been visited by hundreds of noble ladies, gentlemen, clerics, and Members of Parliament, all eager to have boys and maidservants gaze into his crystal ball. Witnesses such as Lady Harry Vane, Archdeacon Robinson (Master of the Temple), the Marchioness of Aylesbury and Bulwer-Lytton were questioned about the situations in which these visions took place and whether Morrison's boys were paid for their clairvoyance. The Arctic visions in particular were brought up and Jane Franklin's name was mentioned as someone who had taken an interest in the crystal ball. The ball itself was produced in court where it was taken 'with much veneration and respect from a plum-coloured velvet bag' by Morrison. Before reaching the hands of the jury, who wanted to inspect it, 'a number of briefless gentlemen seized hold of it to examine it, Mr. Serjeant Ballantine [counsel for defendant] jocularly remarking that they wished to see if possible their future business' ('Zadkiel v Admiral Belcher'). Perhaps surprising for the jury, and no doubt excruciating for the defendant, was the revelation that Belcher himself had consulted Morrison's crystal ball before he departed on his Arctic expedition in 1852. As Mrs Ann Merton, widow of Colonel Merton, deposed:

> At my request the plaintiff brought the crystal ball to my house to show to some friends. A good party was present on the first occasion ... It was brought to my house on five or six occasions. Sir Edward Belcher was present on one or two occasions. After he saw it

> the first time he asked to see it again, and at my request the ball was again brought ('Zadkiel Unearthed – Extraordinary Revelations', *Hampshire Telegraph and Sussex Chronicle*, 1863).

As no proof was brought forward that Morrison had made financial gain from fraudulent activity, he won his case, although significantly he was only awarded 20 shillings and no costs.

This case raised several issues. Clearly, the crystal ball was an enchanting object during this period, moving around salons and aristocratic soirées, immersing adolescent seers in visions of this and other worlds. When passed around in the setting of a courtroom the ball became a banal sign of humbug and ridicule, despite Morrison's reverential attitude towards it. It was a point of contact between Morrison's professional world of astrological predictions and the more sensational context of clairvoyant consultation. As someone who had travelled to the Arctic in search of Franklin, and recognised the falseness of the clairvoyant vision described to Jane Franklin and Cracroft, it is possible that Belcher was criticising his own participation, and the participation of his class (naval officers, nobility), in what he later called 'profane acts' ('Zadkiel v Admiral Belcher', *The Louth and North Lincolnshire Advertiser*, 1863). This points to the increasingly loud boundary work that was taking place in the aftermath of the 'mesmeric mania' and spiritualist craze of the 1850s.

Where mesmerism and clairvoyance were socially acceptable, and even fashionable, things to dabble in around 1850, by the time of Belcher's libel case a decade later there was a growing feeling of discomfort with the participation of the middle and upper classes in magical practices that were now associated with the beliefs of the lower classes. Critics reported gossip about titled gentlemen and ladies visiting old female soothsayers and fortune-tellers in the working-class districts of Lambeth and Southwark in London to gain clairvoyant knowledge of their future or of distant events.[7] The implicit fear here was that superstition, acting like a kind of upwardly mobile virus, travelled from lowly clairvoyants to their paying customers. As one journalist put it: 'A cloud of dupes have ever floated about in the higher regions of society; while it is quite a mistake to suppose then that the refinements and discoveries of the nineteenth century have dispersed them' (Costello, Wills, and Wilson, 1850, 284).

Judging from their surviving correspondence (and there are strong suspicions that some papers were destroyed), Jane Franklin and Cracroft were aware of the growing social stigma associated with spiritualism and the engagement of uneducated mediums, with what one critic termed 'latent Zadkielism' ('More of Zadkiel and Zadkielism', *The Leeds Times*,1863). However, whereas this social critique of upper-class spiritualism came from a modernist position that feared the consequences of superstitious belief, what comes through from the accounts of mesmeric and other séances is that people took many different approaches to otherworldly travelling. Although they were let down by the kind of futures predicted by the clairvoyants, Jane Franklin and Cracroft were desperate for geographical information that they could then cross-compare with information and rumours from other sources.[8] Indeed, although she was the more sceptical of the two, it was Cracroft who raised the idea of consulting several clairvoyants 'on the same day in different parts' (SPRI, MS 248/247/15), as if a mesmeric network might gain more accurate information than a single individual and her operator. Perhaps echoing the thoughts of many during this period, Bulwer-Lytton averred that he was interested in the crystal ball as he was 'endeavouring ... to investigate the natural causes by which strange and wondrous effects might be produced' ('Zadkiel Unearthed – Extraordinary Revelations', *Hampshire Telegraph and Sussex Chronicle*, 1863).

Clairvoyant mobility

In what way did clairvoyants and their audiences actually imagine moving across space and time, and how did this affect their credibility as geographic travellers? Emma conceptualised travelling to the Arctic in material terms as movement across seascapes and landscapes to a particular location. During a séance of 22 September 1849, Emma conversed with the men in the Arctic about how she found them: 'First of all I got into a steam packet – I then went by the right hand, wh. was cold, & when I spit, it went white – I will tell Mr. Haddock, he will be pleased to come here, only it will be bad for his lungs'. Emma also spoke of having a 'warm country' on her left hand when going and on her right when returning (DRO, D3311/81/1 (iii)), and a later séance made clear that she imagined travelling home from the Arctic via Liverpool – that is, a maritime route – before returning home to Bolton. Haddock was unsure about how to conceptualise her mode of travel, given that Emma was also 'wholly ignorant of the mode by which a knowledge of distant things is obtained': he suggested that it be compared to the electric telegraph 'as an expeditious mode of conveyance' that was suited to the purpose (1849, 58), thereby linking Emma's clairvoyance with the tele-technological revolution.

It is interesting that Maconochie noted during one of Emma's séances that 'Time in Bolton now Greenwich Time, from the Railways' (NA, ADM/7/189), because this points to another significant social development – the standardisation of time. The séance may have been a space to contest and debate, but in temporal terms it was aligned with an orthodox national standard time which had spread throughout Britain as a result of the railways. Where local towns and cities once set their own time, railway administrators faced significant challenges in producing nationally accurate timetables until 1848, when *Bradshaw's Railway Guide* published unified times. The telegraph here became a key technology, imposing temporal discipline by spreading the observational time produced at the Greenwich Observatory near London nationally, via telegraphed time signals. This permitted, for the first time, 'the virtually instantaneous synchronization of one place with another distant one' (Stephens, 1989, 11). Just as Bolton was suddenly drawn into a new communication network centred at the Greenwich Observatory (which had long dominated the temporalities of maritime travel through its *Nautical Almanac*), Franklin's time in the Arctic was aligned with this new time in Bolton, further regularising Emma's visions as part of a technological system rather than human trickery.

Linking clairvoyance with the contemporary temporal revolution occurring as a result of the telegraph and the railways also served to project British power onto the Arctic. One of the most consistent ideas associated with the telegraph was that it had caused the annihilation of time and space. One British commentator suggested that the telegraph had established a 'gigantic system of clockwork' whereby 'the clocks of a whole continent move, beat for beat together' (Wilson, 1852, 60), while an American wrote of the ability to send messages worldwide 'with the quickness of thought' (Prescott, 1860, 5). Synchronising events in the Arctic with those in Britain actualised the imperial dream of telecommunications as an instant, precise and reliable form of intelligence gathering. Crucially, this dream was not undone by the bodily presence of the clairvoyant for, from the beginning, telegraphy was imagined through the metaphor of the human nervous system. The analogy between telegraphy and the nervous system worked so well because Victorians' brains, as one scholar has pointed out, 'should be (and be seen to be) in command of their peripheries – their bodies. This also was increasingly what mattered about the Victorian state. The telegraph provided the state with its nervous system and its intelligence' (Morus, 2000, 475). There was nothing paradoxical at all in thinking about the clairvoyant as someone who acted as a conduit of intelligence from the periphery to the centre.

While Emma thought she travelled over the sea, and Haddock thought she travelled by technological transmission, other metaphors of movement were prevalent at the time. The Scottish scientist William Gregory wrote about what happened when one of his clairvoyants, 'Mr D', was sent to a distant place: 'He often finds himself, first, in *no place*, but floating, as it were, on air, or in space, and in a very short time exclaims, "Now, I am there"'. In Gregory's experience, Mr D went on an 'aerial voyage' that was envisioned through a 'panoramic view' of space, usually from a hill or some other high point (1851, 124). Emma similarly spoke of climbing for a better view of things: on being given a letter in Lieutenant G.H. Hodgson's handwriting she stated, 'I can't find him anywhere – I will go to the top of that hill of snow and look – (after a pause) – I hope he is not dead, there is no place to bury him here – no churchyard'. Emma described her travels as 'going away' and in being sent to the Arctic the intention was that she would connect with the thoughts of individual explorers. When requested to go in search of someone, Emma 'begins as it were to look about her' and maintains a grave expression until she 'lights up, & she apparently begins a conversation with those she has been sent to see. "Oh I've found you – Well, you have come a long way since I saw you last – & how are you feeling? & What have you got to eat? & when do you expect to get home?"' (NA, ADM 7/189).

These very specific embodied performances of Arctic experience accord closely with the stereotypes about the Arctic available to audiences in nineteenth-century Britain. Almost by definition, the Arctic was a place that almost nobody could travel to. Because it was so remote from the lives of most people this distance was pared back through things like exploration narratives, fiction, ballads, museum exhibitions and material objects brought back by whalers. Due to this dependence on a media, critics were quick to point out the parallels between clairvoyant visions and popular representations of Arctic exploration. One sceptic satirised Emma's 'spiritual flights', asking:

> Why did not the operator request the fair Emma, while she was perambulating the North Pole, to tell us something we did *not* know? Why did she not reveal to us the secret of the North-west Passage? Why describe only pictures of snowy desolation and

stunted Esquimaux – figures which are familiar to every child who had read any story-book about the Polar Regions? Nay, since Emma is so great a mesmeric prodigy, and since space and time appear to be annihilated during these spiritual flights, why, even now, will not the operator 'will her' to inform us of what is going on in the moon, and what sort of people the Antropophagi really are? If she were only induced even to give us the benefit of her clairvoyance nearer home she would be more useful even to the Government than the telegraph at the top of the Admiralty ('Review: *Somnolism and Psycheism*', *The Medical Times*, 1851, 211).

The publicity surrounding the return of James Clark Ross's expedition in November 1849 and the planning for several more expeditions led to a sustained public interest in the visual aspects of Arctic exploration, a desire fed by a slew of Arctic panorama shows in London from 1849–52 (Potter, 2007; David, 2000, 154–5). Opening at Leicester Square in February 1850, one of the dominant tropes of Robert Burford's panorama, *Description of Summer and Winter Views of the Polar Regions*, was a realism generated by the body of the visitor. The paintings in the panorama were based on originals by William Browne, who served as an officer in the Arctic onboard HMS *Enterprise* from 1848–9, and the panorama located the viewer in a perceptual world that drew directly on the experience of explorers. This overlap and cooperation between Arctic explorers and panorama designers was not new: Henry Aston Barker's *Description of a View of the North Coast of Spitzbergen* (1819) actually constituted the first narrative of David Buchan and John Franklin's voyage north in 1818. Furthermore, in 1834, on his return from the *Victory* expedition, John Ross collaborated with Burford on an exhibition that *The Times* praised for its singular effects, particularly the atmospheric phenomena ('Panorama of Boothia', *The Times*, 1834). Indeed, with these connections between panorama construction and actual exploration, the overlap between artifice and reality became blurred. On the *Prince Albert* expedition sent out by Jane Franklin in 1850, William Parker Snow brought up this uncanny feeling as he approached Leopold Island:

> As we neared the shore, the whole features of the place came fresh upon me, so truthful is the representation given of them by Lieut. Browne in Burford's panorama. I could not mistake; and, I, almost, fancied that I was again in London, viewing the artistic sketch, but for certain undeniable facts in the temperature and aspect of the ice which banished such an idea (1851, 249).

But, unlike earlier panoramas, Burford's *Description of Summer and Winter Views of the Polar Regions* cashed in on the cultural anxiety about the Franklin expedition and the facilitation of 'authentic' polar imagery from explorers added to the reality effect of the experience (Garrison, 2012). The panorama was divided into two sections by a red curtain; one half of the circle showing the ships at midnight in the summer and the other at noon in the winter. *The Penny Illustrated News* described the first scene as a view of desolation and danger:

> a sublimely picturesque scene, of which there exists no parallel. Towering ice-bergs of gigantic size and the most fantastic shapes; immense hummocks; huge masses of ice formed by pressure; columns, pyramids, and an endless multitude of singular forms, heaped together in the wildest disorder, threatening each moment as they are driven in mighty strife by the wind or tide, to crush the ships to atoms ('The Polar Regions', *The Penny Illustrated News*, 1850, 153).

The experience of this panorama was designed to impact on the body and senses of the visitor, and this was memorably described by William Thackeray – aka 'Goliah Muff' – in *Punch*:

> Ah, sir! of what clay are mortals supposed to be made, that they can visit that exhibition. Dreams I have had in my life, but as that view of the Arctic Regions nothing so terrible. My blood freezes as I think of that frightful *summer* even – but what to say of the winter? By heavens, sir! I could not face the sight – the icy picture of eternal snow – the livid northern lights, the killing glitter of the stars; the wretched mariners groping about in the snow round the ship; they caused in me such a shudder of surprise and fright, that I don't blush to own I popped down the curtains after one single peep, and would not allow my children to witness it (1900, 178–9).

The panorama shows were transmission points of information, relaying knowledge of famous battles, disasters and new imperial conquests (see Altick, 1978). But as Thackeray's tongue-in-cheek description suggests, they were also performances of travel that elicited emotional responses that called into question the difference between reality and representation. This 'frieze painting', as *Punch* termed Burford's panorama, provoked comic feelings in its middle-class visitors, who could enjoy the Aurora Borealis on the first floor, marvel at the view of a ship held between walls of ice 'as in a nut-cracker', and look at 'frozen horrors' so natural that it 'sets everybody's teeth on the chatter' ('Climbing up the North Pole', *Punch*, 1850). The visitor to the panorama was both there and not there, inside and outside, travelling and stationary, in Arctic and in Britain (see Figure 3.4). The perspective that Gregory called the 'panoramic view' was a dream of omniscience that clairvoyants shared with most respectable consumers of Arctic spectacles. One could be present and located while one was also 'away', floating down the Mississippi River, travelling in a balloon over the English Channel, or spending the winter in the Arctic.

Thus a certain paradox emerges: in what way did the Arctic become more real to people through mediating technologies? The key thing to remember, as Alison Byerly (2013) points out, is that the imaginative displacement of the panorama visitor was precisely what Victorian realism depended on for its truth value. Novelists, she suggests, borrowed from the panorama shows, 'descriptive techniques and rhetorical gestures that position the reader or viewer as a kind of traveller, a conception of the reader's role that was fundamental to the operations of literary realism'

Figure 3.4 Untitled (portrait of man in front of moving panorama with Arctic theme), c.1850–7. Daguerreotype. Source: Museum purchase, Achenbach Foundation for Graphic Arts Tribute Fund, 1993.2. Image copyright the Fine Arts Museums of San Francisco.

(2013, 2; see also Otto, 2007). For instance, in 'Some Account of an Extraordinary Traveller' (1850) Dickens has Mr Booley visit Burford's panorama in the company of 'two coach painters, a gold-beater and his only daughter, by trade a stray-maker; and several other working-people from sundry parts of Great Britain who had conceived the extraordinary idea of "holiday-making" in the frozen wilderness' (1850, 76). For Booley, the panorama promotes social bonds by offering a cheap and non-exclusive means of 'conveying the results of actual experiences, to those who are unable to obtain such experiences for themselves': the view of Queen Victoria and the working woman is the same. While Dickens satirised this clash between the mundane and the marvellous, the panoramaisation of experience meant that participants had '[n]ew worlds open out to them, beyond their little worlds' that widened 'their range of reflection, information, sympathy, and interest' (Dickens, 1850, 77) – precisely the power of the Victorian realist author. New media were creating virtual worlds that extended the mobility of British consumers beyond the known and into the unknown, meaning that efforts to separate clairvoyant travels from panoramic travels, or fictional travels, were increasingly problematic.

A common theme among reviewers of Burford's panorama was to praise the 'singular condition of light and atmosphere' and 'the transparent brightness of day' ('Burford's Panorama', *Morning Chronicle*, 1850) while another was to focus on the translucency of polar colours – 'vivid emerald and violet tints', 'shades of the most intense blue' ('The Polar Regions', *The Penny Illustrated News*, 1850, 154). This focus on light and colour had long formed a central component of the Arctic imagination for those who consumed panoramas and popular narratives of discovery (see Potter, 2007, 68). It is no surprise, therefore, to find Emma describing the 'beautiful colours of a sort of blue red, like when saltpetre is out in the fire. How dark it is, and the stars they don't twinkle but go round and round, I will go back again, it is so dismal here' ('Sir John Franklin. Further Revelations by the Bolton Clairvoyante', *Preston Guardian*, 1849). Panoramas were representations of Arctic experience, but this does not disqualify them as inauthentic: they were one way in which the Arctic travelled to Britain, showing that these transfers also involved transformations and return voyages by the same bodily route.

Visual representations framed Arctic mobility for British consumers, but making the absent become present also involved a sympathetic connection with the expeditioners. This connection was based on the idea of the mesmeric rapport and the use of material relics. According to William Gregory, who witnessed Emma's travels in 1850, she would crush a letter containing the handwriting of an explorer, or a sample of their hair, in her hands 'and if the person do not at once appear, she will often lay it on her head' (1851, 127). The mechanism of her communications with the missing men was therefore an emotional one. Emma could ascertain the health or illness of subjects and locate lost or hidden objects, but in her travels to the Arctic she was engaging in a deeply intimate geospectral practice. That is, she used materials to hand as if they offered an access to the absent owner. This allowed for an embodied connection, a community of sensation, with the men: she could taste what they tasted, feel what they felt and think what they thought.

While her conversations with the men in the Arctic mostly dealt with their appearance and health, Emma also made claims about their dream life. In a séance in January 1850 Emma was mesmerised and a letter of James Fitzjames was put in her hand. She 'shivered a good deal on the passage, struggled, as if difficult to proceed, drew her apron over her head & neck as Cloak' until she found Fitzjames:

> You seem to be the one who wrote this … I saw you altogether at Prayer that Sunday. Your hair is <u>not</u> so light (<u>Grey</u>) as his – (Franklin's). What's that Spying Glass for? What do you see? You are looking to see if anything is coming to your relief. – You Dreamt that a ship (or ships) was coming to your relief. Three of you all had the same dream – yes: it was my coming to you that made you Dream (NA, ADM 7/189).

What these narratives show is that a 'plain, ignorant, common looking' maidservant from Bromsgrove, Worcestershire, who could neither read nor write was able to maintain a community of sensation binding together elite networks and individuals. Mesmeric knowledge about the Arctic relied on female participation but the traditional role of the maidservant in this scenario, as someone with limited education, mobility or income, was a consequence of social class. The representation of clairvoyants as transmission-machines denied them subjective power, yet it lent them an objective status because – in their normal state – they were so distant from polar knowledge centres. Thus, the particular type of attention and credibility given to the clairvoyant was based on the simultaneous recognition and occlusion of both gender and class.

Not that this smothered the personality of the clairvoyant for, as described by Maconochie, during a séance Emma's unobtrusive manners changed and she became 'familiar, almost pert & childish'. When directed to go in search of someone, she looked around her with her eyes closed 'using a good deal of action also with her hands, as tho' over coming difficulties', and with the eyes of an audience watching her every move, Emma then entered into breezy conversations with men who were international celebrities ('Oh I've found you. Well, you have come a long way since I saw you last – & how are you feeling? & What have you got to eat? & when do you expect to get home?' (DRO, D3311/81/1 (iii)). As one writer put it, after the discovery of clairvoyance, '[t]ravelling is no longer a luxury confined to the rich' (Borrow, 1851, 322).

There is evidence that Emma was aware of the power that she exerted over her employer once publicity about the case had spread. In a letter to a gentleman inquiring about consulting her, Haddock wrote that he had to pay Emma well, as 'from her ignorance & inexperience, and from remarks made by designing and mischievous people, I might have her enticed away just when matters were attracting the most attention'. Haddock therefore gave her half of the fees he received from medical cases, and he was obliged to decline to take on any more consultations into robberies due to Emma's workload (NU, WCT 284/83).[9] Emma's lack of deference as a clairvoyant, her access to the intimate dreams of missing men, and her transmission of geographical information, all add up to a performance less of ventriloquism than of social mobility. During one séance she even went in search of Franklin while still wearing her apron. She drew it over her head as a cloak when she encountered difficulties in travelling (NA, ADM/7/189).

It is also interesting that Haddock gradually began to function as a kind of operating service himself, passing on to Emma letters written by Franklin, James Clark Ross, Crozier, Fitzjames, and other officers from the Franklin expedition. Although she was illiterate, Emma used the letters sourced for her from Maconochie's naval network to direct her travels: in one case she complained that a letter 'wd not let me go the same way as before' (NA, ADM/7/189). Furthermore, Emma told the men she visited in the Arctic that she could write down their accounts: in the séance she went through the motions of 'making Memoranda with her left hand on her right arm'. When she arrived back in Bolton and was interrogated 'she professes to read the result off her right arm, pouring it forth with extreme volubility, & considerable incoherence' (DRO, D3311/81/1 (iii)). Emma's performance of literate power, then, reminds us of the significant role that the mesmeric trance played in social mobility during the Victorian era.

The clairvoyants discussed thus far were typically young women working in service, a sector with limited opportunities for advancement.

Illness, sensitivity, or the unusual symptoms associated with hysteria or animal magnetism could mean less menial work, some financial benefit and national celebrity. Add to this the psychological catharsis and genuine healing that mesmerism offered women, and it becomes clear that the trance became a transferential space in which maid and employer together generated emotional energies that could benefit them in their daily lives. Indeed, Haddock once wrote in a letter to Maconochie that Emma often felt 'low' after being visited by her mother: 'When she is so, she often fancies she sees things which are very strange' (NA, ADM/7/189).

The trance offered a route to the Arctic for both parties. There are plenty of cases in the nineteenth century of influential male professionals who analysed, studied and experimented with working-class women, causing sceptics to question the credibility of both patient and operator. A constant refrain in moralistic discourse about mesmerism was that both parties in the relationship were at risk – the operator from being tricked by the charms of the young somnambule, and the subject by the nefarious spells of her 'Svengali'. Despite this connection, the mobility conjured up in the séance could be embodied differently according to gender, and Emma's mesmerism opened up a geographic and social mobility far beyond the apothecary shop in Bolton. She was certainly aware of the significant cultural currency surrounding the image of the disconsolate Jane Franklin, because she frequently talked to Franklin about his 'Lady'. Female imperial travellers like Jane Franklin and Mary Kingsley came from privileged backgrounds and carried this with them as they travelled: by contrast, Emma moved and spoke differently and, because of this, she relied on an extended network to accredit her voyages.

Examining the network of people that followed Emma's séances gives us an insight into how her information was made credible at the time. Haddock was frequently joined at these by two other local acquaintances – Mr Darbyshire, a magistrate from Rivington, and Mr Martin, probably a professional gentleman from Bolton. Maconochie, meanwhile, brought a more extensive and powerful network to the séance. Firstly, as a former colleague of Franklin and friend to his family, Maconochie became a conduit of information between Emma, Jane Franklin, and Eleanor Gell. Secondly, Maconochie was invested with social authority by virtue of his naval and institutional roles, and his connections with the Royal Geographical Society. Through Hamilton's close following of the case, this led to a relationship between the Admiralty and Emma on the subject of the Franklin expedition. This is evidence that supports Cavell's argument that the 'monopoly of interpretation' that

Barrow exercised on the Arctic broke down after Franklin's disappearance (2008, 17). Not that this meant her revelations were taken seriously by all members of the Admiralty Board: as mentioned, an unidentified reader of one of Maconochie's memorandums scribbled 'Gross Humbug' beside the mention of the Parry Islands as a possible location, while after Haddock wrote of Emma's diseased heart the same pen added 'No doubt of that in her mind too' (NA, ADM/7/189). As for Barrow, he retired in 1845 and died in November 1848 and one suspects he would not have had as open a mind on these matters as his successor Hamilton did. The newspaper press also played a major role in spreading publicity about clairvoyance, and the Bolton correspondent of the *Manchester Guardian* attended Emma's séances in October 1849.

Maconochie was also acquainted with Sir Walter C. Trevelyan, a wealthy naturalist and eccentric landlord from Northumberland who shared his advocacy for penal reform. Like many social reformers in the 1840s, Trevelyan was interested in mesmerism and visited Bolton for two days to investigate Emma's clairvoyance. In order to test out Emma's abilities, Trevelyan asked the Secretary of the Royal Geographical Society, John Hogg, to send him the handwriting of several persons who were unknown to him and were in different parts of the world. Forwarding these to Emma, Trevelyan reported that she located one of the writers by giving a fairly good description of Rome: 'As she generally finds the hour by looking at some clock or watch, it would appear that she had been puzzled by the clocks of Rome, which have 24 hours, instead of 12' (Gregory, 1851, 302). Trevelyan was further linked to Scottish scientific and mesmeric networks (especially in connection with William Gregory), and he became associated with the Arctic schemes of William Parker Snow, an explorer whose eccentricities, as the next chapter will show, far exceeded his own.

A 'crucial instance' of clairvoyance?

For some critics of mesmerism, the phenomena produced at séances were abnormal – 'the result of a derangement of the normal state of the human constitution'. The claims of itinerant lecturers and the antics of the mesmerised patient were decried as incoherent and hysteric jabbering that might explain age-old tales of demonic possession and witchcraft ('Mesmerism', *The Aberdeen Journal*, 1843). From the 1850s, the psychiatrist William Benjamin Carpenter became an influential authority in debates about mesmerism and spiritualism by arguing that it was the loss of the power of 'volitional self-direction', or the Will, which allowed 'sane' people to become suggestible and perceive things that exceed common-sense, as in dreaming (1853, 510). Meanwhile, many who believed in and practised mesmerism as a science or a curative gift from God drew the line at clairvoyance.

In the early months of 1852, the writer Wilkie Collins witnessed a series of mesmeric séances while on holiday in Somerset. Collins described how his friend, known as 'Count P.', placed his wife's companion, 'Mademoiselle V' into mesmeric trances for a parlour game. 'V' was made to follow the hidden movements of the mesmerist, 'just as a needle would have followed a magnet' (1852, 64). During one experiment, 'V' was given a piece of polished coal, a replica of the 'wishing stone' used by the Elizabethan magus Dr John Dee, and Collins asked her to visit a person he was thinking of (his brother in London). 'V' described the long arms, long face and dark or fair hair of the person she was seeing and, after Collins held her hand, guessed the person to be his brother. For Collins, writing in the radical weekly *The Leader*, this experience convinced him of the power of clairvoyance:

> that her spiritual sympathies and mental instincts were so extended in range, and so sharpened in intensity, while she was in the magnetic state, that her mind could act and her thoughts move in the most intimate connection with the minds and thoughts of others (Collins, 1852, 232).

Collins's piece led to a sceptical rebuttal from his editor, George Henry Lewes, who, while agreeing that the evidence for mesmerism was ample, was not convinced about clairvoyance because no '*crucial instance*' of it had ever occurred (1852). Lewes was sure that Collins's clairvoyant could plausibly guess answers based on body language, leading questions and unconscious suggestions ('cold reading', as it is now known). In search of this proof, Lewes then brought up the contemporary sensation Emma of Bolton, challenging her and Haddock to assist him in proving, indisputably, the existence of clairvoyance, presumably by demonstrating something that no other human being could plausibly know. There was obviously a disagreement about what constituted evidence for clairvoyance as Collins, responding to Lewes in 'The Incredible Not Always Impossible', upheld the notion that a genuine clairvoyant could 'fail' in one experiment and 'succeed' in another. He found the idea of a '*crucial instance*' flawed in the testing of clairvoyance, but in the newspaper press this became the standard sceptical response to Franklin visions.[10] Collins returned to the subject of clairvoyance in *The Frozen Deep* in 1856 but, by this stage, when it was woven through the mystery of the Franklin expedition, Collins used it solely as a narrative device.

Elsewhere, William Scoresby was absorbed in his own experiments in what he termed 'zoistic magnetism' at the same time that he was advising the Admiralty and Jane Franklin on the missing Franklin expedition. Scoresby had retired as a whaling master and was now an evangelical Anglican clergyman and an internationally respected member of the Royal Society. Scoresby believed that the same principles of attraction and repulsion present in natural magnetism were also present in the relations between humans. During his mesmeric experiments, he found that 'attracting' magnetised hands (right hand holding subject's left) caused pleasurable sensations in the subject, but non-attracting hands (right with right, or left with left) caused a feeling like an 'electric shock' (1849, 66). Applying this concept of polarities more generally, Scoresby argued that it was important that the mesmerised subject should face magnetic north. Indeed, the female patient was thought of as an '*electrometer*', a delicate instrument (Scoresby, 1849, 92) made by a beneficent divine agency.

Here, then, was a connection between contemporary debates about terrestrial magnetism and animal magnetism: the use of iron in the construction of ships caused major navigational problems because the ship's own magnetism affected the compass. This became a tricky scientific problem that had implications for Britain's role as the dominant naval power on the world stage, but for Scoresby it was not separate from the debates on human magnetism, as both pivoted on powerful influences that had been actualised by God (see Winter, 1994). It was on this basis that Scoresby did not believe in clairvoyance: firstly because, if it were true, it would be a miracle (and such things were only within the 'province of omniscience' (Scoresby, 1849, 48)) and secondly because, aside from the admitted ability of somnambules to gain insight into diseases through *rapport* (usually termed 'introvision'), clairvoyants were unable to determine any really '*useful information*'. As an example of this, Scoresby brought up the Franklin case:

> 'Why', as a lady who was much interested in the fate of the absent Arctic expeditions, said to him when speaking of the pretensions referred to, – 'Why *if* they can tell what is passing at any distance, do they not tell where the discovery ships are, or what is their fate?' (Scoresby, 1849, 50).

When reports spread in the late 1840s that clairvoyants were locating missing items and naming hidden cards, newspaper editors, correspondents and paying audience members demanded that instead of answering trivial things, clairvoyants should make the incredible credible by proving once and for all that this form of perception was indeed a wonder of the Victorian age, a new mental science that could triumph over space, time and matter. It was in this context of calls for sceptical investigation that, in 1849, the mystery of the Franklin expedition was latched onto debates about clairvoyance ('Clairvoyance and its Tests', *The Hull Packet and East Riding Times*, 1849).

Here was a story causing frenzied international speculation about the 'blank spaces' of the Arctic, a *terra incognita* that was by definition geographically distant and inaccessible to most people in Britain. Indeed, the naval experts and explorers who submitted their reports, journals and schemes to the voluminous *Parliamentary Papers* (which are now known as the *Arctic Blue Books*) rarely agreed about anything regarding the fate of Franklin, apart from a general confidence in his survival. This meant that the door was wide open for clairvoyants to make geographical claims about the lost expedition that were capable of being verified or discounted at a future date. As one dismissive commentator in the *Medical Times* put it:

> Let the Mesmerists publish daily or weekly accounts of the proceedings of Sir John Franklin and his companions, or, if unfortunately they are no more, of the expeditions now in search of them, – and surely, if their boasted clairvoyance be concentrated on this one point, they cannot fail, if there be any truth in their so oft-repeated assertions, to mitigate the public anxiety in the meantime (Bushnan, 1850).

Communities of sensation

After news of Emma's visions of the Franklin expedition spread during the winter of 1849, a new series of clairvoyant reports appeared. In Liverpool, a young woman named Sarah, a domestic servant in the service of a Captain Hudson of Chesterfield Street, made new claims about Franklin. Sarah was described as a poor and uneducated girl who had been cured of an injured arm by Hudson's mesmeric treatment, during which he picked up on her clairvoyant abilities. Hudson, like Morrison, was a retired naval officer and probably had some experience commanding a vessel in the northern seas (Hudson, 1852). Apparently responding to a request from Lady Franklin, Hudson placed Sarah in a trance in March and asked her about Franklin.

> 'Did you say', inquired the operator, 'that Sir John Franklin is dead?' And to this and other questions the clairvoyante responded, 'That can not be, for I see him; poor fellow! he looks sad and wearied, and not so well as when I was last here ... He says he is poorly and tired, and almost worn out with hopes deferred, but his men console him and behave nobly. God never made a path through these desolate wastes. What could induce him to try to break through these icy mountains? He frequently thinks of the folly of his daring to do so. Such thoughts humble him, and make him sad and hopeless, yet he thinks he will succeed in returning to England. He is right. He will return in six months and three or four days' ('The Arctic Expedition', *Liverpool Mercury*, 22 March 1850).

Here, then, was a concrete prediction that Franklin would return at a particular time, and this was taken in the press as an opportunity to prove clairvoyance true or false. Indeed, it was favourably noted that both Emma and Sarah thought he would return in September 1850. Gesturing to this mesmeric traffic between Britain and the Arctic, at a later séance in May Sarah mentioned that she met the 'spirits of two clairvoyants' on their way back from a visit to Franklin where they reported that he was safe and well. Although she took the time from Franklin (1.25 p.m. in the Arctic, 9.35 p.m. in Liverpool) Sarah could not locate the ships. However, she said that they would be first heard of at a place called 'the Cape'. During this second séance Sarah repeated her original intelligence that the expedition would return in 'about five months' ('A Night with the Clairvoyants', *Dundee, Perth and Cupar Advertiser*, 1850).

On the same day that the *Liverpool Mercury* published the account of Sarah's clairvoyance, the newspaper sent a correspondent to report on another clairvoyant also causing a sensation in the city. In a report circulated in other metropolitan newspapers, readers were told that Jenny, a Scottish-born domestic servant of around 20 years of age, was sent on an 'aërial journey' to the Arctic by her employer, an amateur mesmerist. This was done with the assistance of a small drinking glass that, when rested on the top of her nose, strengthened her vision. Jenny described reaching a cold place with ice, 'such as you never saw', and met with the expeditioners who were in a sorry state but had enough provisions for another year. Jenny suggested that three ships laden with salt should be dispatched to melt the ice that imprisoned them: 'I wonder they don't try that. But they are a set of stupid blockheads', she noted. Jenny then told the audience that she saw thirteen alive on the ship she found, including Franklin, and they 'ought to get out next summer' with help from the Government. As to the location of his ship, she believed it to be north of Bering Straits but, despite eager questioning, she could find no document that showed the longitude or latitude ('Liverpool Clairvoyantes', *Liverpool Mercury*, 1850) and, on a later occasion, she vaguely said the expedition was lying to the west of Prince Regent Inlet ('Another Visit to Sir John Franklin in the Polar Regions', *Liverpool Mercury*, 1850). 'But how must the vessels laden with salt find Sir John Franklin?', asked the mesmerist. 'Oh', replied Jenny, 'just go straight on till they come to the ice, and then they will see them'. Jenny made up for her obvious lack of geographical information by gesturing towards a comparative clairvoyant truth for, like Sarah, Jenny said that the first news would come from a place called 'the Cape', and again, like Sarah, she demonstrated an awareness of passing mesmeric traffic, saying that on her way home she passed a woman from London who was also heading towards Franklin ('Liverpool Clairvoyantes', *Liverpool Mercury*, 1850).

News of Jenny and Sarah's mesmeric journeys to the Arctic reached Scotland during the next month, appearing in the Aberdeen newspapers on 10 April. Within two weeks a male clairvoyant in the local fishing port of Peterhead travelled north in search of ships. On 22 and 23 April, a 22-year-old tailor named John Park was 'thrown into the mesmeric sleep' by William Reid, a local shoemaker, in the presence of some townspeople. Reid, 'as may naturally be supposed', first asked questions about the fleet of Peterhead whaling ships currently in the Arctic. Park travelled north to 'Old Greenland' (Davis Straits) in search of the vessels, predicting that the *Hamilton Ross* would return first and describing a vision of its captain and surgeon dressing the hand of the second mate after an accident. Reid's report of these séances was apparently sent to the *Aberdeen Herald* shortly afterwards but was put aside in the belief that it was an imposture ('Clairvoyance at Peterhead', *John O'Groat Journal*, 1850). Remarkably, on 3 May, the *Hamilton Ross* did indeed return first with 10,000 seals (153 tonnes) and the hundreds who gathered to greet her were shocked to see the second mate, David Cardno, leave the ship with his arm in a sling after having injured it in a fishing accident ('Peterhead – Mesmerism', *The Aberdeen Journal*, 1850). This incident caused a local sensation with people murmuring 'the mesmerism had come true' ('Mr W. Boyd, Peterhead, on Clairvoyance', *The Aberdeen Journal*, 1891). The story first appeared in the press on 8 May, about two weeks after Reid's séances. This case lived long in local memory and Reid later reported that Park was 'so frightened by the "outstanding" results which followed, that he would never try it again' ('Mr W. Boyd, Peterhead, on Clairvoyance', *The Aberdeen Journal*, 1891).

In the same edition of *The Aberdeen Journal* that published the account of John Park's clairvoyance, it was noted that the *Prince Albert* was on its way to Aberdeen to be fitted out for its Arctic expedition in search of Franklin. Also, on 13 April the Peterhead whaler William Penny departed Aberdeen in command of an Admiralty search expedition made up of the *Lady Franklin* and the *Sophia*. The period of April and May 1850 was a time when 'the eyes of the whole world may be said to be turned towards the frozen regions of the north, where Sir John Franklin and his intrepid companions have in all-likelihood been ice-bound for years' ('Reviews', *Liverpool Mercury*, 1850). There was a routine concern for voyaging whalers and sealers among the inhabitants of the North Sea ports, and several Franklin search expeditions left from Aberdeen with local men and commanders. In this context, the mesmerism at Peterhead might be seen as a practice of remote sensing that offered a perspective on what was happening, or might happen, in the Arctic.

After passing on the information about the *Hamilton Ross*, and despite his desire never to return to the Arctic, Park was again sent in search of the expedition. On this occasion he found Franklin onboard the *Terror* examining a map. Franklin, he said, looked very care-worn and was dressed 'like a common seaman'. Park then visited the *Erebus*, which had sustained damage and was being repaired by the men. Park chatted to one of the men on the deck who said:

> 'That their crew were all well, but that nine were dead, some of them being killed among the ice; that they had plenty of provisions brought from England, but that they were rather scarce of fire, and that the natives were visiting them daily'.

For *The Aberdeen Herald* the whole affair was either 'an extraordinary fact, an extraordinary fraud, or an extraordinary coincidence. Charity and caution lead us to adopt, *ad interim*, the latter alternative'. Could the clairvoyant tell, the newspaper asked, what was passing with Captain Penny's expedition? ('Clairvoyance at Peterhead', *John O'Groat Journal*, 1850). Where an extraordinary coincidence was noted in relation to the *Hamilton Ross*, it was not quite the 'crucial instance' of clairvoyance that many sceptics demanded and Park's false information regarding the

Franklin expedition was later put down to an inability to distinguish 'true' impressions from 'false' ones ('Mr W. Boyd, Peterhead, on Clairvoyance', *The Aberdeen Journal*, 1891).

During May, news of the mesmeric visions from Peterhead travelled further north in Scotland, via the *John O'Groat Journal*, where they reached Shetland. There a party 'of the highest respectability' were inspired to make their own experiments in mesmeric clairvoyance with a man named James Smith. Smith followed Park in placing Franklin onboard the *Terror*, and told his audience that the ship was located opposite 'but some distance from' Fury Beach. (This was the site of Parry's abandonment of the *Fury* in 1825. It harboured the stores and provisions that aided John Ross's *Victory* expedition in 1833).[11] According to Smith, the ship was making some progress out of the ice and would be free in 'two or three days'.

Yet, Smith had a darker vision than Park to relate, speaking of 40 deaths and a 'care-worn' Franklin who 'stated that he was diseased'. Smith then found another ship some distance south-west of the *Terror*: 'We requested him to tell the name, and though he could not see it so distinctly as in the other case on account of the vessel lying over in the ice, he succeeded eventually in spelling the word EREBUS'. Here, the captain was similarly 'unwell and downcast' while the crew were 'dissatisfied, and a party of them had left the ship in search of land'. Responding to the challenge raised by *The Aberdeen Herald*, the clairvoyant mentioned a large vessel approaching Franklin's ships that was named the 'Lady Franklin', obviously taken to be Penny's ship that had left Aberdeen in April ('Clairvoyance in Shetland', *John O'Groat Journal*, 1850).

These mesmeric experiments aroused very different responses from readers of the *John O'Groat Journal*. One correspondent described clairvoyance as nothing more than a form of communication between two parties through the mesmeric fluid, the distance of which could be extended as with the electric telegraph ('Mesmerism', *Aberdeen Journal*, 1843). Also responding to the Shetland clairvoyant was a correspondent named Tom Dixon who had a more down-to-earth interpretation of events:

> Now, I don't pretend to be either a cute or a far-read fellow, but I say it is coming on raything strong to tell us that a man or a woman can see real things with the eyes dead shut. The thing is impossible, and nothing but a farce. Why, what is the use of the eyes if a man can see with them closed, or his nose either, if he can smell without it? ... it seems raything wonderful, that while the eyes were thus able to go

right through the very centre of our solid globe – through rocks and waters and muds and everlasting ice – and count the number of hairs in the beards of the poor tars, the ice about the starn of the Erebus bothered them not a little. Why couldn't the eyes see through the ice … ? … how does it happen that the clairvoyant – a poor, ignorant man, as I suppose – knew 'Fury Beach'? Why here's the mark of an impostor as sure as my name's Tom Dixon. What does a illiterate man know about the name even of 'Fury Beach'? Is there a sign-post stuck up there with the name of Fury on it? or has this prophet been in these cold countries himself and seen before the remains of the old vessel? I ask, how did the clairvoyant know Fury Beach to be Fury Beach? By his sight? Impossible! By his mind? Impossible! By his smell or taste? More impossible still! Depend upon it, Sir, it is all a hoax, and them as believe it are flats. I won't waste your valuable time by making any remarks on the singular quick hearing of this sleeping or dreaming man, for you yourself can't but allow that your being able to hear a quiet chit chat about 3000 or 4000 miles off is decent practice [sic throughout] ('The Humbug of Clairvoyance', *John O'Groat Journal*, 1850).

Despite this criticism, news about Smith's clairvoyance spread, and when an incredulous clergyman visited Shetland in August 1850 he arranged 'to have the matter thoroughly tested'. The clergyman reported that Smith was able to follow him in thought from place to place as he journeyed in his mind, including to his home in Edinburgh, which he correctly described. Although the clergyman was reluctant to use the Franklin expedition as a test case – 'the accuracy of which I could not pronounce upon' – Smith was eventually directed to the Arctic where, shivering from the cold weather, he found the *Erebus* and *Terror* still frozen in the ice. Writing up the case for William Gregory in 1851, the clergyman regretted not making more explicit inquiries about the expedition in order to compare it to other clairvoyant reports (Gregory, 1851, 338–40).

In what way did people deal with these remarkable predictions? Reading Gregory's account of Emma's clairvoyance, a reviewer in *The Lancet* attacked her as an 'artful peasant' who made predictions about Franklin in the knowledge that they would not 'return from the grave to convict her'. Her clairvoyance was a failure and she should therefore be dismissed as a 'hysterical damsel' goaded on by worshippers ('Mesmeric Humbug', 1851, 155). Elsewhere, critics gleefully pointed out that the prophets disagreed on the Franklin mystery – if the clairvoyant process was actually one of illumination, how could one account for such 'variation' in visions? ('Our Weekly Gossip', *The Athenaeum*, 1850b). These criticisms were one way of looking at the matter. Another way was to celebrate them even in their vagueness, as dim 'glimpses of the departed' that were not infallible but might yet be proven to have approached the truth ('Letter from Cleveland to the Readers of the Journal of Man', *Buchanan's Journal of Man*, 1852, 12).[12] Of course the Franklin expedition did not return in the autumn of 1850 as several clairvoyants claimed but we must be careful not to see them simply as failures.

This chapter has argued that we should look at the way that clairvoyance worked by displaying relations between the Arctic and Britain. Information exchange was one purpose and performance of clairvoyants, but they also facilitated those investigating the Franklin mystery to become intimate with the lost expedition. This reveals two underlying conceptions of spatial relations. The first is the Cartesian/Euclidean notion of space as a bounded plane of quantifiable distances and co-ordinates – a passive container that does not stretch. This conception of space draws its power from mathematics and an appeal to an objective framework of space-time (Lefebvre, 1991). In this understanding, Franklin was located at a particular place in the Arctic and the information provided by the clairvoyants was to be judged on the basis of people as objects on a collectively-recognised spatial plane. By this standard, clairvoyance was a failure. By contrast, the second conception is of space as 'atmospherical' (Anderson, 2006), as something that is leaky, that stretches and that involves the unbounded movement of affects between bodies, minds, spirits and things. Building on this notion of space as unstable, elastic and spectral, recent re-formulations of subjectivity posit the idea of a person as equally porous, an unbounded entity through which other subjectivities may flow. The approach to the matter taken by Steve Pile (2012), for instance, links nineteenth-century ideas about telepathy with current emotional understandings of space.

Returning to the subject of mesmerism and clairvoyance, we can draw distinct connections to an unbounded concept of space. Take the idea of an eighteenth-century French mesmerist who thought the human body was 'composed of pipes and pores, beyond conception, and formed of particles, between which, the most minute and extensive porosity is admitted; through which the passage of atoms and fluids of various denominations, circulate in every direction' (Winter qtd. in McCorristine, 2012, II, 12). Such ideas supported the concept of communities of sensation, linking together subjects, mesmerists and distant bodies in emotional relations. For instance, Haddock 'sent' Emma to visit one of his relatives in London. The clairvoyant, on her own volition, began to wander around a 'magnificent residence', which Haddock believed was Buckingham Palace. On further inquiry he found out that his relative had been thinking of the Queen at that moment, and this redirected Emma, via a sympathetic connection to her thoughts, to the Palace (1851, 106).

As a way of thinking about the relations between 'here' and 'there', 'me' and 'you', the community of sensation shows that spaces could be 'worked' into being through intimate relations. Indeed, as a spatially hybrid entity, the British Empire itself only really worked as an emotional space (Thrift, 2006, 144), held together by deeply-felt exchanges and transmissions like letters, prayers, material relics, and even telepathic ghost-seeing. By this standard, clairvoyance collapsed the distance between the Arctic and Britain. Mapping out where the missing are is something that involves more than co-ordinates and time synchronicities. During this period, answering the question 'where is Franklin?' was so difficult that space had to be stretched to take account of the feelings people had about the lost expedition. Disappearance is always a relational process involving different forms of searching, from the physical to the emotional. Clairvoyant travels to the Arctic were geospectral in that they populated absence and gave something tangible to those left behind. It was the quality of these experiences, rather than their credibility or incredibility, which drew people in.

International revelations

These relational geographies between the Arctic and Britain could overflow into another set of relations linking colonial locations with the Arctic. Interest in the Franklin mystery transcended national boundaries and one way of tracking the connections between Britain and its distant colonies during this period is by highlighting the clairvoyants who disrupted the core/periphery model of the British Empire.

The clairvoyant revelations publicised in Britain were picked up frequently by the press in Australia, Van Diemen's Land, and New Zealand, and the 'dead time' between Britain and the Arctic also existed between Britain in its colonies. The temporal aspects of mesmeric visions were important when it came to the Franklin mystery, primarily because of the four-month time-lag that existed between the Antipodean colonies and Britain. The first news of Emma's clairvoyance reached Australia in February 1850, and reports of the Liverpool clairvoyants arrived in August and September. While colonial mesmerisers undoubtedly took their lead from British investigations, their representations of the clairvoyant as a tele-technology opened the door to local speculations independent of the news being transmitted from Britain. Clairvoyance could thereby serve people as a dissenting route of information, something that collapsed space and time and bypassed geographic lags. Interwoven with this utility was the consolation that clairvoyant visions offered to people who felt cut off from the northern hemisphere and at risk of not knowing of injuries or deaths to loved ones far away.

In Australia, Melbourne was the scene of a lively mesmerist culture with several practitioners publishing on the topic and establishing an institute (Donnelly, 2006; Mereweather, 1859, 86–7). In October 1850, Dr J.B. Motherwell, along with some other Melbourne professionals, signed a statement sent to John Elliotson and published in the important British mesmeric journal *The Zoist*, which described their experiments with a young, 'untaught and uneducated' clairvoyant in the town. Using an 1838 letter from John Franklin as a medium, the clairvoyant 'described with complete accuracy several events in Sir John Franklin's life in the Australian colonies, and ultimately followed him to England. She then commenced following him upon his expedition to the North Pole'. The clairvoyant went on to vaguely describe seeing up to four ships among icebergs before Elliotson paused the narrative in order, he stated, to wait until her statements could be verified (1849–50, 71).

While the content of the vision made Elliotson nervous, the Australian press showed no such qualms in reporting that the clairvoyant saw 'the ship that Sir John Franklin sailed for the polar regions in, and that it was enveloped in flames. She also stated that [he] had arrived in London and he had died two weeks after his arrival' ('Mesmerism', *Colonial Times*, 1850). In a subsequent session in November she gave more details of Franklin's route home (from Cape Horn to Plymouth or Portsmouth she said), mentioning that he died off the coast of South America, and even described the details of his naval funeral the previous September ('Domestic Intelligence', *Colonial Times*, 1850; 'Clairvoyance and Sir John Franklin', *Bell's Life in Sydney and Sporting Reviewer*, 1850). These, of course, were facts that would take an extended period of time to disprove in Australia, and this was taken as an impressive leap of faith by some ('Clairvoyance and Sir John Franklin', *Bell's Life in Sydney and Sporting Reviewer*, 1850). However, if these revelations were published by *The Zoist* in London several months later (with no sign of Franklin) they would have embarrassed Elliotson, particularly as most of the British clairvoyant visions were broadly positive about Franklin's chances.

The disappearance of explorers offered mesmerists and their clairvoyants an opportunity to put into practice what the general public could only imagine: the ability to track and follow the routes of missing people and, through the use of geographical information and predictions of arrival, operate alongside official authorities. Indeed, there is evidence that the Melbourne circle were not content with searching for Franklin. Closer to home, the mystery of Ludwig Leichhardt, the Prussian explorer who disappeared in 1848 while attempting to cross Australia from east to west, also drew their attention and they sent their clairvoyant in search of Leichhardt in 1850.[13]

The analogies between the Franklin and Leichhardt expeditions are worth noting. Just like Franklin, Leichhardt had intimated that he may not be heard of for two or three years. As with Franklin, there was a sudden upsurge in anxiety regarding Leichhardt's fate from 1850 onwards, as rumours of rescue, massacre, survival with the natives and geographical utopias circulated throughout the 1850s. Yet, with the government dithering on the matter in 1850, letters began to flow into the newspaper press from former colleagues, geographical authorities and concerned members of the public all asking the same question: 'Where is Dr Leichhardt?'

Many Australians were inspired by the energetic example set by Jane Franklin in mobilising sympathy for her husband's loss. But the *Sydney Morning Herald* argued that while Franklin's was a scientific expedition, it was a different situation with Leichhardt:

> His scheme of an overland route to Swan River, is not simply one in which all lovers of science must take a deep interest, but one in which commerce and civilization, and all the permanent interests not only of the colonies, but of the whole future population of this continent, are deeply involved ('Where is Dr Leichhardt?', *Sydney Morning Herald*, 1850).

Private rescue expeditions were soon proposed and discussed, and running parallel with these developments were idealisations of Leichhardt in popular culture as a pioneer and patriot of the young colony. It was in this context that the Melbourne clairvoyant, fresh from searching for Franklin, '(mentally) wandered through the Australian wilderness in search of the intrepid traveller' and even secured an interview with Leichhardt, who was located between Swan River and Port Essington. Leichhardt revealed to her that all of his party were dead except for two men and himself ('Leichhardt', *Bell's Life in Sydney and Sporting Reviewer*, 1850). In a subsequent update in December 1850, he was described as having reached water, 'but not before having killed a horse and giving [sic] the blood to one of the party' ('Victoria', *South Australian Register*, 1850).

While the classic mesmeric subjects of the period tended to be young and poor women, in his book *Letters to a Candid Inquirer, on Animal Magnetism* (1851), William Gregory particularly highlighted the susceptibility of native Indians and Africans to the mesmeric sleep (1851, 96). In Melbourne, Aboriginies were considered good subjects while in Britain, immigrants from Ireland were prominent experimentees. Power relations therefore formed part of the mesmeric rapport, as racist and hierarchical assumptions dictated who was and who was not considered to be a good and passive subject. Indeed, mesmerism itself operated as an expression of colonial power in Calcutta where British mesmeric medicine, as practised by James Esdaile especially, was seen as an enlightened weapon in the battle against native superstitions and magic (see Ernst, 2004).

In the summer of 1850 the *Bombay Monthly Times* reported on a mesmeric experiment with a 'young lady, a native of and resident in Calcutta' detailing her marvellous travels to Halifax, Nova Scotia, and Scarborough, Yorkshire ('Bengal', *Bombay Monthly Times*, 1850). Over several sessions she was asked by her mesmeriser to 'go to the Arctic Seas in search of Sir John Franklin'. She described seeing Franklin on a ship locked in ice, 'he looks haggard and thoughtful; he has a telescope in his hand'. After some close questioning regarding the details of the ship she saw, the girl mentioned a ship in the distance, and predicted Franklin's return in the middle of September ('Mesmerism and Clairvoyance', *Dumfries and Galloway Standard and Advertiser*, 1850). For those who witnessed the séance, this was remarkable information for someone who had probably never been many miles from Calcutta in her life, but for the clairvoyant herself it seemed to be a wondrous experiment: 'I have seen places and things I never saw before. What is this?' ('Bengal', *Bombay Monthly Times*, 1850). This same report reached Britain in September 1850, and Australia in January 1851 ('Mesmerism and Clairvoyance', *South Australian Register*, 1851).

Closer to Britain, H. Hill Hardy, a Trinity College Dublin mathematician and mesmerist, claimed he investigated Franklin's whereabouts with seven clairvoyants. At one performance in March 1852, Hardy introduced to 'a numerous assemblage of ladies and gentry' one Master Jones, the clairvoyant he placed most faith in. According to Hardy, Jones was:

> a fine lad of about twelve or fourteen years of age ... He described the present situation of Sir John Franklin, whom he said he saw a

> prisoner among the Tartar tribe, on the borders of China. He even pointed out a point on the terrestrial map, when he said the gallant adventurer was now situate. He said Sir John was dressed in a blue coat, but the rest of his costume was Tartarian. His watch was gone, and he seemed closely watched. The young lad, after answering a variety of queries, was released from the 'sleep', and appeared as if bewildered and confused on awaking. Great interest was taken by all present in this part of the proceedings ('Mesmerism – Illustrated Lectures', *Freeman's Journal*, 1852).

Hardy claimed that all of his clairvoyants agreed in locating Franklin in north-east Asia, and some reported that he was blocked up in ice at a longitude of 176½° east, 'north of the country of the Tchekchi'.[14] Much like Haddock and Emma, Hardy judged the accuracy of the visions by looking at the longitudinal agreement between the time where Franklin was stated to be, and the time of the vision. In adding to the truth value of the voyages, Hardy mentioned that one of his clairvoyants even had to be treated for chilblains after being with Franklin for two hours – an extreme form of armchair tourism indeed ('Franklin and the Clairvoyants', *Belfast Newsletter*, 1852).

All of these clairvoyant narratives, generated outside Britain, travelled to British newspapers where they were logged as part of the cumulative clairvoyant quest for the Franklin expedition. In this, they formed part of what Thomas Richards (1993) describes as the 'imperial archive', a storehouse of information, intelligence and data gathered from the peripheries but believed to project British power over the Empire from a great distance. These clairvoyants, however, disrupted the traditional unidirectional model of imperial power, instead pointing to the more fluid notion that information and knowledge were made through multiple trajectories travelling to, from and within locations outside Britain.

4
Spiritual routes and revelations: The Franklin mystery renewed

> *The noblest intellects in the universe require to 'dream' – to have 'visions' – to sleep and be abstracted from the world in which they live, ere they can see any of those brilliant truths, or imbibe those god-like beauties of the mind for which their names afterwards become noted* (Snow, 1862, 171)

The clairvoyant narratives that travelled to Jane Franklin's door from 1849–52 were consoling at the time, even if they proved false and misleading. However, the spread of spiritualism, or 'table-rapping', which arrived in Britain from North America in 1852, made inquiring about the missing or the dead less of a parlour game or scientific experiment and more of a question of belief. High society was split on the question of spiritualism with some thinking it a form of madness or hallucination and others promoting it as Christian or even rational. Whatever the experience one took from a séance room, it was clear that publicly associating oneself with spiritualism was a risky act that opened up respectable people to ridicule and accusations of weakness or lack of common-sense. A pertinent example here is the Arctic explorer Elisha Kent Kane who became romantically involved with, and may have even married, the young medium Margaret Fox. It was at Fox's home in Rochester, New York State that, in 1848, the era of 'table-rapping' began. Fox fell in love with Kane in 1852 but their romance and marriage were denied and covered up for fear of scandal by the Kane family after he died in 1857 (see *The Love-life of Dr. Kane*, 1866; Chapin, 2004).

Clairvoyance, previously considered a kind of geospatial practice under the remit of the quasi-scientific mesmerism, was now part of the even more contested practice of spiritualism, a space where female mediums were controlling narratives and directing the actions of male authorities. Because of this shift in visionary labour practices, engaging people with supernatural knowledge became fraught with social risk and religious controversy. When spiritualist claims about conversations with the post-mortem spirit of Franklin started to circulate in the early 1850s, it is likely that Jane Franklin and Cracroft ceased their interest in clairvoyance out of fear of embarrassment. However, in this chapter I focus on one exceptional case – that of Weesy Coppin – to show that their relationship with spiritualism and the world of ghosts was not as clear-cut as it first appears. Here, I want to make the revisionist argument that Jane Franklin was influenced by ghostly visions in her decision to focus search expeditions on the Prince Regent Inlet area in 1850 and 1851, and this point of view was communicated to several key personalities associated with the Franklin searches. But, to set the scene, I first discuss William Parker Snow (1817–95), who merits his place here as one of the most interesting and eccentric personalities associated with the search for Franklin (see Figure 4.1).

The strange case of William Parker Snow

Snow was the son of a naval lieutenant who served at the Battle of Trafalgar and was educated at the Royal Naval School at Greenwich. He had an adventurous youth, serving on various ships in the navy before he set himself up as a man of letters and acted as an amanuensis for the historian Lord Macaulay. Snow seems to have suffered from periods of psychosomatic ill-health throughout his life that were probably linked to his manic drive to achieve great things. Never one to stick to a single profession, he moved from dream to dream, lecturing, writing and even begging people to gain support for his projects. By 1850, Snow was the most quixotic of the many people who had orientated themselves around the Franklin mystery – this disappearance was something that he became obsessed with and it was something that gave his life meaning.

In a letter to Jane Franklin from New York dated 7 January 1850, Snow volunteered his services in the search for her husband. He put forward his plan for a 100-man land expedition to set out from the Hudson Bay region in three parts – one party heading west towards Bering Strait, a central party towards the North Magnetic Pole, and an eastern party towards Prince Regent Inlet. As to the personnel, Snow wondered if picked men from a group of convicted criminals, 'as is done

Figure 4.1 William Parker Snow. Source: 'Character Sketch: April', *The Review of Reviews*, April 1893.

in exploring Expeditions in Australia', might be selected for discovery service – an unusual idea which, unsurprisingly, was never taken up. In this letter Snow assumed the position of courtly servant that he maintained with his patrons for years, telling Jane Franklin that he would seek no payment for his services 'and look for no other reward than the satisfaction my own heart would give in the knowledge that I had been in some measure instrumental in restoring, or attempting to restore, the long-lost voyagers to their home and mourning friends' (*Hansard*, 1850, 140).

Jane Franklin seems to have been taken with this enthusiastic volunteer and, despite his lack of any Arctic experience, Snow was quickly appointed second-in-command of the *Prince Albert* expedition, the first of her private search expeditions. The expedition, commanded by Charles Forsyth, departed on 5 June 1850 and the plan was to overwinter at Prince Regent Inlet. However, poor ice conditions and an ill-disciplined crew, combined with Forsyth's eagerness to bring home the news of the Beechey Island discoveries, meant that the expedition made an ignominious return in October (Stone, 1993a). This was a cruel end for Snow's ambitions to solve the Franklin mystery but his brief summer in the Arctic furnished him with enough regrets and material for a lifetime of hectoring and dream-weaving.

With the close monitoring, even censoring, of Jane Franklin and Cracroft, Snow then wrote an account of the expedition, *Voyage of the Prince Albert* (1851), and lobbied to be the commander of the next expedition. Jane Franklin, however, preferred to offer the command of the *Prince Albert* to William Kennedy, a half-Cree former Hudson's Bay Company (HBC) officer who, like Snow, had volunteered his services in 1850 (Stone, 1993b). Kennedy was a principled and religious man who resigned his position in the HBC in 1846 over its policy of selling alcohol to the indigenous people of the Labrador area. After being passed over for Kennedy, Snow moved to Australia with his wife and, following some work in Melbourne during the gold-rush, he decided to plough his earnings into his own Franklin search expedition. This haphazard expedition quickly ended in a disastrous return to Sydney but, amazingly, this did nothing to dampen Snow's enthusiasm for the cause (Barr, 1997).

Snow seems to have flirted with mysticism as a youth and believed that 'a more than common power' had singled him out and propelled him forward in life. In an 1889 letter to the spiritualist journal *Light*, he wrote of 'strange experiences' throughout his life and that he 'witnessed much that was extraordinary and beyond my ready comprehension' ('The Franklin Mystery', *Light: A Journal of Psychical, Occult, and Mystical Research*, 1889). He wrote that in Sydney in 1853 he was placed in a mesmeric trance and gained spectral knowledge about the Franklin expedition. From what he could remember years later, he stated that 'the chief himself and some of his officers had died, but several still survived' (1862, 170). It seems that Snow's obsession with Franklin came out of his visionary imagination – this was a mystery that placed a premium on the kinds of remote sensing that people like Snow offered. Certainly, he appears to have been interested in spiritualism by 1860 with one newspaper suggesting that he was the 'dupe of the Spiritualists, and intends, if he ever gets into the Arctic Seas, to follow some route indicated by a "medium"!' ('Spirit-rapping and Arctic Exploration', *The Hereford Journal*, 1860). It is in connection with spiritualism that Snow's story forms a part of this chapter.

* * *

As the years passed, anxiety regarding Franklin's fate grew. In 1853, while Snow was contacting the expedition through mesmeric trances, the Admiralty downgraded its involvement in what was a costly and seemingly never-ending quest. Jane Franklin was therefore forced to rely more on her own money and fundraising from the public to pay for her private expeditions. When the Admiralty stopped paying the wages of the expeditioners in March 1854 – effectively declaring them dead – Jane Franklin reportedly responded by wearing the bright colours of green and pink instead of mourning black – a very public demonstration to the Admiralty that she did not accept their decision (Woodward, 1951, 285). However, the arrival of the Hudson's Bay Company trader and explorer Dr John Rae with news later that year changed everything.

During an expedition to map Boothia Peninsula, Rae encountered Inuit from a place to the north he had previously named Pelly Bay. The Inuit were eager to trade items that Rae recognised as relics from the Franklin expedition. With his Inuk interpreter, William Ouligbuck, Rae learned that the cutlery and other pieces of metal in the possession of the Pelly Bay Inuit came from others who told disturbing stories of the deaths of *qallunaat* a few years previously:

> In the spring, four winters past (spring, 1850), a party of 'white men', amounting to about 40, were seen travelling southward over the ice and dragging a boat with them by some Esquimaux, who were killing seals near the north shore of King William's Land, which is a large island. None of the party could speak the Esquimaux language intelligibly, but by signs the natives were made to understand that their ship, or ships, had been crushed by ice, and that they were now going to where they expected to find deer to shoot. From the appearance of the men, all of whom except one officer looked thin, they were then supposed to be getting short of provisions, and they purchased a small seal from the natives. At a later date the same season, but previously to the breaking up of the ice, the bodies of some 30 persons were discovered on the continent, and five on an island near it, about a long day's journey to the N.W. of a large stream, which can be no other than Back's

> Great Fish River (named by the Esquimaux Oot-ko-hi-ca-lik), as its description and that of the low shore in the neighbourhood of Point Ogle and Montreal Island agree exactly with that of Sir George Back. Some of the bodies had been buried (probably those of the first victims of famine); some were in a tent or tents; others under the boat, which had been turned over to form a shelter, and several lay scattered about in different directions. Of those found on the island one was supposed to have been an officer, as he had a telescope strapped over his shoulders and his double-barrelled gun lay underneath him.
>
> From the mutilated state of many of the corpses and the contents of the kettles, it is evident that our wretched countrymen had been driven to the last resource – cannibalism – as a means of prolonging existence ('The Arctic Expedition', 1854).

Rae had discovered the first evidence of the demise of the expedition and so made the, later controversial, decision to sail south from Repulse Bay in August and journey back with all speed to Britain with this information. The confidential report he sent to the Admiralty was leaked to *The Times* in October 1854, thereby sending shock waves throughout society.

Despite her previous show of force, Jane Franklin realised by this stage that there were no survivors of the Franklin expedition; her priority from then on was to ascertain as far as possible what happened in order to solve the mystery and restore her husband's honour. Rae's evidence mercifully narrowed down the region in which a new search could begin and Jane Franklin began planning the next expedition. One chronicler of the period summed up the new state of affairs:

> Anxiety no longer traced the lost ones in the north. The warlock's spell that bound conjecture there was broken; and common sense, allowed more freedom, pointed to the terrible revelations of the rejected, unsearched south; but Conjecture, though with sight restored, still wandered – she saw, but would not see (Brown, 1858, 402).

In 1857 Leopold McClintock set sail from Aberdeen in command of the *Fox* charged with the task of reconstructing the story of the Franklin expedition. McClintock's return in 1859 with documentary evidence of Franklin's death and the last known location of the *Terror* and *Erebus* provided an 'end of the epic' ('Joven', *The Ladies' Companion, and Monthly Magazine*, 1859) for the British public and consolation to Jane Franklin. For others it was an incitement to further exploration. For Snow, McClintock's seeming validation of his 'central party' plan inspired him to campaign for a new quest to visit King William Island in search of survivors, captives or more relics. Snow was desperate to leave the armchair, writing to John Barrow Jr. in November 1859 of an 'irresistible power urging me on' (BL, MS 35309), and he lectured throughout Britain on the likelihood of survivors. However, he constantly needed emergency assistance to keep himself and his mentally ill wife from destitution. One of the few members of the Royal Geographical Society to pay any attention to him was Walter C. Trevelyan. Trevelyan may already have heard about Snow as he was related to Lord Macaulay by marriage but they had a lot in common: Trevelyan was fascinated by mesmerism and clairvoyance, he was a subscriber to *Zadkiel's Magazine* and he followed the Franklin case closely. Trevelyan and Snow became friends in 1860 and Lady Trevelyan (née Paulina Jermyn) donated funds for a planned Arctic expedition.

Although he managed to purchase a schooner in 1861, Snow's plans for a second expedition collapsed as quickly as the first and he departed for the United States where he scraped out a living as a writer after declining to serve in the Federal Navy during the Civil War. Snow was then hired by the Franklin searcher Charles Francis Hall to edit the journals he had kept on his expedition to Baffin Island (1860–3). Like Snow, Hall was an eccentric egomaniac who was obsessed with the Franklin mystery; indeed, he believed God called him north to locate survivors. It was not long before there was a falling out between the two visionaries, largely due to Snow's tardiness in completing the job. Hall eventually completed the book himself – published as *Arctic Researches and Life Among the Esquimaux* (1864) – and an embittered Snow took legal action against him for compensation, which he lost (see Loomis, 1991, 170–4).[1]

In 1865 Snow attended President Abraham Lincoln's funeral cortege in New York where he was incongruously named as 'commander of the Arctic and Antarctic expedition' by a journalist. At the event Snow managed to have placed in Lincoln's coffin a page from a Book of Common Prayer that had been found under the skull of a Franklin expeditioner (Power, 1872, 48). It is unclear how he came by this relic, or if it was even authentic, but it does show how he was able to inveigle his way into important circles through a combination of brass-neck persistence and an aura of spiritual strength. Coming back to Britain soon afterwards, Snow could not find work but was supported by donations from well-wishers such as John Barrow Jr., Dickens, McClintock, Leslie Stephen, Trevelyan and the Royal Literary Fund (BL, Loan 96 RLF 1/1459).[2]

By this time Snow was putting it about that it was he who first guessed the locality of the Franklin ships in 1849, years before McClintock's expedition actually discovered the evidence ('The New Arctic Expedition', *Newcastle Journal*, 1861). In an 1860 letter to a newspaper, which later appeared in a spiritualist magazine, Snow wrote that in 1849 he had a vision of the missing men 'strongly pictured to my eye', 'exactly as we now know them to have been', which inspired his 1850 plan to search the North Magnetic Pole region. He further claimed that before the *Prince Albert* departed Aberdeen in June 1850 he was visited by a lady, 'well-known to public fame', who told him to write down in his notebook some enigmatic information she had received that the lost expedition would be found 'south of a passage of water with the initials B. S. (Barrow Straits)':

> Other information could be gathered from the initials E. T. (Erebus and Terror), S. J. F. (Sir John Franklin), N. F. and Victory, G. W. and Victoria, and from an outline of the whole locality which was furnished, and of which I hold a *fac-similie* (1862, 169).

Snow did not reveal the source of the information but the lady mentioned was undoubtedly Jane Franklin and Snow's account is an important piece of evidence that she was acting on clairvoyant narratives by discussing them with Arctic explorers heading to the field. Furthermore, it connects Snow with another fascinating clairvoyant that Jane Franklin and Cracroft were discussing in 1850 and which I will turn to in the next section.

In later years, Snow began to embellish the account of his Franklin vision. In a lecture in 1876 he claimed that in 1849:

> he saw in imagination, the whole of Franklin's people, and he put down their position, and in what way they would be able to find them. He thought that they should go in three divisions, and that they would find them wandering about and be able to save them. In fact, it turned out that he was right within thirty miles (NU, WCT 235).

Snow gave the most detailed account of his vision in an 1893 interview published in the *Review of Reviews*, a journal edited by the prominent journalist and social campaigner William T. Stead. Here, in a publication that was sympathetic to spiritualism, Snow said he 'fancied' he saw the Franklin expedition on the morning of 7 January 1850:

> the curtains of my sleeping-room were drawn aside from the bottom and a picture appeared before my eye. This picture represented a flat ice-covered region, which from its configuration seemed to be a triangular extension of James Ross's King William's Land, also a portion round the magnetic Pole and another part embracing the estuary of the Great Fish River with the country, including the Boothian Isthmus and all the land between the longitudes of 90 and 100. Two apparently deserted ships were to be seen, one embedded in the ice south-west of the magnetic Pole and north-west of Point Victory, James Ross's farthest on the off-hand shore of King William's Land. The other ship was away down in a bay – MacLoughlin Bay – or close to O'Reilly Island. Crossing King William's Land and along its shores were a few men, while several bodies lay seemingly lifeless on the ground ... It seemed to me in my waking dream that they were calling aloud to me for aid, and their call appeared to be strongly sounding in my ears ('Character Sketch: April', *Review of Reviews*, 1893, 377).

Snow drew a 'rough outline map' of his 'dream or vision', obviously added to over time (see Figure 4.2). W. Gillies Ross questions why Snow waited 43 years to reveal this spectral information (2003a, 9) but there are reasons why he kept quiet about his vision until his letter of 1860 and why a more detailed version of it was given in the interview in 1893.

The return of McClintock in 1859 sent people scurrying back to the clairvoyant accounts of a decade previously to cross-reference them with the information gained by the *Fox* expedition. Partly there was a desire to show that someone from that period had actually known all along where the Franklin expedition ended up, but also returning to the subject of clairvoyance protected the deeper spiritual meaning that many drew from the Franklin quest. In his campaign to launch a new expedition in search of Franklin survivors, Snow was only really taken seriously by the Trevelyans. To the Royal Geographical Society (RGS), he was something of an embarrassment because he did not stop hounding them and the Admiralty about Franklin survivors, despite McClintock's satisfactory conclusion to the affair. It is certain that Snow's monomania was reinforced by the belief that he had been right all along. He resented McClintock's success and he therefore looked back on his 1850 three-pronged plan as less a rational proposal than an intuition that only he experienced. As it was also certain at this stage that Jane Franklin would not be contributing

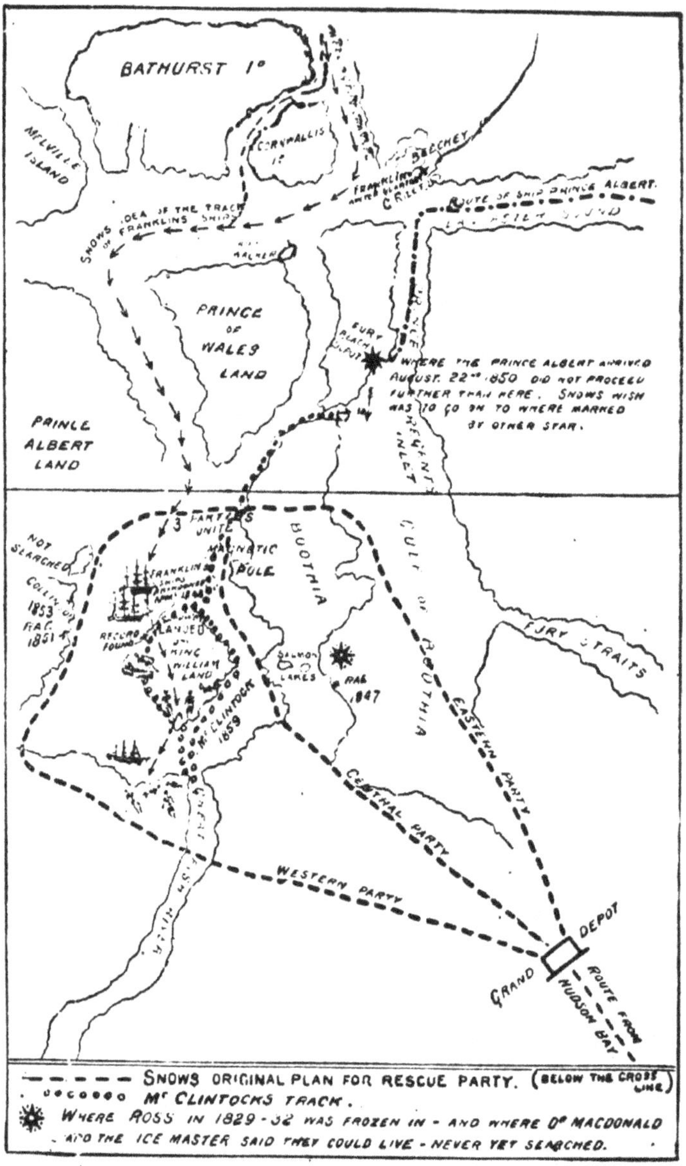

MAP OF THE ARCTIC REGIONS, SHOWING SCENE OF SNOW'S VISION.

Figure 4.2 'Map of the Arctic Regions, Showing the Scene of Snow's Vision'. Source: 'Character Sketch: April', *The Review of Reviews*, April 1893.

any funds to his expedition, Snow probably felt he had nothing to lose in tactfully revealing the clairvoyant background to the *Prince Albert* expedition. It is also significant that the only support Snow received from an Arctic veteran at the RGS was that of William Kennedy ('Notes from our London Correspondent', *York Herald*, 1859). Kennedy had also reacted to McClintock's return by spreading stories about clairvoyant predictions of the location of the *Terror* and *Erebus* dating back to his expedition in 1851 ('Lecture on the Arctic Regions by Captain Kennedy', *Morning Chronicle*, 1860). Although by this stage both Snow and Kennedy had become alienated from Jane Franklin, neither was impolite enough to actually mention her name in connection with the clairvoyance.

As mentioned, Snow was unable to fulfil his dream of returning to the Arctic and his personal life descended into chaos and poverty. By the 1870s he was complaining of 'brain fever' and a 'merciless system of secret as well as open opposition to and counteraction' of all his projects (NU, WCT 235). He believed he was on a publishers' blacklist because of his views on Arctic exploration and in 1876 he applied for a summons against various senior officials in the Admiralty who, he claimed, had suppressed his plans for the recent Nares expedition (BL, Loan 96 RLF 1/1459). Throughout this period he continued to advertise his services as a lecturer, attended meetings of the RGS and worked on obsessive and impossible projects such as an encyclopaedic history of Arctic exploration (which made up 40 folio volumes by 1891) and a limitless reference bureau of news clippings that carpeted the walls of his home ('Character Sketch: April', *Review of Reviews*, 1893, 386). Like the old man in John Everett Millais's painting 'The North-West Passage' (1874), Snow's loyalty to the Franklin quest was a buoy in a chaotic personal life. He once said that he would 'sooner be in [the] stormiest waters than having to content so incessantly with malignant social storms ashore' ('The Franklin Expedition', *Portsmouth Evening News*, 1893). In 1889 he was still writing about the possibility that some of the younger members of the Franklin expedition might be alive among the Inuit, or that they left progeny (Snow, 1889, 7). Snow's decision to reveal more about the clairvoyant search for Franklin in 1893 was his way of having the final word in a very public controversy concerning a ghost in the Irish city of Londonderry that spiralled out to involve Cracroft, McClintock and John Rae.

The Londonderry ghost

When Kennedy assumed the command of the second *Prince Albert* expedition in 1851, one of the first assignments he was set by Jane Franklin was to visit Captain William Coppin in Londonderry (see Figure 4.3). Coppin was a stellar Victorian engineering entrepreneur who worked as a shipbuilder, inventor and specialist in maritime salvage and recovery. He employed hundreds of men in the Londonderry shipyard during its heyday in the 1840s but he suffered a severe financial setback when his innovative screw-propeller vessel, the *Great Northern*, failed to attract any buyers after its launch in 1842 (Malley and McLaughlin, 1992). Coppin had long been interested in Arctic exploration and by 1850 he was in direct contact with Jane Franklin, working for her as a fundraiser and adviser. Kennedy was sent to Londonderry to meet Coppin, to help him make contacts among the merchants of Liverpool, but he was also

Figure 4.3 Portrait of Captain William Coppin, © National Museums NI, Collection Ulster Folk & Transport Museum.

sent by Jane Franklin to investigate for himself a story Coppin told her about the ghost of his dead child.

In May 1849 Coppin's daughter, Louisa or 'Weesy', died of gastric fever at the age of three, following which Coppin's other children reported that Weesy was 'always about' in their home, appearing to them frequently, and once to Coppin, as 'a ball of bluish light' (Skewes, 1889, 71). Coppin's young son William often ran to embrace the ghost when he saw her standing near the walls in the house, injuring himself in the process. Coppin was deeply interested in the supernatural but from the start it was his eldest daughter Anne (aged around nine) who emerged as the chief witness of the ghostly phenomena. She later described seeing Weesy every day around this time, 'very often sitting on my Aunt's knee, of whom she was very fond, dressed in robes of indescribable beauty and radiantly bright' (Skewes, 1890, 313).

In October 1849, around the same time that the Bolton clairvoyant's travels became known, Anne's aunt asked her to ask Weesy about the location of Franklin. Anne claimed that an 'Arctic scene' suddenly appeared on the bedroom floor and she saw 'two ships embedded in the snow, and [said] the room felt so cold' (Skewes, 1890, 311). As recounted in a history of the affair, written almost four decades later, Anne sketched this vision as a chart on some paper and then asked Weesy some further questions that led to her seeing some handwriting on the wall: '*Erebus* and *Terror*. Sir John Franklin, Lancaster Sound, Prince Regent Inlet, Point Victory, Victoria Channel' (Skewes, 1890, 75). Coppin was at first sceptical of the worth of this enigmatic message, because although Victory Point had been named by James Clark Ross during his sledge journey on King William Island in 1830 (Ross, 1835, 418), 'Victoria Channel' was not known to exist on any map of the Arctic. However, reading in *The Times* of Jane Franklin's plans to send the first *Prince Albert* expedition in May 1850, Coppin sent her details of the vision and then met her in London. Jane Franklin was impressed by Coppin's story, but was perhaps more impressed by the credentials of her new supporter. She wanted to visit Londonderry at once but was dissuaded on the grounds that 'the advent of her Ladyship to the "Maiden city" would cause no small stir' (Skewes, 1889, 92).

Using the story of Weesy, Jane Franklin was encouraged in her plans to send the *Prince Albert* down Prince Regent Inlet, as opposed to north towards Wellington Channel. She discussed the Londonderry chart with Snow and Forsyth the night before they departed and Snow, the more interested of the two, noted down the details in his journal. It is worth bearing in mind that Snow's transcription of Weesy's message was significantly different to that circulated by later supporters of the story. Around this time Jane Franklin also visited the wealthy merchant brothers W. and T.B. Horsfall in Liverpool regarding their support for the *Prince Albert* expedition. She told them of Weesy's revelation and the value of a southern route towards the west coast of Boothia in search of Franklin: 'All agreed to be silent concerning the supernatural, but to act upon the route thus made known' (Skewes, 1889, 91; Skewes, 1890, 264). Despite the secrecy surrounding Weesy's revelation (and Snow was not told about the people involved), W.A.B. Hamilton, the Second Secretary of the Admiralty, was informed of the case, most likely because of his open mind on the issue of Emma's clairvoyance (Skewes, 1889, 80).

In any case, the *Prince Albert* was unable to penetrate the ice in Prince Regent Inlet and so Jane Franklin was determined to despatch the ship again in 1851, this time under the command of Kennedy. Coppin was proving a useful ally for Jane Franklin as he supervised the fitting-out of the *Prince Albert* in Aberdeen (Barr, Forestier-Blazart, and Forestier-Blazart, 2014, 5) and organised petitions in Dublin, Edinburgh, Liverpool and Belfast requesting that new steamships be supplied for the Franklin searches (NA, ADM 7/611). The issue of Weesy's vision had not been forgotten though, and Jane Franklin confided in Kennedy about this, even sending him to visit Coppin in Londonderry for three days in March. On 10 April Coppin wrote to Cracroft saying that Kennedy 'has seen all the children, the ice scenes have again commenced & are now seen by the 2d eldest girl' (SPRI, MS 248/107). Some years later, Kennedy remembered speaking to Anne Coppin who:

> related that Sir John with his ships were to be found down Prince Regent Inlet, and that, about places named Victoria, exactly the name of the place where Sir John abandoned his ships, and deposited the only record that has been recovered from the Franklin expedition. How your child could have known these things is the more remarkable, because at the time, she not only had not the slightest intimation as to the whereabouts of poor Franklin, but Lady Franklin herself, was so possessed with the matter that Sir John had gone up Wellington Channel, that most people were carried away with the same impression. I was among this number, and therefore did not attach that importance to these revelations that I ought to have done (qtd. in Skewes, 1890, 141).

Although he did not report seeing anything of Weesy himself, Kennedy must have given solace to the family in 1851 as Coppin wrote to

Cracroft: 'you cannot think with what fresh hopes Mr K.'s visit has inspired us all with & how his opinion with what has occurred & is occurring every day in my home' (SPRI, MS 248/107). By this stage it was not only Anne who was reporting visions. In a letter to Kennedy on 6 May, Coppin said that Dora, the second eldest girl:

> has twice seen Sir John Franklin – since you left here – She never saw him before & she is the most innocent child in my family. From this mysterious matter so often repeated, I cannot but believe that you will soon see Sir John Franklin & his crews, rest assured they are alive & well (SPRI, MS 248/107).

Kennedy was not someone to scoff at such stories because he himself was deeply interested in the supernatural. Jane Franklin noted in her diary that, during an interview in January, Kennedy 'introduced the subject of mesmerism & clairvoyance, presentiments &c. in all of wh he believes. He seemed quite relieved when I told him of the numerous revelations wh had been sent to us, & that they were too remarkable to be disregarded' (SPRI, MS 248/106).

Kennedy's *Prince Albert* expedition was more successful than Forsyth's in penetrating the ice of Prince Regent Inlet, after which he discovered a narrow channel that he named Bellot Strait in honour of his second-in-command, the French lieutenant Joseph-René Bellot.[3] This discovery finally established that the Boothia Peninsula was split in two between Somerset Island to the north and the North American mainland to the south. After passing through Bellot Strait, Kennedy then dog-sledged across the frozen northern extremity of a passage of water that John Rae had named 'Victoria Strait' during his own expedition in the summer of 1851 (Rae, 1852) (the channel of water linking Peel Sound with Victoria Strait is now named Franklin Strait). In 1851 Rae had been unable to force a passage eastwards across Victoria Strait in his boat due to the ice, which meant that King William Island retained its secrets for several more years. At this crucial point Kennedy also turned away from King William Island, striking west across Prince of Wales Land (now Prince of Wales Island) under the erroneous impression that the *Terror* and *Erebus* could not have passed down this western channel due to a barrier of land extending from Somerset Island to Prince of Wales Island (Kennedy, 1853, 134).[4] Returning to Aberdeen in October 1852 without any clues about Franklin's fate, Kennedy concluded that the ships had taken the northern route rather than one south of Cape Walker (Kennedy, 1853, 173). At the time Bellot disagreed with Kennedy's decision and one wonders if the monomaniacal Snow would have been as quick to turn away from a chance to visit the North Magnetic Pole region in search of Franklin's trail.[5] So, in 1851 and 1852, both Rae and Kennedy had come achingly close to the location where the icebound *Terror* and *Erebus* were left by their crews on 22 April 1848.

Although he did not realise it at the time, during his 1851 expedition Rae had discovered pieces of one of Franklin's ships in the form of two wooden poles that had washed up on the shores of Parker Bay. Certain that they came from an Admiralty vessel, Rae nevertheless remained sceptical that the *Terror* and *Erebus* would have taken a route towards the North Magnetic Pole. So when in 1853 he set out again with a small group of men under the auspices of the HBC to survey the west coast of Boothia to Bellot Strait, Rae was exploring for geographical purposes, not with the intention of solving the Franklin mystery. After he reached London with his controversial report in October 1854, Rae received support in private from most Arctic veterans. However, by November a backlash had begun in response to the allegations of cannibalism and Rae was criticised in the newspaper press for not exploring King William Island to verify the word of untrustworthy savages (Owen, 1978, 357; Cavell, 2008, 206–19).[6] After some frosty interviews with Rae, Jane Franklin began plans for a new private expedition that would thoroughly search King William Island and follow up, 'in a more effectual manner, the traces accidentally found by Dr. Rae' (McClintock, 1859, 3). Now that Inuit testimony seemed to pinpoint King William Island as the location where her husband's expedition ended, Jane Franklin looked back on the two *Prince Albert* expeditions with deep regret. As Roderick Murchison put it: had Kennedy 'felt himself able to follow the course indicated by his sagacious employer, there can be no doubt, that much more satisfactory results would have been obtained' (qtd. in McClintock, 1859, xviii–xix). At this point, with Victoria Strait now in existence on the map, and Victory Point a location near where Inuit spoke of bodies, both Coppin and Jane Franklin seemed to believe that Rae's report validated Weesy's enigmatic message of 1849.

In November 1854 Coppin visited Jane Franklin and 'on her own map, marked in pencil, the line as marked out on his little daughter's chart five years before' (Skewes, 1889, 113). This indicates that Jane Franklin may have mislaid (or destroyed) the chart of Anne's vision that he had sent her in 1850. In any case, they both took it that Weesy had been guiding them in the right direction and Jane Franklin discussed making the revelation public, undoubtedly as a way to raise funds for a new expedition, just as she had attempted to do in Liverpool in 1850.

The Admiralty, however, having pronounced the Franklin expeditioners officially dead in March 1854, were in no mood to sponsor any more rescue missions, especially in the context of the Crimean War. At this crucial juncture Jane Franklin gained the support of Charles Dickens who sent her a copy of his article in *Household Words* of 2 December in which he cast doubt on the idea that cannibalism had occurred. This 'cheered her' and she used Carolina Boyle – someone who was interested in mesmerism – as an intermediary with Dickens in order to enlist his help in campaigning for a new expedition. Coppin was urged to come to London to meet Dickens and relate the story as it 'would be a vast power to give impetus to raise money to carry out the proposed expedition' ('The Franklin Mystery', 16 July 1889). Coppin, we are told by his ghost-writer, refused to do so as he regarded the revelation of his child as a 'very sacred thing' (Skewes, 1889, 115). He also probably did not relish the social embarrassment that would come out of such publicity. It is unclear if Dickens was ever informed of the Weesy case (he destroyed his collection of letters in the Gad's Hill bonfire of 1860), but Jane Franklin did gain another devoted ally and it must be more than a coincidence that shortly afterwards Dickens directed a morale-boosting play about Arctic clairvoyance with Wilkie Collins.

When Jane Franklin sent McClintock to the Arctic in 1857 as her latest knight-errant she did not mention the subject of the Londonderry ghost, no doubt sensing McClintock's intolerance of such talk. Yet it was McClintock who brought home the news that Franklin had long been a kind of ghost – dead since 1847. McClintock's return offered Jane Franklin and Cracroft some closure and there is no record of them having any public interest in the supernatural after this point. But for Coppin and Snow this was not the end of the matter.

In a letter to Coppin in 1856 Cracroft called the affair a 'strange and startling episode' and requested that he send her the chart that Anne drew in 1849. Coppin reminded her that the chart was in the possession of Jane Franklin, unless she had mislaid it. After McClintock's return in 1859, Coppin again got in touch with Jane Franklin regarding the chart and the significance of his daughter's message. Perhaps suspecting Coppin was interested in making the chart public, thereby opening her name to ridicule, Jane Franklin wrote back on 22 December:

> I have received your letter of yesterday requesting me to tell you how far the 'mysterious revelations' of your child [Anne] in 1850 respecting the expedition of my late husband corresponded with the facts recently ascertained beyond dispute by Captain McClintock's

researches. In reply, I have no hesitation in telling you that the child's chart, drawn by herself, without, as you assure me, having ever seen an Arctic chart before, represented the ships as being in a channel which we believed at the time to be inaccessible, but which it has since been found they actually navigated.

Moreover, the names 'Victory' and 'Victoria' written by the little girl upon her chart correspond with that of the point (Point Victory) on King William's Land, where the important record of the Erebus and Terror was found, and with that of the strait or channel (Victoria Strait) where the ships were finally lost.

I regret that I have not at hand your very interesting letter of May, 1850, in which you made me these remarkable communications with more detail, but I believe I am quite correct in what I have stated. I have carefully preserved your letter and the child's drawing, and you may be assured that they are in safety and can be referred to, though it would be difficult for me to do so at the present moment. – Ever yours, dear Mr Coppin, most truly and obliged' ('Sir John Franklin – The Secret of the Discovery of his Fate', *Glasgow Herald*, 1889).

Neither the chart nor Coppin's letter of May 1850 are in the papers of Jane Franklin and Sophia Cracroft at the Scott Polar Research Institute today. So what are we to make of the whole affair?

The main reasons why the Weesy Coppin story became just a curious footnote in histories of the Franklin searches relate to the circumstances of its publication and the content of the revelation. Certainly, the story seems to have been known about in Londonderry and London: in 1860 a newspaper report suggested that Snow 'intends, if he ever gets into the Arctic Seas, to follow some route indicated by a "medium"!' ('Spirit-rapping and Arctic Exploration', *The Hereford Journal*, 1860), while in a diary entry in November 1867 William Rossetti gossiped about Coppin and the spirit of his dead child and wrote 'that Coppin holds a letter from Lady F fully acknowledging these facts' (1903, 243). Yet the affair was not made public until 1889, by which time Jane Franklin was long dead and Coppin was a destitute 84-year-old man.

In the mid-1880s Coppin entered into an unsustainable financial arrangement with an evangelical cleric based in Liverpool, the Reverend J. Henry Skewes, about the production of a book on the Weesy visions.[7] Indeed, Coppin was willing to impoverish himself to get the book published (PRONI, D/2666/2/8). Coppin knew Liverpool very well from his piloting and ship-building days and may have encountered Skewes there through a shared interest in psychical research ('The

Rev. J.H. Skewes on Spiritualism', *Liverpool Mercury*, 1883; 'Liverpool Mental Science Association', *Liverpool Mercury*, 1883). Yet Skewes was a poor choice as a ghost-writer for Coppin's book. Hints of his abrasive personality can be found in the fact that he was expelled for life from the Liverpool lodge of the Orange Order due to some unstated offence ('The Orangemen and their Members', *Liverpool Mercury*, 1890), while his flatulent and preaching writing style must have greatly irritated the correspondents he contacted on behalf of Coppin. It is also likely that letters from Skewes to Cracroft and McClintock in 1885 mentioning the interest of the Society for Psychical Research in the case spooked them into taking legal action to block the publication of relevant letters (Skewes, 1890, 309).[8]

With Coppin now finally willing to make his name public, Skewes's book, *Sir John Franklin: The True Secret of the Discovery of his Fate. A 'Revelation'* (1889) told the story of how Weesy's 'revelation' led to the discovery of the remains of the Franklin expedition. Its key argument was that '[b]oth Kennedy and McClintock were machines, whose motor power was a "revelation"' (1889, 150). In the book Skewes summarised, but did not reprint, letters that he suggested proved this story. The sensational content of the book, making explorer-heroes the servants of a girl ghost, meant it garnered a lot of attention in British newspapers and highbrow periodicals. Most reviewers criticised the clumsy structure of the narrative and the style of its author, but spiritualists were supportive of Coppin's claims ('The "Londonderry Vision"', *Hawkes' Bay Herald*, 1889; 'Notes by the Way', 1889). The *Saturday Review* asked why Weesy did not know that Franklin was long dead by 1849 ('How Sir John Franklin was not Found', *Saturday Review of Politics*, 1889) and *The Athenaeum* was sceptical that McClintock would ever have put his life, or the lives of his men, at risk on the word of a dead child ('Book Review', *The Athenaeum*, 1889, 629). The *Pall Mall Gazette* denounced Skewes's 'superfluous rubbish' but noted that 'the book to some extent supplies evidence in support of the story' ('A Strange Tale of Handwriting on the Wall', *Pall Mall Gazette*, 9 May 1889). Skewes received some significant attention, but what about the content of the book?

At this point McClintock, now a retired Rear-Admiral, entered the fray, writing to the *Pall Mall Gazette* to say that although he found the story 'ridiculous' he felt he should respond in case some people 'might be willing to believe that my course was influenced by it'. McClintock, who had a record of policing his Arctic legacy (see Cavell, 2013b), stated that Jane Franklin did not instruct him to follow any revelation because Rae's discoveries in 1854 had already highlighted King William Island as *the* place to look. McClintock then went further and claimed that Jane Franklin had been 'deluged' by clairvoyant revelations during the period:

> She courteously listened to all, but was influenced by none of them. There was no sort of mystery or secrecy observed about any of them. I have yet to learn that any one attached the slightest value to any of them, and least of all the practical people who shared in either the counsels of the Arctic commanders or in the confidence of Lady Franklin ('A Strange Tale of Handwriting on the Wall', *Pall Mall Gazette*, 16 May 1889).

It is true that Skewes had erred in his belief that McClintock was informed of the Weesy story, but the explorer went too far in claiming that Jane Franklin had not been influenced by clairvoyants. As this chapter has shown, Jane Franklin, Cracroft and many other 'practical people' had been in contact with several clairvoyants during the search for the Franklin expedition. Skewes smelled blood and responded by giving descriptions of letters from Jane Franklin and Cracroft indicating their belief in Weesy's revelation ('A Strange Tale of Handwriting on the Wall', *Pall Mall Gazette*, 23 May 1889). Regarding the chart, Skewes said that he and Coppin were unable to get it back, despite threatening legal action against Cracroft as the executor of Jane Franklin's estate (Skewes, 1890, 252). Just as the lack of a smoking gun threatened to put an end to the controversy, help came from a surprising corner.

* * *

When he published the book in 1889, Skewes had assumed that William Parker Snow was dead. Yet, like Coppin, he was an ageing man who had fallen on hard times but looked back to the 1850s with ecstatic longing. Snow exhibited obsessive-compulsive tendencies throughout his life and one of his manias was to keep and catalogue every newspaper-cutting of interest he could get his hands on. So it is no surprise to find he encountered reviews of Skewes's book. On learning of the book Snow mischievously sent John Rae news clippings about Weesy's revelation. This caused Rae to send letters to newspapers in Londonderry, Liverpool and London in the spring of 1889 in which he denied that Snow's opinions or Weesy's revelation had influenced anyone to search King William Island. It was his discussion with McClintock about the Franklin relics, Rae said, which persuaded McClintock to check the area. The discovery of the Victory Point record did not depend on the 'innate genius &c of the gallant explorer, nor perhaps upon the child revelation' (RGS, LMS S 16). Clearly this battle about precedence in the solution to the Franklin mystery was stirring up old emotions. Just as it seemed McClintock and Rae had succeeded in exposing Coppin's story as ridiculous, Snow contacted Skewes to inform him that he had drawn a copy of the chart dictated by Jane Franklin on the night she visited him before the departure of the *Prince Albert* expedition on 5 June 1850.

Snow's chart consisted of a rough outline map of the Boothian region with an internal box containing the sketch in his original notebook of 1850 (see Figure 4.4). In this box Snow drew all that the page 'could take in', later continuing the chart as described to him by Jane Franklin from memory. Skewes pointedly noted, 'How far the additional part, or even the oblong portion, agrees with the child's chart, we cannot say', although Coppin thought it 'a fairly correct reproduction of the one drawn by his little child' (Skewes, 1890, 307–8). By 1889, Snow's account of the initials told to him by Jane Franklin had changed from his 1860 account. Then, he remembered 'B.S.', 'E.T.', 'S.J.F.', 'N.F. Victory' and 'G.W.A. Victoria' (Snow, 1862, 169), but just a year previously, as noted in her letter to Coppin, Jane Franklin had remembered only 'Victory' and 'Victoria' as being the relevant place-names on the chart ('Sir John Franklin – The Secret of the Discovery of his Fate', *Glasgow Herald*, 1889). Although Snow could still not explain the significance of 'N.F.' or 'G.W.A.', the chart he sent Skewes was a creative reconstruction of what he *wanted to believe* he remembered from 1850: it even contains a representation of Bellot Strait, not discovered until 1852. Snow's interview with the

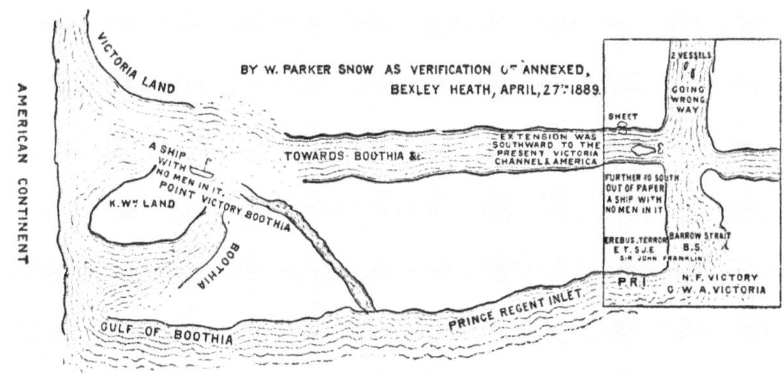

Figure 4.4 Chart of Weesy's vision by William Parker Snow.
Source: John Henry Skewes. *Sir John Franklin: The True Secret of the Discovery of his Fate. A 'Revelation'*. 2nd ed. London: Bemrose, 1890.

Review of Reviews in 1893 was an attempt to assign himself, once again, a predestined role in the conclusion to the Franklin mystery in a periodical read by hundreds of thousands of people. The re-ignition of the Coppin affair gave Snow an opportunity to discuss his colourful career to the press: 'I cannot help but view my own part in this matter as being also marvellous. Small things, and intrinsically of no value, have been preserved by me, with no specific object save as mementos' ('The Franklin Mystery', *Liverpool Mercury*, 22 June1889).

Snow's chart was reproduced in the second edition of Skewes's *Sir John Franklin: The True Secret of the Discovery of his Fate. A 'Revelation'* (1890). Here, to undermine McClintock, Skewes included a new supplement containing copies of letters sent to Coppin from Jane Franklin and Cracroft, detailing their awareness of, and eagerness to discuss, Weesy's revelations between 1850 and 1856. Skewes also included supporting letters from Anne Coppin and her aunt, Harriet Smith, sent to him in 1889, attesting to the accuracy of their claims. It seems clear that Coppin's correspondence was authentic and that this proved deeply embarrassing for Cracroft who, always protective when it came to her aunt's reputation, probably destroyed in 1885 whatever embarrassing papers Jane Franklin had left at the time of her death ten years before.[9] Snow suspected that Cracroft supported McClintock's line because 'like so many people, she didn't like her Aunt's strong addiction to the Supernatural' (qtd. in Owen, 1978, 450). In any case, with her carefully crafted public persona, Jane Franklin would have sought to avoid any association with the Weesy story in the years after 1859, especially in the aftermath of the scandalous Belcher/Zadkiel libel case.

In his article on the Weesy Coppin affair, Ralph Lloyd-Jones suggests there is no relevant correspondence between Coppin and Jane Franklin still extant (2001, 33). However there are several examples to support Skewes's claims. Dartmouth College Library contains a letter from Jane Franklin to W.A.B. Hamilton, dated 3 June 1850, in which she writes 'Mr Coppin continues to write to us, & each time he says the ship is seen at the same place but the ice is breaking all around her' (qtd. in Ross, 2003a, 10).[10] Jane Franklin's midnight meeting in Aberdeen with Snow came just a day later. Furthermore, in a letter to William Scoresby dated 23 July 1850, Cracroft wrote the following:

> We continue to hear of the Supernatural revelations respecting Regent Inlet, the last now some weeks back stated that the ice was breaking up rapidly, but that the vessel had not been able to move. Uncle [John Franklin] was on board. Nothing was said of

> the other ship. The fact, without names, or particulars was lately mentioned to Lord Northampton [Spencer Compton, 2nd Marquess of Northampton; President of the Royal Society 1838–48] who has been staying here & it was interesting to see that a man of his talent & turn of mind recognised the value of such intimations, & the responsibility of disregarding them. Miss Gurney too says that is the opinion of their people [the Gurney family were prominent Norfolk bankers], (I quote her words) 'that the right means have been put into the heart of the Wife'. My Aunt does not feel this particularly in the case of Regent Inlet, because the conviction was arrived by reasoning out the matter, & would have applied with even greater force to Wellington Channel had that as before, been the neglected part (SPRI, MS 1100/1/4).

The Scott Polar Research Institute also contains another two relevant letters from 1851 that prove that Coppin was still in contact with Jane Franklin and Cracroft about Weesy; that they knew of the 'ice scenes' that occurred in Londonderry; that they sent Kennedy to meet Coppin and discuss Weesy; and that they were told that Dora Coppin had 'seen Sir John Franklin' (SPRI, MS 248/107).

Finally, in his modern biography of Franklin, the late Roderic Owen included a transcription of the crucial letter sent, anonymously, by Coppin to Jane Franklin in May 1850. The letter goes into greater detail about the 'ice scenes' and shows the original revelation to have been something very different from the one Snow and Coppin remembered decades later:

> Believing that <u>Sir John Franklin is still alive and well</u> I state this with confidence and entreat of you not to receive it as a visionary dream, it has occurred in a private family, in my own … About 12 months ago I lost a beloved Child and in about six weeks after her death she appeared to her Brothers and Sisters … The deceased Child Louisa appeared distinctly to the 3 Elder Children, and is constantly showing them scenes which I cannot now describe only so far as your interest is concerned the deceased speaks to her <u>sister Anne</u> by some chance the question was put is Sir J. Franklin Alive when to the surprise of Anne, the room they were in appeared to be filled with Ice some Channels and a Ship in one narrow creek or harbour between two Mountains of Snow and Ice in a Sort of dilapidated State with Another in the distance and in a distinct Channel of water two Ships, the first had men on the deck and the second question put is Sir J. Franklin alive, if so make some signal, in a few

> Moments she describes a round-faced Man ascends the Mast and waves his hat … The question being asked what part of the Arctic ocean is S.J. Franklin in, the first scene completely disappears and on the wall are placed in large letters BS then P.RI – NF. These being the first letters shown and constantly lead me to believe that S John is in Prince Regent's Inlet off Barrow's Strait, likely in the Victory in Felix Harbour or not far from it at this moment. I am writing this the letters are placed on the wall the letters also E and T are after shown and SJF shall give you all the letters in rotation on the back of this sheet as they are described by the Child and perhaps you may understand them, from other circumstances which we have found [illegible] out as predicted by this Child. I would impress on your Ladyship the necessity of giving such order to the Commanders of the last Expeditions going out as would cause a diligent search in Prince Regent's Inlet, and into the [illegible] of Cape Walker as I am certain that Sir J. Franklin is there and nowhere else in the Arctic Sea [sic throughout] (qtd. in Owen, 1978, 286–7).

This letter, which may have been uncovered in preparation for a third edition of Skewes's book, had an attestation attached to it dated February 1891 and was signed by John Inglis and David Keigwin, Secretary and Principal Clerk respectively of Trinity House, the British lighthouse and pilotage authority. Inglis and Keigwin stated that they had '[c]arefully compared' this with an original letter in the possession of Cracroft and found it to be 'an exact copy'. They also cross-referenced the handwriting with another letter written by Coppin and found both had been written by the same hand (qtd. in Owen, 1978, 287). Unfortunately Owen adopted a policy of not fully referencing his sources in *The Fate of Franklin* and so the original letter he quoted from has yet to be located.

Yet perhaps the most significant piece of evidence, which directly connects Weesy Coppin with the plans for the first *Prince Albert* expedition, is a letter that Jane Franklin wrote in her typically spidery handwriting to Scoresby on 10 June 1850. Sent just after she returned from Aberdeen, having seen off the expedition, she excitedly told Scoresby:

> I was led to take this long journey, or rather voyage in order to communicate to Captain Forsyth before his departure what I could not have committed to writing & what I am bound to keep secret from all but a chosen few whom I feel sure will not scoff at it. Such was the injunction laid upon me by a stranger from Londonderry who called upon us in Spring Gardens last Friday week at 7 in morning

> eagerly enquiring if I am in town he could not see us at that hour but made an appointment at 12 & remained the rest of the day with us. He had come up from Aberdeen during the night & had intended following us to Aberdeen if he had found us gone there. I went, mainly in consequence of his communications to Aberdeen the next day. I have not time at the moment & it wd be difficult at any moment to impart all he said – suffice it to say that it had nothing to do with mesmerism or clairvoyance, but was a supernatural revelation to him thro' the medium & apparition of a dead child, of the [illegible] of my husband & of his being in Regent Inlet – this apparition has appeared to all the members of his family, but chiefly to another beloved child, the sister of the departed. My stranger friend who is a well known ship builder & engine maker at Londonderry & a pious member of the Ch. of England was long in doubt how to deal with this revelation till reading in the newspaper a paragraph of the ship's being about to sail for Regent Inlet, he hastened to town for the express purpose of [illegible] me a more honest sweet countenance & more simple & truthful manners. I begged him to go to Captn Hamilton at the Admy. feeling sure he wd [illegible] what he had to say & I was right. Captn H. who has already had some personal experiences which predisposed him to listen with interest, was deeply impressed, & moreover said he was sure of the goodness of this man & shd never lose sight of him – he advised also my communicating personally with Captn Forsyth, which I did without I think much [illegible] effort, for tho' he told me at first that he had never felt so odd in all his life before, he slept the impressions away & was disposed to think nothing of it the next morning. My Londonderry friend returned to Liverpool provided with one of our [illegible] charts to show the locality of the part to be searched & [it?] moved some of the chief merchants of Liverpool to consider the matter.

Among these merchants were the Horsfall brothers who advised Jane Franklin not to mention this story to others in Liverpool as it 'wd do more harm than good'. She concluded her letter to Scoresby by reiterating her understanding that Forsyth would search Prince Regent Inlet and the west side of Boothia: 'if he gives faith to the revelation Victory harbour will not be neglected, tho' it does not appear that the ship is there' (SPRI, MS 1100/3/14).

* * *

Taken together, the documents start to reveal a clear story. Ignoring for the moment Skewes's verbose and sensationalist presentation, the evidence supplied by Coppin demonstrates that the Weesy communication supported Jane Franklin's decision to focus the search on the area south of Prince Regent Inlet in 1850 and 1851. This search eventually led to Kennedy's discovery of Bellot Strait, although McClintock was not convinced of its existence until he passed through it in 1858. The evidence also confirms a picture of Jane Franklin and Cracroft as pragmatic people who sought out and used those who could help them in their quest. This included attracting and engaging with clairvoyants when they still believed Franklin to be alive, although this relationship was either at a safe distance or mediated by the credibility of professional men like Haddock, Hands, Maconochie and Coppin. Given McClintock's misinformed interventions in the matter, it seems that Jane Franklin was, however, wary of sharing her beliefs with people she suspected might 'scoff'. As has been demonstrated in other contexts, Jane Franklin and Cracroft could also bury information and speculation that they did not approve of (see Jacobs, 2015). Finally, the fundamental assertions made by Snow, Coppin and Skewes on the matter hold up under scrutiny when compared with extant archival evidence. Indeed, given Skewes's reliability as a source, it now seems likely that Robert Ferguson, Member of Parliament for Londonderry, and Charles Dickens were among the other personalities that were part of Jane Franklin's 'chosen few' who knew about the story. In Dickens's case, this must inform future scholarship on his co-created play *The Frozen Deep*.

As to the accuracy of the revelation, it is true that Victoria Channel/Strait and Victory Point held the key to the Franklin mystery. However, Anne and William Coppin's memory of the handwriting on the wall ('*Erebus* and *Terror*. Sir John Franklin, Lancaster Sound, Prince Regent Inlet, Point Victory, Victoria Channel' (Skewes, 1889, 75)) is an exaggeration of the original, enigmatic message that Anne described in 1849. Skewes and Snow bought into this but pushed the coincidence too far. Although voices arguing for a southerly search were outnumbered by those clambering for a northerly search through Wellington Channel, 'Victoria' and 'Victory' were relatively safe bets when it came to picking locations in the Arctic.

The 'Victoria' that appeared on the wall was perhaps influenced by the existence of Victoria Land (now Victoria Island), the south coast of which had been mapped by Peter Warren Dease and Thomas Simpson in 1839 and mentioned in Barrow's *Voyages of Discovery and Research within the Arctic Regions, from the Year 1818 to the Present*

Time (1846). As Franklin's original instructions had been to voyage south-west once the expedition had reached Cape Walker (Kennedy, 1853, vi), the blank, unmapped zone between the west coast of Boothia and Victoria Island was an obvious place to dream about, even if there was a 'Wellington Channel mania' in the periodical press of the time (see Cavell, 2008, 183–4). 'Victory' was already on maps of the Arctic after Ross's *Victory* expedition, appearing in Cape Victoria on the west coast of Boothia, Victory Point on King William Island, and Victory Harbour (soon after renamed Victoria Harbour) in eastern Boothia. Clearly Coppin also interpreted Weesy's message to indicate that Franklin was near Felix Harbour in the Gulf of Boothia.[11]

All this is not to suggest that Kennedy, Coppin and Jane Franklin were at all consistent in their belief that the expedition would be found in the North Magnetic Pole region. Kennedy, as we have seen, grew to believe that Franklin must have voyaged north; in December 1851 Coppin called for Londonderry Town Council to support the idea that ships be sent into Wellington Channel and Bering Strait; in the same year Jane Franklin wrote in a letter of her conviction that the northern route was the preferred option of her husband, Crozier and Fitzjames (qtd. in 'Return of the Arctic Search Expeditions', *The Nautical Magazine*, 1851, 583) and in 1853 she dispatched Kennedy for the last time towards Bering Strait, although this expedition ended ignominiously at Valparaiso in Chile (see Barr, 1998).

Ultimately, for the impoverished Coppin, the mournful Jane Franklin, the evangelical Skewes and the ecstatic Snow, the news in 1859 that the Franklin expedition had been trapped in the ice in a place named *Victoria* Strait and deposited a crucial document at a place named *Victory* Point seemed to be more than coincidence, especially given the already potent emotional forces swirling around the missing ships.

Sir John Franklin in the spirit world

This chapter and the previous one have shown that the disappearance of the Franklin expedition caused a variety of emotional responses in British society. Different people felt the loss differently, but mesmerists and clairvoyants, who happened to be becoming increasingly active in the late 1840s, utilised a 'second sight' that offered an additional or alternative viewpoint to naval search expeditions. It is no surprise that these revelations received substantial attention in the British and colonial press given the dearth of information available and the consoling messages they seemed to offer. Another theme we might take from these clairvoyant stories is the democratisation of Arctic exploration, as poor young people, mostly women, were able to stake knowledge claims about what was happening in a realm that was socially and geographically distant from them. Yet we have also seen that the 'practical people' assumed by McClintock to have no association with occultism were actually well-informed about clairvoyance and kept track of dozens of otherworldly messages. Indeed, the message transmitted from Weesy Coppin was taken seriously by Jane Franklin and others because it lent support to the theory that the expedition had become stuck in Prince Regent Inlet.

The séance was a liberating space for the human imagination. Whether it was Jane Franklin, eager to try every strategy and listen to every well-wisher, or Admiral Belcher, annoyed with himself for getting involved with Zadkiel's crystal ball, the point is that there was no one legitimate way of dealing with such a remarkable disappearance. The spectral space of the séance had significant geographic power and emotional worth. Indeed, here we might draw alongside a current of research that is moving away from normative notions of 'proper' relationships between the living and the dead or lost. In contrast to advice that the bereaved should 'let go' and 'move on', scholars in the past few decades have discussed the practical and therapeutic values of maintaining bonds with the dead or disappeared. So the bereaved might develop strategies that involve imaginary dialogues, hallucinations, prayers or even the consultation of psychics (see Walliss, 2001).

In the nineteenth and early twentieth centuries, spiritualism was one popular way for people from all classes to get into contact with their dead or missing, and maintain intimate bonds. In many cases, though, the spiritualists who attended séances were also interested in meeting celebrities and learning what happened to the famous dead – people like Benjamin Franklin, William Shakespeare, Charles Dickens and, inevitably, John Franklin. Anne Coppin's questioning of Weesy in Londonderry in mid-1849 seems to be the first documented time a person asked a dead person or spirit about Franklin. There are a number of publicised examples of such communications in the 1850s and this growth in spirit contact tells us two things: that people who suspected Franklin was dead were still unwilling to 'let him go'; and that versions of Franklin were now circulating through unregulated new spiritualist geographies that imagined the polar regions to have deep cosmological significance.

Unsurprisingly, given the rapid spread of spiritualism from New York State in 1848, some accounts of mediums claiming contact with the spirit of Franklin came from North America. In May 1850 an account of a séance was published in a newspaper in New York State which claimed that the expedition had completed the Northwest Passage but had been taken prisoner in Japan ('"Rappings" in Cortland Co.', *New York Daily Tribune*, 1850; Chapin, 2004, 71). Some years later, in February 1854, a medium in Halifax, Nova Scotia, named Alfred Cridge, channelled the spirit of Franklin, who revealed that the expedition had ended in disaster:

> The cause of our failure was a season which set in with unusual severity, at an earlier period than usual. The indifferent manner in which our provisions were packed spoiled many of them, and compelled me to detach too large a party to hunt, so that we could not prevent the ships being crushed by ice. Thus driven from our refuge, all who had not previously been drowned or died of hardship perished from the combined effects of cold and hunger (Cridge, 1854, 74).

Later spiritualists went into greater detail. In 1860 Francis H. Smith described his communications with the spirit of Franklin, mediated through the 'dial' – an instrument that pointed to letters in the alphabet when affected by the tilting of the table. Smith described séances in January and February 1856 in which Franklin revealed that the expedition had discovered the land beyond the mythical Open Polar Sea and encountered a new primitive race of people who had huge hands and tough feet 'peculiarly adapted for travelling on snow and ice' (1860, 158). Franklin's North was not a barren polar waste, but rather a tropical wonderland filled with new species of animals and insects. Remarkably, the spirit of Sir Humphrey Davy then appeared to support Franklin's claims. The land beyond the Open Polar Sea was warm and mild, Davy said, inhabited by a race of 'quiet, inoffensive people, who know nothing of you except as a strange race of men of whom a wandering Esquimaux may have brought occasional accounts'. Unfortunately for interested explorers, Davy revealed than humans would not be able to visit this place until someone invented a mariner's compass that was not affected by polar magnetism (Smith, 1860, 161–2).[12]

Back in Britain, in 1856 John George Henry Brown, a Christian spiritualist from Nottingham, asked the angel Gabriel whether Franklin was alive. The angel replied that Franklin had perished from the cold and was now undergoing 'purification' in the 'progressive circles of the atmospheric regions' (1857, 156). At a séance Brown invoked the spirit of Franklin who then appeared, dressed 'in a long loose brown garment' and read from a scroll. The spirit recounted a fantastic tale of disaster and shipwreck in the Arctic ending in his bodily death by polar bears on 24 September 1853. However, two companions who had been separated from him on the ice were still living and 'at a short period hence, will return to England, and bear living testimony of all the assertions up to the period of our separation' (Brown, 1857, 167). A later 'mesmerist' in London claimed to receive spiritual information that indicated that Franklin had died on 2 May 1858 ('Spirit Rapping', *Taunton Courier, and Western Advertiser*, 1858).

While the return of McClintock in 1859 halted such clairvoyant and spiritualist speculations about Franklin, the London-born actress and medium Emma Hardinge Britten continued to channel the spirit of Franklin throughout her career as an advocate for spiritualism, describing him as her guide and telling an audience in Manchester in 1869 that she was his 'adopted child' ('Mrs. Hardinge's Lectures', *Manchester Weekly Times*, 1869). Britten reached ecstatic heights redolent of William Parker Snow in her identification with Franklin, and seems to have regarded him also as 'Metron' the 'Spirit of the North'. The spirit once told her:

> 'Look to the north when the pencilled glory of the Boreal lights are flaming through the evening skies! Look to the silent finger of the magnetic compass pointing out the mariner's path through the boundless wastes of ocean, yet ever faithful to the invisible polar brain of the earth, fixed in the Arctic regions!' (1876, 396)

In 1911, meanwhile, the spirit of Franklin intervened in the infamous dispute between Frederick Cook and Robert Peary over who reached the North Pole. This was announced in a letter from William T. Stead, who claimed to receive a message from Franklin stating that the explorer had 'personally conducted Cook to the pole and then left him to complete the journey himself'. He did not say anything about Peary ('Spirits for Cook').

Although the proofs of Franklin's spirit life were ultimately as insubstantial as the other clairvoyant revelations, rumours, hoaxes and theories about the fate of the expedition, the séance offered people a space, a language and a set of practices that drew them nearer to a lost or dead celebrity. In this they were representing and capturing the 'affective forces and sensations that weave and fold the séance together' (Holloway, 2006, 185): the feeling of awe at seeing the 'dial' move; the sense of power in knowing that the lost Franklin could be contacted; the tears shed and 'heart-rending' emotions displayed in his presence

(Brown, 1857, 168). In creating a shared space for the living and the dead – a dance between presence and absence – the séance made concrete the spectral geographies of the Arctic.

In her copy of John Brown's *The North-West Passage and the Search for Sir John Franklin* (1858) Jane Franklin highlighted the sections where the author stated 'We prefer Arctic facts to Arctic opinions' and 'Where we sent him, it was our duty to follow' (Woodward, 1951, 270). This and the previous chapter have shown that Arctic facts were always opinions, and that Jane Franklin and others were more than willing to listen to the opinions of those who were far from official centres of expertise. In doing this, she and others were performing their duty in following Franklin into *terrae incognitae*. Emotions and affects, then, were not separate from the quest; they were part of an extended field of Arctic exploration and knowledge that directly involved women. The next chapter will further explore the role of gender in understanding the power of the spectral in Arctic exploration.

5
Polar queens, ghosts and mummies: Women in Arctic discourses

Introduction

John Rae's revelation that the Inuit witnessed signs of cannibalism during the Franklin expedition created, according to one contemporary, a 'shock of horror that ... swept across the civilized world' (qtd. in Brannan, 1966, 14). Joseph Conrad later described the demise of the expedition as 'the darkest drama perhaps played behind the curtain of Arctic mystery' (2010, 10). So in what way did people process this disaster?

The publication of Rae's report in *The Times* meant that the Franklin expedition came to be seen by many in Britain as a catastrophic disaster, as something so disturbing that people struggled to gather up the threads of narrative and express it as anything other than a tragedy. Janice Cavell (2008) argues that this recuperation process revealed the 'connected narrative' of the Northwest Passage quest – a set of heroic geographical stories that were read much like people read serial fiction at the time. While it goes too far to say that the loss of the Franklin expedition ruptured British aesthetic engagement with the Arctic (Loomis, 1977, 111), it certainly affected public feelings of optimism about the quest for a Northwest Passage. As a Canadian poet put it decades later: 'No man could ever live to reach that place, / And horror seized me of that haunted world, / That I should die there and be froze for aye, / Amid the ice-core of its awful heart' (Campbell, 1893, 67–8). This pervasive unease regarding geographical discovery in a 'haunted world' surfaced elsewhere in a piece of fiction published in *Harper's New Monthly Magazine* in 1854. This told a rip-roaring tale of an American who discovered the Northwest Passage before Robert McClure, only for the narrator to actually reveal himself to be 'the Khan of Tartary' and an inhabitant of the mad-house ('Who Discovered the Northwest Passage?', 464).

In this chapter I argue that stories like this show how people were able to become affected by the Arctic in different ways after the Franklin expedition. One way that writers dealt with the horror of the Franklin loss was by telling stories of romance and intimacy that bridged the divide between men in the Arctic and women in Britain. In many examples of poetry, ballads, and serial and sensational fiction, it is clear that the loss inspired a strikingly gendered response as the themes of love and ghostly women became associated with the expedition. Male absence and female (spectral) presence became bound together in imaginative re-tellings of the Franklin disaster. Therefore I want to make a case for the significance of emotions in histories of Arctic exploration by focusing on the intersections between exploration, gender and haunting. By looking at some marginal and ephemeral Arctic narratives I show that the emotions mobilised by the Franklin expedition were complex forces that reflected contemporary ideas of a gothic Arctic, but also feelings of anxiety regarding the role of women in Arctic expeditions. I conclude by looking at the importance of mummies in the way that Arctic exploration was thought of as a haunting enterprise.

* * *

The Franklin loss upturned several assumptions that British people had about the Arctic explorations carried out by the Admiralty: that expeditions were well-planned, powerful and scientifically useful, that explorers like Franklin were heroes and that the Admiralty's geographical aim of a Northwest Passage was achievable and beneficial. As the power of the Admiralty's voice over the Arctic waned, the voices of people who could not be described as 'experts' emerged – many of them were female. As we have seen, clairvoyants and spiritualists visited Franklin in the Arctic through the séance, while metropolitan audiences visited panorama shows to experience the senses of polar terror and sublimity for themselves. There were also developments in traditional literary and media culture that allowed British Arctic exploration to be presented in a multitude of ways to the reading public.

From 1818 onwards it seemed that one particular polar publishing network might come to dominate, comprising John Barrow, the John Murray publishing house, and a range of 'approved' Arctic authorities (explorers and scientists) (Craciun, 2011, 440). Through vitriolic policing of knowledge about Arctic exploration in the conservative journal the *Quarterly Review*, Barrow tried to freeze out critical, literary or otherwise unauthorised voices, while contracts with John Murray promised preferred commanders a prestigious publisher for their narratives. In reality, Barrow was not always successful in his policing efforts (see Cavell, 2013a) and some officers were not beholden to John Murray at all: John Ross and Alexander Fisher published with Longmans for instance. Nevertheless, what did happen in the 1840s, alongside the deaths of John Murray II and John Barrow, was a transformation of the media landscape by spiritualism, the telegraph, penny presses and mass readership, allowing voices very different to Barrow's to increase in volume, make claims and seek credibility on the Arctic.

The subject of the Franklin expedition did not receive as much attention in the Houses of Parliament as might be assumed and, when it was discussed, it was typically after lobbying on the part of Jane Franklin (Stone, 1996). In contrast to the reticence of politicians, Arctic narratives were incessantly constructed and disseminated in the armchairs and lending libraries of the public sphere – independent of naval authorities – and these amateur voices could come into conflict with actual explorers (see Osborn, 1852, 207). Booming newspaper and periodical presses dissected and criticised Admiralty policy on the Arctic, celebrating newcomer-explorers such as Penny, Bellot and Kennedy for their strength and daring, while denigrating established explorers like Belcher and Rae for their incompetence or perceived closeness to the Admiralty (see Cavell, 2008, 206). In serial fiction and ghost stories, meanwhile, the Arctic became a setting for spectral happenings and hauntings. For many writers, the associations between the Franklin expedition and female clairvoyance on the one hand, and the instinctual moral horrors of cannibalism on the other, called for new emotional expressions that would alternately omit, suppress, redirect or transform the raw material afforded by such a traumatic national event.

The 1857 performances of *The Frozen Deep*, a play co-written by Collins and Dickens, stand out as moments of public catharsis, when the traumatic details of the expedition's demise were recreated and then reconfigured to console those who had been affected (Potter, 2007, 139). First performed as an amateur theatrical at Dickens's Tavistock House residence, *The Frozen Deep* was a three-act melodrama that centred on the threat of a murder on an Arctic expedition in search of a Northwest Passage. Richard Wardour (played by Dickens) felt he was jilted by the weak-willed Clara Burnham, and swore revenge on the man she loves. Unknown to Wardour, the man is Frank Aldersley (played by Collins), a fellow expeditioner with whom he is suffering in the Arctic as the expedition collapses. The women back home are in an anxious state about this because Clara's Scottish nurse Esther, who claims to possess 'second sight', has seen Wardour kill Aldersley in her mind's eye. Despite the prophecy, Wardour, who has figured out who Aldersley is, resists the urge to kill the debilitated expeditioner and in a final scene of sentimental pathos, carries Aldersley in his arms to a cave in Newfoundland where he is reunited with Clara (see Figure 5.1).

Wardour's urge, obviously linked to the Franklin cannibalism controversy, provided Dickens with an opportunity to show the way that British Arctic explorers acted manfully, nobly and did not slide into savagery despite every temptation. Yet, as Lillian Nayder (1991) argues, this redemption came at the expense of an aggressive silencing of the Inuit, who do not feature in the play, and the neutralisation of Nurse Esther, a Highland servant whose visionary claims about Arctic disaster are seen as a subversive threat to the power relations in Clara's household. Dickens played a key role in the development of Esther's character, and she represents the savagery undermining Arctic heroism in *The Frozen Deep*, a dissenting working-class voice who is also a symbol of racial and sexual otherness. As if to demonstrate the closure of an era of spectral threats to a noble narrative of the Franklin expedition, *The Frozen Deep* was followed by a performance of Elizabeth Inchbald's farce *Animal*

Figure 5.1 'Private Theatricals at Tavistock House – Scene from *The Frozen Deep*'. Source: *Illustrated London News*. 17 January 1857.

Magnetism, in which Dickens played a doctor deluded into believing in mesmerism while trying to win the affections of his young ward.

The Frozen Deep was an important and popular resolution to the 'epistemological crisis' caused by Rae's return (Davis-Fisch, 2012, 167). While it seemed to provide a closure of sorts to the thousands who witnessed the defeat of spectral testimony and wept at the death of Wardour during the Manchester performances in August 1857, the play did not silence the voice of ghostly women in cultural representations of the Arctic. Ghost stories and other gothic tales set in the Arctic pre-dated the Franklin expedition, but the emergence of scores of ghostly women into poetic and literary representations of the Arctic after 1845 highlights this motif as a creative means of making sense of the loss.[1]

Gender, emotions and the Arctic

From the mid-nineteenth century onwards the theme of love in relation to British Arctic exploration was expressed in popular ballads, poetry and supernatural and sensational fiction. Writers constructed this theme by contrasting masculine endeavour in the face of suffering with feminine fidelity on the home front (see Spufford, 1996, 62). In this relational motif women were psychically connected to their male lovers across the cartographic divide, transgressing even the boundaries of what was natural in the physical world. Such was the power of this polar love to unite souls across space and time that it was inextricably linked to the supernatural, to the world of ghosts, haunting memories and celestial melodies – features which were all performed in an environment of death or impending death. An erotic rhetoric permeated this writing on exploration: although the Arctic was occasionally imagined in masculine terms (Porden, 1818, 23; 'The Arctic Expeditions', *The Aberdeen Journal*, 10 April 1850), by the time of the Franklin expedition it was more common for the Arctic to be feminised and imagined to have 'wooed' and 'drawn' men into her realm only for them to be attacked by 'white teeth' which could grip like 'a vice' (Gilder, 1908, 108; Dixon, 1864, 49).

Historically prevalent discourses ensured that the Arctic was commonly imagined as a space of masculinist fantasy, a space where white men could test their bodies while at the same time performing their political strength by flag-planting, mapping and other nationalist 'ceremonies of possession' (Bloom, 1993). Yet this is only half the story, for in Victorian fiction the Arctic became a space 'complicated' by the presence of women. When possible, it was common for British explorers to have sexual intercourse with Inuit and other indigenous women. The most famous case is that of Green Stockings, a Chipewyan teenager fought over by Robert Hood and George Back during Franklin's first Arctic expedition. Green Stockings was celebrated in a Valentine's Day poem written to Franklin by his first wife, Eleanor Porden, entitled 'The Esquimaux Girl's Lament':

> Return! and the ice shall be swept from thy path,
> I will breathe out my spells o'er the land and the sea;
> Return! and the tempest shall pause in his wrath,
> Nor the winds nor the waves dare to be rebels to thee!
> Spread thy canvas once more, keep the Pole-star before thee,
> 'Tis constancy's type, and the beacon of glory;
> By the lake, by the mountain, the forest and river,
> In the wilds of the north, I am thine, and for ever!
> (qtd. in Kay, 1874, appendix ii).

Yet haunting the language of such idealisations of polar romance were the realities of sexual exchange, disease and abandonment. Green Stockings and other women were used by male explorers as informants, geographers and sexual objects. They were occasionally made pregnant (George Lyon, Robert Peary, Matthew Henson and Vilhjalmur Stefansson left children behind) and risked contracting syphilis. By contrast with these embodied encounters with women who were actually present, after Franklin's loss Arctic exploration was imagined to involve spectral relations between men and the absent women back home.

Explorers imagined and wrote about the presence of imaginary women all the time. A poem entitled 'A Thought of Home' written for the shipboard publication *The North Georgia Gazette and Winter Chronicle* during Parry's first Northwest Passage expedition placed the active male facing danger in contrast with the passive, soothing woman back home, whose 'endearments procure us release'. The woman is therefore a figure of solace and her 'love-bearing glance' has a role in the construction of the north for the poet: 'In those virtues we happiness feel; / The source of our transport below, / Not the charms of the sex can reveal; / From the mind, soul-enchantment must flow' (Sabine ed., 1821, 34). Later in the nineteenth century, Fridtjof Nansen imagined his family celebrating a birthday back home: 'Many a thought will be sent northwards but they know not where to look for us; are not aware that we are drifting here embedded in the ice in the highest northern latitude ever reached, in the deepest polar-night ever penetrated' (1897, II, 59). Explorers knew that loving thoughts about the Arctic and the people in it did not simply evaporate: their poetry and reveries suggest that these thoughts were relational and magnetic, travelling ever northwards. Western women, the great missing category in Arctic exploration, became spectrally present in Arctic discourses.[2]

How was this presence manifested? As a rule of thumb, when emotions and emotional states were explicitly stated in nineteenth-century narratives of Arctic exploration, references to women, whether figures of support or opposition, were not far behind. From lovers, relatives, women in general, to the Arctic environment feminised, rigidly regulated female categories became crucial in how men orientated themselves in all-male environments considered desolate, dangerous and heartless. For instance, on New Year's Day in 1854 Edward Belcher looked out at the snow surrounding his expedition ships and was struck with the idea of a 'watchful mother spreading her graceful arms around some cherished object, and protecting it from injury; the greater elevation of the snow astern representing the breast, and the gradual tapering to the bow the arms' (1855, II, 87). Echoing this, the relationships between sailors and their wives were frequently idealised as part of the 'two spheres' framework of nineteenth-century marriage, with the privations of the whaling trade and exilic nature of Arctic voyaging placed in contrast to a soft and consoling welcome back home (see Stamp and Stamp, 1976, 12–13). Prolonged periods of separation and distance caused stress and pent-up emotions for explorers, sailors, whalers and their families. For instance, William Scoresby's description of being reunited with his pregnant wife in 1812 demonstrates the intense emotional relationship between the whaler and his lover:

> The agony of parting, the gnawing anxiety and distress attendant upon our separation, was thus fully compensated by the feelings, the delights experienced on our reunion. This extreme sensibility, whilst it subjects its possessor to pain and anguish unknown to coarser minds – reaps, when circumstances are favourable, a mighty and full return in an ecstasy and weight of enjoyment which minds of other moulds can neither participate in nor understand (qtd. in Stamp and Stamp, 1976, 47).

Another example of this dynamic was the intimate relationship between Elisha Kent Kane and Margaret Fox. Kane referred to their relationship as 'a dream' and even carried a portrait of his loved one 'strapped to his back, through the dreary Arctic wastes' (*The Love-Life of Dr. Kane*, 1866, 117). Furthermore, in a development that might have been taken from the plot of a sensational novel, Charles Francis Hall was poisoned and killed on his *Polaris* North Pole expedition in 1871 by the ship's doctor, Emil Bessels, who discovered that they were both in love with the same woman, a young artist named Vinnie Ream (Potter, 2016, 114).

While life onboard Arctic ships involved brutal violence, misogyny and casual racism, several accounts also suggest the power of emotions and tenderness in everyday practices. For instance, Joseph P. Faulkner's wonderful *Eighteen Months on a Greenland Whaler* displays an awareness of the reveries, dreams and occurrences of 'transcendental import' that could characterise the situation of the whaler (1878, 42). Crucially, emotions were here not imagined in an hydraulic sense – as 'venting' or pressure-releases – but rather as the 'bundles' that 'tie' the men together through hopes, fears, 'affections, enjoyments and endurances' (Faulkner, 1878, 243). Faulkner particularly highlighted 'Jack's' [the sailor] 'devotion' to his feminine vessel:

> The 'she' fairly entwines itself round Jack's heart, and unless when just leaving her with the view of meeting that other 'she', Jack's own wife 'Susan', or his sweetheart 'Sally', when he gets into port, it is generally with husky voice and a half-brushed away tear, that he turns his back toward her (Faulkner, 1878, 65–6).

Women were also present in the ribald rhymes that sailors, including those on the Franklin expedition, would have sung (see Cyriax and Jones, 1954), while rituals of mapping involved a conjuration of female presence, an important practice that underwrote the ideology of exploration as 'revelation' and 'penetration' (see McClintock, 1995, 24).

In poetry, the fantasy of the polar queen, or Arctic-as-woman, was another way of conjuring non-native women into presence.[3] In Amelia C. Jennings's poem 'Song of the Polar Night' (1854), the narrative voice is a female spirit of the Arctic whose domain is conquered and her secrets revealed: 'He traversed my empire's farthest bound, / Through that mysterious way / I hid so long in my garb profound / From the babbling tongue of Day' (117). John Moultrie's 'The Witch of the North' (1828; see Moultrie, 1838) and Thomas D'Arcy McGee's Our Ladye of the Snow! (1858; see D'Arcy McGee, 2000) also imagined the polar agency that attacked vulnerable men as supernatural and feminine. Elsewhere,

Figure 5.2 'A Cold Reception' and 'A Warm Welcome'. Source: *Punch, or the London Charivari*, 71 (1876).

in 'The Snow Queen' (1844; see Andersen 1911) and 'The Ice-Maiden' (1863) Hans Christian Andersen imagined castrative ice queens whose power over men was their deathly embrace and a kiss which froze. Finally, in the saccahrine poem *The Arctic Queen* (1857), dedicated to Kane, Franklin was imagined as someone who had gone in search of the queen of the 'Frigid Zone' to plead for the lives of imprisoned lovers. These treatments all had in common an idea of the Lady as a cold and distant being, an objectified abstract, and not as a passionate and loving female.

The popular comic magazine *Punch* provided a striking demonstration of this gendered Arctic in its visual commemoration of the return of the expedition led by George Nares in 1876 (see Figure 5.2). This image drew upon the dualist interpretation of feminine nature/culture, placing the cold Arctic ice queen in contrast to the warm embrace of Britannia back home. A related fantasy appeared in the Christmas edition of *Punch*, released the previous year (see Figure 5.3). In this piece Mr Punch thinks of the 'gallant' explorers of the Nares expedition while imagining the sovereignty of a feminine spirit named 'The Everlasting Silence' ruling over a 'realm' dangerous to men:

> Can *she* be a Woman, by the way, as I have limned her? And if she is, how tired she must be of herself! How fain, methinks, to fling herself into the arms of the gallant mariners who come to break

Figure 5.3 Mr. Punch and the Everlasting Silence. Source: *Punch, or the London Charivari*, 68 (1875–6).

> her – and substitute the silvern speech for her pale and frosted gold! ('Preface', *Punch*, 1875–6, iii).

In alternately naming this feminine being 'the Polar Queen' and 'the Ice Maiden', the kneeling Mr Punch exposes a long-standing western cosmology: the difficulties of exploration presume a frigid North capable of freezing the male explorer (indeed, the repulsion of the Nares expedition by the polar ice in 1876 reinforced this representation). Not that this romantic geography was simply a media construction, for just a few years later an officer who served on this very expedition, Albert Hastings Markham, wrote an untitled poem which encapsulates many of the same themes:

> At her feet the Frozen Ocean round her head the Auroral Lights
> Through cycles, chill & changeless, of six month days & nights.
> In her bride veil, fringed with icicles, and of the snowdrift spun,
> Sits the White Ladye of the Pole, still waiting to be won.
>
> What suitors to her palace-gates have hoisted daring sail,
> Though eye of man has never seen the face behind her veil!
> So long sighed for, so hard served for, as this Queen, was never none,
> Since the days of brave adventure & true service first begun.

But still the White-Witch Maiden, that sits above the Pole,
In the snow-bound silver silence whose cold quells aught but soul
Draws manly hearts with strange desire to lift her icy veil;
The bravest still have sought, and will seek, whoever fail
(NMM, MRK/48).[4]

Love and laments

After the Franklin loss the themes of love and lament start to inform much of the creative writing about the Arctic. Indeed, the earliest poetic imaginings of the disaster were laments that were sung to traditional tunes and spread widely through broadside publications in ports, towns and onboard ships. In one example – 'A Ballad of Sir John Franklin', published in May 1850, by the American poet George Henry Boker – the idea of multivocality stands out, as competing voices – both legitimate and illegitimate – form part of the search expeditions:

O, whither sail you, Sir John Franklin?
Cried a whaler in Baffin's Bay.
To know if between the land and the pole
I may find a broad sea-way.

I charge you back, Sir John Franklin,
As you would live and thrive;
For between the land and the frozen pole
No man may sail alive.

When the 'little Esquimaux' and the 'little Indian' both stress the necessity of fur clothing in the Arctic, and sledging rather than sailing, Franklin and his crew laugh off this unauthorised advice (Boker, 1850, 323). As the 'cruel ice', 'as strong as death', closes behind the expedition, they sink into despair and the authority of Franklin and the Admiralty is questioned: "'Twas cruel, Sir John, to send us here, / So far from help or home, / To starve and freeze on this lonely sea: / I ween the lords of the Admiralty / Would rather send than come' (Boker, 1850, 324). The images surrounding the publication of this poem in *Sartain's Union Magazine* aptly display the affects of disaster as indigenous and bawdy, and female perspectives are re-imagined as being central to Arctic exploration (see Figure 5.4). The crews are absent from representation while a kayak crowns the pathetic image of a British ship crushed by the ice and surrounded by savage animals. Recast as a folly, the quest for a Northwest Passage becomes a personal and national tragedy, but with the crucial addition of Franklin's love for his wife as a saving grace for masculine nobility: 'Be still, be still, my brave sailors! / Think not such thoughts again. / But a tear froze slowly on his cheek: / He thought of Lady Jane' (Boker, 1850).

In the majority of treatments, however, it is not the voice of Franklin but that of his wife Jane, which drives the tone of lament, making audible a woman imagined as Penelope-like, and 'more steadily hopeful than the

Figure 5.4 'A Ballad of Sir John Franklin', by G.H. Boker.
Source: *Sartain's Union Magazine*, 6 (1850).

Ithacan wife of old' (Dowe, 1853, 634). Despite her voluminous travel writings, exciting life, and powerful personality, Jane Franklin eventually became an object conflated with the tragedy of her husband – her archive significantly stored in the Scott Polar Research Institute, Cambridge. Going through her letters and diaries reveals a complicated woman who disguised her independence of thought and mobility through a carefully fabricated 'rhetoric of wifeliness' (Russell, 2005, 47). From the beginning of the era of the Franklin searches, the position, perspective, and voice of Jane Franklin moved centre-stage: she was now a household name and recurring character in periodicals and newspapers (Spufford, 1996, 115–29; Cavell, 2008, 219–22). She even appeared as a Staffordshire earthenware figure, for sale alongside a figure of her husband in full naval uniform. This configuration helped redefine male activity in the Arctic while also legitimising a female perspective on Arctic policy, if only through a male-networked influence. Described by Emily Dickinson as 'the lone British Lady' (qtd. in Morris, 1997, 89), Jane Franklin's imagined virtues ('Patience, Perseverance, and Fortitude') (Abrahall, 1856, dedication page) became the epitome of *Femina Domestica*: she waits and hopes. Jane Franklin quickly became an emotional conduit for the nation with the explorer and writer Sherard Osborn hailing her as an example of how a 'sailor's wife' and an 'Englishwoman' should feel: 'untiring exertions, that zeal which has never wavered, that hope so steadfast … that patience under misconstruction, that forgiveness for the sneer of jealousy, and that pity for the malicious' (1852, 5–6). Jane Franklin's emotional power began to have real public force following her open letter of supplication to President Taylor in April 1849 and, by September of that year, she was featuring as an emotional presence in the narratives of Emma, the Bolton clairvoyant.

Throughout many of the Arctic narratives that I have surveyed, Jane Franklin's emotional power is traced to the love she has for her husband: this was imagined as a highly sentimentalised relationship, a 'love no Arctic winter bound' (Rawnsley, 1893, 54). In ballad treatments this attachment to her husband either places her in conflict with the Admiralty ('The government in this present year / Did pensions give to their families dear; / But Lady Franklin refused the grant / Crying give me my husband I no money want' ('A Lament on the Fate of Sir J. Franklin and his Crews')), or causes her to initiate journeys for his succour ('With my goodly Ship in motion, / No longer here I'd stay, / But athwart the rolling ocean, / For thee I'd bear away') ('Lady Franklin's Lament', c. 1852). The most popular ballad on the subject, 'Lady Franklin's Lament for her

Husband' (c.1852), narrates the vision of a sailor ('I dream't a dream which I thought was true') in which a female voice is heard:

> She wept aloud and seem'd to say,
> Alas! My Franklin is long away.
> Her mind it seem'd in sad distress,
> She cried aloud, I can take no rest,
> Ten thousand pounds I would freely give,
> To say on earth that my husband lives.

These ballads express an intimate connection between home and abroad, between Britain and the Arctic, mediated through the voice of the loving woman. This connection, symbolised in an illustration of joined hands in the broadside of 'Lady Franklin's Lament' (c.1851–2), is heightened due to the mystery of the expedition's disappearance and the relentless efforts of Jane Franklin to organise its rescue. 'Lady Franklin's Appeal to the North', a poem published in the *New York Times* in 1851, imagines her taking on the very conditions of the Arctic environment in her emotional pleas for information from the 'North'. In this scenario the Arctic is a silent impediment to the connection between lovers:

> Tell me, oh dreary North! for now
> My soul is like thine Arctic zone;
> Beneath the darkened skies I bow
> Or ride the stormy sea alone!
> Tell me of my beloved! for I
> Know not a ray my lord without!
> Oh, tell me, that I may not die
> A sorrower on the sea of doubt! (Bourne, 1851)

The poetics of this connection come about through emotional states and affects, through the sending and receiving of thoughts across environments considered inhospitable for people. While in the Victorian era of 'geography militant' (Driver, 2001) exploration was thought of as a thoroughly masculine enterprise, the North was also imagined as a theatre for the disembodied performance of gender. Although the only domesticities in the Arctic were supposed to be within the homosocial world of the ship, or what Dickens infamously termed the Inuit 'domesticity of blood and blubber' (1854, 392), female presences kept invading the literature of Arctic exploration.

Spectral geographies of love

In the winter of 1859 the *Toronto Daily Colonist* told its readers a story about a young English sailor named Jones who volunteered to join the Franklin expedition because he was dissatisfied with the conduct of his sweetheart, Miss Cook, who was found in a 'flirtation with another swain from Falmouth'. However, on learning that she had not been unfaithful to him, Jones married the woman just before the departure of the *Erebus* and *Terror*. The narrator reported that in the years following the disappearance Mrs Jones, accompanied by their son, would climb up to Pendennis Castle on Sunday afternoons to gaze out into the English Channel, 'waiting and watching for the vessels that never came'. When last heard of, Mrs Jones was eking out her widow's pension, and 'remained still constant to her first love' ('An Episode of the Franklin Expedition', *Paisley Herald and Renfrewshire Advertiser*, 1859). While this is a touching story, it remains just that; no person named Jones was actually present on the Franklin expedition. Yet the image of Mrs Jones gazing into the horizon would have been deeply affecting to readers, showing how the expedition was mourned as an ambivalent loss.

Geographies of love and geographies of ghosts irresistibly blend in examples like this: entangled in the absences and presences of memory and emotion, they speak to the ruptures of space in Britain's relationship with the Arctic. Turning to Victorian supernatural and sensational fiction, we find that the silences and melodies of the Arctic were articulated through spectres of ghostly women. Ghosthood was something that women and spirits shared in Victorian culture and ghost stories were frequently stages for examining the ambivalence and power/powerlessness of the female (Dickerson, 1996). Western folk traditions host a pantheon of female spirits, elementals, banshees, and 'white ladies', but Arctic spirits seem particularly related to a kind of 'melodic' haunting linked to the deconstruction of the male explorer.

The first tale I examine explores the spectral nature of male desire. 'The Shadow of a Shade' (1869) by the caricaturist and writer Tom Hood (son of the better-known poet Thomas Hood (1799–1845)) tells the story of the elderly Lettie, whose 'old story of a lost lover' has given her a habitual grave and melancholy look (Hood, 2003, 150). She was engaged to George Mason, a sailor who had volunteered to join one of the expeditions seeking Franklin. To celebrate this, his portrait was painted by Lettie's younger brother in full naval costume. Before the departure of the expedition a Scottish colleague onboard the ship was invited to dinner with the family. This man, Vincent Grieve, was an unpleasant character whose attentions made Lettie uncomfortable. However, Grieve took an instant dislike to the painting of Mason on the wall:

> 'I have an inherited horror of such pictures. My mother married against her father's will, and when I was born she was so ill she was hardly expected to live. When she was sufficiently recovered to speak without delirious rambling she implored them to remove a picture of my grandfather that hung in the room, and which she vowed made threatening faces at her. It's superstitious, but constitutional – I have a horror of such paintings!' (Hood, 2003, 152)

Mason lets it be known that Grieve was 'pleasant enough company among men at the inn', but was not to be trusted in female company. Despite this, Grieve manages to find opportunities to pester Lettie with his attentions and declares his love for her on the day the expedition is due to sail. Receiving a blunt refusal, Grieve makes a vague threat regarding Mason's safety on the expedition. While Lettie does not mention the incident to Mason 'for fear it should lead to a duel', the painting seems to develop moisture on it and the face of Mason assumes a ghastly pallor (Hood, 2003, 153). The restrictions on sexual choice, it seems, causes paranoia in the male subject, centred on the power of the representation of his rival. Conceived of as an animate object, the painting becomes an icon of judgement, restricting the romantic and sexual feelings travelling between the Arctic and Britain.

Two years of near-silence follow the departure of the expedition until, one balmy evening, a 'deathly cold' swept into Lettie's dining room and the narrator perceives a grinning spectral skull where Mason's face once was (Hood, 2003, 154). The date of this occurrence is noted and, in a well-known trope of Victorian supernatural tales, the arrival of the news of a significant death on that day is expected. Sure enough, a newspaper reporting on the return of the expedition mentions the death of Mason while out shooting on the ice with Grieve. Soon Grieve comes to visit Lettie, but he is noticeably thinner and stooped, and has acquired a habit of 'glancing sideways every instant, as if unconsciously. It looked as if he heard someone behind him' (Hood, 2003, 158). Again, he evinced a total repugnance of the picture of Mason and demanded that it be covered. However, while giving the particulars of Mason's death to Lettie's brother, the shroud covering the portrait falls down and the sight of the bloody face of Mason causes Grieve to have a fit. On leaving, it is revealed that Grieve is in possession of two shadows, his own and 'something always at his side' (Hood, 2003, 160). On returning once more to court Lettie, Grieve's head is cut open when Mason's portrait falls on him. He subsequently commits suicide, begging the 'haunting spirit to leave him' (Hood, 2003, 162). The shadow of Mason seems to operate here as a literary device for articulating the experience of self-division; it is a doppelgänger and reflects on the weird status of love in Arctic exploration. Mason and Grieve are different personalities with different libidinal natures but both leave on their search for Franklin in love with the same woman. The trace of Mason left behind in the portrait is part of his soul-force and communicates his death and vengeance in the domestic sphere. In common with other gothic tales of haunted portraits (Edgar Allan Poe's 'The Oval Portrait' and Oscar Wilde's *The Picture of Dorian Gray* for example), the psychological disruption that love causes reveals a narcissism that refuses to accept 'separation from the libidinous object (or subject)' (Chodorow, 1985, 279). Grieve's persistent courting of Lettie might actually disguise an attachment to Mason, the more typical Arctic hero (with a 'fine Italian-looking head' (Hood, 2003, 151)), a fact then diverted into a horror for his representation and self-dissolution. The presence of women and children on nineteenth-century whaling voyages challenged the idea of home at sea, especially in the context of commercial expeditions that overwintered in the Arctic. These tensions about domesticity found their way into fiction where the presence of women made the contrast between brutality and sympathy more obvious.

The short periodical tale 'The Spectre of the Ice' (*Every Week*, 1872) is set within the context of male violence on a whaling voyage, 'the old story of brutality and tyranny' ('The Spectre of the Ice', *Every Week*, 1872, 241). In this piece the young hero, Harry Elting, endures abuse and bullying from the captain of the *Mentor* for talking to his daughter Blanche: 'she whispered regrets and sympathy into the ears of the brave boy' ('The Spectre of the Ice', *Every Week*, 1872, 242). Elting is in love with Blanche but nurses a deep resentment against the captain and plots his revenge. His opportunity comes when he and the captain are stranded alone on the ice after an abortive whale hunt. The act of murder in such a situation is imagined as something intrinsically easy and clean, and recalls examples from *The Frozen Deep* and 'The Shadow of a Shade'. In this case Elting's passion for Blanche causes him to lose his moral balance and contemplate pushing the sleeping captain off the ice to his death, 'when suddenly a soft, sweet voice was heard to breathe, "Harry!"'. Elting hears his name called again by the voice of Blanche and then he sees the 'spirit semblance' of his love which hovers over him for a moment, extending her arms in benediction and halting the crime ('The Spectre of the Ice', *Every Week*, 1872, 243). It is the perversion of the captain that he enjoys inflicting pain on Elting, both physically and – by separating him from Blanche – emotionally. The captain, who had dreamed of Elting's vengeance while sleeping on the ice, is subsequently reconciled with him and allows his daughter to marry the young man, thus ending the circuit of desire and prohibition. The fact that Blanche had the same dream as her father is left as an unexplained mystery in this family romance, figuring as an implicit challenge to any easy dichotomy between natural and supernatural, dream and reality.

In these Arctic tales, jiltings, romantic misunderstandings and prolonged separation from women form preludes to a conservative reassertion of social and moral order. However, they also speak to the vicissitudes and impossibility of desire. The tale 'The Spectre Ship' (*A London Magazine*, 1876), by Percy Bolingbroke St. John, repeats many of the motifs discussed thus far. In this periodical story the domestic tranquillity of Mary Stone is disrupted when a man she thought was dead returns to Britain from abroad. Robert Rankin, a violent and disreputable sailor had gained a reluctant promise from Stone for her hand in marriage just before he departed on a voyage to India. After three years, and reports of Rankin's death in India, Stone married the Hull whaling captain, Harry Medhurst. Rankin is disgusted at the news, revealing that he had sustained years of hardship for her love: 'You have wrecked my life; when I have wrecked that of your husband I shall be satisfied, and never until then' (518). The constancy of the woman – the cherished illusion of the man at sea – has been denied to Rankin: masculinity is here defined in relation to femininity. Stone's impending sense of dread leads her to persuade her husband to allow her to travel on the next Arctic whaling voyage. However, in a sensational turn of events, Rankin manages to get himself employed on Medhurst's ship, under an assumed name. Fearing the exposure of her past, and the possibilities of mortal violence, Stone keeps her husband in the dark while Rankin plots his revenge as the ship overwinters in the Arctic. The following spring he drugs and kidnaps Stone, escaping on a raft after sabotaging the ship, and heading for Greenland. Yet the raft is seemingly followed by a spectre ship, 'its huge fabric moved or glided as it were over the surface of the sea, it was a thing unreal, the mere phantom of the thing that was, the shadow of the strong fabric of iron and wood' ('The Spectre Ship', *A London Magazine*, 1876, 533). In terror at the vision, Rankin falls to his death into the sea. Stone is later rescued by her sceptical husband with the phantom appearance left unexplained: 'but in the solitude of her own heart she never forgot that terrible incident which connected her so strangely with the spectre ship' ('The Spectre Ship', *A London Magazine*, 1876, 534).

In 'The Spectre Ship' the introduction of women into the Arctic disrupts male activity and moral certainty. Again, the dramatisation of romance and melodrama in the Arctic becomes a stage for unravelling one of the fundamental illusions of western thought – the boundary between reason and magic. The particular geographies of this breakdown – the desolation, icescapes and sublimity of the popular Arctic imagination – set the scene for the transformation of male identities through the supernatural experience. Thus, spectral geographies of love reveal the contingent links between the domestic and the Arctic.

'The captain of the "*Pole-star*"'

The Scottish doctor and author Arthur Conan Doyle spent eight months onboard the Peterhead whaler the *Hope* in 1880 as a ship's surgeon. This was a formative experience for the young medical student and it resulted in material for two journalistic articles and an interesting supernatural tale that focused on the ghostly presence of a woman in the Arctic.

In Doyle's view, whaling was a practice that demanded vigilance, intelligence and manly prowess – the difficulties of whale-hunting, he writes, 'dwarfs all other experiences' (2012, 320). While Doyle was writing in the context of the decline of the industry and a general rise in levels of anxiety and frustration among whalers, he still imagined the Arctic as a realm of romance and enchantment. He wrote of the 'glamour about those circumpolar regions which must affect everyone who has penetrated to them' (Doyle, 2012, 323). Fundamentally, it was a region where men acted strangely due to isolation and solitude in the face of physical hardship and environmental 'purity':

> My heart goes out to that old, grey-headed whaling captain who, having been left for an instant when at death's door, staggered off in his night gear, and was found by his nurses far from his house and still, as he mumbled, 'pushing to the norrard' (Doyle, 2012).

In an article published in the *Strand Magazine* in 1897 Doyle expanded on the homosocial environment of the whaling voyage, painting a picture of simmering violence, comradeship and initiation rites. He also discussed melody and sound at sea, writing of the 'beautiful and sympathetic tenor voice' of the steward who sang songs of women and love which 'filled us all with a vague, sweet discontent, which comes back to me now as I think of it' (Doyle, 2012, 327). All of these elements – masculine power, Arctic purity and haunting melody – are present in the fictional tale that Doyle wrote following his whaling voyage, 'The Captain of the "*Pole-star*"' (1883).

This gothic tale is presented as a series of extracts from the journal of a young ship's surgeon, John McAlister Ray, onboard the *Pole-star*, a whaler of Dundee. Commanded by Captain Craigie, the ship becomes stuck in an ice-field north of Spitsbergen in September, a time when she should be directing her way homeward. Craigie is a wild monomaniac in the style of Captain Ahab who loves the dangers of whaling and possesses something of a death-wish. Yet for Ray, who engages in a 'psychological study' of the captain, he retains a 'depth of tenderness' in his eyes (Doyle, 2012, 336). He is a gallant companion and his countenance is 'manly and resolute', but again Doyle places these characteristics in contrast with his emotional life: Craigie frequently displays a 'look of fear' and has trouble sleeping (Doyle, 2012, 337). He has a peculiar attitude to women (or female representation), as seen in his violent outburst when Ray happens to show him a vignette of his fiancée. The mystery of Craigie's double life seems to be connected with a peculiar outbreak of 'superstition' (Doyle, 2012) among the men onboard the ship, a superstition involving a ghostly woman.

Shortly after leaving Shetland the men at the wheel heard 'plaintive cries and screams' following the ship (Doyle, 2012, 338). The second mate reported hearing sounds 'sometimes like a bairn crying and sometimes like a wench in pain' and then seeing a tall, white, shadowy figure moving along the ice seemingly waiting for someone (Doyle, 2012). Symbolising the attributes of a particular form of western rationality, Ray approaches these accounts as absurd superstitious beliefs but fears an epidemic if such superstitions spread. Ray begins to fear for Craigie's sanity when the captain also sees this ghost on the ice:

> He was staring out over the ice with an expression in which horror, surprise, and something approaching to joy were contending for the mastery. In spite of the cold, great drops of perspiration were coursing down his forehead, and he was evidently fearfully excited. His limbs twitched like those of a man upon the verge of an epileptic fit, and the lines about his mouth were drawn and hard.
>
> 'Look!', he gasped, seizing me by the wrist, but still keeping his eye upon the distant ice, and moving his head slowly in a horizontal

> direction, as if following some object which was moving across the field of vision. 'Look! There, man, there! Between the hummocks! Now coming out from behind the far one! You see her – you *must* see her! There still! Flying from me, by God, flying from me – and gone!' (Doyle, 2012, 340).

Mirroring the increasing tension onboard the *Pole-star* are the worsening ice conditions and the 'horrible', 'deathly silence' of the ice-fields (Doyle, 2012, 341). As the ghost continues to be seen flitting around the ship, the captain mumbles to himself, 'But a little time, love – but a little time!' (Doyle, 2012, 345). Ray's faith in rationality is finally shattered when he hears the sounds of the ghost: 'a mere sound, and that was all' (Doyle, 2012), he writes with some understatement. After noting the deep silences and strange hums that pervade the Arctic ice-fields, Ray hears 'a cry, sharp and shrill, upon the silent air of the night' culminating in a 'long wail of agony, which might have been the last cry of a lost soul' (Doyle, 2012, 346). These are the sounds of grief, but also of longing and enchantment: the ghost's intentions and the dangers of the ship's position are interlinked, forcing the men to wait until she releases them.

The denouement to 'The Captain of the "*Pole-star*"' comes when Craigie keeps his 'tryst' with this ghost and suddenly jumps off the ship onto the ice where he runs towards what seems to be a 'wreath of mist' (Doyle, 2012, 348). The next day the ship's crew find Craigie's body face down on the ice with a 'bright smile' and outstretched arms, as though grasping something (see Figure 5.5). As the men approach the body, a puff of wind catches the snowflakes that covered him and whirl around before blowing out towards the sea: 'To my eyes', Ray notes, 'it seemed but a snow-drift, but many of my companions averred that it started up in the shape of a woman, stooped over the corpse and kissed it' (Doyle, 2012, 349). Ray had previously found occasion to enter the captain's cabin where he saw a watercolour of a young lady with 'languid, dreamy eyes' and a 'clean-cut, prominent jaw' (Doyle, 2012, 343). Judging from this portrait, Ray believes her to have been a woman of extraordinary will-power. On entering the cabin again, he finds that this picture had been cut from the frame, a portrait of a woman, Doyle's postscript tells us, who had 'died under circumstances of peculiar horror' while engaged to Craigie, who was then at sea (Doyle, 2012, 350).

This gothic tale forms one example of a consistent theme in Doyle's fiction, that of passion and love from beyond the grave. 'De Profundis' (Doyle, 2016 (originally 1892; published alongside Doyle's

Figure 5.5 'He was lying face downwards upon a frozen bank', by Charles Kerr. Source: A.C. Doyle. *The Captain of the Polestar and Other Tales*. London: Smith, Elder & Co., 1912.

'The Glamour of the Arctic' in the same issue of the *Strand Magazine*)) features the ghost of a dead man who emerges from the ocean to his shocked wife at the very moment that he died in a hospital at Madeira. In a related tale, 'The Ring of Thoth' (1890), an Egyptian sneaks into a mummy exhibit in Paris to bring his ancient love back to life. Love as a means of exploring the relationship between the living and the dead speaks, of course, to the whole area of relics and fetishes. Material objects bearing memories, pieces or representations of the loved one mediate processes of intimacy in Doyle's supernatural fiction and highlight the deep connections between bodies and ghosts, presences and absences.

Craigie's portrait of his fiancée, much like the portrait of Mason in 'The Shadow of a Shade', acts as a substitute for an absent lover – an already spectral object with its own context of loss and desire. The ghostly woman who haunts the men of the *Pole-star* also suggests the spectralisation of sexuality, its sublimation into sounds, images and rumours. It is no coincidence that, in many of these works of Arctic fiction, the link between the male and the female remains tenuous due to the physical and emotional separation between home and Arctic. Lovers have not married yet and the supernatural experience seems to express sexual tension and a desire or fantasy for bonding. Remembering his own whaling experience, Doyle leaves us with no doubts regarding the emotional and carnal desires experienced by whalers onboard ship:

> To appreciate a woman one has to be out of sight of one for six months. I can well remember that as we rounded the north of Scotland on our return we dipped our flag to the lighthouse, being only some hundreds of yards from the shore. A figure emerged to answer our salute, and the excited whisper ran through the ship, 'It's a woman!' The captain was on the bridge with his telescope. I had the binoculars in the bows. Every one was staring, She was well over fifty, short skirts and sea boots – but she was a 'wumman'. 'Anything in a mutch!' the sailors used to say, and I was of the same way of thinking (1989, 37).

In many Arctic narratives women were elevated into inaccessible Things – impossible objects – to such an extent that simple desire cannot be fulfilled. Stefan Zweig famously defined the adventurer as one who 'is in flight from women' (1974, 61), but there is perhaps something more complicated going on here.

In the world of female ghosts and spirits, victimisation is often expressed through sound and noise. The wailing and siren calls of the ghost and Craigie's alternating pursuit and waiting motions might be examined from the perspective that desire is fundamentally a paradox. As

Žižek has outlined, 'the drive's ultimate aim is simply to reproduce itself as a drive, to return to its circular path, to continue its path to and from the goal. The real source of enjoyment is the repetitive movement of this closed circuit' (1997, 5). Anxiety, in this scenario, centres not on lack but on the danger of losing lack and thereby desire. In this understanding, the Arctic/woman is not valued because of the obstacles she places in front of the man but because she functions as a kind of emptiness around which the male subject's desire is structured. The techniques of courtly love identified here are therefore 'techniques of holding back, of suspension, of *amor interruptus*' (Lacan qtd. in Žižek, 1999, 156). Remember Craigie's intonation: 'But a little time, love – but a little time!'

The attributes of female sexuality in 'The Captain of the "*Pole-star*"' reflect the tension between waiting and pursuing: the flighty and ambient characteristics of the ghost as she embraces Craigie's corpse (the appearance is described as being like a 'vortex' (Doyle, 2012, 349)) plays into historic definitions of female desire as irrational, dangerous, unpredictable and ethereal (see Castle, 1995). These attributes, it should be noted, were also frequently used to describe the Arctic. For instance: 'Yea, awful art thou in thy beauty; with white fingers beckoning in mists and shadows of the frozen sea; / drawing to thee the hearts of heroes' (Gilder, 1908, 109). Yet Craigie's 'bright smile', with his hands 'outstretched as though grasping at the strange visitor which had summoned him away into the dim world that lies beyond the grave' signifies, I argue, the endless circulation of desire in Arctic fiction, and the fear that this inspires (Doyle, 2012, 350). Of course, Craigie's death is yet another ordeal and postponement: he has 'a leaning for metempsychosis and the doctrines of Pythagoras' (Doyle, 2012, 344). Craigie's frozen smile – seeking to grasp the ghost – suggests the essential paradox of desire: his Arctic embrace is a version of the courtly love trial.

Arctic mummies

In 1934 a strange story about the 1876 *Pandora* Arctic expedition was published in a British newspaper. Its narrator, William J.A. Grant, the photographer on the expedition, recalled some spooky incidents onboard the ship as it prepared to leave Greenland for home. Grant developed his photographs in a darkroom beside the engine-room and one day the stoker, a man nicknamed 'Deaffy', ran up to deck claiming he heard a ghost in the darkroom: 'To which his messmates said: "Rubbish: ghosts did not make noises, and if they did, how could a deaf man hear them?"' Yet, as the ship approached Cape Farewell on the southern tip of Greenland, Grant himself heard a 'woman's shriek' from the room and the commander, Allen Young, was informed. With everyone alerted, Grant unlocked the door and found a long box that was brought up on deck and found to contain 'the body of a woman, cut up, her legs and arms having been sawn off'. It was then discovered that the ship's surgeon, A.C. Horner, had been paid £100 by the 'Anthropological Society of London'[5] to acquire 'the bones of an Eskimo woman'. The crew, keen to rid the ship of this macabre passenger, performed a funeral service and the body was consigned to the sea. 'From that moment', Grant wrote, 'the wind shifted and blew from dead aft, and in a very short time we had passed Cape Farewell and soon arrived in Bantry Bay, Ireland' ('Ghost Story of the Arctic', *Western Morning News*, 1934). Although he did not mention this story in his private journal, Horner did note that the crew 'blackballed' him during the 1875 journey of the *Pandora* for 'killing skinning & to make matters worse cutting up birds':

> Only yesterday I banged away at a Tern overhead. At the time there was a favourable breeze springing up. The smoke was not out of the muzzle of the gun before the Captn. was on deck and wanting to know what the Dickens anyone meant by shooting the wind away now he had one. I was floored at once. Such a thing never entered my head. Again it was only the other day Benyen [Lieutenant Koolemans Benyen of the Royal Dutch Navy] came and entreated me to throw overboard a birdskin that he did not approve of ... It will be my fate to be chucked over soon I am certain should the calm continue (SPRI, MS 713).

These kinds of mummy stories should affect how we think of Arctic exploration because they raise troubling and gothic questions about how expeditions acted towards native peoples and cultures. Steve Pile (2006) examines the 'occult entanglements' that link western cities with non-western and colonial space, showing the circulation of magical beliefs, practices and objects through particular routes. One only has to recall the vast literature on fin-de-siècle occultism and psychical research in Britain to see that there was a fundamental cross-pollination of scientific, pseudo-scientific and occult cosmologies at the time. The exposure of the West to the mysterious, occult and unseen forces of the East, of Africa, or of the Celtic or European peripheries, created a literary mode identified by Patrick Brantlinger (1985) as 'imperial gothic'. This can be seen in the ubiquity of vampires, Egyptian mummies and Indian fakirs in late nineteenth-century and early twentieth-century fiction. Echoing the work of scholars of the gothic who look at how supernatural forces relate to political forces, I am interested in the way that the noisy ghosts haunting Arctic expedition ships can inform us about acts of colonial violence.

As Grant's ghost story relates, during this period the Arctic was imagined, like Egypt, to be a site of magic linked to acts of disinterment and despoiling. The pulp tale 'A Cry from the Ice' (1911) by Ernest Elliott Stock echoes Grant's story in recounting the mental collapse of a scientist onboard a ship in the Arctic and is unusual in its appeal to native ontologies. In the story, Dr Muttlebery has been sent North by a learned society 'with instructions to record the Arctic in all its moods' (Stock, 1911, 96). Muttlebery finds himself drawn to the icy landscape, 'holding yet repelling', and begins to feel an 'eerie resistless temptation' to tramp northwards. In the familiar motif, cries and an 'eerie wail' are heard on the ship by the crew, mostly Scottish as behoves the stereotype of their superstitious disposition. When the ship moves southwards Muttlebery starts to behave irrationally and seems to be mesmerised by the North itself: his outstretched and pleading hands remain, like Craigie's, empty. This results in a kind of collapse and degeneration into savagery. Muttlebery becomes 'a crouching, dishevelled, haggard creature', and he leaps overboard to his death (Stock, 1911, 121). When the men search the ship for the origin of the weird cries they discover a case that Muttlebery had kept hidden: in this case is the half-frozen corpse of 'a young Esquimaux girl' which he had disinterred for phrenological examination in London (1911, 124). 'But the North can guard her ain', the captain concludes, 'that I've heard weel these mony years; and the poor doctor laddie keens it too now' (Stock, 1911, 130).[6] With some reverence, the crew carry the case on to the deck and deposit the corpse back into the sea.

Just as in the tales of the mummy's curse, there are colonial histories at work in these two stories, alongside a straightforward warning against the antiquarian impulse and the desecration of cultures one does not understand. The preserved body of the Other is a paradigmatic magic object that contains 'a reserve of supernaturalism' (Luckhurst, 2010), and the movement of such an object outside a realm imagined as an otherworld of mystery and secrecy opens up the relic-hunter to feelings of guilt and moral failure. The degeneration of civilised man into superstition is something that happens on the periphery of the Empire and therefore has implications for the social health of the metropolis. 'A Cry from the Ice' demonstrates that non-western ghosts were harnessed into a western emotional language about Arctic place and its spectral attributes.

Entertaining and spooky as these mummy stories are, they pale in comparison to real acts of colonial despoiling and grave-robbing which occurred in the 1890s. The American explorer Robert E. Peary looms large in this context as someone who was more than willing to snatch mummies and other body parts in order to fund his expeditions in the far north of Greenland. For instance, Peary's Second Greenland Expedition of 1891–2 was part-funded by the Peabody Museum of American Archaeology and Ethnology at Harvard University whose curator, F.W. Putnam, was eager for a full skeleton of one of the 'Arctic Highlanders' (now known as Inughuit) to display at the anthropological section of the Chicago World's Fair of 1893 (Peary, Putnam and Dexter, 1969, 178). Despite donating the huge sum of $2000 to the expedition, Putnam was not satisfied by the materials gathered by Peary and his surgeon (and later rival) Frederick A. Cook. In the inventory of photographs, tools and other artefacts from northwest Greenland that Peary sent back to Harvard in October 1891, Putnam was disappointed to read listed only '1 Eskimaux skull from grave at Nettik' (Peary, Putnam and Dexter, 1969, 183). In the end Putnam realised that Peary gave some specimens to other scientific bodies, leaving only a few crania for his display, but the official account of the expedition tells a macabre story of illicit procurement.

According to this narrative, when the expedition ship, the sealer *SS Kite*, reached a village near Cape Parry in July the expeditioners distracted the local Inughuit in order to dig for bodies. Their search was rewarded by the discovery of a mummified corpse wrapped in a bearskin. Afraid of alerting the Inughuit to this 'despoiling', the men covered the body in an old coat and brought it onto the vessel (Keely and Davis, 1892, 126). As the ship was passing the eastern shores of Disko Island some time later the *Kite* ran aground in calm weather, a sign 'some of the more superstitious sailors attributed ... to the presence of the Eskimo skulls which had been obtained further north' (Keely and Davis, 1892, 195). Years later a crew-member of the expedition sent a story to the press that went into greater detail about this incident. He said that despite their best efforts, the expeditioners were unable to purchase skeletons from the Inughuit because of superstitions that, when taken from their homeland, 'the bones of such a transported Esquimaux are chewed up by snakes, and the spirit perishes beyond redemption'. Realising this, the men entertained the Inughuit with 'the mighty wonders of New York jack-knives' while others, the scientific crew, raided the grave of the mummified male whom they termed the 'chief'. The grave-robbing was supposedly concealed from the crew as they would have refused to sail 'with so ghostly a burden onboard'. Further collections of skulls at Herbert Island and Godhavn turned a bunk on the *Kite* into a 'regular graveyard' but stormy weather caused the crew to rebel. Forming a deputation they told Peary that there would be no luck 'until "something" was thrown overboard':

> The men at the wheel declared in turn that while in the act of steering some stronger hand than theirs was constantly turning the ship shorewards. One veteran helmsman ran us into a sand-bank. He said 'he couldn't help it, "somebody" seized the wheel and ran the ship aground'. The superstitious sailors were firmly persuaded that ghostly 'Huskies' – as they call the Esquimaux – were piloting the ship landwards to induce us to give up their chief's body for decent burial.

The next morning one of the sailors spotted a ghostly kayaker at sea who 'kept waving and beckoning with mysterious gestures' and hailed the ship 'with a mournful wail'. An officer on watch also reported seeing a procession of six Inuit walk the poop deck and vanish through the bulwark, following which six skulls were found to be missing from the storage bunk ('Arctic Body-snatching', *The Hampshire Telegraph*, 1898).

So what do these three mummy stories tell us? Firstly, it is clear from Grant's story and the account of the haunting of the *Kite* that sailors had certain beliefs about what constituted the proper behaviour of a sailor. The desire for a decent burial was an important part of these beliefs, something which body-snatching disrupted. This moral dimension found expression through the sailor's superstitions and the superstitions that were ascribed to them. On the *Pandora* in 1875, Horner was a figure of suspicion for the crew both for his relentless desire for animal and human remains and his status as a greenhorn who drove away the wind. Secondly, all three tales demonstrate considerable tension between the crew of Arctic expedition ships and the scientists onboard. Clearly one group had to manage navigation and had the ultimate responsibility for the safe passage of all, while the other group gathered data and specimens. Given that the scientific cargo already represented a point of fracture between the two types of expeditioner, the fact that skeletal remains were involved provided an opening for dissent and interpersonal conflict. The recognition of the spectral co-presence of Inughuit onboard the ship is another theme here and it is remarkable, in this regard, to note how closely Stock's fictional story echoes real events in Greenland. Whether a 'woman's shriek', 'eerie wail' or 'mournful wail', the repressed spectral woman shadows the expedition ship, demanding justice through the lament. The work of Arctic exploration is suddenly recognised as haunting when the mummy wakes up, when the moral dimension of scientific practice hits home, when this *something* becomes *somebody*. Mummies disturb because they are the actors of colonial haunting par excellence; rarely mentioned at all in narratives of Arctic exploration, they come from the dark depths beneath the icy surface. Frequently female, they attack western knowledge with all the force and power of repressed hatred and a desire for justice. These were feelings that were not simply limited to the pages of pulp fiction or memories of a maritime expedition but were forces that followed Peary around and continue to haunt Arctic exploration and science to this day.

Although the mummy of the 'chief' mentioned above was given to the Academy of Natural Sciences in Philadelphia ('Additions to the Museum', 1891, 510), Peary continued to supply human remains for Putnam and his colleague, the anthropologist Franz Boas, who both went on to work at the American Museum of Natural History in New York. Indeed disinterments, as well as other acts of biological and cultural appropriation, were normative practices for nineteenth-century explorers, anthropologists and antiquarians (see Garson and Read, 1892, 5; Roque, 2010).[7] Peary long coveted the large meteorites near Cape York known to the Inuit as 'the tent', 'the woman' and 'the dog'. These meteorites had provided the locals with iron for centuries and, although they were less dependent on this metal source by the 1890s, Peary's removal of them was considered something that threatened bad luck for the community. Before he left on his 1897 trip to take the largest meteorite – 'the tent' – Boas requested that Peary send him a live Inuk for ethnological study. Peary returned from Greenland with six people and the remains of others in 'five big barrels' (Herbert, 2012, 107). This human cargo caused a sensation when it arrived in New York and 30,000 people reportedly visited the ship, with admission by ticket only.

The Inughuit, who included one of Peary's hunters Qisuk and his seven-year-old son Minik (also known as Kishu and Menee), were kept in the basement of the museum until the authorities knew what to do with them. In the autumn heat of New York they quickly contracted tuberculosis and four had died by 1898, including Qisuk. Minik, now a sickly orphan, was determined to bury his father according to traditional ritual but the museum authorities staged a phoney funeral in the grounds in order to keep a hold of the corpse of one of 'Peary's Eskimos'. Minik's foster father William Wallace later confessed to the trick:

> While Minik stood sobbing by, the museum men lingered around watching the proceedings. The thing worked well. The boy never suspected, and when the grave was complete he made his mark on the north side of it. You see that is the Eskimo way. They think that the mark prevents the spirit of the dead coming back to haunt them, and the mark is always made between the home of the living and the resting place of the dead (qtd. in Harper, 1986, 93).

While Minik mourned over a mound of stones containing a log of wood, students at Bellevue hospital dissected his father's corpse. At this point he may have remembered how he and his father were photographed naked on arriving at Bellevue. These photographs later appeared in a short scientific study – *An Eskimo Brain* – along with an analysis and more photographs of Qisuk's dissected brain (Hrdlička, 1901). After dissection Qisuk's disarticulated skeleton was then sent to the museum where it was put on display. Some years later Minik learned of his deception from the newspapers and confronted the museum authorities, but his call for his father's burial was ignored (see Figure 5.6). His appeals to be brought back to Greenland were also ignored by Peary who, after selling the meteorites to the museum for the fabulous sum of $40,000, became firmly focused on his quest to reach the North Pole. As recounted by Kenn Harper in the biography *Give Me My Father's Body* (1986), Minik kept up the pressure on Peary with a public campaign until he was eventually given passage to Greenland in 1909.

The story of Qisuk and Minik reminds us that mummies and skeletons matter; just because people, alive or dead, are tagged as specimens they do not lose their capacity to resist objectification. Haunting therefore names resistance. It was not until 1993 that the American Museum of Natural History sent back four of the Inughuit bodies, including Qisuk, to Qaanaaq in Greenland for burial. The American actor Kevin Spacey was so enthralled by the story that he acquired the movie rights for Harper's narrative and wrote a foreword

Figure 5.6 'Why Arctic Explorer Peary's Neglected Eskimo wants to shoot him'. Source: *San Francisco Examiner*, Magazine supplement, 9 May 1909.

to a 2000 edition of *Give Me My Father's Body*. It is clear that the past does not simply vanish with the passage of time and indigenous people in the Arctic continue to think of Euro-American exploration and science in terms of violence, racism and injustice.

6
The spectral place of the Franklin expedition in contemporary culture

> *The most northern portion of our globe will not always be a terra incognita. When Arctic expeditions for the sake of the missing navigators have long ceased to be familiar to the public ear, and wars and rumours of wars have passed away, the interest in those geographical and other problems which were left unsolved in the year 1854 will again appear worthy of a great national effort for their solution; and then will arise in touching association, the memory of the men who, in pursuit of this knowledge, and in obedience to their country's command, first penetrated into the fastness of the north and were left there to their fate* (Franklin, 1854, 11).

Introduction

At the end of the twentieth century, several novels and other literary treatments were published that re-imagined the career of John Franklin and the tragic circumstances of the expedition under his leadership. As we have seen, the disappearance of this expedition, one of the most prominent episodes in the history of exploration, incited frenzied speculations about its fate throughout the Victorian era and beyond in which spiritualists and clairvoyants, as well as writers and investigators, endeavoured to imagine what really happened.

In this chapter I suggest that through the mystery of its disappearance, the Franklin expedition has come to occupy a spectral place in contemporary culture: as Margaret Atwood put it, 'Because Franklin was never really "found", he continues to live on as a haunting presence' (Atwood, 1995, 10). The impact of the loss of the *Terror* and *Erebus*, 129 men and subsequent revelations of cannibalism on Victorian society has been compared to that of the *Challenger* space shuttle disaster in late-twentieth-century society (Stein, 2007, 224), and the inheritance of the Franklin expedition represents a compelling ghost story that continues to haunt many modern Canadians. If the North has functioned in Canada as a grand national myth for the past century – the 'True North, Strong and Free' – an idea more than a location (see Grace, 2007), then this disaster occupies a central role in the way that the nation deals with its Arctic possessions.

My primary approach in this chapter is to highlight the spectral analogies between the attempts to discover the fate of the Franklin expedition in the 1850s, and the sudden eruption of novels, documentaries and archaeological projects between the 1980s and 2010s dealing with the demise of the expedition. Just as with the motif of the ghostly woman, in both cases supernatural tropes had a role in how western audiences confronted Arctic discourses and thereby invited varied speculations on, and spectralisations of, the mysterious disappearance of so many explorers. Recent decades have seen a boom in 'Franklin fiction' and many of these novels use spectral motifs in reconstructing the traumas of the disaster. For instance, *The Emigrant's Farewell* (2006) by Liam Browne brings out the explicitly supernatural aspects of the Franklin mystery through the dramatisations of Victorian clairvoyance, while at the heart of William T. Vollmann's *The Rifles* (1994) is the spectral presence of Franklin in Arctic history and in a present day that is irrevocably haunted by the past. In these novels writers use the haunting nature of the Franklin expedition as a vehicle of representation to express both the horrors of its disappearance and the present-day legacy of Victorian exploration. An examination of them locates the Franklin disaster at the heart of recent Arctic fiction and establishes the ghostly presence of Franklin in modern poetics as a reminder of how the disappearances of the past can act on the present in a manner that demands recurring articulation.

This book has so far focused on nineteenth-century history and culture: in this chapter I bring some of the themes I have discussed up to the present day, demonstrating their continuing significance. I therefore offer a fresh perspective on the death rituals surrounding the Franklin searches by tracking the huge upsurge in interest from the 1980s in locating Franklin bodies and relics. When in 2008 the Canadian federal government signalled its intention to sponsor a marine hunt for the sunken and lost Franklin ships, one of the main reasons given was the need to assert their claims to Arctic sovereignty in an unstable and tense circumpolar geopolitical environment. The wrecks of the *Erebus* and

Terror in this context were seen as important due to their historic associations with the development of Canada as a nation. One of the most important lynch-pins of Canadian Arctic sovereignty is the fact that most of the Arctic archipelago was mapped and explored by the British vessels searching for Franklin between 1848 and 1859. Canadian sovereignty in the Arctic, so the argument goes, rests upon its inheritance of British attempts to solve the mystery of Franklin's disappearance (Sutherland, 1985, vi). Discussing the searches for Franklin as ghost stories therefore involves discussions of haunted history, possession and geopolitical sovereignty.

Haunted history

Supernatural and gothic motifs have never been far from any mention of the Franklin expedition in narrative, whether in Franklin fiction or in the academic language used by professionals investigating the mystery. Indeed, long before the release of the famous photographs of the frozen bodies of John Torrington, William Braine and John Hartnell, dug up on Beechey Island in 1984, Margaret Atwood referred to the important symbolic exhumations taking place in Canada that could, she argued:

> be viewed as archaeology, necrophilia, or resurrection, depending on your viewpoint. The digging up of ancestors, calling up of ghosts, exposure of skeletons in the closet which are so evident in many cultural areas – the novel, of course, but also history and even economics – have numerous motivations, but one of them surely is a search for reassurance. We want to be sure that our ancestors, ghosts, and skeletons really are there, that as a culture we are not as flat lacking in resonance as we were once led to believe (Atwood, 1977, 100).

Alongside Atwood's many allusions to the ghostliness of Canadian cultural memory, the fascination with the Franklin expedition in Canadian literature especially can be seen in texts from Gwendolyn MacEwen's verse play *Terror and Erebus* (1987), to Mordecai Richler's novel *Solomon Gursky was Here* (1990), to David Solway's prize-winning poem *Franklin's Passage* (2003). In popular culture, the quest for the Northwest Passage has also inspired many documentaries and ballads (Stan Rogers's 'Northwest Passage' becoming an alternative Canadian national anthem by the 1990s), and tourists can now book a cruise along part of the

Northwest Passage, stopping off to view relics and burial sites associated with the expedition.[1] In Canadian politics, the Franklin expedition is frequently mobilised as a sign of Arctic inheritance. The visit of Joseph Bernier's *Arctic* expedition to Beechey Island in 1906 stands out in this regard, as does 'Project Franklin' of 1967, a centennial military exercise and search for Franklin relics (see Cavell, 2006; Wonders, 1968). In the wider world meanwhile, performances of obsession and possession have been at the heart of how this trauma was faced, going back to the very time of the disappearance. Narratives are prototypical in the discursive strategies that make up national ceremonies of possession and, in the case of Canada, Franklin represents both a territorial claim and a conduit for self-understanding.

As with many ghost stories, the spectralisation of the Franklin expedition can be traced to disturbed graves, in this case the three graves discovered on Beechey Island in 1850 – the first real evidence of the route of the expedition, and the first indications of its tragic demise. For over 150 years visitors to the graves have reported feeling haunted by the scene. Searching for Franklin in 1852, E.A. Inglefield visited the burial site and wrote of 'a huge bear' that was seen 'continually sitting on one of the graves keeping a silent vigil over the dead' (1853, 186). While describing his exhumations of the same graves in 1984, the anthropologist Owen Beattie wrote of 'a ghostly image taking shape through the ice – a frightening, shimmering face of death' (Beattie and Geiger, 1998, 115). The artist Toni Onley referred to Beechey Island as a 'frightening place, guarding the great Franklin mystery. The silence is deafening. The spirits of the dead are there, prisoners forever in the ice' (1989, 39); while, in a recent documentary, the historian Russell Potter describes Beechey Island as a 'haunting and haunted place' (*Arctic Passage*, 2006). These examples illustrate how consistently the sense of the supernatural has been used among the Franklin searchers from the mid-nineteenth century to the present day. In recent fiction, however, supernatural motifs have been employed not just rhetorically but in a very literal way. One of the main ways that people have imaginatively dealt with the spectral Franklin expedition has been through the theme of 'haunted history'.

Amid the contemporary thirst for information about the expedition, the first work of Franklin fiction was published – not surprisingly given the dearth of testimony – in the form of an 'authentic' narrative of a 'survivor' from the expedition. *The Extraordinary and All-absorbing Journal of Wm. N. Seldon* (1851) recounted the trek of three of Franklin's men south from the frozen ships to 'the most beautiful land in the world', where an eternal spring reigned and the local inhabitants seemed to speak a form of Spanish (18–19). This was a narrative firmly within the genre of the fantastic, one that drew upon theories of a polar paradise and the public speculation surrounding the fate of Franklin. Coming shortly after the Beechey Island discovery, Seldon's narrative concluded on a positive note:

> I am pleased to say that when we left Sir John Franklin, eight months ago, there was strong hopes of his soon getting free from the ice, and evidently a prospect of finding out the north-west pass. He was gleeful and happy, as was also his adventurous crew [sic throughout] (Seldon, 1851, 36).

Elsewhere, the discovery of the Beechey Island graves, rather paradoxically, inspired collective fantasies that the expedition had in fact thrived, and was more than likely trapped in the hypothetical 'Open Polar Sea' (see Sutherland, 1852; Kane, 1856).

This sense of the spectral presence of the Franklin expedition has been maintained in the large number of ballads, poems and novels produced since Seldon. Yet the 1980s witnessed a sudden upsurge in Franklin fictions that developed the notion that history itself was a haunted process and that the fate of Franklin was something still echoing in the contemporary world. The emergence of these cultural developments was aided by the success of Sten Nadolny's novel *The Discovery of Slowness* (1983), which retold the life of Franklin with the addition of a supposed trait of 'slowness', right up to the leaden entrance of the expedition into the Arctic. Alongside this novel, several forensic investigations carried out by the University of Alberta anthropologist Owen Beattie and others from 1981–6, which suggested that lead poisoning was a factor in the demise of the expedition, dramatically opened up the horrors of the expedition for speculative fiction – creating, in effect, the groundwork for a Franklin mythology.

The findings of these forensic investigations seeped into popular culture and literary criticism, with Atwood noting in a preface for a new edition of Beattie and John Geiger's account of the exhumations – *Frozen in Time* (2004) – that Geiger had actually read her Franklin-themed short story 'Age of Lead' and it had 'caused him to give further thought to lead as a factor in northern exploration and in unlucky nineteenth-century sea voyages in general' (Atwood, 2005, 375). Running alongside these developments was the emergence of postmodernism which, in its assertion that historical discourse is essentially speculative and conjectural, freed historical fiction from its mimetic shackles. As Herb Wylie argues, postmodernism gave novelists the opportunity to deal with the 'dark areas' of history for which there was little documentary evidence (2002, 18). So, aside from the innumerable historical and cultural studies of the Franklin expedition, since the 1990s it has become the subject of at least six historical novels (Edric, 1992; Flanagan, 2009; Fortier, 2008; O'Loughlin, 2016; Wilson, 1999; Edge, 2011), a comic novel (Richler, 1990), two fantasy/horror novels (Hopkins, 1997; Simmons, 2007), a spiritualist communiqué (Rule, 1998), and a speculative conspiracy theory (involving a 'Shaman Light' believed to cause vanishing and transportation across time) (Latta, 2001). I think it is important that in some of these examples, writers use the supernatural as a means of coming to terms with the legacy of 'the most famous vanisher of the Victorian era' (Macfarlane, 2003, 26).

I take my cue for my main argument from critiques of historicism and the recent emergence of various 'hauntologies' in postcolonial and critical discourses. In their note 'On the Theory of Ghosts', Horkheimer and Adorno (2002) posit the notion of a 'proper relationship' with the dead that involves a memory politics and a mourning that are not watered down. This would bring the living into a new intimacy with ghosts as co-occupants of life:

> Only when the horror of annihilation is raised fully into the consciousness are we placed in a proper relationship to the dead: that of unity with them, since we, like them, are the victims of the same conditions and of the same disappointed hope (2002, 178).

Jacques Derrida's more recent idea – in *Specters of Marx* – that learning to live involves speaking with and questioning the ghost – 'perhaps the hidden figure of all figures' (2006, 120) – also deconstructs any stable point for the individual subject in secular historical time. For Derrida – perhaps reflecting on Horkheimer and Adorno's tentative theory – 'this being-with specters would also be, not only but also, a *politics* of memory, of inheritance, and of generations' (Derrida, 2006, xix). The crucial thing is that the 'scholar' (which Derrida embodies in the figure of Horatio from *Hamlet*) must address the ghost and break down 'the sharp distinction between the real and the unreal, the actual and the inactual' through a hauntology – a theory of being for spectres/a spectral theory of being (Derrida, 2006, 11–12).

Dipesh Chakrabarty is one such Horatian scholar, arguing in *Provincializing Europe* (2000) that Eurocentric discourse is haunted by the others of subaltern modernity. South Asian political modernity suggests for him 'that historical time is not integral, that it is out of joint with itself': societies and spirits emerge in a coeval fashion and the European idea that 'the human is ontologically singular' is exposed in the occultism, violence and peripherality of Europe-in-the-world (2000, 16). The sign of the Franklin expedition, or what we could also term the 'Franklin text', fits in well to this contemporary critique of historicism. This is because it *was* the modern: a representative of imperial exploration culture travelling into absence. The 'History' of the Franklin expedition – its mystery and disappearance – continues to operate as a site of struggle: whether a bungler or tragic hero, the cultural space mapped out by contemporary Franklin fiction uncovers a contested 'spectral unconscious'.[2] In Franklin fiction this spectral unconscious emerges through a critique of secular historical time.

Spectral time

Liam Browne's *The Emigrant's Farewell* draws upon the idea of haunted histories by conjuring up the spectral presence of the Franklin expedition to explore the nature of loss in the present day. Indeed, Browne prefaces his novel with a quote by G.M. Trevelyan that exemplifies the sensibility that history haunts the present:

> The poetry of history lies in the quasi-miraculous fact that once, on this earth, on this familiar spot of ground, walked other men and women, as actual as we are today, thinking their own thoughts, swayed by their own passions, but now all gone, one generation vanishing after another, gone as utterly as we ourselves shall shortly be gone like ghosts at cockcrow (2006, i).

The Emigrant's Farewell is set in modern-day Derry city and deals with the tragic death of Joe O'Kane's only daughter Ciara in an accident. O'Kane, who is shut out of his attempts to grieve with his wife, turns to local history and finds, in the career of a personality from Victorian Londonderry, a way to work through his loss and put to bed the ghosts of the past. As a researcher in the local Heritage Centre, O'Kane is commissioned to write a study of William Coppin. O'Kane discovers the story that Coppin and his deceased daughter Weesy were directly involved in the searches for the Franklin expedition. As he delves deeper into this unusual history, O'Kane finds the spectral strands that connect his situation with the tragedies of Franklin and Coppin, thereby completing a journey about loss. History, Karl Marx once wrote, is not made as people please 'but under circumstances existing already, given and transmitted from the past. The traditions of all dead generations weighs like a nightmare on the brains of the living' (qtd. in Solomon ed., 1979, 54). O'Kane researches history but is also possessed by this history: the past assumes new status as something that eludes capture according to secular historical time.

Browne's novel echoes many aspects of Joan Didion's memoir of mourning, *The Year of Magical Thinking* (2005), and is also comparable to A.S. Byatt's *Possession: A Romance* (1990), not just in terms of the similar structure, which flits back and forth from the present to an historical past, but in that the strands that connect the past and the present in both novels are identified as spectral:

> He was intimate with the history of his city, its rings of growth, so that, as the poet's eye sees symbol and metaphor in the everyday, his eye saw distant battles, vanished buildings and old ghosts: the past and present overlapping (Browne, 2006, 9–10).

With the death of his daughter, O'Kane feels like 'an indeterminate ghost caught between two worlds', between a past and present that, on the one hand, should offer a fixed point for distinguishing the 'actual' and 'real' but, on the other, reinforces a feeling of alienation from a city that was like 'a ship trapped in polar ice' (Browne, 2006, 49, 46). Learning to live, as Derrida reminds us, must take place between life and death and only through '[talking] with or *about* some ghost. So it would be necessary to learn spirits' (2006, xviii). This identification between O'Kane and the ghosts of the Franklin expedition would seem a tenuously metaphorical one were it not for the real-life Weesy Coppin ghost story that allows Browne to meditate on the nature of loss from an Irish perspective. *The Emigrant's Farewell* is therefore a haunted history in more ways than one, as Browne uses this curious episode to reinforce the spectral presence of the Franklin expedition in the present.

As in Collins's and Dickens's *The Frozen Deep*, the use of clairvoyance as a means of expressing spiritual connections with loved ones informed the dynamics of Franklin fiction at the turn of the twenty-first century. Furthermore, just as during the period of the Franklin searches, the themes of emigration from home and hearth, of traumatic disaster and of an inability to mourn, make up the spectral poetics circulating around the Franklin expedition. Aware of this contiguity, Browne gives his protagonist the dual role of ghost and ghost-seer. On watching a home video of his daughter, O'Kane finds that he simply cannot accept her death:

> He heard her voice, by turns blithe and querulous. He could see the small mole on her left thigh. Her smile to the camcorder was really to him for she was too young to recognize its intermediary role. He did not understand how someone so extravagantly alive could be no more. This was no grey, insipid ghost, no half-glimpsed apparition, the child cavorting before him exhibited all the colours of the spectrum, emitted a high-voltage energy. Where had that life force gone? He could not believe that it had just flickered out and died (2006, 154).

Like William Coppin, whose daughter seemed to return as a ghost, and Jane Franklin, whose husband was spectralised, O'Kane finds that he begins an engagement with magical thinking that at first manifests itself in an attraction towards the explicitly supernatural phenomenon of clairvoyance but soon fosters the view that death, rather than the apparent spiritual limbo world of Weesy and Franklin, itself provides a means by which the bereaved can be comforted:

> There were occasions when he had comforted himself by likening Ciara's fate to a journey on an emigrant ship and his own to being the relative left behind at the quayside. She was dead to him, he told himself, for he would never see her again, and yet she still lived, existing in a place well beyond his comprehension from where he hoped she had not entirely forgotten her past (Browne, 2006, 273).

O'Kane imagines his daughter, like the three men buried in the Beechey Island graves, frozen in an Arctic landscape, dead but undecayed, gone but not forgotten. The temporal rupture of the spectral, its existence 'out of joint' with secular time, forces us to realise that 'haunting is historical … but it is not *dated*' (Derrida, 2006, 4). This notion that haunting is historical but not dated has opened the door to an upsurge in neo-Victorian fiction that plays upon the strangely spectral intimacies and reciprocities that exist between the nineteenth-century past and a present haunted by its legacies (see Arias and Pulham eds., 2010; Hadley, 2010). This spectralisation of the Victorian period creates multiple possibilities for framing dialogues between past and present. In line with this, Browne ties the Franklin expedition to other spectral traumas by adding to the mix the gothic memory of the Irish Famine, an imperial disaster contemporaneous with the Franklin expedition and a site of considerable haunting in Irish culture and the culture of the Irish diaspora (see Morash, 1995). As Browne writes:

> Unknown to each other, thousands of miles apart, had not Franklin's men and the Irish peasantry been linked by a shared sense of inevitability, by the terrifying realization that no-one could or would help them, that their past had become the totality of their lives (2006, 180).

Franklin possession

The Franklin expedition has functioned as a kind of spectral synecdoche since its disappearance, as a marker for the hopes and horrors of contemporary culture. I return again to Henry David Thoreau's meditation on the questions raised by the Franklin disappearance:

> Is not our own interior white on the chart? Is it … a North-West Passage around this continent, that we would find? … Is Franklin the only man who is lost, that his wife should be so earnest to find him? … Be rather the Mungo Park, the Lewis and Clarke and Frobisher, of your own streams and oceans; explore your own higher latitudes, – with shiploads of preserved meats to support you, if they be necessary; and pile the empty cans sky-high for a sign (1895, 343).

This metaphor of the Northwest Passage as a spiritual journey was appropriated by John Everett Millais for his symbolic painting 'The North West Passage' (1874) and by the Situationists during the 1950s (who had in turn taken it from Thomas de Quincey's 'psychogeographical' search for routes to find his spectral love Ann in *Confessions of an English Opium-eater* (1821). It is clear then that the geographical journey of the Franklin expedition was also understood along alternate levels of meaning, including that of the spiritual quest.

This was the perspective of Joseph Conrad who, as a boy, was enthralled by McClintock's narrative of his search for traces of the Franklin expedition, *The Voyage of the 'Fox' in the Arctic Seas* (1859). Conrad's *Heart of Darkness* (1889) utilises McClintock's narrative as an intertext and, in its opening pages, refers to explorers like Franklin as 'knights all, titled and untitled—the great knights-errant of the sea' (Conrad, 1902, 53). Indeed, although Franklin died before cannibalism occurred on the expedition, it is easy for the modern reader to see some of Franklin in the character of Kurtz from *Heart of Darkness*: both were representatives of the colonial order dispatched into an unmapped region where horror and savagery were imagined to reign. This is not due to interaction with the natives, however, but due to the very assumptions and delusions of the western mind where whiteness and darkness become confused and, ultimately, interrelated. By the time Kurtz is captured by Marlow he is crawling on all fours through and towards the darkness: this degeneration exemplifies the magnetism of what Conrad calls 'the fascination of the abomination' (Conrad, 1902, 57). Conrad's idea of 'geography militant' was inspired by the classic era of nineteenth-century exploration, but in *Heart of Darkness* it morphs into a kind of *Katabasis*, a journey to the underworld – a journey into a personal 'heart of darkness' (see Driver, 2001).

In *Heart of Darkness* Conrad was at pains to stress the multinational aspect of the imperial project, where the map of the world is variously painted red, blue, green, orange and purple, according to the colonial conquests of different European nations. The idea that Franklin was a shared loss and possession of the civilised world was more than a metaphor during the Victorian era.[3] At the end of the twentieth century, however, it was clear that the possession of Franklin now stood for a renewed expression of sovereignty in the Arctic. While searches for bones and bodies happened in the 1980s, the past three decades have witnessed an escalation in multinational attempts to locate Franklin's sunken vessels, the *Erebus* and *Terror*. As I will discuss later, the game-changing plan to locate the vessels, made by Robert Grenier for the International Polar Year (2007–08), was enthusiastically funded as a national priority by the Canadian government, eager to exert its authority in a geopolitical region of growing importance (Geiger, 2008). Unsuccessful searches took place in the region west of King William Island in the summers of 2008 and 2010–13, but this did not dampen enthusiasm among searchers and many people following the story in the media. Ironically, with global warming and melting ice almost making the Northwest Passage a navigable reality, the possession of the Franklin expedition assumed renewed symbolic status in a new era of Arctic activity.

Marx saw, in the revolutionary crisis of movement to the future, a paradoxical possession by the past: at such times, he wrote, people 'anxiously conjure up into their service the spirits of the past, assume their names, their battle cries, their costumes to enact a new historic scene in such time-honoured disguise and with such borrowed language' (1919, 9–10). The *presentness* of the past is the subtext of the ghost story, and this situation is echoed in the idea that Canada has somehow inherited the legacy (as well as the territory) of British exploration (Prentice, 2009–10, 94). With Canada's 'inheritance' of British exploration comes the trauma of disaster as well as the imperial framework of hegemony, for while nations need ghosts and unsettled remains in order to memorialise the past and move forward, they are also drawn backwards to repeat the injustices, strategies, and politics of the past in the name of sovereignty. History has the knack of being distant and uncomfortably proximate at the same time. Haunting, therefore, belongs to the structure of every hegemony, and the disjointed nature of the sign of Franklin (its 'radical untimeliness' (Derrida, 2006, 25)) makes it an especially spectral presence in modern Canadian culture.

The poet Earle Birney wrote in 1947 'it's only by our lack of ghosts / we're haunted' (1975, 296). Almost as a rejoinder to this famous statement, Atwood has written widely on the spectral presences haunting Canada, none more so than the ghost of Franklin. She particularly used the findings that some members of the Franklin expedition were afflicted with lead poisoning in her short story 'The Age of Lead' in which television footage of the Beechey Island exhumations is woven through memories of the peculiar romance between the characters Jane and Vincent, and the even more peculiar death of the latter. With the almost perfectly preserved face of John Torrington emerging from the Arctic permafrost, Atwood suggests that the malady that crippled the glorious Franklin expedition is analogous to the diseases that affect all people in the modern 'Age of Lead', such as AIDS, cancer, poverty or suicide: 'It was as if they had been weakened by some mysterious agent, a thing like colourless gas, scentless and invisible, so that any germ that happened along could invade their bodies, take them over' (Atwood, 1991, 172). Atwood's spectre of the Franklin expedition, with lead poisoning as a metaphor for mortality, is echoed in Vollmann's Franklin novel, *The Rifles* (1994), where Franklin is featured as a vital and spectral presence in a haunted landscape.

The idea of possession by the spirit of Franklin drives Vollmann's text, written as the 'sixth dream' in his series of symbolic histories of expeditions and settlements (1994). Perhaps the most striking things about *The Rifles* are the threads that link it to other examples of Franklin fiction. Like *The Emigrant's Farewell*, Vollmann's novel features two main historical loci that irresistibly overlap: the events of the Franklin expedition and the state of Inuit society in the 1980s and 90s. *The Rifles* recounts

Vollmann's present-day travels in the High Arctic with 'flashbacks' to the departure and events of the Franklin expedition and 'flashforwards' to Inuit settlements in the Arctic region 150 years later. If Browne's haunted history gave articulation to the three ghosts of Joe O'Kane, William Coppin and John Franklin, Vollmann's novel is multivocal in the extreme, radically de-centered by multiple voices from letters, memoirs, reports and dreams. Also, much like Atwood's musings on 'The Age of Lead' that unite the period of the Franklin expedition with the late-twentieth century, Vollmann similarly locates a pestilence at the heart of the civilising process, especially as it relates to the encounter between the native Inuit culture and the bumbling, destructive and cynical forces of western hegemony. Finally, echoing the recurring symbolic use of the Northwest Passage as a psychogeographical idea, Vollmann writes about finding the Northwest Passage through a lover's legs and about the anxiety of disorientation in a frozen world of ice and snow, a 'mirrorless house of mirrors' (1994, 3):

> you felt disconcerted; this center of things was not what you had expected. There was nothing wrong with anything, but you could not place yourself anywhere. Everything was below you and in the wrong direction. The wind blew numbingly cold, and a fog began to seep up onto the plain so that you saw that if you stayed there very long you would be well and truly lost, and then you might die, so you went back to your river while you could still locate it and descended tricked and bewildered (Vollman, 1994, 7).

In Vollmann's exploration, the figure of Franklin functions as a spectral synecdoche: this face from the 'mirrorless mirror' of the Arctic is used as a gateway into a haunted history that exposes the injustices of the past. Vollmann's text is morally oriented around the suffering of the High Arctic relocations, in which Inuit families from northern Quebec were sent far north to Resolute Bay and Grise Ford in the 1950s due to a mixture of welfare and sovereignty concerns (see Smith ed., 2014). This tale of dislocation, loss and hardship makes it another ghost story in the Franklin mythology for Vollmann, a continuity of the same 'lead-poisoning' introduced by the cultural arrogance of British explorers, only this time symbolised by the spread of rifles. Franklin, however, is just one of the spectral narrative's voices, or dreamers – there is also Captain Subzero, a modern-day Arctic tourist who feels that he is the 'supernatural twin' of Franklin (Vollmann, 1994, 137). This perception is maintained because he seems to be possessed by Franklin and is married to 'Jane', but is also in love with a modern-day Inuk named Reepah. Vollmann himself is also a significant character in the novel, but sometimes, like Captain Subzero, becomes conflated with/possessed by the identity of Franklin: 'Why did Franklin go north again? … Subzero believed that he did it for love, or perhaps to solve the world's problems (that is, Reepah's) … Of course Franklin himself, who is myself, never thought in those terms' (Vollman, 1994, 107). *The Rifles* is comprised, therefore, of overlapping Arctic ghost stories and the novel shows how the ghost of Franklin possesses and haunts the living, none more so than the petrol-sniffing Reepah who, the reader is informed by Vollmann, has or will commit suicide with her grandfather's shotgun. Even Franklin is haunted by his own doomed expedition. In *The Rifles* Vollmann reproduces the apocryphal incident when Jane Franklin was said to have laid a flag she was sewing over her husband as he slept one evening before the expedition departed: 'Don't you know that they lay the Union Jack over a corpse?' (Vollman, 1994, 110).

The Rifles shows the way that history comes to inhabit people's dreams and thereby exposes notions of a single identity in a particular place and time. Vollmann describes his primary world as a 'dream world' that co-exists with other worlds, none of which take precedence because all are 'equally unreal' (qtd. in McCaffrey, 1993, 9). The most telling moments of crossover between the world of Franklin and the modern dream world of Reepah-Subzero-Vollmann occur through the clairvoyance of love. For instance, Vollmann has Franklin chatting to his fellow Arctic explorer James Clark Ross about how he was obsessed with Reepah, 'who existed, of course, only to the extent that Sir John was Subzero; and precisely to that extent Sir John was beyond Sir James's ken—another sort of creature entirely, from another time!' (1994, 120). In his postmodern intermingling of past and present, of here and there, Vollmann suggests that ultimately it is Franklin as a 'supernatural twin', as a spectral presence entombed but unburied, that has caused the degeneration of Inuit culture. Indeed, Vollmann criticises the reader's fixation on the 'real' Franklin alone:

> you don't see what Reepah has to do with anything; you want to watch Mr Franklin die; and you will (you know me) … by Mr Franklin's time the rifles were spreading faster than smallpox and it was too late to be anything but a dupe; it was merely his weird death that brought us to the Arctic for good, first in the form of search parties, and then as traders, missionaries, police, resettlement administrators, our purpose long and sharp and spiraled like a narwhal horn; and the only reason that Mr Franklin is germane at

all has to do with a certain coincidence of rifles and starvation that I cannot put out of my mind (Vollmann, 1994, 123).

Dan Simmons's bestselling fantasy/horror novel, *The Terror* (2007), recently filmed for television by AMC in the USA, synthesises many of the themes I have discussed thus far and represents a striking confirmation of the spectral place that the Franklin expedition occupies. Instead of Franklin, Simmons focuses on the figure of Francis Crozier, Franklin's second-in-command. Crozier, having had his romantic advances rejected by Sophia Cracroft, jumped at the chance of polar service, despite, or even because of, premonitions of disaster and death. Such a biographical situation allows Crozier to emerge in *The Terror* as the most interesting character in the expedition, a psychological case study in polar melancholia and repressed sexuality.[4]

The plot of *The Terror* involves the destruction of the ice-bound expedition by a malevolent monster on the ice, variously imagined as a huge polar bear, an evil god, the spirit of Leviathan, and an evil Inuit spirit called the *Tuunbaq*. As it picks off the men one by one, the spectral monster soon comes to represent the metaphysical horror at the heart of humanity, literally represented in the descent of the expedition into cannibalism and brutality. Fitting seamlessly among other examples of Franklin fiction touched on above, Simmons's Crozier has clairvoyant abilities and can see the ships searching for his expedition in 1848; he also receives visions of the Fox sisters and their rappings in New York State in the same year. As the last man alive following the massacres by the monster and by cannibals among his crew, Crozier is nursed back to health by a clairvoyant Inuk with whom he falls in love. Echoing Vollmann's condemnation of the Franklin ghost-hunt as heralding the end for Inuit culture, Simmons has this psychic couple foresee a future in which westerners will invade the Arctic causing its ice to melt and its people to degenerate.

The Terror reacts to the huge blanks in the historical narrative in a hyperactive manner, combining speculation with supernatural sensationalism. As John Clute (2007) noted in his review of Simmons's novel:

> there is no way to understand Franklin's insane blundering assault against the arctic ice north of mainland Canada, nor the 'supernatural' intensity of the experience of dying there of cold at the top of the world, as a simple narrative whose terminus is mundanely inevitable. The story of the Franklin expedition is not inherently a realistic story — not a tale that can plausibly be told within the framework of a conventional mimetic narrative process.

Searching for Franklin

In 1833 the emigrant Catharine Parr Traill wrote that Canada was a 'too matter-of-fact country' for ghosts to visit (1839, 153) while her sister Susanna Moodie mentioned the settler belief that the country was 'too new for ghosts' (1852, II, 13) (on the gothic implications of these quotes see Sugars and Turcotte, 2009; Goldman, 2006, 3–35). Such pronouncements foregrounded a cultural imagination that laid emphasis on taming and domesticating the Canadian landscape, seen as wild and neglected, as part of the colonial logic of expansion. A survey of early Canadian poetry demonstrates the dominance of pastoral and neoclassical conventions of landscape and a relationship with the landscape predicated on economic progressivism and development (Mazoff, 1995). In a context in which Canada as a settler-nation was desperately seeking to expand territorially and demographically, this banishing of ghosts and battle against the malevolent wilderness were central components of the 'agrarian myth' of nationhood. This rhetoric of nation-building through the agricultural development of the western prairies was the dominant Canadian myth of the nineteenth century, not the lure of the North (Cavell, 2002). While the quest to traverse the Northwest Passage through the Arctic was a recurring imperial objective, in 1865 Matthew Macfie, a resident in Vancouver Island, penned an article in *The Fortnightly Review* pointing out that a land route and inter-oceanic railway across Canada would have much more commercial value than any maritime passage and so might become the 'true' Northwest Passage (see Cavell, 2002, 372). Indeed, the transfer of the Arctic territories from Britain to Canada in 1880 did not elicit much enthusiasm from Canadian authorities who did not know what to do with the vast and largely unknown territories they were receiving (Smith, 1961, 69).

By the early twentieth century, with the East-West axis achieved, and the political geography of Canada becoming more rationalised, policy makers moved beyond a purely sublime reading of Arctic landscape and began to take seriously voices that called for the political integration and economic and social development of the North, in accordance with a new imagined community encapsulated in the refrain 'True North Strong and Free'. When, over a century after Traill, Birney reformulated Canada's canniness by suggesting that 'it's only by our lack of ghosts / we're haunted' (1975, 296), a whole new set of 'ideas of the north' gave the lie to Canadian perceptions of immunity from ghosts – for the ghosts of the Northwest Passage returned again, but this time to a Canada in which the Arctic archipelago, and the newly created territory of Nunavut, occupied a core rather than peripheral location in national politics and mythology.

Building upon long-standing tradition, nineteenth-century British and Euro-Canadian explorers emphasised the harshness, malevolence and challenging nature of the northern landscape. Running alongside this myth was the idea of wilderness sublime – the importation of sublime and picturesque conventions into textual and visual representation – to such an extent that some expeditions collapsed or were retarded because of a decision-making process fundamentally based on aesthetics (Sandlos, 2001, 7). The boreal forest featured in this imaginary as a repository of fears that had to be challenged and faced down if northern progress was to be made. Susanna Moodie found it difficult, nonetheless, to shake off her 'foolish dread' of the woods: 'The cracking of an old bough, or the hooting of an owl, was enough to fill me with alarm, and try my strength in a precipitate flight' (1852, II, 22). Traill's *The Backwoods of Canada* contains a striking illustration of a road-track carved through a thick pine forest, leading to a farm that she named 'Glen Morrison' 'partly from the remembrance of the lovely Glen Morrison of the Highlands, and partly because it was the name of the settler that owned the spot' (1839, 111): here possession and the picturesque unite in a familiar process of colonial legitimacy.

One factor that played a role in the co-emergence of national identities and the idea of a 'northern gothic' was the rhetoric of an Arctic lure which, becoming engrained from the early twentieth century on, emphasised the friendly, floral and soulful nature of the north to Canadian audiences. The Manitoba-born explorer Vilhjalmur Stefansson was a pivotal figure in this context, predicting great northern futures for Canada in writings such as *The Friendly Arctic* (1921) and *The Northward Course of Empire* (1922). In 1907 the poet Robert Service referred to the 'whisper on the night-wind' and the call of the Wild (1907b, 32), while soon after, the author Ernest Thompson Seton tied a positive image of the north to predictions of its colonisation and development by white southerners (1920, 67; see also Mitcham, 1975). Meanwhile the Group of Seven artist and theosophist Lawren Harris imagined a Canada 'on the fringe of the great North and its living whiteness, its loneliness and replenishment, its resignation and release, its call and answer – its cleansing rhythms' (qtd. in Larisey, 1993, 62). The strength of these 'calls of the Arctic', and their presence in narratives of tourism and self-development (Davis, 1981), feeds into a contemporary climate in which Canada's unconscious is imagined to lie due north.

A scene from the final episode of the Canadian television series *Due South* demonstrates how the Franklin expedition has come to represent a kind of contemporary ghost story in popular culture. Produced from 1994–9, the series centred on the crime-fighting adventures of a Canadian Mountie in Chicago. As a show which, of necessity, used Canadian stereotypes and themes it is not surprising to find a reference to the Franklin expedition, but the extent to which it to hits upon many of the spectral strands of the story is revealing. The scene takes place by a campfire in the Yukon and begins when Kowalski asks Fraser, the Mountie, a question:

> 'Fraser, you ever get the feeling that you're lost?'
> 'No, a quick look to the stars or the sun and you can always find your location'.
> 'No, I don't mean where you are, I mean who you are'.
> 'Oh [tune of Stan Rogers's 'Northwest Passage' begins]. When I first came to Chicago I felt as though I were from another planet'.
> 'Which you are'.
> 'Which I have come to accept. Everything was unknown and at times it was frightening. And I felt as though I was an explorer – an urban explorer'.
> 'Urban explorer ... '
> 'I remember one time we were on a stakeout and I was trying to explain the sense of otherworldliness to the detectives. I was telling them the story of Sir John Franklin who set out to discover the Northwest Passage. But I realised as I was telling the story that they'd all fallen a ... ' [Kowalski is asleep] (*Due South*, 1999).

First we have the rhetorical connection between being lost in a geographical way and being lost in a psychological way. This is an important area in Canadian criticism, with Atwood pointing out the theme of the 'will to lose' in literature and Northrop Frye (1971) declining to ask Kowalski's question of himself, 'Who am I?', and instead asking the question of his country, 'Where is here?' (1971, 220). Yet Fraser never gets the feeling he is lost, unlike his American counterpart: 'A quick look to the stars or the sun and you can always find your location', he says. Despite this native assurance, he uses an unstable spatial metaphor to describe his reverse, southern expedition, in which the Canadian Mountie is in the position of the naïve explorer, this time an urban explorer, seeking his own Northwest Passage. The mention of trying to explain a 'sense of otherworldliness' through the story of John Franklin highlights the status of this event as a myth, or a haunted history. The realities of mass death are put aside as the spiritual power that the polar explorer has in western culture comes to the fore. Franklin is remembered here positively, the bedtime story of the expedition is the story of this man, but it is a ghost story, slightly eerie but ultimately heart-warming. As seen in this example, therefore, the Franklin expedition continues to function as a kind of spectral synecdoche.

If spectres haunt the body politic through their clamour for justice and recognition, recent Canadian criticism suggests that one should look at the level of hegemony and the uncanniness of the nation to begin the project of conversing with the past (see Edwards, 2005; Goldman and Saul, 2006; Kertzer, 1998). A constant refrain among settlers and visitors to Canada during the colonial era was that it was a new land, a state of nature lacking any previous civilised human labour and, indeed, lacking a human past. As Traill put it: 'its volume of history is yet a blank' (1839, 155). Therefore one of the projects of Canadian writers from the 1960s was the effort to 'haunt' Canada by populating it with ghosts, monsters and the dead who do not die, thereby destabilising the colonial logic of *terra nullis*. It is no coincidence then that the Franklin mythology started to be strongly associated by writers and politicians with Canadian identity from the mid-twentieth century on, when there was a growing realisation of the spectral history of Canada – its ghostly indigenous peoples, minorities and immigrants. Sherrill Grace argues that, by the last quarter of the twentieth century, Franklin:

> was firmly ensconced as a Canadian myth, a Canadian place name, and a Canadian victim. At times, I think, Canadians have delighted in the image of this arrogant, foolish old Brit trapped in *our* Arctic ice: the telling of Franklin can sometimes be a Canadian revenge tragedy (2002, 223).

And so, since the 1970s, many revisionist Canadian critics, historians and writers have viewed Franklin in a largely negative light (Berton, 1988; MacLaren, 1984b; Wiebe, 1995).

So why did Canada take possession of the Franklin expedition and how does it haunt the nation? Atwood has suggested 'it's because – as they say in china shops – if you break it, you own it. Canada's North broke Franklin, a fact that appears to have conferred an ownership title of sorts' (2005, 381). Whether or not this is the case, the fact is that Canada actually has an ownership of sorts. In light of increasing Canadian federal attention on the geopolitics of the Northwest Passage and North Pole, and the huge international interest surrounding the material culture of the Franklin expedition, with many private expeditions mapping the seabed, a Memorandum of Understanding was signed in 1997. By this Great Britain assigned custody and control of the shipwrecks *Terror* and *Erebus* to Canada, thus forming a central plank of Canada's new assertive cultural and heritage policy in the region. The designations of Franklin as a Canadian Person of National Significance in 1945, and of the shipwrecks as National Historic Sites in 1992 ('Erebus and Terror National Historic Site of Canada'), can be read as turning Franklin from a ghost into an ancestor who lived again in Canadian modernity, but this disguised the inherently ghostly nature of the situation: Franklin is a missing, placeless body and, until very recently, the protected sites of the *Terror* and *Erebus* were unlocated.

The sense of an absent presence also represents a repetition of the discourses in place during the searches for Franklin in the 1850s when the men were imagined to be locked up in a 'Polar dungeon' (Parsons, 1857, 70) or lodged in an 'adamantine prison', 'chained up by the Polar Spirit' (qtd. in Simmonds, 1852, 196) waiting for 'succour' (Bray, 1992, 100). Seeking Franklin in this context was variously imagined as a 'crusade' (Kane, 1856, I, 393), a 'glorious mission ... a *great national duty* [that] ranked amongst the noblest efforts in the cause of humanity any nation ever engaged in' (McClintock, 1859, 11), and a 'holy cause' (McClintock, 1859, xix). Following the return of McClintock, *The Times* – a newspaper sceptical of polar exploration – picked up on this language, derisively noting 'there can be no longer those sad wailings from an imaginary Tintagel to persuade the credulous that an ARTHUR still lives' (Editorial, *The Times*, 23 September 1859). The language in contemporary Canadian cultural policy is less melodramatic, preferring to emphasise the potential of recovering the shipwrecks for heritage, but its possession of the Franklin expedition merely reinforces the spectrality of Arctic history.

While there are not multiple claimants for the bodies and material culture of the Franklin expedition, the Northwest Passage and the North Pole region are different stories. In those cases the detritus of a British imperial disaster have become symbolic of circumpolar sovereignty. The main issue in current Canadian Arctic policy is, as it was for the British over 150 years ago, the Northwest Passage, a 7000 kilometre shorter route between Europe and Asia. Due to the effects of global warming and climate change many parts of this route will become ice-free in the coming decades, although scientists differ as to how long this process will take. While, aside from a minor squabble with Denmark over Hans Island, there is no dispute regarding Canada's territorial claims, for decades there has been a legal impasse between the United States and Canada as to whether this body of water represents an international strait in Canadian territory, like the Strait of Magellan, or whether it represents Canada's internal waters (Charron, 2005–06).

The dispute regarding the Lomonosov Ridge, which covers the central floor of the Arctic Ocean and may contain one quarter of the world's oil and gas reserves, has complicated Arctic relations between Denmark, Norway, Canada, Russia and the United States. Russia claimed this area as an extension of their continental landmass in 2001 and in 2007 planted a rust-proof flag in an assertive gesture: this prompted Canada's then Foreign Affairs Minister Peter Mackay to comment. 'You can't go around the world these days dropping flags somewhere. This isn't the 14th or 15th Century. They're fooling themselves' (qtd. in Reynolds, 2008). Yet despite this criticism from a Canadian politician, people in the Arctic would be forgiven for thinking that they are indeed witnessing a traditional territorial dispute involving claims and counter-claims, with hydrographers and scientists from the circumpolar nations submitting reports to the United Nations Convention on the Law of the Sea.

While a Department of Foreign Affairs report in 2000 noted a decline in public concern about Arctic sovereignty (Huebert, 2001, 88), the Canadian Conservative Party made it a centrepiece of their 2008 re-election campaign with Prime Minister Stephen Harper taking on board a 'use it or lose it' approach to the region. Harper promised to fund a new Coast Guard icebreaker for the region and committed to purchasing 65 Lockheed Martin F-35 fighter jets to replace the Cold War fleet, although both objectives have since been mired in scandal and long-term delays. In a more tangible annual exercise, Harper visited the Arctic every summer between 2007 and 2015 to witness military exercises, open new facilities and discuss resource development. This happened in a context in which there were over 50 incidents between 2007–10 of Russian war planes approaching North American airspace in a show of force (although under the Open Skies treaty Russia and Canada routinely send unarmed observation flights into each other's airspace). A statement from the Department of Foreign Affairs and International Trade declared: 'The Arctic is fundamental to Canada's national identity', it is also 'embedded in Canadian history and culture, and in the Canadian soul. The Arctic also represents tremendous potential for Canada's future' ('Statement on Canada's Arctic Foreign Policy'). With the indigenous communities of the North now held up as standard bearers of Canadian-ness, the Conservative government argued that its Arctic sovereignty was founded on past inhabitants and explorers. Indeed, as then Environment Minister

Jim Prentice declared: 'Policy that is designed to shape the future ... must have a firm footing in the past' (2009–10, 94).

This acute concern with the overlap of past and present came across most clearly when the wreck of HMS *Investigator* was precisely located and imaged by Parks Canada in July 2010. In a column praising the team involved – three southern Canadians and an Inuk – Prentice drew strong rhetorical analogies between the Victorian explorers who sought the Northwest Passage and this 'typically Canadian' archaeological team – a team he believed was representative of modern, dynamic, multi-ethnic Canada:

> This group reflects the best of today's Canada: young, well-educated, committed and passionate about our responsibilities in the Arctic and about who we are as a country. All that was reflected in their relentless determination – and optimism – in the face of drudgery, icy water and harsh weather. (Personally, I also will remember their voracious appetites – as I saw them hunched in a wind-blown kitchen tent, wolfing down macaroni, clearly invigorated by the prospect of success) (2010).

Here, the appeal to traditional discursive formations of the Arctic (masculine struggle, heroism) discloses the neo-colonial underpinning of aspects of Canadian Arctic policy: Prentice engaged in an exercise of 'writing the nation' by highlighting the Inuk's place among a growing circle of national subjects (see Bhabha, 1994). Reflecting this ambivalence towards indigenous actors in Arctic policy, in August 2007 Harper hailed the end of the 'paternalistic federal policies of the past so Northerners have more control over their own economic and political destiny' (2007b) while, just two days later, he reinscribed a (southern) romantic, nationalist and patriarchal image of the Arctic (2007a). Fundamentally, Prentice's modern, ultra-Canadian, Franklin explorers highlighted the basic paradox of (political) fantasy: the subject's presence at the very act of its own conception (Žižek, 1991, 197). This discloses a strategy that would fix Canadian national time-space by rebranding indigenous actors as both historical objects (giving them Arctic authority) and as (perennial) national subjects, 'as living principles of contemporaneity' (Bhabha, 1994, 145).

The history of British Arctic exploration forms an integral part of this Arctic strategy, a fact reflected in the financial and political investments in Arctic conservation and the messy interweaving of political and conservation concerns. A prime example of this was the search and salvage of the HMS *Breadalbane* shipwreck near Beechey Island in 1980. This expedition was jointly funded by governmental and private agencies and was primarily intended to demonstrate the technical capacity of Canadian divers to operate below the ice. It was 'never intended as having primarily archaeological aims' and Canadian archaeologists were only invited to participate after the shipwreck was located (MacInnis, 1985, 182). The secondary aim of the expedition was actually to practise for a future attempted recovery of the Franklin ships. This ambition was taken up some years ago by Parks Canada, the national heritage agency, which led several federal missions to locate the Franklin shipwrecks in collaboration with the government of Nunavut between 2008 and 2016. The challenge for Parks Canada since its establishment has been to fit things that pre-dated Confederation in 1867 into a national narrative and, while this has proved problematic in the heritage and historic sites of First Nations and aboriginal communities, in the case of Franklin, heritage has been successfully frozen in deference to a linear version of history. Just as in the search for the *Breadalbane*, Parks Canada's quest for the Franklin shipwrecks was as much a search for a conclusive historical narrative as it was for any archaeological or heritage aims.

As part of its 'Guidelines for Evaluating Shipwrecks of National Historical Significance', Parks Canada assigns the *Terror* and *Erebus* a 'symbolic' status:

> The symbolic aspect that may be recognized in a shipwreck can be variable. It might be spiritual or religious, aesthetic or educational in nature. It might be manifested by the impact of a given event (shipwreck, rescue, salvage, creation of folklore) on a cultural community. Such impact may have arisen at the time of a wreck or even long after it. Symbolic value might also lie in the significance of the ship's construction and career, or even the human tragedy associated with it, as kept alive in tradition. For instance, such value might be attributed to a ship which is a war memorial, exploration ships, or other vessels with strong evocative power (e.g. the *Terror* and *Erebus*, *Bluenose*, *Marco Polo*, *Empress of Ireland*) ('Guidelines').

The type of language used by the federal authorities in their justification for the Franklin searches serves to reinforce the contention that the lure of heritage and conservation threatens to eclipse history by offering personal immediacy and mythologies that support national narratives. This federal push saw other private (and non-national) search expeditions frozen out and refused archaeological permits. In one case an application was refused on the grounds that it did not consult with the local Inuit communities ('Not Looking for Franklin's Ships', 2009). Just as the 2010 search for *Investigator* also had the research aim of evaluating the impact that naval debris and equipment had upon the Inuvialuit people, so too the justifications for the search for the Franklin shipwrecks always contained references to the validation of historical Inuit oral testimony alongside the aim of reasserting sovereignty. Such strategies, as well as the employment of Inuit as Canadian Rangers, seek to reinforce the idea of the Arctic as an indigenous, homeland territory of Canada (Williams, 2010).

Conclusion

In the summer of 2010, a six-man survey team on board a Canadian Coast Guard Vessel with 50 crew members searched for shipwrecks in the Arctic. The lead scientist on the expedition, marine archaeologist Ryan Harris, pointed to the ghostliness of the subject when he said that the disappearance of the Franklin expedition was for Canadians 'a Victorian gothic horror story that played out across the Arctic' (qtd. in MacDonald, 2010). Harris also stated that the *Investigator* wreck was, in anthropological terms, 'the most important shipwreck in history', while, along with Minister Prentice, he declared it to be fundamental to Arctic sovereignty (qtd. in Griffiths, 2010). The sedimentation of Arctic landscapes within layers of gothic tradition and heritage represents a significant problem for cultural policy-makers in Nunavut. Shifts have taken place recently in the arts that have complicated the Franklin myth and old romantic ideas of the north in the light of Inuit heritage and culture (see Grace, 2010).

In this context why should Nunavummiut participate in an uncomplicated celebration of the Franklin expedition as a symbol of Canadian Arctic sovereignty? Echoing and extending this train of thought, Adriana Craciun notes that the search for the shipwrecks 'has unexamined connections to pressing issues in Arctic sovereignty, heritage and energy exploration, which will play a role in any commemorative effort' (2012, 4). Following the dramatic locations of the *Erebus* and *Terror* in recent years, pressure will grow for differentiation or reconciliation between the ghost-seeing of particular geopolitical strategies and emergent regional economies, identities and historiographies. Questions remain to be answered about what impacts new commemorations and celebrations of Franklin heritage will have on public discourse in Canada, especially in relation to the Northwest Passage, potential energy exploitation in the area where the ships were found and the role of the Conservative Party in the interpretation of colonial history.

The great mystery of the Franklin expedition continues to be the fact that while certain facts about its demise are well-known (where and when the ships went, where the men died, even what killed some of them), the details remain remarkably sketchy. Speculations that draw upon the supernatural and the gothic are an irresistible response to this vacuum of information as contemporary writers merely build on a nineteenth-century framework that encoded the Franklin mystery with the spectral from the moment of its disappearance into the unknown.[5] In the appearance and reappearance of themes such as haunted history, clairvoyance and love, and the possession of or by bodies across an intersected historical time period, Franklin discourses similarly reveal consistent tableaux of expression. Indeed, in one of the most recent poetic treatments of the Franklin expedition, David Solway constructed a poem that amalgamated – in a consciously 'cannibalistic' manner – thoughts about Franklin and thoughts about thoughts about Franklin (citing Nadolny, Latta, and Beattie, and so on).

In the years since the Franklin expedition was originally lost to linear historical narrative, its spectral presence was manifested across a wide spectrum of cultural discourses. Where for Canada the past was a foreign country, in the next decade Victorian history will increasingly become a strategic weapon as British corpses and ships along the Northwest Passage become positioned and curated as 'national bodies' (Hill, 2008) and as ghosts of Canada past. While the Canadian federal authorities may be at risk of 'forgetting to remember' by calling back into existence the violent sign of imperialism (Bhabha, 1994, 160) in the context of geopolitical strategising and energy exploitation, the ghost stories of the Franklin expedition continue to haunt audiences, thereby opening up alternative modes of knowing and engaging with the past.

One such alternative came from the Inuit ability to retain 'the memory of important and strange incidents' relating to sixteenth-century British explorers, a kind of trans-historical oral archive that was celebrated by Charles Francis Hall (1864, vii). Elsewhere in *The Rifles* Vollmann replaced the act of historical sequencing with a series of ruptures, reflecting the inability of western historicism to find truth in the past. In contrast to the end-driven discourse of the Franklin searches, these authors recognise a Franklin-time 'out of joint', a temporality that haunts rather than ends. Haunting, Avery F. Gordon writes, 'is a part of our social world, and understanding it is essential to grasping the nature of our society' (1997, 27), but this necessitates a recognition of the 'double-time' of history and the nation (Bhabha, 1994, 144), an acknowledgement that just as the future is uncertain, so too the past is a complex site of spectral ruptures.

Afterword
The discoveries of the *Erebus* and *Terror*

> *On King William Island, Inuit used to say that if you found a white man's grave, you'd never find it a second time – because it had ghosts around it* (Eber, 2008, 134).

On 9 September 2014, Parks Canada announced that the multi-agency Franklin search expedition it was leading that year had located a well-preserved shipwreck, later identified as the *Erebus*. This discovery of Franklin's own ship made headlines across the world and gave Prime Minister Harper an opportunity to showcase a key success in his northern vision to national and international audiences. Given the political and cultural capital invested in the searches, it was no surprise that government spokespeople weren't shy in tethering the ship to a geopolitical narrative about Canada's place in the Arctic. In promoting the find, Harper drew direct analogies between the British Arctic explorers of the nineteenth century and the 'heroes' of 2014 who had located the *Erebus* and participated in Canada's assertion of Arctic sovereignty. Harper, his wife Laureen, an aide named Jeremy Hunt, and over two hundred other members or friends of the expedition even received the 'Erebus Medal', specially commissioned by the Royal Canadian Geographical Society to commemorate the discovery (the Harpers were made Honorary Fellows of the RCGS in 2013).

The euphoria surrounding the event allowed Harper, Parks Canada and the RCGS to flood the media with a particular set of assumptions about Arctic exploration (as heroic mapping) and the role of Inuit communities in its commemoration (as trusted informants). However, despite the location of the *Erebus*, the ghostliness of this National Historic Site was not exorcised in the flash of underwater cameras and press conferences. Rather, enlisted in a story of Canadian nationalism, Franklin's reappeared ship was made to act out a role in disappearing other stories that were much less comfortable for the expeditioners of 2014.

In this book I have highlighted the roles of ghosts and dreams in some of the narratives, experiences and images associated with the Northwest Passage quests of the nineteenth century. Throughout I have been keen to complicate the figure of the British explorer, to stress the utter strangeness of men navigating, mapping and overwintering in the Arctic. I have discussed the spectre of women and shown how the idea of a female presence in the Arctic revealed the intimate and emotional forces that travelled between the Arctic and Britain during the Victorian period. This strategy of questioning accepted ideas of what exploration was, and of holding up a cultural-historical mirror to explorers, would probably have made as little sense to Franklin in 1845 as it would to Harper in 2014. This is because both believed they were involved in disinterested projects of mapping out *terrae incognitae*. There was little awareness in the press releases of 2014 that the practices of exploration should be analysed – that they were linked to colonialism, gender discrimination and historical injustice, or that they were part of the long history of anthropogenic climate change. There was no feeling of how odd it was for the voices of Victorian expeditioners to ring out in pidgin Inuktitut:

> We are in search of two English ships / Which have been five years in the ice / Have you heard anything of such ships? / Make it known among all the Eskimós or Innuít / That the Queen of England will give a large reward / To any of the Innuít who will bring news of them / Should you meet any white men / Treat them kindly, and you shall be rewarded (*Eskimaux and English Vocabulary, for the Use of the Arctic Expedition*, 1850, 105).

Rather, Harper's version of Franklin harked back to the tragic hero model that dominated Canadian culture before cultural and political ties with Britain loosened in the mid-twentieth century. In this model, the Euro-American mapping of the Arctic was normal and heroic, not strange and complicated, and the cultural impact of explorers on indigenous peoples almost totally ignored. Although revisionist and postcolonial writers have deployed the 'bumbling imperialist' image of Franklin since the 1970s (see Cavell, 2007), Harper used an older and uncritical version of Franklin because he needed an historical story (minus allusions to cannibalism and disaster) that prefaced the kind of tradition he wanted to invent for Canada:

> As I've said before, Sir John's exploration and discovery of parts of Canada's North are an important part of our history and have contributed to Canada becoming the wonderful country we enjoy today. The search for the fabled Northwest Passage is something that Canadians have celebrated in stories and songs for generations — it's even the subject of the Stan Rogers song that we consider our 'unofficial national anthem' — because that story is the story of Canada. Just look at the list of explorers who tried even before Sir John: Cabot, Frobisher, Davis, Cartier, Hudson, La Salle, Cook, Vancouver, MacKenzie. These are the giants of our history, and the story of the search for the Northwest Passage is essentially the history of Canada's North. The Franklin expedition is part of that broader story — the most tragic, and most mysterious part, to be sure. For almost 200 years Canadians — not just Canadians, people around the world — have wondered what happened to the Franklin expedition. Now that we've found the first of the two ships we can begin unlocking the mystery of what happened to them (qtd. in Geiger 2014).

Finding Franklin here contributes to settling the nation – even at the cost of silencing other, unsettling, voices and stories.

The discovery of the *Erebus* came after years of public controversy about the cost and aims of the searches. The 2012 searches by Parks Canada were particularly attacked by online commentators as red herrings, designed to distract people from the travails of the government. Some of the most cutting criticisms of Harper's prioritisation of the Franklin searches – in the midst of what was a period of economic austerity – came in the letters and comments sections of newspaper articles and op-eds about the quest: why was the government wasting money in the Arctic when jobs were being lost elsewhere? Why was the Franklin search being prioritised over women's refuges, social programmes for indigenous communities, and scientific research? Why should we be looking for dead British explorers? Why was the Canadian Broadcasting Corporation – a state-sponsored corporation – paid by Parks Canada to cover its searches? Strangest of all, why was Parks Canada facing job cuts and reduced budgets nationally, but was feted and bankrolled for its particular endeavours around King William Island? Or, as one commentator put it: 'Cash for sunken junk. Great. And if they find them, more cash to resurrect them, more cash to find a home for them, more cash to look after them. The Inuit don't care about a failed white mans [sic] expedition, in fact, neither do white men' ('Monkeewerks' qtd. in Baluja, 2012).

By the time the sixth expedition commenced in 2014 some of the commentary focused on the government's refusal to establish an inquiry to investigate the circumstances behind the murder and disappearance of over 1000 aboriginal women since 1980. Even after the discovery of the *Erebus*, angry letter-writers contrasted Harper's obsession with a Victorian mystery with an apparent lack of curiosity about a contemporary one ('Solving the Franklin Expedition Mystery', *The Star*, 2014). Meanwhile, the archaeologist Patricia Sutherland, whose work focuses on evidence of Norse presence on Baffin Island around 1000 AD, believes she was dismissed from her position in the Canadian Museum of Civilisation (now re-branded as the Museum of Canadian History) because her research and views were out of step with the government's view of Arctic history. In contrast to the rich pre-Columbian histories of the Arctic, the Franklin expedition reflects, Sutherland noted, 'the government's interest in sovereignty, the military, and Canada's historical ties to Britain' ('A Crucible That May Change the Way we See Canada's North', CBC Radio).

If cannibalism, disaster and climate change are other obvious themes downplayed in the story of the Franklin expedition advanced by Harper and Parks Canada, two themes that were drawn out were Canada's technological power over the North and the value of Inuit oral records. In a speech to the Royal Canadian Geographical Society in March 2015, Harper drew lines of connection between Franklin as a heroic seeker of knowledge, and the team of researchers, hydrographers, archaeologists, pilots and for-profit companies that assisted in the location of the *Erebus*. Indeed Harper highlighted this public–private aspect of the expedition as a metaphor for modern Canada. The modern Franklin searches always had the secondary aims of mapping the sea bed and testing the Royal Canadian Navy's ability to operate in the Arctic. The technology used in the searches (autonomous underwater vehicles) are a means by which Canada gains wider knowledge and power in the North, and this makes the Franklin story relevant to contemporary geopolitics. Add to this the fact that Shell Canada was a part of the Parks Canada team that located the *Erebus*, and it is clear that Franklin's reappearance is also linked to long-term interests in exploiting the Arctic's oil and gas reserves. Finally, questions have been raised about the role and perspective that the RCGS has taken in publicising and interpreting the *Erebus* alongside Harper (Murphy, 2015).

The *Erebus* was found west of the Adelaide Peninsula in a region named Utjulik or Ootgoolik ['place of bearded seals'], precisely the area where Inuit witnesses told McClintock and Hall they saw and visited an immobile ship before it sunk (Woodman, 1991, 248–61). At press conferences Harper and Parks Canada therefore paid tribute to Inuit oral records from the King William Island region – both the testimony collected by the early Franklin searchers, and the information and artefacts collected by researchers like David Woodman and Louie Kamookak more recently. Yet this was a superficial positioning of Inuit testimony as accurate knowledge in order to suit a dominant narrative – in this case geographic information, the most amenable to western modes of conceptualising space. Traditional Geographic Knowledge, as one might call it, appears to be the only kind of indigenous knowledge that has been officially ratified by the locations of the *Erebus* and *Terror*. With these successes, oral history has been 'modernised', local Inuit are recognised as being part of one of Canada's great creation myths, and a story is produced that is consistent with state interests (see Irlbacher-Fox, 2009, 112).

Yet the spectres of the Franklin expedition continue to disturb any settlement of the mystery. Elders in Nunavut still tell stories of Inuit who fear the ghosts of Franklin expeditioners; some are linked to horror at their cannibalism and desperate situation, other stories are linked to the shamanic curse said to have been placed on King William Island (Watson, 2017, 227). Indeed, feelings of ghostliness played a role in the discovery of *Terror* in 2016. A crew-member of one of the vessels searching for Crozier's ship that year, Sammy Kogvik, told the director of operations that years previously, when he was hunting near Terror Bay off King William Island, he had seen what looked like a mast sticking out of the sea ice. After posing for some photographs with the mast, Kogvik returned home only to find the camera had fallen out of his pocket: remembering the ghost stories told about the Franklin expedition, he felt this was a bad omen and didn't report the find at the time. However, years later Kogvik's tip proved crucial as the search vessel made a detour and located the *Terror* in excellent condition on the sea floor (Watson, 2016).

Although they provide good copy, ghost stories of the Franklin expedition are difficult to integrate into a narrative of tragic heroism. Well-known stories and memories of *qallunaat* seen wandering with human meat, in strange clothing, with dry, bleeding, black mouths, and assumed to be spirits of some kind, will of course disturb Harper's discourse because they do not fit into the normalised narrative surrounding the discoveries of the ships: explorers cannot be thought of as seaborne strangers, aliens who do not speak the local language. The arrival of the *Erebus* to Utjulik was not a scene of 'first contact' between the British and the Inuit – nor is there any evidence here of brutality, disease exchange, or any of the other immediate horrors of the colonial encounter – but this ship did herald an utter transformation in the lives of Inuit when the Franklin expeditioners were followed by more explorers, traders, settlers, missionaries, policemen and representatives of the Canadian state. The removal of strangeness from sonar images of British shipwrecks resting on the Arctic seabed means that the colonial and neo-colonial histories that form part of the Franklin expedition, then and now, are laundered out of official discussions, and the kind of legacy issues brought up by the likes of Vollmann and Atwood in their fiction are not heard in mainstream commentary.

As of 2017, there has been little in-depth discussion about what the location of the ships might mean for Inuit communities along the Northwest Passage route today, still living with the social upheaval caused by sedentarisation after the 1940s. Certainly there has been nothing to compare with John Walker's documentary film on John Rae and the Franklin expedition – *Passage* (2008) – which flitted back and forth between the past and present in a jarring but exhilarating format. Walker saw his film-making practice as being rooted in oral traditions and had an affinity with Rae's approach to local sources of information (Varga 2012, 79). In *Passage* Walker filmed a remarkable encounter in the Admiralty Board Room in London between the Nunavut politician, Tagak Curley, and Ernie Coleman, a retired naval officer and Franklin searcher. In the scene Curley opposes the idea that Franklin 'discovered' the Northwest Passage, as the statue commemorating him at Waterloo Place in London suggests. 'A dead man cannot find something, it just could not happen, so I am absolutely amazed. Incredible', he says. Curley goes on to defend the honour and honesty of Rae and his Inuit informants who reported tales of cannibalism among the expeditioners. Using Dickens's *Household Words* articles as a source, Coleman upholds the heroism of Franklin and his men, denies that cannibalism took place, and advances the theory that the expeditioners were massacred by the Inuit. Curley is appalled by this opinion but receives no apology for it from Coleman, apparently representing the perspective of the British Empire in an unreconstructed way. The climax to the film comes later when Curley meets Gerald Dickens, the great-great grandson of Charles Dickens. As they both stand among the actors who are playing the roles of Rae, Jane Franklin and other Franklin era figures, Gerald Dickens apologises for the hurt caused by his great-great grandfather's racist comments on Inuit testimony, a cathartic moment that suggests that the Franklin expedition is made up of many different stories spread over time – some of them traumatic and unsettling, but all of them ultimately symbolic.

For Walker, the actors and the other participants in *Passage*, history is not simply past time – it is rather a living thing still capable of wounding. The Franklin ships might be fetish objects to some, but to others they are symbols of particular mindsets or repositories of memories and bodies. Perhaps most disturbing from a British perspective, the ships were material resources which, when dismantled, actually made a positive impact on local lives. After all, throughout the 1850s the *Erebus*, just like earlier wrecks, was repeatedly visited and looted by local Inuit for its useful wood, glass and iron. As the *Erebus* and *Terror* become multi-year archaeological sites and have curators, politicians, lawyers, experts and twenty-first-century digital technology unleashed upon them, it is crucial that discussions of the Franklin era are not impoverished by political narratives that reduce its significance to that of a series of retrospective sovereignty missions inherited from Britain. The mystery of what happened to the expeditioners will not come down to maps and claim-staking.

The image of the Victorian explorer that Harper and others rely on in their 'idea of the north' is made up of complex constructions, repressions and fantasies. Harper's genealogy of explorers leading up to Franklin is as just as mythic as the Iglulingmiut creation myth of how Paarri came to visit them in 1821. The Franklin expeditioners were also *qallunaat* and, just like them, the Inuit were not passive bystanders, actors on a stage or recording devices while things happened around them. The *Erebus* was a Royal Navy bomb vessel, but it was also a 'white-man's umiak' (qtd. in Woodman, 1991, 11). In this book I have argued that British Arctic exploration was made up of a multiplicity of stories that speak about encounters, emotions, dreams and the relationship between the space and the 'geo-spectral' – between people and things appearing, disappearing and then reappearing. I hope these stories inspire a shift in scale, with non-explorers made part of the history of exploration, and inspire a shift in sequentiality, as historical time is recognised as being 'out of joint'. This encounter with the history of exploration has allowed me to understand the power of the spectral anew. The past does not simply vanish – it hangs around in landscapes, bodies, dreams and stories. It is *ongoing*, like an unexploded mine. This should not be forgotten.

Notes

Introduction

1. E.g. Hains, 2002, 16; Feeney, 1997, 79. See also Nansen's celebration of Roald Amundsen's 'quiet and strong' character. Cited in Amundsen, 1912, I, xxxi.
2. On this topic see Guneriussen, 2008. A recent tourist brochure promises that visitors will enjoy a 'dreamscape' in the Canadian North (Cruise North Expeditions). One academic has even promoted the idea of an Arctic 'spell' in interesting young scholars to conduct research on the region in the future (Sturm, 2000). Historically, fears about the psychological consequences of the long Arctic night have been widespread in other regions. These stereotypes feature in recent movies and television shows such as *The Last Winter* (2006), *30 Days of Night* (2007), and *Fortitude* (2015–17).
3. In his influential essay 'The Arctic Sublime' (1977) Chauncey Loomis emphasises the unromantic and factual voices of explorers such as William Edward Parry and John Franklin: 'For explorers and scientists, it [the Arctic world] all was natural and therefore subject to the scientific explanations that they gave in their accounts. Even they sometimes wondered about the Creator of such a world, however, and for readers with imaginations more romantic than theirs, the Arctic became almost unearthly in its sublimity'. Loomis's model is unidirectional in its assumption that explorers' disinterested descriptions were transformed by 'imaginative' audiences into the sublime and romantic Arctic of popular myth (102). By contrast I show how the accounts of explorers and exploration (including the classic accounts that Loomis focuses on) were more complex, involving dreams, emotions and other pressing voices.
4. On the mental and physical maladies associated with living and working in British India see Ernst, 1991. See also Arnold, 2000.
5. For other examples of Shackleton's dream language see his *The Heart of the Antarctic* (1909, I, 1, 39, 64, 69). Frank Worsley, one of Shackleton's men on the Imperial Trans-Antarctic Expedition (1914–17), apparently applied to join the expedition after an 'absurd dream' about navigating a ship along Burlington Street, London. He later saw a sign advertising Shackleton's expedition on the same street and volunteered to join (see Shackleton, 1983, 164).
6. On this see Barraclough, Cudmore and Donecker eds., 2016.
7. In 1868 the Franklin searcher Charles Francis Hall was told by the Inuit of Melville Peninsula that a man named Kia saw a stranger wearing a long cape that was not made of skin some 13 years previously. 'He saw that he (the stranger) had *strange* clothes on & carried something *strange* in a *strange* way on his shoulder' (qtd. in Woodman, 1995, 15). Hall suspected this was one of the last survivors of the Franklin expedition.
8. The diaries of the members of the Andrée expedition in 1897 attest to the frequent occurrence of diarrhoea and constipation during arduous sledging journeys. See Uusma, 2014, 110–47.

Chapter 1

1. On the quixotic attempt by François-René de Chateaubriand to gain support from the United States for a Northwest Passage expedition in the 1790s, see Chateaubriand, 1849, 260–1.
2. Despite his key role in all this, Scoresby was offered only a junior role as pilot in one of the expedition ships of 1818. Scoresby turned down the offer in disgust, although this probably

signified less a snobbish disregard for whaling experience on the part of Barrow than the pressing need to find employment for the scores of Royal Navy officers on half-pay after the end of the wars (see Jackson, 2007, 14).

3. On the subject of polar publishing routes see MacLaren, 1994; Cavell, 2008; 2013b. The accounts of Arctic whaling masters had a very different route to print – see Ross, 1985, 127.
4. There were particular rituals and superstitions on Arctic service such as the 'King Neptune' initiation for 'greenhands' who crossed the Arctic Circle for the first time (*Arctic Miscellanies*, 1852, 15–17). For other whaling superstitions see 'Superstitions of the Whaler'; 'Superstition of Whale-Fishers'; 'The Loss of the Polar Star'; Young, 1876, 7; SPRI, MS 713. For superstitions about the naming of ships see 'The Arctic Expedition', *The Morning Post*, 17 February 1852.
5. The whaling captain William Penny clashed with naval officers during his search for Franklin in 1851–2. One of his grievances on returning to Britain was that his private journals were kept for a long time and used against him (Penny, 1852, 11). For another controversy about the impounding or destruction of officers' journals see Miertsching, 1967, 201, 230. In a narrative, purporting to be written by an officer on the *Griper* on the 1819–20 expedition, Parry's 'Classical Production' was contrasted with the author's 'journalistic' style (*Letters Written*, 1821, iii).
6. See Elce, 2003.
7. Although Richard King, the naturalist on Back's 1833 Arctic expedition, only received 12 copies of his book as payment from the publisher Richard Bentley (Craciun, 2016, 111). For other examples of 'unauthorised' publications see Marra, 1775; Godfrey, 1857; Fisher, 1821; Huish ed., 1835. On the lost or hidden journals of crew see Pesso-Miquel, 2013. Edward Belcher is an unusual example of a naval commander who frequently deployed an emotional tone in his published journals. Despite this, in a communiqué of 1854, describing the difficulties of finding a safe place to overwinter, he wrote: 'To explain my feelings does not come within the scope of official correspondence' (qtd. in *Further Papers Relative to the Recent Arctic Expeditions*, 1854–5, 27). On the negative press reaction to Belcher's style see Cavell, 2008, 48, 227.
8. Although the editing of Cook's journals by John Hawkesworth and John Douglas also contributed to Cook's literary and national personae (see O'Sullivan, 2008, 36–47).
9. This is perhaps a by-product of the overwhelming focus on the themes of geographical discovery and biography in polar history compared to, for example, the history of African exploration. For recent work which brings emotions and performativity into polar history see Berg, 2006; Davis-Fisch, 2012.
10. Although it lies beyond the scope of this study, I hope that my strategies will assist others in seeking to describe the 'middle ground' (White, 1991) or 'in-between space' (Bhabha, 1994) that existed between explorers and indigenous inhabitants of the Arctic. One key concern of my research to date has been to demonstrate unequivocally why casting western/Inuit relationships in terms of dichotomous secular versus spiritual values is fundamentally misleading, historically and philosophically (see McCorristine, 2013).
11. This particular trend culminated in Ernest Shackleton's (1920) description of his 1914–17 Antarctic expedition as heroic 'White Warfare of the South', set in connection with the 'red' conflict taking place at the same time in Europe.
12. 'Ulysses' was a favourite poem of Kane, who named an unusual geological feature in the Arctic 'Tennyson's Monument' in honour of the poet ('Tennyson's Arctic Monument'). The deaths of Franklin and Scott have traditionally been linked through their association with heroism, patriotism, and martyrdom. For a contemporary poem that links the death of Scott with that of Franklin see 'I.E.'
13. For discussions on the convergences of Arctic exploration and disaster, see Craciun, 2016.
14. Ralph Lloyd-Jones notes a 'missionary attitude' among many Arctic officers which may have led to evangelical candidates being preferred when it came to selecting expeditioners (1997, 331).
15. E.g. Officer and Page, 2001; Coleman, 2006; Berton, 1988; Swerling, 2015.
16. On the dominance of these notions see Stefansson, 1921.
17. Translations of the words 'dream' and 'ghost' in an English-Inuktitut vocabulary used by the Admiralty in the 1850s indicates that explorers were at least interested in when or how Inuit used them. See *Eskimaux and English Vocabulary, for the Use of the Arctic Expedition*, 1850.

Chapter 2

1. In his book on Greenland (a prominent source for British naval officers), the Moravian missionary David Crantz denied that shamans were all 'jugglers'. Instead he believed there to be three types: the 'genuine angekoks' or wise men, who have knowledge of the environment and can heal through 'Legerdemain'; 'phantasists' who can deceive themselves into believing they possess supernatural powers; and 'mere deceivers' who perform fraudulent tricks and pull the wool over the eyes of viewers. Crantz believed that the latter type predominated (1767, I, 212–14).
2. For a related study of Maori-European encounters see Salmond, 1991.
3. For evidence of whalers requesting séances see Oosten, Laugrand and Remie (2006). The fur trader George Nelson conducted his own séance during a period of hunger (1988, 9). Vilhjalmur Stefansson wrote of one shaman who 'had for a familiar spirit the spirit of a white man, and in séances spoke "white men's language"' (1913, 255).
4. See McCorristine, 2013.
5. Greg Dening reminds us that the machinery of the ship was only energised through the bodily exertions of the sailor and that the most skilled sailor was frequently also the best dancer: 'Speed, reflexivity, coordination married aesthetics with practicality' (1992, 57).
6. The journal of Matthew Liddon, Parry's second-in-command, records that at this time a wolf 'came & watched against the sides of the Hecla, which Lieut. Parry heard as he was lying in bed indisposed'. The presence of wolves, and their attacks on the ship's dogs, was noted frequently by the expedition's surgeon and naturalist Alexander Fisher (NA, ADM 55/59).
7. On this topic see Schivelbusch, 1988; Bachelard, 1961.
8. See Mackenzie, I, ccxxxii; Hayes, 1881, 12.
9. Feet have been at the heart of some of the most touching cross-cultural interactions in the Arctic. On Parry's second expedition (1821–23), Lyon recorded how one of the seamen with a frostbitten toe was cared for by Toolemak who 'supplied him with a warm pair of fur boots, and sat above an hour chafing and exorcising his foot' (1824, 292). During John Ross's *Victory* expedition (1829–33) a local Boothian man named Tulluahiu was fitted for a wooden leg by the ship's carpenter, an incident that lived long in regional oral memory. While travelling with the Inuit in the early 1860s Charles Francis Hall went to sleep one night with half-frozen feet and awoke to see 'no less than three pairs of warm feet all woven and interwoven, so that some difficulty was experienced to tell which were my own' (1864, I, 214).
10. For some, the Arctic could certainly become homely. John Pead, a seaman who served on three of Parry's expeditions, often wished he could have mustered the courage to ask to be left behind to live happily among the Inuit ('The Voice of an Old Arctic Seaman', *The Times*, 1856).
11. The snow bunting was symbolic for British and American explorers, variously serving as a cheerful reminder of 'a better country' (Parry, 1821, 199) and as a reminder of life in the winter (Parry, 1824, 312). Following the burial of a marine who suffered from a long illness during his *Terror* expedition, George Back wrote: 'Soon after the mournful ceremony was concluded, a little snow-bunting was observed to hover for a few seconds over the aperture through which the body had been lowered, and then to fly away' (1838, 325). After passing the 'vacant and dead' region of Hassel Sound during his North Pole expedition, Frederick Cook described how one morning his party was awoken 'by a strange sound. Our surprised eyes turned from side to side. Not a word was uttered. Another sound came – a series of soft, silvery notes – the song of a creature that might have come from heaven. I listened with rapture. I believed I was dreaming. The enchanting song continued – I lay entranced. I could not believe this divine thing was of our real world until the pole of our tent gently quivered. It was a bird – a snow bunting thrilling its ethereal song – the first sound of life heard for many months' (1911, 330–1).
12. For another snow bunting poem – perhaps written by Lyon's wife Lucy – see *A Peep at the Esquimaux*, 1825.
13. In his narrative of 1633 Thomas James mentioned that he left two greyhounds ashore near Cape Henrietta Maria in Hudson Bay (1975, 47).

Chapter 3

1. For another theatre rumour, and accompanying broadsheet, see Owen, 1978, 320.

2. Another Bolton clairvoyant, possibly the same one mentioned by Haddock (1851, 96), was involved in a strange assignment during August and September 1849, just as the shocking 'Bermondsey Murder' case received extensive attention in the national and provincial press of the British Isles. A correspondent who signed the letter 'W.' wrote to the police from Bolton with the news from a clairvoyant that a concealed pistol was to be found in a cellar in the building where the murder took place. But after a search no pistol was uncovered ('The Bermondsey Murder', *The Times*, 1849). Haddock went to some effort to state that he had nothing to do with the affair (Elliotson, 1849–50, 323).
3. Discussing an earlier case in which Emma was consulted, Haddock expanded on how these conversations took place: 'she began to talk with an imaginary personage, as if present in the room with us; but as it subsequently proved, although, invisible and imaginary to us, he was both *real* and *visible* to her ... and was conversing with his mind' (1849, 60).
4. Haddock wrote to the newspapers following Ross's return, seeking to maintain the validity of Emma's overall revelations: 'Three things stated in her examination respecting the northern expeditions, have now proved to be correct; viz., that two ships were coming home, that Sir J. Ross was nearer home than at the first examination, and that Sir James Ross had not seen Sir J. Franklin. On being asked how it was she had described Sir J. Ross's ships as being in the ice, at a time when they must have been sailing homeward, she said she supposed them to be Sir J. Ross's because Sir J. Franklin told her he had not seen him' ('The Bolton Clairvoyante', *Newcastle Courant*, 23 November 1849).
5. On average, most medical physicians charged between five shillings and one guinea for consultations during the Victorian period (Digby, 1994, 186).
6. Jane Franklin mentioned that she once placed a Union Jack flag she was making over her sleeping husband, not realising the superstitious belief that this was something reserved for those about to be buried at sea (Traill, 1896, 436).
7. This was also the period when Robert Fitzroy popularised the claims of scientific meteorology by publishing weather forecasts and storm warnings in national newspapers. Fitzroy's Met Office was attacked from both sides: by his superiors who saw forecasting as superstitious prognostication and by Zadkiel's 'Astro-Meteorological Society'. A series of incorrect weather forecasts, and a campaign against Fitzroy's credibility (possibly involving Zadkiel) led to his suicide in 1865 (Perkins, 1996, 224).
8. In her diary for 1 June 1849, Caroline Fox wrote: 'poor Lady Franklin ... She spends most of her days in a room she has taken in Spring Gardens, where she sees all the people who can tell or suggest anything ... she is in such a restless, excited state of feeling' (1883, 295).
9. For consultations on 15 October and 6 November 1849, Trevelyan paid Emma five shillings and Haddock one pound and three pence (NU, WCT 266).
10. For instance, after the French mesmerist Adolphe Didier offered to solve the Franklin mystery in 1853, a letter-writer to *The Morning Post* asked 'in what manner is the connection of the mesmerist to be tested, or how is his report to be made of any service? ... His information can only be valuable by being both precise and certain'. The correspondent, who signed as 'Open to Conviction', proposed that a committee be established, a member of which would be stationed at a distant town. At an agreed time Didier would be asked to write down the circumstances of the member, following which the statement would be compared with a telegraph sent by the member at the exact same time ('Mesmeric Divination', *The Morning Post*, 1853).
11. During a séance later in the year Smith claimed the *Erebus* was located 'a great distance to the north and west of Cape Riley, in lat. 89, lon. 170 E.' ('Wonderful Case of Clairvoyance', *John O'Groat Journal*, 1850).
12. A later commentator believed the clairvoyant predictions had failed because 'Sir John Franklin was dead beforehand, and probably all his companions. Mesmerism does not extend beyond death' ('A Hint to Mesmerists if they can take it', *The Dundee Courier and Argus*, 1881).
13. One critic who seemed unaware of this wrote in to the Melbourne *Argus*: 'Could not the Mesmerists of Port Philip, who appear to be not a whit behind those of the mother country, make inquiries of the clairvoyants after the missing Leichhardt and his brave companions?' ('Mesmerism: To the Editor of the *Argus*', *The Argus*, 1850).
14. There was some debate at the time about whether the Franklin expedition had travelled through an 'Open Polar Sea' and had reached Russian-controlled territory. A naval officer named Bedford Pim believed in this scenario and proposed a small expedition to search the north-east coast of Siberia in 1851, although this came to nothing (see Barr, 1992).

Chapter 4

1. While overwintering at Repulse Bay during his second Arctic expedition, Hall visited a shaman named Artooa to have his boils treated. During the séance, Artooa told him that the main cause of the affliction was an enemy. As Loomis relates, 'Hall's ears pricked up at this: "There was one man in America who was a great enemy to me – he sought to do me all the injury he could – would rejoice in my sickness & greatly so at my death – if he had the opportunity, he was such a bitter enemy he would kill me"'. Hall recognised this enemy as William Parker Snow (1991, 187).
2. Just as his financial situation became increasingly desperate, so too his marriage appears to have entered a critical phase. Snow had long claimed that his wife had a mental illness (in 1860 he told Trevelyan she 'will know everything I say or will do, and if not satisfied immediately, works herself up into all sorts of imaginations') and in 1869 he wrote that she had fallen down some stairs and broke her leg (NU, WCT 229; 235). In 1874 Snow became embroiled in a scandal after he brought a prostitute, Emma Cann aged 33, to a police station for incessantly knocking on his door and assaulting his wife. Snow refused to press charges on this occasion but, in 1883, Cann was again charged with assaulting Mrs Snow. At the court hearing, Snow claimed she had lived with them for several years at Bexleyheath in Kent and that he had been trying to rescue her from a 'degraded life'. On her part, Cann claimed that Snow had taken her to Oxford and Scotland as his wife, pretending he was on business (BL, Loan 96 RLF 1/1459).
3. Bellot was circumspect on whether the Strait actually existed or not (Bellot, 1855, II, 179).
4. Cracroft later wrote of her aunt's prescience in this context: 'It is some comfort to be reminded as she now is on all sides, that the Expeditions she sent out year after year, were the only ones which, provided for that Search, which if it had been carefully carried out upon her own comprehensive views, would have revealed the truth to us long ago. It is indeed almost wonderful to look back & perceive the complete accuracy of her views and reasoning' (SPRI, MS 1100/1/31).
5. For Rae's criticism of Kennedy's westward route see Rae, 1953, 231–5.
6. It is interesting to read of the quick deterioration in the relationship between Rae and Jane Franklin. In a letter sent to Scoresby, dated 7 November 1854, Cracroft wrote: 'Rae is now exhausting language in maintaining against all opposition & diversity of opinion, his own assumptions, and I must honestly tell you that his head appears to be completely turned by being for the moment a lion. He is not like the same man, and seems to think that no one has a right to make even a representation for the sake of fair argument, & getting at the truth. Everyone says the same of him, & we hear he has made himself very ridiculous & very offensive besides … with one voice Rae's revolting details [of cannibalism] are rejected, & himself condemned for having made them known. At one time, we were told, he was sorry for having done so – now his mood is changed, for he defends that, as well as every other point; his vanity really seems to have carried out of himself & this will no doubt be exhibited at the Geographical' [Rae was scheduled to deliver a lecture at the Royal Geographical Society on 13 November but he cancelled it] (SPRI, MS 1100/1/31).
7. A benefactor, Lydia Cunningham, occasionally sent Coppin money but he neglected her advice to withhold money from Skewes until he could see the result (PRONI, D/2666/2/8). Despite his poverty, Coppin gave Skewes £57 towards the cost of publishing the second edition and commenced lobbying Members of Parliament to support his cause (PRONI, D/2666/2/10; PRONI, D2666/2/11). Cunningham, suspecting foul play, contacted Skewes directly about his relationship with Coppin but Skewes replied that he had acted unselfishly in the matter and worked on the book 'for the mere love of doing good – caring very little about remuneration' (PRONI, D/2666/2/11).
8. McClintock, Jane Franklin and Cracroft policed Franklin's legacy for decades. Jane Franklin and Cracroft censored Snow's *Voyage of the Prince Albert* at proof stage in 1850; they sought to 'cross-examine' Hall about his discoveries in the mid-1860s; in 1877 they sought to have McClintock approve the proofs of J.E. Nourse's narrative of Hall's last journey; McClintock self-censored the evidence of cannibalism he encountered in the Arctic before publishing *Voyage of the 'Fox'*; and in 1880 McClintock wrote to Frederick Schwatka begging him not to repeat the evidence of cannibalism in his account (Craciun, 2016, 241, 69). Some time later Snow asked: 'Why has an arbitrary private injunction lately been served upon the Press as to "publishing any letter or part of a letter &c., purporting to have been written on the subject by Lady Franklin or any members of her family or testamentary representative?"' (Snow, 1889, 16).

9. Many of Jane Franklin's journals for the period of the Franklin searches in the 1850s are absent from the relevant archive, supporting speculations that Cracroft censored any difficult material (see Jacobs, 2015, 359). Another possibility is that Jane Franklin self-censored after hearing the gossip about Elisha Kent Kane and the publication of his love letters to Margaret Fox through Henry Grinnell in the 1860s.
10. This accords with Hamilton's interest in clairvoyance and supports Skewes's claim that Coppin actually visited Hamilton to inform him of the case: 'To the gallant officer the child's story came as a remembrancer of some hallowed associations of his own home. He also had once a little child that spake as with other tongues. "Do not disbelieve the child", said Captain Hamilton, and with the advice was a promise that he would lay the case before "my lords", minus the supernatural part of the matter' (Skewes, 1889, 80).
11. In 1851, meanwhile, the whaler and Franklin searcher William Penny told Coppin that he got into a 'passion' with the cartographer John Arrowsmith over the latter's refusal to accept the name 'Queen Victoria Channel' for the region north of Wellington Channel (SPRI MS 248/2241; BJ).
12. In his book Smith included a letter from Nathaniel P. Tallmadge, a spiritualist and politician who had briefly been Governor of Wisconsin Territory, claiming that he attended a séance in Washington with Kane and the Fox sisters around 1853. After Kane questioned the spirit of John Torrington, one of the Franklin expeditioners buried on Beechey Island, Tallmadge asked if Franklin was still alive. To this he received the rapped answer: 'Franklin is no more – thick-ribbed ice, sterner than warriors' steel, encases his form – the home of his triumphs is his grave' (Smith, 1860, 216).

Chapter 5

1. Angela Byrne has noted an 'overlap between common perceptions of the northerner and of women as more spiritually inclined and disposed to the supernatural than the metropolitan man' (2013, 15).
2. For a survey of the wives of famous male explorers, and their contrasting roles, see Herbert, 2012.
3. This fantasy also existed in accounts of Antarctic exploration. For instance, Roald Amundsen wrote: 'Inviting and attractive the fair one lies before us. Yes, we hear you calling, and we shall come. You shall have your kiss, if we pay for it with our lives' (1912, I, 179).
4. I am grateful to Janice Cavell for pointing out this poem to me.
5. This society is likely to have been the Anthropological Institute of Great Britain and Ireland, which had a keen interest in Arctic items at the time (Markham et al., 1873).
6. Explorers and whalers were known to disinter Inuit graves for artefacts and human bones. See Ross, 1997, 164–5; Murray, 1856, 11; Faulkner, 1878, 136.
7. On the relationship between science, colonialism and head-hunting during this period see Larson, 2014, 17–45. On the phrenological head-hunting of John Ross see Huish ed., 1835, 272–81.

Chapter 6

1. The origins of Franklin hunting as a kind of extreme tourism can be traced to a bizarre set of aborted solo expeditions by the Irishman Francis Kennedy Pease. In 1934 it was reported that he would search for Franklin relics for two years with his fox terrier ('Arctic Hunt for Relics', *Singapore Free Press and Mercantile Advertiser*, 1934). In 1939 another report stated that his hopes of success were based on 'a sketchily drawn map made by a member of the Franklin Expedition. It was given to him by the Danish explorer, Rasmussen, shortly before he died, and indicates the position of Franklin's grave on King William Island and the probable position of the logbook' ('Search for Franklin's Arctic Log', *The Straits Times*, 1939).
2. On Franklin revisionism see Davis, 2002; Durey, 2008.
3. British expeditions were joined by American-organised efforts during the period of the Franklin searches, and many expeditions availed of the considerable support and hospitality

of Danish-administered Greenland. Furthermore, of the crews and officers of ships searching for Franklin, many were made up of multinational personnel. Of the former, Irish-born officers such as McClintock and McClure excelled while the Frenchman Joseph René Bellot was considered a martyr by Jane Franklin after his death in Wellington Channel in 1853.

4. Crozier's known assumption of leadership, despite the ensuing tragedy, meant he is imagined as a complex figure more in tune with the Arctic than his colleagues. See Wilson, 1999; Hanlon, 1990; Smith, 2006.
5. Franklin's biographer Roderic Owen acknowledged this sense of the ghostly when researching the expedition: 'I would like to draw attention to a phenomenon which many writers experience but are too shy to mention – the Unseen. When writing *Beautiful and Beloved* I couldn't fail to notice that time and time again I was being helped by influences directing me to look at this or at that particular paper out of a huge heap of documents. The same sort of thing went on during the *Fate of Franklin* – perhaps even to a greater degree, as there were so many things from which to choose' (1978, 11).

Bibliography

Unpublished primary sources

British Library, London (BL)
Add MS 35309: Barrow Bequest.
Loan 96 RLF 1/1459: Royal Literary Fund.
Derbyshire Record Office, Matlock (DRO)
D3311/51/2; D3311/74/1; D3311/81/1(iii): Papers of the Gell family of Hopton.
Glenbow Museum Calgary (GM)
M-141: George Brown. *The Story of My Life*, 1876.
National Archives, London (NA)
ADM 7/189: Documents relating to Arctic Expeditions.
ADM 7/611: Cases: Petitions as to the search for Sir John Franklin (143).
ADM 55/59: Lieut. Liddon's Private Journal, H.M. Brig 'Griper', 1819–1820.
National Maritime Museum, Greenwich (NMM)
MRK/48: Albert Hastings Markham. Untitled poem dated March 1879.
Newcastle University, Newcastle upon Tyne (NU)
WCT 229; 235; 266; 284/83: Walter Calverley Trevelyan Papers.
Public Record Office of Northern Ireland, Belfast (PRONI)
D2666/2/8-11: Cunningham Papers.
Royal Geographical Society, London (RGS)
GB402WHH, SSC/73: The Lt. William Harvey Hooper Collection.
LMS S 16: Book of News Cuttings on Skewes's Book on Franklin, 'Sir John Franklin: A Revelation'.
Scott Polar Research Institute, Cambridge (SPRI)
MS 248/106-7; MS 248/184; D; MS 1100/3/14: Jane Lady Franklin Correspondence.
MS 248/118; BJ: Jane Lady Franklin Papers.
MS 248/108; BJ: Jane Lady Franklin Journals.
MS 248/247/15; MS 248/247/17; MS 248/247/21; MS 248/2241; BJ; MS 1100/1/4; MS 248/267/1-4: Sophia Cracroft Papers.
MS 248/335; D: Undetermined author.
MS 655/3; BJ: Sir John Ross Papers.
MS 713: Arthur C. Horner Collection.
MS 1100/1/31: Sophia Cracroft Correspondence.
MS 1503/47/1: Richardson-Voss Collection.

Film and radio sources

Due South. CTV, episode 67, original air date 14 March 1999.
Arctic Passage: Prisoners of the Ice, by Chris Schmidt. Dir. Louise Osmond. NOVA/WGBH. PBS. 28 February 2006.
'A Crucible That May Change the Way we See Canada's North'. *As it Happens*, CBC Radio. Broadcast 5 December, 2014.

Primary and secondary sources

Abrahall, Chandos H. *Arctic Enterprise. A Poem*. London: Hope, 1856.

Adams, W.H. Davenport. *The Arctic: A History of its Discovery, its Plants, Animals and Natural Phenomena*. Edinburgh: G. Tod, 1876.

'Additions to the Museum'. *Proceedings of the Academy of Natural Sciences of Philadelphia*, 43 (1891): 510–17.

Adey, Peter. *Aerial Life: Spaces, Mobilities, Affects*. Chichester: Wiley-Blackwell, 2010.

'A Lament on the Fate of Sir J. Franklin and his Crews' (c.1854). Firth c.12(438), Allegro Catalogue of Ballads, Bodleian Library, University of Oxford.

Altick, Richard D. *The Shows of London*. Cambridge, Massachusetts: Belknap Press of Harvard University Press, 1978.

Amundsen, Roald. *Roald Amundsens Dagbøker: Belgicaekspedisjonen, 1897–1899: Den Første Overvintring i Antarktis*. Geir O. Kløver ed. Oslo: Fram Museum, 2009.

Amundsen, Roald. *My Life as an Explorer*. London: Heinemann, 1927.

Amundsen, Roald. *The South Pole: An Account of the Norwegian Antarctic Expedition in the 'Fram', 1910–1912*. 2 vols. A.G. Chater trans. London: John Murray, 1912.

Amundsen, Roald. *'The North West Passage': Being the Record of a Voyage of Exploration of the Ship 'Gjöa' 1903–1907*. 2 vols. New York: E.P. Dutton & Company, 1908.

Andersen, Hans Christian. *Stories from Hans Andersen*. New York and London: Hodder & Stoughton, 1911.

Andersen, Hans Christian. *The Ice-Maiden: And Other Tales*. Fanny Fuller trans. Philadelphia: F. Leypoldt, 1863.

Anderson, Ben. 'Becoming and Being Hopeful: Towards a Theory of Affect'. *Environment and Planning D: Society and Space*, 24 (2006): 733–52.

'Another Visit to Sir John Franklin in the Polar Regions'. *Liverpool Mercury*, 2 April 1850.

Anthi, Per. 'Freud og Nansen – Rivalisering og Respekt'. *Tidsskrift for Norsk Psykologforening*, 53:1 (2016): 26–33.

Anthi, Per. 'Roald Amundsen: A Study in Rivalry, Masochism and Paranoia'. *International Journal of Psychoanalysis*, 80 (1999): 995–1010.

Aporta, Claudio. 'Old Routes, New Trails: Contemporary Inuit Travel and Orienting in Igloolik, Nunavut'. PhD Dissertation: University of Alberta, 2003.

Appelbaum, David. *The Stop*. Albany: State University of New York Press, 1995.

'Arctic Body-snatching'. *The Hampshire Telegraph*, 8 October 1898.

'Arctic Dreams of Food'. *Daily Mail*, 16 January 1913.

'The Arctic Expedition'. *The Times*, 23 October 1854.

'The Arctic Expedition'. *The Morning Post*, 17 February 1852.

'The Arctic Expedition'. *Liverpool Mercury*, 22 March 1850.

'The Arctic Expeditions'. *The Aberdeen Journal*, 10 April 1850.

'Arctic Hunt for Relics'. *Singapore Free Press and Mercantile Advertiser*, 2 October 1934.

Arctic Miscellanies: A Souvenir of the Late Polar Search. London: Colburn & Co., 1852.

The Arctic Queen. S.l.: s.n., 1857.

Arias, Rosario and Patricia Pulham eds. *Haunting and Spectrality in Neo-Victorian Fiction*. New York: Palgrave Macmillan 2010.

Arnold, David. '"Illusory Riches": Representations of the Tropical World, 1840–1950'. *Singapore Journal of Tropical Geography*, 21:1 (2000): 6–18.

'Arrival of Sir J. Ross from the Arctic Regions'. *Elgin Courier*, 9 November 1849.

'Arrival of the "Truelove"'. *Hull Packet*, 5 October 1849.

Atwood, Margaret. *Writing with Intent: Essays, Reviews, Personal Prose: 1983–2005*. New York: Carroll & Graf, 2005.

Atwood, Margaret. *Strange Things: The Malevolent North in Canadian Literature*. Oxford: Oxford University Press, 1995.

Atwood, Margaret. *Wilderness Tips*. London: Bloomsbury, 1991.

Atwood, Margaret. 'Canadian Monsters: Some Aspects of the Supernatural in Canadian Fiction'. In *The Canadian Imagination: Dimensions of a Literary Culture*. David Staines ed. Cambridge, Massachusetts and London: Harvard University Press, 1977: 229–53.

Bachelard, Gaston. *The Poetics of Space*. Maria Jolas trans. New York: Orion Press, 1994.

Bachelard, Gaston. *The Poetics of Reverie: Childhood, Language, and the Cosmos*. Daniel Russell trans. Boston: Beacon Press, 1971.

Bachelard, Gaston. *La Flamme d'une Chandelle*. Paris: Presses Universitaires de France, 1961.

Back, George. *Narrative of an Expedition in H.M.S. Terror, Undertaken with a View to Geographical Discovery on the Arctic Shores, in the Years 1836–7*. London: John Murray, 1838.
Back, George. *Narrative of the Arctic Land Expedition to the Mouth of the Great Fish River, and along the Shores of the Arctic Ocean, in the Years 1833, 1834, and 1835*. London: John Murray, 1836.
Baluja, Tamara. 'Search Launched for the Franklin Ships' Watery Arctic Grave'. *The Globe and Mail*, 23 August 2012. Accessed at http://www.theglobeandmail.com/news/politics/search-launched-for-the-franklin-ships-watery-arctic-grave/article4495549 on 10 September 2013.
Barr, William, Nadine Forestier-Blazart, and Jean-Claude Forestier-Blazart. '"The Last Duty of an Officer": Lieutenant de Vaisseau Joseph-René Bellot, 1826–1853, in the Franklin Search'. *Polar Record*, 50:1 (2014): 1–30.
Barr, William. '"The Cold of Valparaiso": The Disintegration of William Kennedy's Second Franklin Search Expedition, 1853–1854'. *Polar Record*, 34:190 (1998): 203–18.
Barr, William. 'Searching for Franklin from Australia: William Parker Snow's Initiative of 1853'. *Polar Record*, 33:185 (1997): 145–50.
Barr, William. 'Franklin in Siberia? – Lieutenant Bedford Pim's Proposal to Search the Arctic Coast of Siberia, 1851–52'. *Arctic*, 45:1 (1992): 36–46.
Barraclough, Eleanor Rosamund, Danielle Marie Cudmore, and Stefan Donecker eds. *Imagining the Supernatural North*. Edmonton, Alberta: University of Alberta Press, 2016.
Barrow, John. *Voyages of Discovery and Research within the Arctic Regions, from the Year 1818 to the Present Time, etc.* London: John Murray, 1846.
Barrow, John. *A Chronological History of Voyages into the Arctic Regions; Undertaken Chiefly for the Purpose of Discovering a North-East, North-West, or Polar Passage between the Atlantic and Pacific, etc.* London: John Murray, 1818.
Beattie, Owen and James M. Savelle. 'Discovery of Human Remains from Sir John Franklin's Last Expedition'. *Historical Archaeology*, 17:2 (1983): 100–05.
Beattie Owen and John Geiger. *Frozen in Time: The Fate of the Franklin Expedition*. Vancouver: Greystone Books, 1998.
Bebbington, D.W. *Evangelicalism in Modern Britain: A History from the 1730s to the 1980s*. London and New York: Routledge, 1989.
Belcher, Edward. *The Last of the Arctic Voyages; Being a Narrative of the Expedition in H.M.S. Assistance. Under the Command of Captain Sir Edward Belcher, C.B., in Search of Sir John Franklin, during the Years 1852–53-54 etc.* 2 vols. London: Lovell Reeve, 1855.
Bell, Bill. 'Authors in an Industrial Economy: The Case of John Murray's Travel Writers'. *Romantic Textualities*, 21 (2013). Accessed at http://www.romtext.org.uk/issues/issue-21 on December 14, 2014.
Bell, Karl. *The Magical Imagination: Magic and Modernity in Urban England, 1780–1914*. Cambridge: Cambridge University Press, 2012.
Bellot, Joseph René. *Memoires of Lieutenant Joseph René Bellot, etc.* 2 vols. London: Hurst and Blackett, 1855.
Belyea, Barbara. 'Captain Franklin in Search of the Picturesque'. *Essays on Canadian Writing*, 40 (1990): 1–24.
Belyea, Barbara. 'Mackenzie meets Moodie at the Great Divide'. *Journal of Canadian Studies*, 23 (1988): 118–29.
'Bengal'. *Bombay Monthly Times*, 24–25 June 1850.
Bennett, John Hughes. *The Mesmeric Mania of 1851, with a Physiological Explanation of the Phenomena Produced*. London: Simpkin, Marshall & Co., 1851.
Berg, Roald. 'Gender in Polar Air: Roald Amundsen and his Aeronautics'. *Acta Borealia: A Nordic Journal of Circumpolar Studies*, 23:2 (2006): 130–44.
'The Bermondsey Murder'. *The Times*, 14 September 1849.
Berton, Pierre. *The Arctic Grail: The Quest for the Northwest Passage and the North Pole, 1818–1909*. Toronto: Viking Books, 1988.
Bessels, Emil. *Polaris: The Chief Scientist's Recollections of the American North Pole Expedition, 1871–73*. William Barr ed. and trans. Calgary: University of Calgary Press, 2016.
Bhabha, Homi K. *The Location of Culture*. London: Routledge, 1994.
Bird, Louis. *Telling our Stories: Omushkego Legends and Histories from Hudson Bay*. Jennifer S.H. Brown, Paul W. DePasquale, and Mark F. Ruml eds. Peterborough, Ontario and Orchard Park, New York: Broadview Press, 2005.
Birney, Earle. *The Collected Poems of Earle Birney*. Toronto: McClelland and Stewart, 1975.
Blake, Richard. *Religion in the British Navy 1815–1879: Piety and Professionalism*. Woodbridge, Suffolk: The Boydell Press, 2014.
Blake, Richard. *Evangelicals in the Royal Navy, 1775–1815: Blue Lights & Psalm Singers*. Woodbridge, Suffolk: The Boydell Press, 2008.

Bloch, Ernst. *Literary Essays*. Stanford, California: Stanford University Press, 1998.
Bloom, Lisa. *Gender on Ice: American Ideologies of Polar Expeditions*. Minneapolis: University of Minnesota Press, 1993.
Boker, George H. 'A Ballad of Sir John Franklin'. *Sartain's Union Magazine of Literature and Art*, 6 (1850): 323–4.
'Book Review'. *The Athenaeum*, 3212 (1889): 628–9.
Borrow, George. 'Lavrengo'. *Blackwood's Edinburgh Magazine*, 69 (1851): 322–37.
Boss, Pauline. 'Ambiguous Loss Research, Theory, and Practice: Reflections after 9/11'. *Journal of Marriage and Family*, 66:3 (2004): 551–66.
Bourne, William Oland. 'Lady Franklin's Appeal to the North'. *New York Times*, 18 October 1851.
Bradford, William. 'Life and Scenery in the Far North'. *Journal of the American Geographical Society of New York*, 17 (1885): 79–124.
Braithwaite, John. *Supplement to Captain Sir John Ross's Narrative of a Second Voyage in the Victory, in Search of a North-West Passage, etc.* London: Chapman & Hall, 1849.
Brannan, Robert Louis ed. *Under the Management of Mr. Charles Dickens: His Production of 'The Frozen Deep'*. Ithaca, New York: Cornell University Press, 1966.
Bratlinger, Patrick. 'Imperial Gothic: Atavism and the Occult in the British Adventure Novel, 1880–1914'. *English Literature in Transition, 1880–1920*, 28:3 (1985): 243–52.
Bravo, Michael. 'Science and Discovery in the Admiralty Voyages to the Arctic Regions in Search of a North-west Passage (1818–25)'. PhD Thesis: University of Cambridge, 1992.
Bray, Emile Frédéric de. *A Frenchman in Search of Franklin: De Bray's Arctic Journal, 1852–1854*. William Barr trans. Toronto and London: University of Toronto Press, 1992.
'British Adventure'. *Illustrated London News*, 15:394 (1849): 241–2.
Britten, Emma H. *Ghost Land; or Researches into the Mysteries of Occultism*. Boston: s.n., 1876.
Brown, John. *The North-West Passage, and the Plans for the Search for Sir John Franklin. A Review*. London: E. Stanford, 1858.
Brown, John George Henry. *A Message from the World of Spirits, Shewing the State of Men after Death, etc.* London: Holyoake & Co., 1857.
Browne, Liam. *The Emigrant's Farewell*. London: Bloomsbury, 2006.
'Burford's Panorama of the Arctic Regions'. *Morning Chronicle*, 11 February 1850.
Burnett, D. Graham. *Masters of All they Surveyed: Exploration, Geography, and a British El Dorado*. Chicago: University of Chicago Press, 2000.
Bushnan, J. Stevenson. 'Desultory Sketches'. *Medical Times*, 21 (1850): 313.
Byerly, Alison. *Are We There Yet? Virtual Travel and Victorian Realism*. Ann Arbor: University of Michigan Press, 2013.
Byrne, Angela. *Geographies of the Romantic North: Science, Antiquarianism, and Travel, 1790–1830*. Basingstoke: Palgrave Macmillan, 2013.
Cameron, Emilie. *Far Off Metal River: Inuit Lands, Settler Stories, and the Making of the Contemporary Arctic*. Vancouver: UBC Press, 2015.
Cameron, J.M.R. 'John Barrow, the *Quarterly*'s Imperial Reviewer'. In Jonathan Cutmore ed. *Conservatism and the Quarterly Review*. London: Pickering & Chatto, 2007: 133–49.
Campbell, William W. *The Dread Voyage: Poems*. Toronto and Montreal: W. Briggs, 1893.
Carpenter, William B. 'Electro-Biology and Mesmerism'. *Quarterly Review*, 93 (1853): 501–57.
Castle, Terry. *The Female Thermometer: Eighteenth-Century Culture and the Invention of the Uncanny*. New York and Oxford: Oxford University Press, 1995.
Cavell, Janice. 'Making Books for Mr Murray: The Case of Edward Parry's Third Arctic Narrative'. *The Library*, 14:1 (2013a): 45–69.
Cavell, Janice. 'Publishing Sir John Franklin's Fate: Cannibalism, Journalism, and the 1881 Edition of Leopold McClintock's *The Voyage of the 'Fox' in the Arctic Seas*'. *Book History*, 16 (2013b): 155–84.
Cavell, Janice. 'Lady Lucy Barry and Evangelical Reading on the First Franklin Expedition'. *Arctic*, 63:2 (2010): 131–40.
Cavell, Janice. *Tracing the Connected Narrative: Arctic Exploration in British Print Culture, 1818–1860*. Toronto: Toronto University Press, 2008.
Cavell, Janice. 'Comparing Mythologies: Twentieth-Century Canadian Constructions of Sir John Franklin'. In Norman Hillmer and Adam Chapnick eds. *Canadas of the Mind: The Making and Unmaking of Canadian Nationalisms in the Twentieth Century*. Montreal and Kingston: McGill-Queen's University Press, 2007: 15–45.
Cavell, Janice. 'Arctic Exploration in Canadian Print Culture, 1890–1930'. *Papers of the Bibliographic Society of Canada*, 44:2 (2006): 7–43.

Cavell, Janice. 'The Second Frontier: The North in English-Canadian Historical Writing'. *Canadian Historical Review*, 83 (2002): 364–89.
Chakrabarty, Dipesh. *Provincializing Europe: Postcolonial Thought and Historical Difference*. Princeton, New Jersey, and Oxford: Princeton University Press, 2000.
Chapin, David. *Exploring Other Worlds: Margaret Fox, Elisha Kent Kane and the Antebellum Culture of Curiosity*. Amherst and Boston: University of Massachusetts Press, 2004.
'Character Sketch: April. Mr. W. Parker Snow – Sailor, Explorer, and Author'. *Review of Reviews*, 7:4 (1893): 371–86.
Charron, Andrea. 'The Northwest Passage in Context'. *Canadian Military Journal*, 6 (2005–06): 41–8.
Chateaubriand, François-René de. *Memoirs of Chateaubriand, etc.* London: Henry Colburn, 1849.
Chodorow, Nancy Julia. 'Beyond Drive Theory: Object Relations and the Limits of Radical Individualism'. *Theory and Society*, 14:3 (1985): 271–319.
'Clairvoyance'. *The Morning Post*, 25 May 1850.
'Clairvoyance and its Tests'. *The Hull Packet and East Riding Times*, 6 July 1849.
'Clairvoyance and Sir John Franklin'. *Bell's Life in Sydney and Sporting Reviewer*, 9 November 1850.
'Clairvoyance at Peterhead'. *John O'Groat Journal*, 24 May 1850.
'Clairvoyance in Shetland'. *John O'Groat Journal*, 7 June 1850.
'Climbing up the North Pole'. *Punch, or the London Charivari*, 18 (1850): 87.
Clute, John. 'In the Belly of the Thing'. *Sci-Fi Weekly*, 513 (2007). Accessed at http://www.scifi.com/sfw/books/column/sfw15092.html on 14 November 2012.
Coleman, Ernest C. *The Royal Navy in Polar Exploration: From Frobisher to Ross*. Stroud: Tempus, 2006.
Coleridge, Samuel Taylor. *Samuel Taylor Coleridge: Poems*. London: Faber and Faber, 2011.
Collins, Wilkie. 'The Incredible Not Always Impossible'. *The Leader*, 3 April 1852: 328–9.
Collins, Wilkie. 'Magnetic Evenings at Home'. *The Leader*, 17 January 1852: 63–4; 14 February 1852: 160–1; 21 February 1852: 183–4; 28 February 1852: 207–8; 6 March 1852: 231–3; 13 March 1852: 256–7.
Collinson, Richard ed. *The Three Voyages of Martin Frobisher, in Search of a Passage to Cathaia and India by the North-West, A.D. 1576–8*. London: Hakluyt Society, 1867.
Colombo, John R. *The Big Book of Canadian Ghost Stories*. Toronto: Dundurn Press, 2008.
Conrad, Joseph. *Last Essays*. Harold Ray Stevens and J.H. Stape eds. Cambridge: Cambridge University Press, 2010.
Conrad, Joseph. *Youth: A Narrative. And Two Other Stories*. Edinburgh and London: W. Blackwood and Sons, 1902.
Cook, Frederick A. *My Attainment of the Pole: Being the Record of the Expedition that First Reached the Boreal Center, 1907–1909, etc.* New York: Polar Publishing Co., 1911.
Cooke, Christopher. *Curiosities of Occult Literature*. London: Arthur Hall, Smart, and Allen, 1863.
Costello, Dudley, W.H. Wills, and T.H. Wilson. 'The Magic Crystal'. *Household Words*, 2 (1850): 284–8.
Coulton, David T. 'Art. IV. 1. Narrative of an Expedition to the Shores of the Arctic Sea, in 1846 and 1847, etc.' *Quarterly Review*, 92 (1853): 386–421.
Crabtree, Adam. *From Mesmer to Freud: Magnetic Sleep and the Roots of Psychological Healing*. New Haven, Connecticut, and London: Yale University Press, 1993.
Craciun, Adriana. *Writing Arctic Disaster: Authorship and Exploration*. Cambridge: Cambridge University Press, 2016.
Craciun, Adriana. 'The Franklin Mystery'. *Literary Review of Canada*, 20:4 (2012): 3–5.
Craciun, Adriana. 'Writing the Disaster: Franklin and *Frankenstein*'. *Nineteenth-Century Literature*, 65:4 (2011): 433–80.
Crantz, David. *The History of Greenland: Containing a Description of the Country and its Inhabitants, etc.* 2 vols. London: Brethren's Society, 1767.
Cridge, Alfred. *Epitome of Spirit-Intercourse: A Condensed View of Spiritualism, in its Supernatural, Historical, Actual and Scientific Aspects, etc.* Boston: B. Marsh, 1854.
Crouch, David. 'Spatialities and the Feeling of Doing'. *Social and Cultural Geography*, 2 (2001): 61–75.
Cruise North Expeditions (2007). Accessed at http://www.cruisenorthexpeditions.com/Cruise_North_Brochure.pdf on 25 March 2012.
Cyriax, Richard J. *Sir John Franklin's Last Arctic Expedition: The Franklin Expedition. A Chapter in the History of the Royal Navy*. London: Methuen, 1939.
Cyriax, Richard J. and A.G.E. Jones. 'The Papers in Possession of Harry Peglar, Captain of the Foretop, H.M.S. Terror, 1845'. *The Mariner's Mirror*, 40 (1954): 186–95.

D'Arcy McGee, Thomas. *Selected Verse of Thomas D'Arcy McGee*. Toronto: Exile Editions, 2000.

David, Robert G. *The Arctic in the British Imagination, 1818–1914*. Manchester: Manchester University Press, 2000.

Davis, Richard C. '"Once Bitten, Twice Shy": Cultural Arrogance and the Final Franklin Expedition'. *Polar Geography*, 26 (2002): 21–38.

Davis, Richard C. 'From Conquest to Cognition: 20th Century Exploration Narratives'. *Arctic*, 34:1 (1981): 85–90.

Davis-Fisch, Heather. *Loss and Cultural Remains in Performance: The Ghosts of the Franklin Expedition*. Basingstoke: Palgrave Macmillan, 2012.

Dening, Greg. *Mr Bligh's Bad Language: Passion, Power and Theatre on the Bounty*. Cambridge: Cambridge University Press, 1992.

De Quincey, Thomas. *Confessions of an English Opium-eater*. London: London Magazine, 1821.

Derrida, Jacques. *Specters of Marx: The State of the Debt, The Work of Mourning, and the New International*. Peggy Kamuf trans. New York and London: Routledge, 2006.

Dickens, Charles. 'The Lost Arctic Voyagers'. *Household Words*, 10 (1854): 385–93.

Dickens, Charles. 'Some Account of an Extraordinary Traveller'. *Household Words*, 1 (1850): 73–7.

Dickerson, Vanessa D. *Victorian Ghosts in the Noontide: Women Writers and the Supernatural*. Columbia, Missouri, and London: University of Missouri Press, 1996.

Digby, Anne. *Making a Medical Living: Doctors and Patients in the English Market for Medicine, 1720–1911*. Cambridge: Cambridge University Press, 1994.

Dixon, Richard W. *Historical Odes and Other Poems*. London: Smith, Elder, and Co., 1864.

'Domestic Intelligence'. *Colonial Times*, 15 November 1850.

Donnelly, Tiffany. 'Mesmerism, Clairvoyance, and Literary Culture in Mid-Century Australia'. In Martin Willis and Catherine Wynne eds. *Victorian Literary Mesmerism*. Amsterdam and New York: Rodopi, 2006: 105–26.

Dowe, W. 'The Polar Seas and Sir John Franklin'. *Putnam's Monthly Magazine*, 1 (1853): 629–37.

Doyle, Arthur Conan. *Gothic Tales*. Oxford: Oxford University Press, 2016.

Doyle, Arthur Conan. *'Dangerous Work': Diary of an Arctic Adventure*. Jon Lellenberg and Daniel Stashower eds. London: British Library, 2012.

Doyle, Arthur Conan. *Memories and Adventures*. New York and Oxford: Oxford University Press, 1989.

'Dream Fortunes'. *Western Times*, 3 September 1903.

Driver, Felix. 'Hidden Histories Made Visible? Reflections on a Geographical Exhibition'. *Transactions of the Institute of British Geographers*, 38 (2013): 420–35.

Driver, Felix. *Geography Militant: Cultures of Exploration and Empire*. Oxford: Blackwell, 2001.

DuBois, Thomas A. *An Introduction to Shamanism*. Cambridge: Cambridge University Press, 2009.

Dubow, Jessica. '"From a Vision of the World to a Point of View in it": Rethinking Sight, Space and the Colonial Subject'. *Interventions*, 2 (2000): 87–102.

Eadon, S. 'Visit to the Celebrated Clairvoyant of Bolton'. *The Sheffield and Rotherham Independent*, 21 March 1853.

Eber, Dorothy H. *Encounters on the Passage: Inuit meet the Explorers*. Toronto, Buffalo, and London: University of Toronto Press, 2008.

Eber, Dorothy H. *When the Whalers Were up North: Inuit Memories from the Eastern Arctic*. Kingston, Ontario and London: McGill-Queen's University Press, 1989.

Edge, Arabella. *Fields of Ice*. London: Picador, 2011.

Editorial. *The Times*, 23 September 1859.

Edric, Robert. *The Broken Lands*. London: Jonathan Cape, 1992.

Edwards, Justin D. *Gothic Canada: Reading the Spectre of a National Literature*. Edmonton, Alberta: University of Alberta Press, 2005.

Egerton, Francis. 'Barrow on the Arctic Voyages'. *Quarterly Review*, 78 (1846): 45–8.

Elce, Erika B. '"Far as the Eye can Reach": Scientific Exploration and Explorer's Poetry in the Arctic, 1832–1852'. *Victorian Poetry*, 41:1 (2003): 73–92.

Elce, Erika B. 'Voices of Silence, Texts of Truth: Imperial Discourse and Cultural Negotiations in Nineteenth-Century British Arctic Exploration'. PhD Thesis: Queen's University, Kingston, 2002a.

Elce, Erika B. 'On the Trail of an Arctic Tale: Tracing Sir John Franklin in Wilkie Collins's and Charles Dickens's *The Frozen Deep*'. In Irene Blayer and Monica Sanchez eds. *Storytelling: Interdisciplinary and Intercultural Perspectives*. New York and Oxford: Peter Lang, 2002b: 58–71.

Elliotson, John. 'The Clairvoyance of Mr. Haddock's Subject'. *The Zoist: A Journal of Cerebral Physiology & Mesmerism, and Their Applications to Human Welfare*, 7 (1849–50): 318–23.

'An Episode of the Franklin Expedition'. *Paisley Herald and Renfrewshire Advertiser*, 31 December 1859.
'Erebus and Terror National Historic Site of Canada'. Accessed at http://www.historicplaces.ca/en/rep-reg/place-lieu.aspx?id=19683 on 27 December 2014.
Ernst, Waltraud. 'Colonial Psychiatry, Magic and Religion: The Case of Mesmerism in British India'. *History of Psychiatry*, 15:1 (2004): 57–71.
Ernst, Waltraud. *Mad Tales from the Raj: The European Insane in British India*. London and New York: Routledge, 1991.
Esdaile, James. *Natural and Mesmeric Clairvoyance, with the Practical Application of Mesmerism in Surgery and Medicine*. London: H. Baillière, 1852.
Eskimaux and English Vocabulary, for the Use of the Arctic Expedition. London: John Murray, 1850.
'Extraordinary Case of Clairvoyance'. *The New Monthly Belle Assemblée*, 30 (1849): 108–9.
Fabian, Johannes. *Time and the Other: How Anthropology Makes its Object*. New York: Columbia University Press, 1983.
Faulkner, Joseph P. *Eighteen Months on a Greenland Whaler*. New York: s.n., 1878.
Fawcett, J. 'Case of Clairvoyance'. *The Spiritual Magazine*, 1 (1860): 281–3.
Feeney, Robert E. *Polar Journeys: The Role of Food and Nutrition in Early Exploration*. Washington, DC, and Fairbanks: University of Alaska Press, 1997.
Fisher, Alexander. *A Journal of a Voyage of Discovery to the Arctic Regions, in His Majesty's Ships Hecla and Griper, in the Years 1819 & 1820*. 4th ed. London: Longman, Hurst, Rees, Orme, and Brown, 1821.
Flanagan, Richard. *Wanting*. London: Atlantic Books, 2009.
Fleming, Fergus. *Barrow's Boys*. London: Granta, 1998.
Fluhmann, May. *Second in Command: A Biography of Captain Francis Crozier R.N., F.R.S., F.R.A.S.* Yellowknife: Department of Information, Northwest Territories, 1976.
Fortier, Dominique. *Du Bon Usage des Étoiles*. Québec: Alto, 2008.
Fox, Caroline. *Memories of Old Friends: Being Extracts from the Journals and Letters of Caroline Fox of Penjerrick, Cornwall, from 1835 to 1871*. Horace N. Pym ed. London: Smith, Elder & Co., 1883.
'Franklin and the Clairvoyants'. *Belfast Newsletter*, 29 December 1851.
Franklin, Colleen M. '"An Habitation of Devils, a Domicill for Unclean Spirits, and a Den of Goblings": The Marvelous North in Early Modern English Literature'. In Helen Ostovich, Mary V. Silcox, and Graham Roebuck eds. *The Mysterious and the Foreign in Early Modern England*. Newark: University of Delaware Press, 2008: 27–38.
Franklin, Jane. *As Affecting the Fate of My Absent Husband: Selected Letters of Lady Franklin Concerning the Search for the Lost Franklin Expedition, 1848–1860*. Erika B. Elce ed. Montreal: McGill-Queen's University Press, 2009.
Franklin, John. *Sir John Franklin's Journal and Correspondence: The First Arctic Land Expedition, 1819–1822*. Richard C. Davis ed. Toronto: Champlain Society, 1995.
Franklin, John. *Narrative of a Journey to the Shores of the Polar Sea, in the Years 1819, 20, 21, and 22*. London: John Murray, 1823.
'The Franklin Expedition'. *Portsmouth Evening News*, 12 August 1893.
'The Franklin Mystery'. *Light: A Journal of Psychical, Occult, and Mystical Research*, 9:445 (1889): 339–40.
'The Franklin Mystery'. *Liverpool Mercury*, 16 July 1889.
'The Franklin Mystery'. *Liverpool Mercury*, 22 June 1889.
Frye, Northrop. *The Bush Garden: Essays on the Canadian Imagination*. Toronto: Anansi, 1971.
Fulford, Tim. 'The Sound of the Shaman: Scientists and Indians in the Arctic'. In Tim Fulford and Kevin Hutchings eds. *Native Americans and Anglo-American Culture, 1750–1850*. Cambridge: Cambridge University Press, 2009: 171–96.
Fulford, Tim, Debbie Lee, and Peter J. Kitson. *Literature, Science and Exploration in the Romantic Era: Bodies of Knowledge*. Cambridge: Cambridge University Press, 2004.
Further Papers Relative to the Recent Arctic Expeditions in Search of Sir John Franklin and the Crews of H.M.S. 'Erebus' and 'Terror'. House of Commons Sessional Papers, Accounts and Papers 35:1898 (1854–5).
Garrison, Laurie. 'Virtual Reality and Subjective Responses: Narrating the Search for the Franklin Expedition through Robert Burford's Panorama'. *Early Popular Visual Culture*, 10:1 (2012): 7–22.
Garson, John G. and Charles Hercules Read. *Notes and Queries on Anthropology edited for the Council of the Anthropological Institute*. 2nd ed. London: The Anthropological Institute, 1892.

Geiger, John. 'Prime Minister Stephen Harper on the Franklin Find'. *Canadian Geographic* (2014). Accessed at http://www.canadiangeographic.ca/magazine/dec14/interview-stephen-harper-franklin-expedition.asp on 5 May 2015.

Geiger, John. *The Third Man Factor: Surviving the Impossible*. Edinburgh: Canongate, 2010.

Geiger, John. 'Ottawa to Mount Search for Lost Franklin Ships'. *Globe and Mail*, 13 August 2008.

'Ghost Story of the Arctic'. *Western Morning News*, 10 December 1934.

Gibson, James J. *The Ecological Approach to Visual Perception*. Boston and London: Houghton Mifflin, 1979.

Gieryn, Thomas F. *Cultural Boundaries of Science: Credibility on the Line*. Chicago: University of Chicago Press, 1999.

Gilder, Richard W. *The Poems*. Boston and New York: Houghton Mifflin Company; The Riverside Press, 1908.

Glickman, Susan. *The Picturesque and the Sublime: A Poetics of the Canadian Landscape*. Montreal and London: McGill-Queen's University Press, 1998.

Godfrey, William C. *Godfrey's Narrative of the Last Grinnell Arctic Exploring Expedition, in Search of Sir John Franklin, 1853–4-5, etc.* Philadelphia: J.T. Lloyd, 1857.

Goldman, Marlenne and Joanne Saul. 'Talking with Ghosts: Haunting in Canadian Cultural Production'. *University of Toronto Quarterly*, 75:2 (2006): 645–55.

Goode's Universal Dream Book. London: T. Goode [1854?].

Gordon, Avery F. *Ghostly Matters: Haunting and the Sociological Imagination*. Minneapolis and London: University of Minnesota Press, 1997.

Grace, Sherrill E. 'From the "Hand of Franklin" to *Frobisher*: Opera in the Canadian North'. In Anka Ryall, Johan Schimanski, and Henning Howild Wærp eds. *Arctic Discourses*. Newcastle: Cambridge Scholars, 2010: 283–300

Grace, Sherrill E. *Canada and the Idea of North*. Montreal and London: McGill-Queen's University Press, 2007.

Grace, Sherrill E. 'Reconfiguring North: Canadian Identity in the 21st Century'. In Marc Maufort and Franca Bellarsi eds. *Reconfigurations: Canadian Literatures and Postcolonial Identities*. Brussels and Oxford: P.I.E.-P. Lang, 2002: 215–30.

Grace, Sherrill E. 'Gendering Northern Narrative'. In John Moss ed. *Echoing Silence: Essays on Arctic Narrative*. Ottawa: University of Ottawa Press, 1997: 163–81.

Gran, Tryggve. *The Norwegian with Scott: Tryggve Gran's Antarctic Diary, 1910–1913*. Geoffrey Hattersley-Smith ed. Ellen Johanne McGhie trans. Greenwich: National Maritime Museum, 1984.

'The Greely Expedition'. *London Standard*, 18 August 1884.

Greenblatt, Stephen. *Marvelous Possessions: The Wonder of the New World*. Chicago: University of Chicago Press, 1991.

Gregory, William. *Letters to a Candid Inquirer on Animal Magnetism*. Philadelphia: Blanchard and Lea, 1851.

Griffiths, Sian. 'Canadian Archaeologists Hunt Long-Lost Arctic Explorers'. *BBC News: US & Canada*. Accessed at http://www.bbc.co.uk/news/world-us-canada-10705564 on 21 July 2010.

'Guidelines for Evaluating Shipwrecks of National Historical Significance'. Parks Canada. Accessed at http://www.pc.gc.ca/docs/pc/guide/res/arch4_a.aspx on 23 March 2011.

Guneriussen, Willy. 'Modernity Re-enchanted: Making a "Magic" Region'. In Jørgen Ole Bærenholdt and Brynhild Granås eds. *Mobility and Place: Enacting Northern European Peripheries*. Aldershot: Ashgate, 2008: 233–44.

Hacquebord, Louwrens. 'Five Early European Winterings in the Atlantic Arctic (1596–1635): A Comparison'. *Arctic*, 44:2 (1991): 146–55.

Haddock, Joseph W. *Somnolism & Psycheism: Otherwise Vital Magnetism, or Mesmerism: Considered Physiologically and Philosophically*. London: J.S. Hodson, 1851.

Haddock, Joseph W. *Somnolism and Psycheism: Otherwise Vital Magnetism, or Mesmerism: Considered Physiologically and Philosophically*. London: J.S. Hodson, 1849.

Hadley, Louisa. *Neo-Victorian Fiction and Historical Narratives: The Victorians and Us*. Basingstoke: Palgrave Macmillan, 2010.

Hains, Brigid. *The Ice and the Inland: Mawson, Flynn, and the Myth of the Frontier*. Carlton South, Victoria: Melbourne University Press, 2002.

Hall, Charles F. *Narrative of the Second Arctic Expedition made by Charles F. Hall: His Voyage to Repulse Bay, Sledge Journeys to the Straits of Fury and Hecla and to King William's Land, and Residence*

among the Eskimos during the Years 1864-'69. J.E. Nourse ed. Washington: Government Printing Office, 1879.
Hall, Charles F. *Life with the Esquimaux: the Narrative of Captain Charles Francis Hall, of the Whaling Barque 'George Henry', from the 29th May 1860, to the 13th September 1862*. 2 vols. London: S. Low, Son, and Marston, 1864.
Hands, Joseph. 'Mesmeric Cure of a Case Pronounced by Different Physicians to be Consumption, Dropsy, and Disease of the Kidneys, with Numerous Instruments of Clairvoyance that Appeared in it'. *The Zoist: A Journal of Cerebral Physiology & Mesmerism, and Their Applications to Human Welfare*, 5 (1847–8): 328–43.
Hanlon, Sean. *The Frozen Franklin*. New York: Pocket Books, 1990.
Hansard, 1850. 7 January 1850: 138–41.
Harper, Kenn. *Give Me My Father's Body: The Life of Minik, the New York Eskimo*. Newmarket, Ontario: Blacklead Books, 1986.
Harper, Stephen. 'Prime Minister Announces Expansion of Canadian Forces Facilities and Operations in the Arctic'. Prime Minister of Canada (2007a). Accessed at http://pm.gc.ca/eng/media.asp?id=1787 on 21 March 2011.
Harper, Stephen. 'Prime Minister Announces Expansion of Nahanni National Park Reserve'. Prime Minister of Canada (2007b). Accessed at http://pm.gc.ca/eng/media.asp?id=1781 on 21 March 2011.
Harvey, David A. *Beyond Enlightenment: Occultism and Politics in Modern France*. DeKalb: Northern Illinois University Press, 2005.
Hayes, Edward. 'Sir Humphrey Gilbert's Voyage to Newfoundland'. In Charles W. Eliot ed. *Voyages and Travels, Ancient and Modern*. Vol. 33. New York: P.F. Collier, 1910: 271–308.
Hayes, Isaac I. *Pictures of Arctic Travel: Greenland*. New York: G.W. Carleton, 1881.
Hayes, Isaac I. *The Open Polar Sea. A Narrative of a Voyage of Discovery towards the North Pole, in the Schooner 'United States'*. London: Sampson Low, 1867.
Heidegger, Martin. *The Fundamental Concepts of Metaphysics: World, Finitude, Solitude*. William McNeill and Nicholas Walker trans. Bloomington, Indiana: Indiana University Press, 1995.
Hendrik, Hans. *Memoirs of Hans Hendrik, the Arctic Traveller, serving under Kane, Hayes, Hall and Nares, 1853–1876*. Henry Rink trans. London: Trübner & Co., 1878.
Herbert, Kari. *Polar Wives: The Remarkable Women behind the World's Most Daring Explorers*. Vancouver: Greystone Books, 2012.
Hill, Jen. *White Horizon: The Arctic in the Nineteenth-Century British Imagination*. Albany, New York: State University of New York Press, 2008.
'A Hint to Mesmerists, If they can take it'. *The Dundee Courier and Argus*, 23 December 1881.
Holland, Clive and F.F. Hill. 'Sir William Edward Parry's Barrel Organ'. *Polar Record*, 16:102 (1972): 413–4.
Holland, Clive and James M. Savelle. 'My Dear Beaufort: A Personal Letter from John Ross's Arctic Expedition of 1829–33'. *Arctic*, 40:1 (1987): 66–77.
Holloway, Julian. 'Enchanted Spaces: The Séance, Affect, and Geographies of Religion'. *Annals of the Association of American Geographers*, 96:1 (2006): 182–7.
Holloway, Julian and James Kneale. 'Locating Haunting: A Ghost-hunter's Guide'. *Cultural Geographies*, 15:3 (2008): 297–312.
Home, Daniel D. *Incidents in My Life*. 5th ed. New York: A.J. Davis & Co., 1864.
Hood, Edwin P. *Dream Land and Ghost Land: Visits and Wanderings there in the Nineteenth Century*. London: Partridge and Oakey, 1852.
Hood, Thomas. 'The Shadow of a Shade'. In Michael Cox and R.A. Gilbert. *The Oxford Book of Victorian Ghost Stories*. Oxford and New York: Oxford University Press, 2003: 150–62.
Hopkins, Brian A. and Donald W. Schank. *Cold at Heart*. Pasco, Washington: Starlance, 1997.
Horkheimer Max and Theodor W. Adorno. *Dialectic of Enlightenment: Philosophical Fragments*. Gunzelin Schmid Noerr ed. Edmund Jephcott trans. Stanford, California: Stanford University Press, 2002.
'How Sir John Franklin was not Found'. *Saturday Review of Politics, Literature, Science and Art*, 67 (1889): 520.
Hrdlička, Aleš. *An Eskimo Brain*. New York: The Knickerbocker Press, 1901.
Hudson, H. *An Attempt to Explain Some of the Wonders and Mysteries of Mesmerism, Biology, and Clairvoyance*. Chorley: Geo. Houghton, Stamp-Office, 1852.
Huebert, Rob. 'Climate Change and Canadian Sovereignty in the Northwest Passage'. *Isuma: Canadian Journal of Policy Research*, 2 (2001): 86–94.

Huish, Robert ed. *The Last Voyage of Capt. Sir John Ross, R.N. Knt. to the Arctic Regions: for the Discovery of a North West Passage; performed in the years 1829–30-31–32 and 33 etc.* London: J. Saunders, 1835.
'The Humbug of Clairvoyance'. *John O'Groat Journal*, 19 July 1850.
Huntford, Roland. *Nansen: The Explorer as Hero*. London: Abacus, 1997.
Huntford, Roland. *Shackleton*. New York: Antheum, 1986.
'I.E.' 'Dirge of the Antarctic'. *The Cheltenham Looker-on*, 15 February 1913: 10.
Inglefield, Edward Augustus. *A Summer Search for Sir John Franklin: With a Peep into the Polar Basin*. London: Thomas Harrison, 1853.
Ingold, Tim. *Being Alive: Essays on Movement, Knowledge and Description*. London and New York: Routledge, 2011.
'Interesting Case of Clairvoyance'. *The Journal of Health: A Monthly Magazine, Devoted to the Illustration and Advocacy of the Principles of Health and Longevity*, 1 (1849): 78–9.
Irlbacher-Fox, Stephanie. *Finding Dahshaa: Self-Government, Social Suffering, and Aboriginal Policy in Canada*. Vancouver and Toronto: UBC Press, 2009.
Jackson, Colin. 'Three Puzzles from Early Nineteenth Century Arctic Exploration'. *Northern Mariner*, 17:3 (2007): 1–17.
Jacobs, Annaliese. 'Arctic Circles: The Franklin Family, Networks of Knowledge, and Early Nineteenth-Century Arctic Exploration, 1818–1859'. PhD Thesis: University of Illinois at Urbana-Champaign, 2015.
James, Thomas. *The Strange and Dangerous Voyage of Captaine Thomas James: A Critical Edition*. Colleen M. Franklin ed. Montreal: McGill-Queen's University Press, 2014.
James, Thomas. *The Strange and Dangerous Voyage of Capt. Thomas James*. W.A. Kenyon ed. Toronto: Royal Ontario Museum, 1975.
Janvier, Thomas A. *Henry Hudson: A Brief Statement of his Aims and Achievements*. New York: Harper, 1909.
Jennings, Amelia C. *Linden Rhymes*. Halifax: E.G. Fuller, 1854.
Jerdan, William. *Men I have Known*. London: G. Routledge, 1866.
Johnston, R. *The Arctic Expedition of 1875–6: Compiled from Official Sources with a Summary of Previous Adventures in the Arctic Seas*. London: F. Warne & Co., 1877.
Joven. 'The End of an Epic'. *The Ladies' Companion, and Monthly Magazine*, 16 (1859): 242–6.
Kane, Elisha K. *Arctic Explorations: The Second Grinnell Expedition in Search of Sir John Franklin, 1853, '54, '55*. 2 vols. Philadelphia: Childs and Peterson, 1856.
Kane, Elisha K. *The U.S. Grinnell Expedition in Search of Sir John Franklin: A Personal Narrative*. New York: Harper and Brothers, 1854.
Kaplan, Fred. *Dickens and Mesmerism: The Hidden Springs of Fiction*. Princeton, New Jersey: Princeton University Press, 1975.
Karamanski, Theodore J. 'The Heroic Idea: Romantic Literature and the British Exploration of the Antarctic, 1901–1914'. *Fram: The Journal of Polar Studies*, 1:2 (1984): 461–9.
Kay, Mary A. *A Brave Man and his Belongings: Being some Passages in the Life of Sir John Franklin, etc.* London: S. Taylor, 1874.
Keats, John. *The Complete Poetical Works and Letters of John Keats*. Boston and New York: Houghton, Mifflin, and Company, 1899.
Keely, Robert N. and Gwylim George Davis. *In the Arctic Seas: The Voyage of the 'Kite' with the Peary Expedition, Together with a Transcript of the Log of the 'Kite'*. Philadelphia: R.C. Hantranft, 1892.
Keenleyside, Anne, Margaret Bertulli, and Henry C. Fricke. 'The Final Days of the Franklin Expedition: New Skeletal Evidence'. *Arctic*, 50:1 (1997): 36–46.
Kennedy, William. *A Short Narrative of the Second Voyage of the Prince Albert, in Search of Sir John Franklin*. London: W.H. Dalton, 1853.
Kertzer, Jonathan. *Worrying the Nation: Imagining a National Literature in English Canada*. Toronto and London: University of Toronto Press, 1998.
Knight, Charles. *Passages of a Working Life during Half a Century: A Prelude to Early Reminiscences*. 3 vols. London: Bradbury & Evans, 1864.
'Lady Franklin's Lament'. Allegro Catalogue of Ballads, Bodleian Library, University of Oxford, (c.1852) Firth c.12(81).
'Lady Franklin's Lament for her Husband'. Allegro Catalogue of Ballads, Bodleian Library, University of Oxford, (c.1852) Firth c.12(83).
Lambert, Andrew. *Franklin: Tragic Hero of Polar Navigation*. London: Faber and Faber, 2010.

Lamont, Peter. *The First Psychic: The Peculiar Mystery of a Notorious Victorian Wizard*. London: Abacus, 2006.

Landy, Joshua and Michael Saler eds. *The Re-enchantment of the World: Secular Magic in a Rational Age*. Stanford, California: Stanford University Press, 2009.

Larisey, P. *Light for a Cold Land: Lawren Harris's Work and Life – An Interpretation*. Toronto: Dundurn Press, 1993.

Larson, Frances. *Severed: A History of Heads Lost and Heads Found*. London: Granta, 2014.

Latta, J.B. *The Franklin Conspiracy: Cover-up, Betrayal, and the Astonishing Secret behind the Lost Arctic Expedition*. Toronto and Tonawanda, New York: Hounslow Press, 2001.

Learmonth, L.A. 'Ross Meets the Netchiliks'. *The Beaver*, 279 (1948): 10–13.

'Lecture on the Arctic Regions by Captain Kennedy'. *Morning Chronicle*, 20 December 1860.

Lefebvre, Henri. *The Production of Space*. Donald Nicholson-Smith trans. Oxford: Blackwell, 1991.

Lehmann, H. 'Two Dreams and a Childhood Memory of Freud'. *Journal of the American Psychoanalytic Association*, 14 (1966): 388–405.

'Leichhardt'. *Bell's Life in Sydney and Sporting Reviewer*, 9 November 1850.

'Letter from Cleveland to the Readers of the Journal of Man'. *Buchanan's Journal of Man*, 3 (1852): 7–19.

Letters Written during the Late Voyage of Discovery in the Western Arctic Sea. By an Officer of the Expedition. London: R. Phillips & Co., 1821.

Levere, Trevor H. *Science and the Canadian Arctic: A Century of Exploration, 1818–1918*. Cambridge: Cambridge University Press, 1993.

Lewes, George Henry. 'The Fallacy of Clairvoyance'. *The Leader*, 27 March 1852: 305.

'Lieut. Chipp's Father's Dream'. *New York Times*, 22 December 1881.

Lincoln, Margarette. 'Shipwreck Narratives of the Eighteenth and Early Nineteenth Century: Indicators of Culture and Identity'. *Journal for Eighteenth-Century Studies*, 20:2 (1997): 155–72.

Lipman, Caron. *Co-habiting with Ghosts: Knowledge, Experience, Belief and the Domestic Uncanny*. Farnham, Surrey and Burlington, Vermont: Ashgate, 2014.

'Liverpool Clairvoyantes'. *Liverpool Mercury*, 26 March 1850.

'Liverpool Mental Science Association'. *Liverpool Mercury*, 30 April 1883.

Lloyd-Jones, Ralph. 'The Paranormal Arctic: Lady Franklin, Sophia Cracroft, and Captain and 'Little Weesy' Coppin'. *Polar Record*, 37:200 (2001): 27–34.

Lloyd-Jones, Ralph. 'An Evangelical Christian on Franklin's Last Expedition: Lieutenant John Irving of HMS *Terror*'. *Polar Record*, 33:187 (1997): 327–32.

Lloyd-Jones, Ralph. 'Parry's Polarities: Lord Byron and William Parry, Arctic Explorer'. *The Byron Journal*, 24 (1996): 59–67.

'The "Londonderry Vision"'. *Hawke's Bay Herald*, 29 September 1889.

'Long Arctic Experiences'. *Daily Mail*, 3 December 1902.

Loomis, Chauncey C. *Weird and Tragic Shores: The Story of Charles Francis Hall, Explorer*. Lincoln and London: University of Nebraska Press, 1991.

Loomis, Chauncey C. 'The Arctic Sublime'. In U.C. Knoepflmacher and G.B. Tennyson eds. *Nature and the Victorian Imagination*. Berkeley, California: University of California Press, 1977: 95–112.

'The Loss of the Polar Star'. *Dundee Courier*, 17 November 1899.

The Love-life of Dr. Kane; Containing the Correspondence, and a History of the Acquaintance, Engagement, and Secret Marriage between Elisha K. Kane and Margaret Fox, with Facsimiles of Letters, and her Portrait. New York: Carleton, 1866.

Luckhurst, Roger. 'The Mummy's Curse: A Study in Rumour'. *Critical Quarterly*, 52:3 (2010): 6–22.

Lutz, John S. 'First Contact as Spiritual Performance: Encounters on the North American West Coast'. In Lutz ed. *Myth and Memory: Stories of Indigenous-European Contact*. Vancouver and Toronto: UBC Press, 2007: 30–45.

Lyon, George. *A Brief Narrative of an Unsuccessful Attempt to reach Repulse Bay: Through Sir Thomas Rowe's 'Welcome' in His Majesty's Ship Griper, in the Year 1824*. London: John Murray, 1825.

Lyon, George. *The Private Journal of Captain G.F. Lyon, of H.M.S. Hecla during the recent Voyage of Discovery under Captain Parry*. London: John Murray, 1824.

MacDonald, Alistair. 'Failed Search Deepens Mystery of Vanished Explorers'. *Wall Street Journal*, 31 August 2010.

MacEwen, Gwendolyn. *Afterworlds*. Toronto: McClelland and Stewart, 1987.

Macfarlane, Robert. 'Read it on the Autobahn'. *London Review of Books*, 25:4 (2003): 26.

MacInnis, J.B. 'The Breadalbane Project: Implications for the Discovery of Franklin's Ships'. In P.D. Sutherland ed. *The Franklin Era in Canadian Arctic History, 1845–1859*. Ottawa: National Museums of Canada, 1985: 174–84.
Mack, John. *The Sea: A Cultural History*. London: Reaktion, 2011.
Mackenzie, Alexander. *Voyages from Montreal through the Continent of North America to the Frozen and Pacific Oceans in 1789 and 1793*. 2 vols. New York: New Amsterdam Book Co., 1902.
MacLaren, Ian S. 'Booking a Northwest Passage: Thomas James and *The Strange and Dangerous Voyage* (1633)'. In Frédéric Regard ed. *The Quest for the Northwest Passage: Knowledge, Nation and Empire, 1576–1806*. London: Pickering & Chatto, 2013: 89–102.
MacLaren, Ian S. 'From Exploration to Publication: The Evolution of a 19th-Century Arctic Narrative'. *Arctic*, 47:1 (1994): 43–53.
MacLaren, Ian S. 'Samuel Hearne's Accounts of the Massacre at Bloody Fall, 17 July 1771'. *Ariel: A Review of International English Literature*, 22:1 (1991): 25–51.
MacLaren, Ian S. 'Arctic Exploration and Milton's "Frozen Continent": A Note'. *Notes and Queries*, 31 (1984a): 325–6.
MacLaren, Ian S. 'Retaining Captaincy of the Soul: Response to Nature in the First Franklin Expedition'. *Essays on Canadian Writing*, 28 (1984b): 57–92.
Macnish, Robert. *The Philosophy of Sleep*. New York: D. Appleton, 1834.
Maitland, S.R. *Illustrations and Enquires Relating to Mesmerism. Part 1*. London: William Stephenson, 1849.
Malley, Annesley and Mary McLaughlin. *Captain William Coppin: 'Neptune's Brightest Star'*. Londonderry: Foyle Civic Trust, 1992.
Markham, Clements R. et al. 'Report of the Arctic Committee of the Anthropological Institute'. *Journal of the Anthropological Institute of Great Britain and Ireland*, 2 (1873): 291–306.
Marra, John. *Journal of the Resolution's Voyage in 1772, 1773, 1774 and 1775, on Discovery to the Southern Hemisphere, etc.* London: F. Newbery, 1775.
Martineau, Harriet. *Harriet Martineau's Autobiography: With Memorials by Maria Weston Chapman*. 3 vols. London: Smith, Elder & Co., 1877.
Marx, Karl. *The Eighteenth Brumaire of Louis Bonaparte*. D. de Leon trans. 3rd ed. Chicago: Charles H. Kerr, 1919.
Mazoff, C.D. 'Strategies of Colonial Legitimation in the Early Canadian Long Poem'. *Canadian Poetry*, 36 (1995): 81–113.
McClintock, Anne. *Imperial Leather: Race, Gender and Sexuality in the Colonial Contest*. New York and London: Routledge, 1995.
McClintock, Francis L. *The Voyage of the 'Fox' in the Arctic Seas: A Narrative of the Discovery of the Fate of Sir John Franklin and his Companions*. London: John Murray, 1859.
McClure, Robert. *The Discovery of the North-West Passage, etc.* Sherard Osborn ed. 2nd ed. London: Longman, Brown, Green, Longmans, & Roberts, 1857.
McCorristine, Shane. '"Involuntarily we Listen": Hearing the Aurora Borealis in Nineteenth-Century Arctic Exploration and Science'. *Canadian Journal of History*, 48:1 (2013): 29–61.
McCorristine, Shane. ed. *Spiritualism, Mesmerism and the Occult, 1800–1920*. 5 vols. London: Pickering & Chatto, 2012.
McCorristine, Shane. *Spectres of the Self: Thinking about Ghosts and Ghost-seeing in England, 1750–1920*. Cambridge: Cambridge University Press, 2010.
McGoogan, Ken. *Lady Franklin's Revenge: A True Story of Ambition, Obsession and the Remaking of Arctic History*. London: Bantam, 2006.
McGoogan, Ken. *Fatal Passage: The Untold Story of John Rae, the Arctic Adventurer who Discovered the Fate of Franklin*. London: Bantam, 2002.
McIlraith, John. *Life of Sir John Richardson*. London: Longmans, Green and Co., 1868.
'Melville's Wife's Story'. *The New York Times*, 21 May 1882.
Mereweather, John D. *Diary of a Working Clergyman in Australia and Tasmania etc*. London: Hatchard and Co., 1859.
'Mesmeric Divination'. *The Morning Post*, 29 April 1853.
'Mesmeric Humbug and Quackery'. *The London Lancet*, 2 (1851): 154–5.
'Mesmerism'. *The Aberdeen Journal*, 28 June 1843.
'Mesmerism'. *Colonial Times*, 8 November 1850.
'Mesmerism and Clairvoyance'. *South Australian Register*, 20 January 1851.
'Mesmerism and Clairvoyance'. *Dumfries and Galloway Standard and Advertiser*, 11 September 1850.
'Mesmerism – Illustrated Lectures by Hill H. Hardy, A.M., T.C.D.' *Freeman's Journal*, 20 March 1852.
'Mesmerism: To the Editor of the *Argus*'. *The Argus*, 8 November 1850.

Miertsching, Johann. *Frozen Ships: The Arctic Diary of Johann Miertsching, 1850–1854*. L.H. Neatby trans. Toronto: Macmillan, 1967.

Mitcham, Allison. 'Northern Utopia'. *Canadian Literature*, 63 (1975): 35–9.

Moodie, Susanna. *Roughing it in the Bush; or, Life in Canada*. 2 vols. London: R. Bentley, 1852.

Morash, Chris. 'Spectres of the Famine'. *Irish Review*, 17–18 (1995): 74–9.

'More of Zadkiel and Zadkielism'. *The Leeds Times*, 11 July 1863.

Morris, Timothy. 'Dickinson's Arctic'. *The Emily Dickinson Journal*, 6:1 (1997): 89–108.

Morus, Iwan Rhys. '"The Nervous System of Britain": Space, Time and the Electric Telegraph in the Victorian Age'. *British Journal for the History of Science*, 33:4 (2000): 455–75.

Motherwell, J.B. et al., 'Mesmerism in Australia'. *The Zoist: A Journal of Cerebral Physiology & Mesmerism, and Their Applications to Human Welfare*, 9 (1851–2): 69–71.

Moultrie, John. *Poems*. London: William Pickering, 1838.

'Moving (Dioramic) Experiences'. *All the Year Round*, 17 (1866–7): 304–7.

'Mrs. Hardinge's Lectures'. *Manchester Weekly Times*, 20 February 1869.

'Mr. W. Boyd, Peterhead, on Clairvoyance'. *The Aberdeen Journal*, 16 May 1891.

Murphy, Jessica. 'Canada Shipwreck claims another victim 170 years later: a Muck-Raking Journalist'. *The Guardian*, 11 July 2015.

Murray, T.B. *Kalli, the Esquimaux Christian*. London: Society for Promoting Christian Knowledge, 1856.

Nadolny, Sten. *The Discovery of Slowness*. Ralph Freedman trans. Edinburgh: Canongate, 2003.

Nansen, Fridtjof. *Farthest North: Being the Record of a Voyage of Exploration of the Ship Fram, 1893–96, and of a Fifteen Months' Sleigh Journey*. 2 vols. Westminster: Archibald Constable & Co., 1897.

Nayder, Lillian. 'The Cannibal, the Nurse, and the Cook in Dickens's "The Frozen Deep"'. *Victorian Literature and Culture*, 19 (1991): 1–24.

Nelson, George. *'The Orders of the Dreamed': George Nelson on Cree and Northern Ojibwa Religion and Myth, 1823*. Jennifer S.H. Brown and Robert Brightman, eds. Winnipeg, Manitoba: University of Manitoba Press, 1988.

Neumann, Roderick P. *Imposing Wilderness: Struggles over Livelihood and Nature Preservation in Africa*. Berkeley, California, and London: University of California Press, 1998.

'The New Arctic Expedition'. *Newcastle Journal*, 2 August 1861.

'A Night with the Clairvoyants'. *Dundee, Perth, and Cupar Advertiser*, 14 May 1850.

Northern Regions. A Relation of Uncle Richard's Voyages of Discovery of a North-West Passage, and an Account of the Overland Journies of Other Enterprizing Travellers, 2nd ed. London: J. Harris, 1826.

'Notes by the Way'. *Light: A Journal of Psychical, Occult, and Mystical Research*, 9 (1889): 197–8.

'Notes from our London Correspondent'. *York Herald*, 19 November 1859.

'Not Looking for Franklin's Ships This Year, Private Researcher Says'. *CBC News*, 15 September 2009. Accessed at http://www.cbc.ca/news/canada/north/story/2009/09/15/franklin-search.html on 14 October 2010.

Nuttall, Mark. *Arctic Homeland: Kinship, Community and Development in Northwest Greenland*. London: Belhaven Press, 1992.

Officer, Charles and Jake Page. *A Fabulous Kingdom: The Exploration of the Arctic*. Oxford: Oxford University Press, 2001.

O'Loughlin, Ed. *Minds of Winter*. London: Riverrun, 2016.

Onley, Toni. *Onley's Arctic: Diaries and Paintings of the High Arctic*. Vancouver: Douglas & McIntyre, 1989.

Oosten, Jarcih, Frédéric Laugrand, and Cornelius Remie. 'Perceptions of Decline: Inuit Shamanism in the Canadian Arctic'. *Ethnohistory*, 53 (2006): 445–77.

'The Orangemen and their Members'. *Liverpool Mercury*, 19 March 1890.

Osborn, Sherard. *The Career, Last Voyage, and Fate of Captain Sir John Franklin*. London: Bradbury and Evans, 1860.

Osborn, Sherard. *Stray Leaves from an Arctic Journal; Eighteen Months in the Polar Regions, in Search of Sir John Franklin's Expedition, in the Years 1850–51*. New York: G.P. Putnam, 1852.

O'Sullivan, Daniel. *In Search of Captain Cook: Exploring the Man through his Own Words*. London and New York: I.B. Tauris, 2008.

Otto, Peter. 'Between the Virtual and the Actual: Robert Barker's Panorama of London and the Multiplicities of the Real in Late Eighteenth-Century London'. *Romanticism on the Net*, 46 (2007). Accessed at http://www.erudit.org/revue/ron/2007/v/n46/016130ar.html on 20 May 2011.

'Our Weekly Gossip'. *The Athenaeum*, 1163 (1850a): 160.
'Our Weekly Gossip'. *The Athenaeum*, 1173 (1850b): 420–1.
'Our Weekly Gossip'. *The Athenaeum*, 1112 (1849): 169.
Owen, Roderic. *The Fate of Franklin*. London: Hutchinson, 1978.
'Panorama of Boothia'. *The Times*, 14 January 1834.
Parry, Edward. *Memoirs of Rear-Admiral Sir W. Edward Parry*. 4th ed. London: Longman, Brown, Green, Longmans & Roberts, 1858.
Parry, William E. *Journal of a Third Voyage for the Discovery of a North-West Passage from the Atlantic to the Pacific, etc.* London: John Murray, 1826.
Parry, William E. *Journal of a Second Voyage for the Discovery of a North-West Passage from the Atlantic to the Pacific, etc.* London: John Murray, 1824.
Parry, William E. *Journal of a Voyage for the Discovery of a North-West Passage from the Atlantic to the Pacific, etc.* London: John Murray, 1821.
Parsons, James. *Reflections on the Mysterious Fate of Sir John Franklin*. London: J.F. Hope, 1857.
Peary, Robert E., F.W. Putnam, and Ralph W. Dexter. 'Correspondence between Lieutenant R.E. Peary and Professor F.W. Putnam on Arctic Ethnology'. *Ethnohistory*, 16:2 (1969): 177–89.
A Peep at the Esquimaux; or, Scenes on the Ice. 2nd ed. London: H.R. Thomas, 1825.
Penny, William. *Letter to the Lords Commissioners of the Admiralty*. London: G. Barclay, 1852.
Percy, Carol E. '"To Study Nature Rather than Books": Captain James Cook as Naturalist Observer and Literary Author'. *Pacific Studies*, 19:3 (1996): 1–30.
Perkins, Maureen. *The Reform of Time: Magic and Modernity*. London: Pluto Press, 2001.
Perkins, Maureen. *Visions of the Future: Almanacs, Time, and Cultural Change 1775–1870*. Oxford: Clarendon, 1996.
Pesso-Miquel, Catherine. '"In the Company of Strangers": Shedding Light on Robert McClure's Claim of Discovery (1850–7)'. In Frédéric Regard ed. *Arctic Exploration in the Nineteenth Century: Discovering the Northwest Passage*. London: Pickering and Chatto, 2013: 61–78.
'Peterhead – Mesmerism'. *The Aberdeen Journal*, 8 May 1850.
Petitot, Émile. *Travels around Great Slave and Great Bear Lakes, 1862–1882*. Paul Laverdure, Jacqueline Moir, and John S. Moir trans and eds. Toronto: Champlain Society, 2005.
Pierce, Richard A. 'Edward Belcher (1799–1877)'. *Arctic*, 35:4 (1982): 552–3.
Pile, Steve. 'Distant Feelings: Telepathy and the Problem of Affect Transfer over Distance'. *Transactions of the Institute of British Geographers*, 37:1 (2012): 44–59.
Pile, Steve. 'The Strange Case of Western Cities: Occult Globalisations and the Making of Urban Modernity'. *Urban Studies*, 43:2 (2006): 305–18.
Podmore, Frank. *Mesmerism and Christian Science: A Short History of Mental Healing*. Philadelphia: George W. Jacobs & Company, 1909.
Podruchny, Carolyn. *Making the Voyageur World: Travelers and Traders in the North American Fur Trade*. Lincoln, Nebraska: University of Nebraska Press, 2006.
'The Polar Regions'. *The Penny Illustrated News*, 1:20 (1850): 153–5.
Porden, Eleanor Anne. *The Arctic Expeditions. A Poem*. London: John Murray, 1818.
Potter, Russell A. *Finding Franklin: The Untold Story of a 165-Year Search*. Montreal: McGill-Queen's University Press, 2016.
Potter, Russell A. *Arctic Spectacles: The Frozen North in Visual Culture, 1818–1875*. Seattle: University of Washington Press, 2007.
Potter, Russell A. 'Open Polar Sea'. In Mark Nuttall ed. *Encyclopedia of the Arctic*. Vol. 3. New York and London: Routledge, 2004: 1578–80.
Power, J.C. *Abraham Lincoln: His Great Funeral Cortege, from Washington City to Springfield, Illinois. With a History and Description of the National Lincoln Monument*. Springfield, Illinois: E.A. Wilson, 1872.
Pratt, Mary L. *Imperial Eyes: Travel Writing and Transculturation*. London and New York: Routledge, 1992.
'Preface'. *Punch, or the London Charivari*, 68 (1875–6): iii–iv.
Prentice, Jim. 'Reclaiming a Piece of Our History'. *National Post*, 9 August 2010.
Prentice, Jim. 'Ships Frozen in Ice, Crew Gets out Alive' [Review of Brian Payton. *The Ice Passage: A True Story of Ambition, Disaster and Endurance in the Arctic Wilderness*, 2009]. *Policy Options*, 31 (2009–10): 94.
Prescott, George B. *History, Theory, and Practice of the Electric Telegraph*. Boston: Ticknor and Fields, 1860.
'Proposed Magnetic Expedition to the North Pole'. *Punch, or the London Charivari*, 24 (1853): 223.

Rae, John. *John Rae's Correspondence with the Hudson's Bay Company on Arctic Exploration 1844–1855*. E.E. Rich ed. London: Hudson's Bay Record Society, 1953.

Rae, John. 'Recent Explorations along the South and East Coasts of Victoria Land'. *Journal of the Royal Geographical Society*, 22 (1852): 82–96.

'"Rappings" in Cortland Co. – Fate of Sir John Franklin'. *New York Daily Tribune*, 14 May 1850.

Rasmussen, Knud. *The Netsilik Eskimos: Social Life and Spiritual Culture*. Gyldendal: Copenhagen, 1931.

Rawnsley, H.D. *Valete: Tennyson and Other Memorial Poems*. Glasgow: J. MacLehose & Sons, 1893.

Rees, W.G. 'Polar Mirages'. *Polar Record*, 24:150 (1988): 193–8.

'Return of the Arctic Search Expeditions'. *The Nautical Magazine*, 20 (1851): 569–91.

'The Rev. J.H. Skewes on Spiritualism'. *Liverpool Mercury*, 1 February 1883.

'Review of New Publications'. *The Gentleman's Magazine: and Historical Chronicle*, 90 (1820): 609–17.

'Review: *Somnolism and Psycheism*'. *The Medical Times*, 3 (1851): 211–2.

'Reviews'. *Liverpool Mercury*, 7 May 1850.

'Reviews of *The Mesmeric Mania of 1851, with a Physiological Explanation of the Phenomena Produced*. By J.H. Bennett, M.D.; *Chambers' Journal for March, 1851*, (No. 371); *Somnolism and Phycheism* [sic], *or the Science of the Soul, and the Phenomena of Nervation*. By J.W. Haddock, M.D.' *The Westminster Review*, 55–6 (1851): 161–9.

Reynolds, Paul. 'Trying to Head Off an "Arctic Gold Rush"' *BBC News*, 29 May 2008. Accessed at http://www.news.bbc.co.uk/1/hi/in_depth/7423787.stm on 14 October 2014.

Richards, Thomas. *The Imperial Archive: Knowledge and the Fantasy of Empire*. London: Verso, 1993.

Richler, Mordecai. *Solomon Gursky was Here*. London: Chatto & Windus, 1990.

Riffenburgh, Beau. *The Myth of the Explorer: The Press, Sensationalism, and Geographical Discovery*. Oxford: Oxford University Press, 1994.

Robinson, Michael F. *The Coldest Crucible: Arctic Exploration and American Culture*. Chicago: University of Chicago Press, 2006.

Roque, Ricardo. *Headhunting and Colonialism: Anthropology and the Circulation of Human Skulls in the Portuguese Empire, 1870–1930*. Basingstoke: Palgrave Macmillan, 2010.

Rose, Gillian. *Feminism and Geography: The Limits of Geographical Knowledge*. Cambridge: Polity Press, 1993.

Ross, D. *Poem on the Death of Lieutenant Bellot of the French Navy, etc.* Paisley: J. & R. Parlane, 1855.

Ross, James and James M. Savelle. 'Retreat from Boothia: The Original Diary of James Clark Ross, May to October 1832'. *Arctic*, 45:2 (1992): 179–94.

Ross, John. *Narrative of a Second Voyage in Search of a North-West Passage, etc.* London: A.W. Webster, 1835.

Ross, John. *A Voyage of Discovery made under the Orders of the Admiralty, in His Majesty's Ships Isabella and Alexander, for the Purpose of Exploring Baffin's Bay, and Inquiring into the Probability of a North-West Passage*. London: 1819.

Ross, M.J. *Polar Pioneers: John Ross and James Clark Ross*. Montreal and Buffalo: McGill-Queen's University Press, 1994.

Ross, W. Gillies. 'The Arctic Council of 1851: Fact or Fancy?' *Polar Record*, 40:213 (2004a): 135–41.

Ross, W. Gillies. 'The Admiralty and the Franklin Search'. *Polar Record*, 40:215 (2004b): 289–301.

Ross, W. Gillies. 'Clairvoyants and Mediums Search for Franklin'. *Polar Record*, 39:208 (2003a): 1–18.

Ross, W. Gillies. 'False Leads in the Franklin Search'. *Polar Record*, 39:209 (2003b): 131–60.

Ross, W. Gillies. *This Distant and Unsurveyed Country: A Woman's Winter at Baffin Island, 1857–58*. Montreal and Buffalo: McGill-Queen's University Press, 1997.

Ross, W. Gillies. *Arctic Whalers, Icy Seas: Narratives of the Davis Strait Whale Fishery*. Toronto: Irwin Publishing, 1985.

Rossetti, William Michael. *Rossetti Papers, 1862 to 1870*. London: Sands, 1903.

Rule, B.J. *Polar Knight: The Mystery of Sir John Franklin*. New Smyrna Beach, Florida: Luthers, 1998.

'Rumoured Discovery of Sir J. Franklin'. *Kentish Gazette*, 31 December 1850.

Russell, Penny. 'Wife Stories: Narrating Marriage and Self in the Life of Jane Franklin'. *Victorian Studies*, 48:1 (2005): 35–57.

Sabine, Edward, ed. *The North Georgia Gazette, and Winter Chronicle*. London: John Murray, 1821.

'Safety of Sir John Franklin's Expedition'. *London Standard*, 5 October 1849.

Said, Edward. *Orientalism*. London: Penguin, 1995.

Salmond, Anne. *Two Worlds: First Meetings between Maori and Europeans, 1642–1772*. London: Viking, 1991.

Sandlos, John. 'From the Outside Looking In: Aesthetics, Politics, and Wildlife Conservation in the Canadian North'. *Environmental History*, 6:1 (2001): 6–31.

Schivelbusch, Wolfgang. *Disenchanted Night: The Industrialisation of Light in the Nineteenth Century*. Angela Davies trans. Berkeley, California and London: University of California Press, 1988.

Scoresby, William. *Memorials of the Sea: Sabbaths in the Arctic Regions*. 2nd ed. London: Longman, Brown, Green, and Longmans, 1850a.

Scoresby, William. *The Franklin Expedition: Or, Considerations on Measures for the Discovery and Relief of Our Absent Adventurers in the Arctic Regions*. London: Longman, Brown, Green, and Longmans, 1850b.

Scoresby, William. *Zoistic Magnetism: Being the Substance of Two Lectures, Descriptive of Original Views and Investigations Respecting this Mysterious Agency*. London: Longman, Brown, Green, and Longmans, 1849.

Scoresby, William. *An Account of the Arctic Regions, with a History and Description of the Northern Whale-Fishery*. 2 vols. Edinburgh: Archibald Constable, 1820.

Scott, Robert Falcon. *Scott's Last Expedition*. 2 vols. New York: Dodd, Mead and Company, 1913.

'Search for Franklin's Arctic Log'. *The Straits Times*, 15 May 1939.

Seldon, W.N. *The Extraordinary and All-absorbing Journal of Wm. N. Seldon, etc.* Detroit: E.E. Barclay, 1851.

Service, Robert W. *Songs of a Sourdough*. Toronto: William Briggs, 1907a.

Service, Robert W. *The Spell of the Yukon and Other Verses*. New York: Barse & Hopkins, 1907b.

Seton, E.T. *The Arctic Prairies: A Canoe-Journey of 2,000 Miles in Search of the Caribou, etc.* New rev. ed. New York and London: Constable & Co., 1920.

Settle, Dionyse. *A True Reporte of Martin Frobisher's Voyage, 1577*. London: Henry Bynnyman, 1577.

Shackleton, Ernest. *Shackleton: His Antarctic Writings*. London: British Broadcasting Corporation, 1983.

Shackleton, Ernest. *South: The Story of Shackleton's Last Expedition, 1914–1917*. London: William Heinemann, 1920.

Shackleton, Ernest. *The Heart of the Antarctic: Being the Story of the British Antarctic Expedition 1907–1909*. 2 vols. London: William Heinemann, 1909.

Sheller, Mimi and John Urry. 'The New Mobilities Paradigm'. *Environment and Planning A*, 38 (2006): 207–26.

Shelley, Mary. *Frankenstein; or, The Modern Prometheus*. London: Henry Colburn and Richard Bentley, 1831.

Shelley, Percy Bysshe. *The Complete Poetical Works of Percy Bysshe Shelley*. Cambridge, Massachusetts, 1901.

Simmonds, P.L. *Sir John Franklin and the Arctic Regions: With Detailed Notices of the Expeditions in Search of the Missing Vessels under Sir John Franklin*. Buffalo, New York: G.H. Derby, 1852.

Simmons, Dan. *The Terror: A Novel*. London: Bantam, 2007.

Simpson-Housley, Paul. *The Arctic: Enigmas and Myths*. Toronto: Dundurn Press, 1996.

'Sir J. Franklin and the Clairvoyants'. *Manchester Times*, 18 February 1852.

'Sir John Franklin'. *The Derby Mercury*, 3 July 1851.

'Sir John Franklin'. *The Standard*, 8 March 1850.

'Sir John Franklin'. *The Morning Post*, 4 October 1849.

'Sir John Franklin. Further Revelations by the Bolton Clairvoyante'. *Preston Guardian*, 27 October 1849.

'Sir John Franklin – The Secret of the Discovery of his Fate'. *Glasgow Herald*, 20 April 1889.

Skewes, John H. *Sir John Franklin: The True Secret of the Discovery of his Fate. A 'Revelation'*. 2nd ed. London: Bemrose, 1890.

Skewes, John H. *Sir John Franklin: The True Secret of the Discovery of his Fate. A 'Revelation'*. London: Bemrose, 1889.

Smith, Bernard. *European Vision and the South Pacific*. 2nd ed. New Haven and London: Yale University Press, 1985.

Smith, Francis H. *My Experiences, or Foot-prints of a Presbyterian to Spiritualism*. Baltimore: The Author, 1860.

Smith, Gordon W. 'The Transfer of Arctic Territories from Great Britain to Canada in 1880, and some Related Matters, as seen in Official Correspondence'. *Arctic*, 14:1 (1961): 53–73.

Smith, Keith D. ed. *Strange Visitors: Documents in Indigenous-Settler Relations in Canada from 1876*. Toronto: University of Toronto Press, 2014.

Smith, Michael. *Captain Francis Crozier: Last Man Standing*. Cork: The Collins Press, 2006.

Snelling, William J. *The Polar Regions of the Western Continent Explored, etc.* Boston: W.W. Reed, 1831.
Snow, William P. 'The Franklin Expedition'. *The Evening News*, 12 August 1893.
Snow, William P. *The Franklin Mystery. Plain Facts and Arguments Relating to the Lost Polar Expedition, etc. Pt. 1.* Bexley Heath, Kent: Printed for the Author, 1889.
Snow, William P. 'Letter XL'. In *An Exposition of Spiritualism; Comprising two Series of Letters, and a Review of the 'Spiritual Magazine', etc.* ['Sceptic']. London: George Manwaring, 1862: 166–72.
Snow, William P. 'Franklin and the North-West Passage'. *London Standard*, 29 September 1859.
Snow, William P. *Voyage of the Prince Albert in Search of Sir John Franklin: A Narrative of Every-day Life in the Arctic Seas.* Paris: A. and W. Galignani, 1851.
Solnit, Rebecca. *Wanderlust: A History of Walking*. New ed. London: Verso, 2002.
Solomon, Maynard, ed. *Marxism and Art: Essays Classic and Contemporary*. Detroit: Wayne State University Press, 1979.
'Solving the Franklin Expedition Mystery'. *The Star*, 20 September 2014.
Solway, D. *Franklin's Passage*. Montreal and London: McGill-Queen's University Press, 2003.
'The Spectre of the Ice'. *Every Week*, 6:146 (1872): 241–3.
'Spirit Rapping'. *Taunton Courier, and Western Advertiser*, 26 May 1858.
'Spirit-rapping and Arctic Exploration'. *The Hereford Journal*, 7 November 1860.
'Spirits for Cook'. *The Citizen*, 11 January 1911.
Spufford, Francis. 'Ice'. In *Patterned Ground: Entanglements of Nature and Culture*. Stephan Harrison, Steve Pile, and Nigel Thrift eds. London: Reaktion, 2004: 279–81.
Spufford, Francis. *I May Be Some Time: Ice and the English Imagination*. London: Faber and Faber, 1996.
Stafford, Robert A. 'Scientific Exploration and Empire'. In Andrew Porter and Alaine Low eds. *The Oxford History of the British Empire*. Vol. 3. Oxford and New York: 1999: 294–319.
St. John, Percy B. 'The Spectre Ship'. *Belgravia: A London Magazine*, 8 (1876): 517–34.
Stamp, Tom and Cordelia Stamp. *William Scoresby, Arctic Scientist*. Whitby: Caedmon, 1976.
Standish, David. *Hollow Earth: The Long and Curious History of Imagining Strange Lands, Fantastical Creatures, Advanced Civilizations, and Marvelous Machines Below the Earth's Surface*. Cambridge, Massachusetts: Da Capo Press, 2006.
'Statement on Canada's Arctic Foreign Policy: Exercising Sovereignty and Promoting Canada's Northern Strategy'. Foreign Affairs and International Trade Canada (2010). Accessed at http://www.international.gc.ca/polar-polaire/canada_arctic_foreign_policy-la_politique_etrangere_du_canada_pour_arctique.aspx?lang=eng on 30 September 2013.
Stefansson, Vilhjalmur. *The Friendly Arctic: The Story of Five Years in the Arctic Regions*. London: G.G. Harrap & Company, 1921.
Stefansson, Vilhjalmur. *My Life with the Eskimo*. New York: The Macmillan Company, 1913.
Stein, Glenn. 'Scattered Memories and Frozen Bones: Revealing a Sailor of the Franklin Expedition, 1845–48'. *Journal of the Orders and Medals Research Society*, 46 (2007): 224–32.
Stephens, Carlene. '"The Most Reliable Time": William Bond, the New England Railroads, and Time Awareness in 19th-Century America'. *Technology and Culture*, 30:1 (1989): 1–24.
Stiegler, Bernd. *Traveling in Place: A History of Armchair Travel*. Chicago: University of Chicago Press, 2013.
Stock, Ernest Elliott. *The Ring of Ug, and Other Weird Tales*. London: John Ouseley Limited, 1911.
Stocking, George W. 'Animism in Theory and Practice: E.B. Tylor's Unpublished "Notes on 'Spiritualism'"'. *Man*, 6:1 (1971): 88–104.
Stone, Ian R. 'The Franklin Search in Parliament'. *Polar Record*, 32:182 (1996): 209–16.
Stone, Ian R. 'An Episode in the Franklin Search: The *Prince Albert* Expedition, 1850. Part 1'. *Polar Record*, 29:169 (1993a): 127–42.
Stone, Ian R. 'An Episode in the Franklin Search: The *Prince Albert* Expedition, 1850. Part 2'. *Polar Record*, 29:170 (1993b): 197–208.
'A Strange Story'. *The Times*, 13 September 1849.
'A Strange Tale of Handwriting on the Wall'. *Pall Mall Gazette*, 23 May 1889.
'A Strange Tale of Handwriting on the Wall'. *Pall Mall Gazette*, 9 May 1889.
'"A Strange Tale of Handwriting on the Wall"'. *Pall Mall Gazette*, 16 May 1889.
Sturm, Matthew. 'The Spirit of the Arctic and the Next Generation of Arctic Researchers'. *Arctic*, 53:3 (2000): iii-iv.
Suedfeld, Peter and Jane S.P. Mocellin. 'The "Sensed Presence" in Unusual Environments'. *Environment & Behavior*, 19 (1987): 33–52.

Sugars, Cynthia and Gerry Turcotte. 'Introduction: Canadian Literature and the Postcolonial Gothic'. In Sugars and Turcotte eds. *Unsettled Remains: Canadian Literature and the Postcolonial Gothic*. Waterloo, Ontario: Wilfrid Laurier University Press, 2009: vii–xx.

'Superstitions of the Whaler'. *Evening Telegraph and Post*, 3 April 1911.

'Superstition of Whale-Fishers'. *Manchester Courier and Lancashire General Advertiser*, 23 May 1881.

Sutherland, P.C. *Journal of a Voyage in Baffin's Bay and Barrow Straits, in the Years 1850–1851, etc.* 2 vols. London: Longman, Brown, Green, and Longmans, 1852.

Sutherland, P.D. 'Introduction'. In Sutherland ed. *The Franklin Era in Canadian Arctic History, 1845–1859*. Ottawa: National Museums of Canada, 1985.

Swerling, Gabriella. 'There are No Worlds Left to Conquer, Mourns Fiennes'. *The Times*, 6 May 2015.

Taylor, Thomas G. *With Scott: The Silver Lining*. London: Smith, Elder & Co., 1916.

'Telepathic Experiment'. *Lancashire Evening Post*, 3 September 1921.

'Tennyson's Arctic Monument'. *The Newcastle Courant*, 13 August 1898.

Thackeray, William Makepeace. *Contributions to Punch, etc.* New York and London: Harper, 1900.

Thomas, Keith. *Religion and the Decline of Magic: Studies in Popular Beliefs in Sixteenth- and Seventeenth-Century England*. London: Penguin, 1991.

Thompson, David. *David Thompson's Narrative, 1784–1812*. New ed. Richard Glover ed. Toronto: The Champlain Society, 1962.

Thoreau, Henry D. *Essays and Other Writings*. Will H. Dircks ed. London: Walter Scott, 1895.

Thrift, Nigel. 'Space'. *Theory, Culture & Society*, 23:2–3 (2006): 139–46.

Traill, Catharine Parr. *The Backwoods of Canada*. 4th ed. London: Charles Knight, 1839.

Traill, H.D. *The Life of Sir John Franklin, R.N.* London: John Murray, 1896.

Trattner, Walter I. 'God and Expansion in Elizabethan England: John Dee, 1527–83'. *Journal of the History of Ideas*, 25:1 (1964): 17–34.

'A Treasure House of Romance'. *The Western Morning News and Mercury*, 14 August 1925.

Tylor, Edward Burnett. *Primitive Culture: Researches into the Development of Mythology, Philosophy, Religion, Art, and Custom*. 2 vols. London: John Murray, 1871.

The Universal Fortune Teller, Being Sure and Certain Directions for Discovering the Secrets of Futurity. London: s.n., 1850.

Uusma, Bea. *The Expedition: A Love Story*. Agnes Broomé trans. London: Head of Zeus, 2014.

Van Schlun, Betsy. *Science and the Imagination: Mesmerism, Media, and the Mind in Nineteenth-Century English and American Literature*. Glienicke, Berlin; Madison, Wisconsin: Galda + Wilch Verlag, 2007.

Varga, Darrell. *John Walker's 'Passage'*. Toronto, Buffalo, and London: University of Toronto Press, 2012.

'Victoria'. *South Australian Register*, 9 December 1850.

'The Voice of an Old Arctic Seaman'. *The Times*, 20 December 1856.

Vollmann, William T. *The Rifles*. New York: Viking, 1994.

Wallace, Anne D. *Walking, Literature and English Culture: The Origins and Use of Peripatetic in the Nineteenth Century*. Oxford: Clarendon Press, 1993.

Wallace, Hugh N. *The Navy, the Company, and Richard King: British Exploration in the Canadian Arctic, 1829–1860*. Montreal: McGill-Queen's University Press, 1980.

Walliss, John. 'Continuing Bonds: Relationships between the Living and the Dead within Contemporary Spiritualism'. *Mortality*, 6:2 (2001): 127–45.

Walsham, Alexandra. 'The Reformation and "The Disenchantment of the World" Reassessed'. *The Historical Journal*, 51 (2008): 497–528.

Wamsley, Douglas W. *Polar Hayes: The Life and Contributions of Isaac Israel Hayes, M.D.* Philadelphia: American Philosophical Society, 2009.

Warren, William F. *Paradise Found: The Cradle of the Human Race at the North Pole*. 11th ed. Boston: Houghton, Mifflin, 1898.

Watson, Paul. *Ice Ghosts: The Epic Hunt for the Lost Franklin Expedition*. New York: W.W. Norton and Company, 2017.

Watson, Paul. 'Ship Found in Arctic 168 Years After Doomed Northwest Passage Attempt'. *The Guardian*, 12 September 2016.

'Where is Dr. Leichhardt?' *Sydney Morning Herald*, 6 August 1850.

'Whitby'. *Hull Packet and East Riding Times*, 9 May 1845.

White, Richard. *The Middle Ground: Indians, Empires, and Republics in the Great Lakes Region, 1650–1815*. Cambridge: Cambridge University Press, 1991.

'Who Discovered the Northwest Passage?' *Harper's New Monthly Magazine*, 9 (1854): 453–64.

Wiebe, Rudy. *A Discovery of Strangers*. Toronto: Vintage Canada, 1995.
Wilkins, Hubert and Harold Sherman. *Thoughts Through Space: A Remarkable Adventure in the Realm of the Mind*. New York: Creative Press, 1942.
Williams, Glyn. *Voyages of Delusion: The Search for the Northwest Passage in the Age of Reason*. London: HarperCollins, 2002.
Williams, Lisa. 'Telling an Arctic Tale: Arctic Discourses in Canadian Foreign Policy'. In Anka Ryall, Johan Schimanski, and Henning Howild Wærp eds. *Arctic Discourses*. Newcastle: Cambridge Scholars, 2010: 240–58.
Wilson, Eric. *The Spiritual History of Ice: Romanticism, Science and the Imagination*. New York and Basingstoke: Palgrave Macmillan, 2003.
Wilson, George. *Electricity and the Electric Telegraph: Together with the Chemistry of the Stars; An Argument Touching the Stars and their Inhabitants*. London: Longman, Brown, Green, and Longmans, 1852.
Wilson, John. *North with Franklin: The Lost Journals of James Fitzjames*. Markham, Ontario and Allston, Massachusetts: Fitzhenry & Whiteside, 1999.
Winter, Alison. *Mesmerized: Powers of Mind in Victorian Britain*. Chicago and London: University of Chicago Press, 1998.
Winter, Alison. '"Compasses all Awry": The Iron Ship and the Ambiguities of Cultural Authority in Victorian Britain'. *Victorian Studies*, 38:1 (1994): 69–98.
Wolfreys, Julian. *Victorian Hauntings: Spectrality, Gothic, the Uncanny*. Basingstoke: Palgrave, 2002.
'Wonderful Case of Clairvoyance'. *John O'Groat Journal*, 22 November 1850.
Wonders, W.C. 'Project "Franklin"'. *Polar Record*, 14:90 (1968): 333–6.
Woodcock, Henry. *The Gipsies; Being a Brief Account of their History, Origin, Capabilities, Manners, and Customs, etc.* London: William Lister, 1865.
Woodman, David. *Strangers Among Us*. Montreal and Kingston: McGill-Queen's University Press, 1995.
Woodman, David. *Unravelling the Franklin Mystery: Inuit Testimony*. Montreal and Kingston: McGill-Queen's University Press, 1991.
Woodward, Frances J. *Portrait of Jane: A Life of Lady Franklin*. London: Hodder & Stoughton, 1951.
Woodward, Josiah. *The Seaman's Monitor; or, Advice to Sea-faring Men with Reference to their Behaviour Before, In, and After their Voyage, etc.* 17th ed. London: F. & C. Rivington, 1806.
Wråkberg, Urban. 'The Quest for Authenticity in Narratives of Northern Borderlands'. *Nordlit*, 22 (2007): 193–209.
Wylie, Herb. *Speculative Fictions: Contemporary Canadian Novelists and the Writing of History*. Montreal and Ithaca, New York: McGill-Queen's University Press, 2002.
Wylie, John. 'A Single Day's Walking: Narrating Self and Landscape on the South West Coast Path'. *Transactions of the Institute of British Geographers*, 30:2 (2005): 234–47.
Young, Allen. *Cruise of the 'Pandora'. Extracts from the Private Journal Kept by Allen Young, R.N.R., F.R.G.S., F.R.A.S., &c., Commander of the Expedition*. London: Wm. Clowes & Sons, 1876.
Young, Allen. *The Search for Sir John Franklin: From the Journal of Allen Young, Esq., F.R.G.S.* London: J. Griffin & Co., 1875.
'Zadkiel Unearthed – Extraordinary Revelations'. *Hampshire Telegraph and Sussex Chronicle*, 4 July 1863.
'Zadkiel v Admiral Belcher'. *The Louth and North Lincolnshire Advertiser*, 4 July 1863.
Žižek, Slavoj. 'Courtly Love, or Woman as Thing'. In Elizabeth Wright and Edward Wright eds. *The Žižek Reader*. Oxford: Blackwell, 1999: 148–73.
Žižek, Slavoj. *Looking Awry: An Introduction to Jacques Lacan through Popular Culture*. Cambridge, Massachusetts and London: MIT Press, 1997.
Žižek, Slavoj. *For They Know Not What they Do: Enjoyment as a Political Factor*. London: Verso, 1991.
Zweig, Stefan. *The Adventurer*. London: Dent, 1974.

Index

www.ingramcontent.com/pod-product-compliance
Lightning Source LLC
LaVergne TN
LVHW052017300826
846742LV00020B/79
* 9 7 8 1 7 8 7 3 5 2 4 6 9 *